The international politics of Russia and the successor states

Mark Webber

Manchester University Press
Manchester and New York
distributed exclusively in the USA and Canada by St. Martin's Press

Published by Manchester University Press
Oxford Road, Manchester M13 9NR, UK
and Room 400, 175 Fifth Avenue, New York, NY 10010, USA

Distributed exclusively in the USA and Canada
by St. Martin's Press, Inc., 175 Fifth Avenue, New York, NY 10010, USA

British Library Cataloguing-in-Publication Data
A catalogue record for this book is available from the British Library

Library of Congress Cataloging-in-Publication Data
Webber, Mark.
The international politics of Russia and the successor states / Mark Webber
p. cm.
ISBN 0–7190–3960–6. — ISBN 0–7190–3961–4 (pbk.)
1. Former Soviet republics—Foreign relations. 2. National security—Former Soviet republics. 3. Former Soviet republics—Economic conditions. 4. Soviet Union—Politics and government—1985–1991. 5. World politics—1989– I. Title.
DK293.W43 1996
947.085'4—dc20 95–4960
CIP

ISBN 0 7190 3960 6 *hardback*
0 7190 3961 4 *paperback*

First published 1996

00 99 98 97 10 9 8 7 6 5 4 3 2

Typeset in Great Britain
by Northern Phototypesetting Co Ltd, Bolton
Printed in Great Britain
by Redwood Books, Trowbridge

Contents

Tables and boxes

Tables

Boxes

Abbreviations

ATTU	Atlantic to the Urals
AzPF	Azerbaijani Popular Front
BSEC	Black Sea Economic Co-operation
BSF	Black Sea Fleet
CFE	Conventional Forces in Europe
CIS	Commonwealth of Independent States
CMEA	Council for Mutual Economic Assistance
COCOM	Co-ordinating Committee for Multilateral Export Control
CPSU	Communist Party of the Soviet Union
CSBMs	Confidence and Security Building Measures
CSCE	Conference on Security and Co-operation in Europe (since December 1994 known as the Organisation on Co-operation and Security in Europe)
EBRD	European Bank for Reconstruction and Development
EC	European Community
ECO	Economic Co-operation Organisation
EU	European Union
FRY	Federal Republic of Yugoslavia
FSU	Former Soviet Union
G7	Group of Seven
GATT	General Agreement on Tariffs and Trade (superseded in January 1995 by the World Trade Organisation)
GPALS	Global Protection against Limited Strikes
IBRD	International Bank for Reconstruction and

	Development
ICBM	Inter-Continental Ballistic Missile
IDA	International Development Association
IMF	International Monetary Fund
INF	Intermediate Nuclear Forces
IRP	Islamic Renaissance Party (Tajikistan)
MAD	Mutually Assured Destruction
MFN	Most-Favoured Nation
MPF	Moldovan Popular Front
NACC	North Atlantic Co-operation Council
NATO	North Atlantic Treaty Organisation
NPT	Non-Proliferation Treaty
PFP	Partnership for Peace
RSFSR	Russian Soviet Federated Socialist Republic
SALT	Strategic Arms Limitation Treaty
SCSE	State Committee for the State of Emergency
SDI	Strategic Defence Initiative
SLBM	Submarine-Launched Ballistic Missile
START	Strategic Arms Reduction Treaty
TLE	Treaty-Limited Equipment
UN	United Nations
UNPROFOR	United Nations Protection Force
UNSCR	United Nations Security Council Resolution
USSR	Union of Soviet Socialist Republics
VOPP	Vance–Owen Peace Plan
WEU	Western European Union
WTO	Warsaw Treaty Organisation

Preface

This book is designed to introduce students to the international politics of Russia and the Soviet successor states. It has been written in the midst of rapid and monumental change. It was conceived shortly after the collapse of the USSR in early 1992. Three years on many of the dire predictions of chaos and instability that attended this event seem well-founded. Some, thankfully, do not. The 'post-Soviet' period is still an uncertain one. Many of the observations that are offered in the text are necessarily tentative. Nonetheless, it is hoped that the reader profits from the material and analysis that is offered and that this may form a basis for further investigation. The chronological cut-off date of events covered in the book is 12 December 1994.

I have been helped by a number of people. Roy Allison, Michael Smith and Dave Allen took time out to read all or parts of the various manuscripts and to offer helpful advice. The exacting observations of the anonymous referee also proved invaluable. The Department of European Studies, University of Loughborough, provided funds for a research trip to Russia. My partner Della Cohen furnished emotional sustenance and much more.

Map 1. *Russia and the successor states*

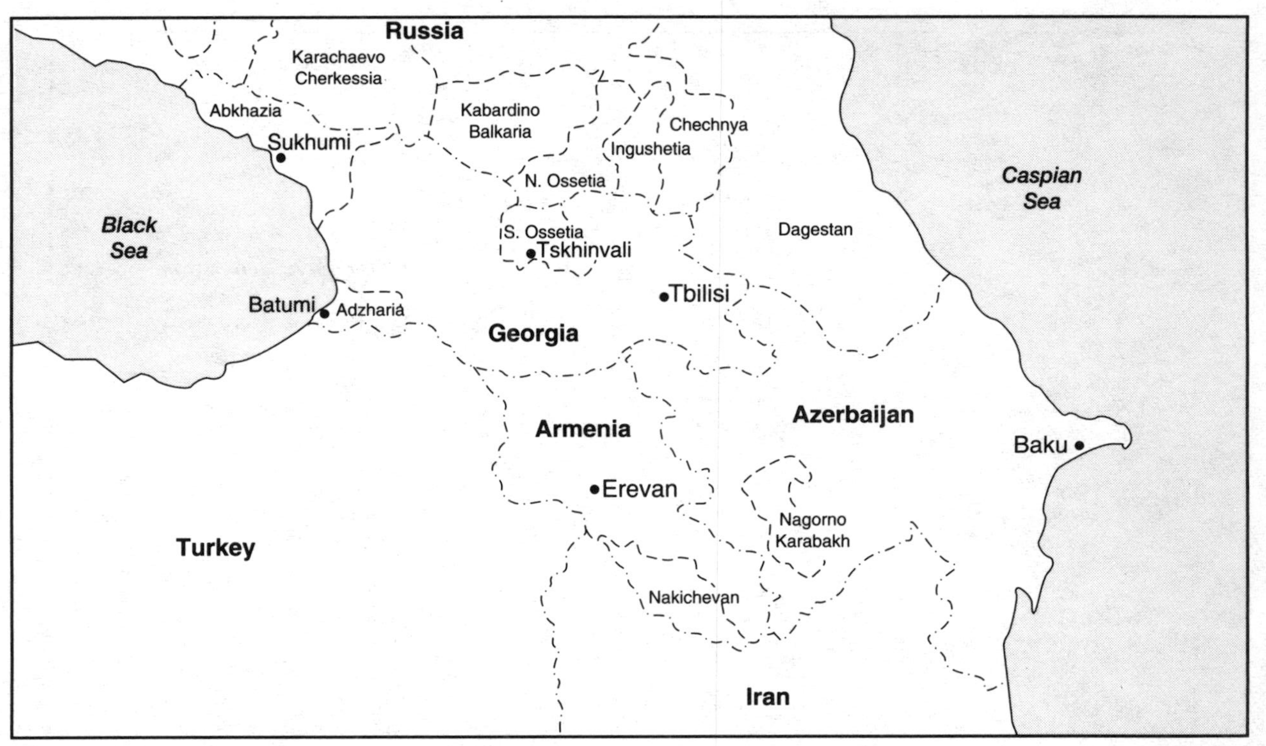

Map 2. *The Transcaucasus*

Map 3. *The Black Sea and the surrounding states*

Map 4. *Central Asia*

Map 5. *The Baltic states*

For Della

Introduction

The study of the international politics of Russia and the successor states

In 1985 Mikhail Gorbachev embarked upon a course intended to reform the USSR domestically and revive its fortunes internationally. Gorbachev certainly presided over a radical overhaul of the USSR, this was not, however, along the lines he had envisaged. Just six years after his accession to power, the USSR – the world's first socialist state, slayer of Nazism in World War II, the superpower equal of the United States and the feared head of the Warsaw Pact alliance system – was no more. In its place, fifteen states stepped on to the international stage. Consequently, during the 1990s many of the certainties of international politics have been removed. Students and practitioners are confronted with a world quite different from that they knew just ten or even five years ago. The USSR and the Cold War are no longer defining features of international politics. An uncertain era, 'a new world disorder', has been entered. This is a world of both threats and opportunities, of resurgent conflict and emergent co-operation. It is also a world in which the states of the former Soviet Union occupy a central space.

This book offers a guide to the manner in which change came about during the Gorbachev years and outlines the consequences of the Soviet collapse both within what was the USSR and beyond. In studying these issues the reader will encounter many basic questions central to the discipline of international politics. In this opening chapter we shall consider some of the discipline's theoretical approaches. This will provide us with reference points in later chapters. We shall also encounter the bones of an analytical framework which will be followed during the course of the book. We shall begin, however, in good academic fashion, with a definition of some terms.

Definitions

International politics

To what activities exactly does the term 'international politics'[1] refer? Any student of politics will have encountered a number of definitions of 'politics'. These usually orientate around notions of power, influence, conflict and its resolution. To use Harold Lasswell's now famous description, this boils down to asking 'who gets what, when and how?'[2] A question of this sort is as applicable in the international arena, as it is within the borders of a single state. In domestic politics, the shaping and sharing of power is influenced by political parties, pressure groups and politicians. In international politics, a similar process occurs, mediated by states, international organisations and diplomats. In fact, the boundary between the domestic and the international spheres is increasingly fuzzy as a multitude of international forces now exert a considerable sway over national policies. Where the two are quite different, however, is in regard to the location of ultimate authority. Domestic politics operates under the administration of government, exercising authority on behalf of the state. It is this body in all its manifestations (central, local etc.) that those engaged in politics seek to enter or to influence. A defining characteristic of international politics, by contrast, is its anarchic structure, the absence of a universally recognised governing authority. In consequence, the manner and likelihood of conflict and co-operation under anarchy are central concerns of scholars working within the field. Does anarchy result in a world of power maximising states, concerned primarily with issues of national security and balance of power politics? Does it inspire states to construct mechanisms of co-operation that might substitute for the absence of authority? Or does the existence of anarchy have more explicitly economic effects, facilitating the development and expansion of world capitalism? We shall return to these themes below in our discussion of theoretical approaches.

International politics is not simply politics between states. The state (and government which carries out policies on its behalf) may be a central character on the international stage and often the most important one, but equally, the state now co-exists with a range of other actors, spanning intergovernmental organisations (e.g. the United Nations [UN]), international financial institutions (e.g. the International Monetary Fund [IMF]), cross-national pressure groups (e.g. Greenpeace) and multinational companies (e.g. oil companies). These all in various ways temper its autonomy and affect its actions. A state may be subjected to sanctions or even invasion because it is in defiance of UN resolutions; it may have to tailor its economic policies to meet the conditions of the IMF; it may alter its environmental policies in response to the lobbying efforts of Greenpeace; and its prosperity may be boosted by the investment decisions of a large oil company. As we shall see below, theoretical approaches differ in the importance they attach to the state, but this is a debate which centres only on a question of degree. All are sensitive to the role of a variety of international actors which moderate or mediate state behaviour. It is how much or how little impact they have that is in dispute.

The USSR and its republics, Russia and the successor states

The current study is concerned with the international politics of a particular region, one which is made up of a group of states whose common origin lies within the now dissolved USSR. The study of this region and its Soviet precursor, however, presents us with a number of lexicographical challenges. What terminology does one use when referring to the new states that have emerged from the USSR? A variety of labels have been employed; 'former republics', 'post-Soviet republics', 'Eurasian states' and 'successor states' among others. In the main, we shall adopt the last of these.The term successor state does, it is true, have a specific meaning in international law, and as we shall discover in Chapter 3, the Baltic states have shunned the label, as has Russia. In fact, the latter has claimed the title of the USSR's 'continuing' state, a position which carries certain obligations and rights in the international community and which alludes to Russia's superior standing among its peers. Nonetheless, there are a number of reasons why the label of 'successor state' is to be preferred above others. The first is a practical consideration: it has already fallen into common usage. If one tag above others tends to be favoured in academic and diplomatic discourse it is this one. Second, it has a descriptive utility, suggestive of the shared past and common, recently acquired status of the new states. Third, notwithstanding the legalistic point noted above, there is one important respect in which all the new states are, in fact, the USSR's successors – their current frontiers conform to the principle of *uti possidetis, ita pos-*

sidetis ('have what you have had') that establishes succession to borders formerly of an administrative nature. Thus in this case, the boundaries of the USSR's Union Republics have become the borders of the new states.[3]

A second problem is what to now call the totality of the area once constituted by the USSR? Eurasia is problematic (it is not just the successor states which occupy the Eurasian landmass) and for this reason we have simply plumped for 'the former Soviet Union' (FSU). The confusing practice of using the term 'former Soviet Union' when referring to the Soviet Union during its period of existence is avoided. In the text, when referring to developments pre-1992 the 'Soviet Union' or 'USSR' are used.

A final difficulty concerns the manner in which the names of some Union Republics/successor states have been altered. The long-winded Russian Soviet Federated Socialist Republic (RSFSR) became the Russian Federation (or simply Russia) at the end of 1991; Moldavia became Moldova in June 1990; Byelorussia became Belarus in September 1991. In this regard we shall use a synchronic approach, citing the name by which a republic/successor state is known at the point in time being considered.

Foreign policy

In that all the successor states have acquired legal recognition as independent sovereign states it is only proper to consider their external relations as foreign policy. This applies equally whether one is referring to their interactions with one another or with the wider world. Hence, as used throughout the text, 'foreign policy' can refer as much to say Kazakhstan's relations with Ukraine as it can Russia's dealings with the US. This rather legalistic point, should, however, not blind us to the qualitative difference between the two types of relationship, a point we shall discuss below in reference to the FSU's 'inward' and 'outward' orientations.

Theoretical approaches to the study of international politics

Attempting to place the great diversity of analysis of international politics into neat categories is not an easy task. Scholars placed in one category often share many assumptions of another; some take great pride in their eclecticism, or in their efforts to marry or synthesise different approaches. Nonetheless, as the study of international politics has developed, different and discernible approaches have emerged in order to guide scholars in their attempts to tackle some central and abiding preoccupations. Viotti and Kauppi, have identified three different approaches (what they call 'alternative images') – realism, pluralism and globalism.[4] These are considered below.

Realism

Realism has, in the post-war period been the dominant Western approach in the study of international politics. Its early formulation, referred to here as 'classical' realism, is somewhat different from the more contemporary version of 'neo' or 'structural' realism, even if some common themes are apparent.

Classical realism as a distinctive approach to the study of international politics coalesced following World War II as a reaction to what were regarded as the mistaken assumptions of political 'idealism'. The latter, with its faith in the goodness of human nature and the utility of international law and organisations as mediums of preventing war, was rejected as naive and moralistic. Idealism, it was suggested, underestimated the 'realities' of power politics and was thus partly responsible for the slide to war in 1939.[5] The 'classical' realist approach, by contrast, was informed by a pessimistic philosophical outlook. Human nature was held to be essentially bad, motivated above all by an ineradicable striving for power. As Hans Morgenthau put it, political phenomena involve either the desire 'to keep power, to increase power, or to demonstrate power'.[6] This results in competition, suspicion and ultimately war between states. To cite Morgenthau again, '(a)ll history shows that nations active in international politics are continuously preparing for, actively involved in, or recovering from organised violence in the form of war'.[7]

To these philosophical premises was married the observation that the distinguishing feature of international politics is a condition of anarchy. No central or superordinate authority exists above the state (i.e. a world government) capable of holding in check its appetitive drive for power. International law and international organisations are ineffective substitutes for this missing authority. Both lack the autonomy and element of compulsion (i.e. a legal monopoly of the use of force) that the state possesses in the domestic realm. A body such as the UN may claim a wide mandate and even a moral purpose, but it exists simply as a vehicle for the pursuit of the particular interests of powerful states.[8] International politics was thus seen as the inverse of its domestic equivalent. According to Martin Wight, 'while in domestic politics the struggle for power is governed and circumscribed by the framework of law and institutions, in international politics law and institutions are governed and circumscribed by the struggle for power'.[9]

In the condition of anarchy, states must resort to strategies of self-help. The obvious course of action is the build-up of military power, increasing one's power position relative to that of other states. Such a course, however, is not without its drawbacks as states are confronted with the 'security dilemma'. The more one state increases its military capability the more threatening it appears to others. The resulting arms race rather than increasing security through the possession of greater arsenals only diminishes it by heightening the feeling of distrust between states. A second course open to states is to join with others in the form of alliances. Here the principle of self-help is partially suspended as states recognise the necessity of temporarily pooling their capabilities in order to counteract a state or group of states that appears to be accumulating a disproportionate amount of power. In light of these two strategies, the concept of the 'balance of power' looms large amongst the concerns of classical realists. Put simply, it is argued that stability and the avoidance of war will result from the maintenance of a balance of power among states, carefully constructed by the efforts of skilled diplomats.[10] The benefits of the balance of power, however, can never be permanent. *Raison d'état* – defined in terms of the acquisition of power and survival by the state – is the highest end of international politics. This not only excludes any concern for the long-term interests of other states (these are simply regarded as being in conflict with one's own)[11] but also rules out considerations of a moral nature (these are considered either subordinate to the immediate objective of power, or characteristic of a misplaced idealism).[12] Alliances may be sought and a balance of power desired, but ultimately these are merely transient devices by which the competition between states is only suspended, never eradicated.

The classical realist perspective is at first sight a persuasive one. It has an intuitive plausibility, describing the world as it really is, rather than how we might like it to be. Its focus on power, states and war appeared to offer 'the keys to the universe', a simple yet illuminating set of guidelines to understanding the complexities of international politics.[13] Yet the seeming verities of classical realism notwithstanding, the approach has suffered at the hands of some damning criticisms.

Among its critics was a group of scholars who were to become associated with realism's reformulation in a 'neorealist' or 'structuralist' guise. Neorealists haven taken classical realism to task for its reliance on historical and philosophical interpretation rather than testable hypotheses. In place of this 'unscientific' methodology, they have sought to formulate a 'rigorous theoretical framework for the study of world politics' that draws on 'the insights of the older realism' but which 'is more systematic and logically more coherent'.[14] Thus, neorealism abandons assumptions regarding human nature and elaborates more fully the notion of anarchy and its consequences. Kenneth Waltz, whose *Theory of International Politics* is often regarded as central to neorealist analysis, attempts this with an approach in which international politics is viewed as a system with structural properties. For Waltz, anarchy ('the absence of agents with system-wide authority') is the ordering principle of the international political system. From this flow a number of assumptions: the functional similarity of states and their rational character (i.e. in a self-help system, all will recognise and pursue the imperatives of security and survival – power, which for Waltz is the guiding principle of international politics, is sought as means to these ends); limits to international co-operation owing to insecurity and distrust; and the limited role of international organisations.[15]

Two further aspects of the neorealist approach are worth stressing. First, what is seen as the inevitable tendency of the international system towards recurrent balances of power as states ally and wage war as a consequence of the insecurities of anarchy. In this connection, neorealists argue that an international system dominated by a bipolar balance of two, relatively equal, great powers is more stable and less likely to result in system-wide wars than a multipolar balance. Bipolarity is more peaceful for three main reasons: there are fewer 'conflict dyads', resulting in fewer possibilities for war; deterrence is easier 'because imbalances of power are fewer'; and 'the prospects for deterrence are greater because miscalculations of relative power and of opponents' resolve are fewer and less likely'.[16] Second, neorealism's view of change is also important. Waltz doubts the likelihood of a change from one type of international system to another. A move from an anarchic to a 'hierarchic' realm is a transformation as yet unknown in the modern state system. Change which does occur is strictly 'within-system', the most significant being an alteration in the type of balance of power – a move from bipolarity to multipolarity or vice versa. This is triggered by alterations in the distribution of capabilities (population, territory, economic and military strength etc.) between states. It is worth adding that Waltz does not view change of such magnitude as a common occurrence. Multipolarity lasted three centuries until it was finally put to rest by World War II and the bipolar post-war dominance of the US and Soviet Union, the two military superpowers, is considered in *Theory of International Politics* as likely to endure to at least the end of the century.[17]

Pluralism

The pluralist approach to the study of international politics embraces a wide range of perspectives.[18] At its heart, however, is a set of common assumptions that stand in sharp contrast to those of the realists. In the first place, the pluralist outlook is shaped by a liberal political philosophy that emphasises co-operation rather than conflict. Hence, while the liberal would agree with the realist that the international realm is characterised by anarchy (s)he would be far more sanguine about the possibility of a harmony of interests between states. A number of arguments are forwarded to justify this optimism. The expansion during recent decades of the international economy, the spread of democratic political systems and the widening scope of international law and organisations all render war an increasingly costly and unacceptable form of inter-state behaviour and promote trust between states.

The pluralist perspective also offers a particular view of the state-as-actor. Pluralists have adopted an interest group approach to decision-making that explores the complex procedures by which foreign policies are made. Decisions are the result of a complex inter-play between various agencies of government, pressure groups, organisations and influential individuals at both a domestic and international level. From this it follows that the state is neither a unitary nor a rational actor. The realist view that the state acts in a coherent, determined fashion in the calculated pursuit of an agreed national interest dominated by the pursuit of power and military security is, for the pluralist, a gross oversimplification. This, in turn, distances pluralism from what might be regarded as the determinism of neo-realism. The Waltzian view that the structure of the international system (the 'system level') is the key to understanding international politics is clearly undermined by the pluralists' case that other levels of analysis are also germane – state, society, organisation and individual.

The realist view of a world of dominant, autonomous states is contradicted by the pluralist image of 'complex interdependence' in which the state is not the only, or necessarily the most important, actor and in which 'multiple channels' connect societies.[19] Summarising pluralist literature, Hocking and Smith have outlined five types of network or patterns of activity in the world arena:

1 subnational networks involving groups whose activities might spill over into international politics (e.g. secessionist movements);
2 transnational networks in which organisations such as multinational companies conduct activities across countries that challenge the economic autonomy of states;
3 transgovernmental networks refer to contacts between different agencies and departments of government, that is, ministries and so forth;
4 intergovernmental networks are those central to realist assumptions, involving contacts between political leaderships;
5 finally supranational networks refer to those which subordinate states to a common authority; the Commission of the European Union is the exemplar of this type.[20]

Pluralism's shift away from an emphasis on the state offers one attempt to overcome the growing anomalies in the realist view, in this case the increasing role of non-state actors and international organisations in international politics in the post-war period. Similarly, realism was found wanting in the face of growing evidence of co-operation between states. The realist perspective which views co-operation as merely a function of the balance of power and something that is only an expedient for states, has been challenged by pluralism, which has emphasised its durability and pervasiveness in international politics.[21] Co-operation is promoted by international organisations and regimes, the latter being defined as 'sets of implicit or explicit principles, norms, rules and decision-making procedures around which actors' expectations converge in a given area of international relations'.[22] Regimes exist to deal with, amongst other things, trade, monetary issues, arms control, the environment, the exploitation of space, transport and fishing. For pluralists, international organisations and regimes are a way of mitigating the uncertain effects of anarchy. They create mutual restraint, promote trust and alter states' expectations about how other states will behave – '(s)tates become more willing to co-operate because they assume others will do the same'.[23] It follows that the more issues that become subject to such oversight the greater the overall level of trust and stability in international politics.

Globalism

The 'globalist' perspective embraces varieties of Marxist analysis and non-Marxist approaches. Scholars operating within this field, however, share a number of common preoccupations, in particular an analysis of global political economy and the economic underdevelopment of the Third World. Viotti and Kauppi in their summary of the diverse literature of globalism identify its four key assumptions.[24] The first concerns the necessity of understanding the global context within which states and other international actors operate. In common with neorealism, it is suggested that the behaviour of individual actors can only be comprehended by grasping the structure of the international system. The nature of that system, however, is conceived of entirely differently. The existence of a capitalist world economy, rather than the condition of anarchy, is taken as its defining characteristic. True, the existence of anarchy is recognised, but this is only regarded as consequential to the degree that it allows for the development and spread of a world capitalist system unimpeded by a central regulating force. From this starting point follows the globalists' second assumption – the importance of historical analysis – and, in particular, an attention to the evolution and the rise to dominance of capitalism.

The two assumptions considered so far are central to the 'world system' theory of Immanuel Wallerstein.[25] For Wallerstein, the contemporary world system equates with the capitalist 'world-economy'. Capitalism took root firstly in Europe in the 'long' sixteenth century (1450–1640) and expanded piecemeal thereafter, such that by the end of the nineteenth century it had come to geographically embrace the entire world. The structure of this world economy Wallerstein analyses in terms of the existence of 'a three-layered structure' – a core, periphery and semi-periphery – which corresponds to a global division of labour. The core has historically embraced the advanced economies of Western Europe and during the twentieth century came to include Japan and the US. The countries of the core are seen as the dominant force, undertaking 'an appropriation of surplus of the whole world economy', and reinforcing their position by the imposition of a cultural dominance and the exercise of 'political–military advantage in the interstate system'.[26] If countries in the core are regarded as the exploiter then those in the periphery – situated largely in the Third World – are the exploited. These provide raw materials, cheap labour and so on to fuel the core's economic expansion.

The semi-periphery, finally, is both exploiter and exploited, economically subordinate to the core, but wresting its own advantages from the periphery. Countries enjoying this status include the relatively developed countries of the Third World (India, Brazil), the relatively underdeveloped countries of the core (Greece, Portugal) and those geographically isolated countries with strong links to the core (Australia, South Africa). For Wallerstein the existence of a socialist bloc of countries in which production has been largely socialised did not contradict his basic framework. These countries were seen as being tied to the world capitalist economy through trade, investment and borrowing. The *modus operandi* of enterprises in socialist countries was regarded as identical to those in countries with a property owning class, that is, 'a more favourable allocation of the surplus of the world economy'. Indeed, he regarded the USSR as having achieved after World War II the status of a core country owing to its role as a major industrial and trading nation.[27]

The third and fourth assumptions of the globalist approach refer to the existence of mechanisms of domination by which the countries of the Third World are prevented from developing, and the centrality of economic factors in understanding the nature of this subordination. These two assumptions are evident in the work of Wallerstein, and also in that of the so-called 'dependency theorists'.[28] This school of thought emerged in the 1960s and 1970s, partly in response to what were regarded as discredited American analyses of development.[29] The failure of the Third World or the 'South' to experience an upward curve of economic growth as predicted by development theorists, resulted in a greater attention to the constraints these countries faced in the international economy. In particular, it was argued that their dependence on the major industrialised countries of the 'North' (through unequal terms of trade, the operation of multinational companies, international banks and multilateral lending agencies) had relegated them to a subservient position in which they had little control over their economic fortunes. In some versions, this subservience was seen as being reinforced by transnational class coalitions; the property-owning classes in the advanced capitalist economies (the international bourgeoisie) allying with 'comprador' classes (a national bourgeoisie) in the Third World, to the detriment of the peasantry and proletariat.

Theories of international politics and the collapse of the USSR

The chronological period covered in this book extends roughly from 1985, to the end of 1994. These years witnessed amongst the twentieth century's most profound changes in international politics, 'the triple collapse of communism as an ideology, the Soviet Union as a European power and the USSR as a united country'.[30] As with previous historical junctures during this century (the two World Wars, the Russian revolution, decolonisation of the Third World), that occasioned by the collapse of communist power has had truly global consequences – the retreat of Soviet hegemony in Eastern Europe and the disappearance of the USSR as the military, political and economic rival of the liberal capitalist order headed by the United States, *in toto* an end to the Cold War. In addition, in place of the USSR a new geopolitical region has emerged, occupied by the successor states, dominated by Russia, and characterised by political, military and economic transition. Sheer size alone mean changes in this region affect a significant portion of the globe. Andrei Kozyrev, the first post-Soviet Russian Foreign Minister, has written eloquently on the significance of this dramatic transformation and its continuing repercussions. For him, it resembles, 'a tectonic shift, a global change in the world's political landscape … One sixth of the world land mass that at different times has been known as the Russian Empire or the Soviet Union is now in a state of flux. It is undergoing a major facelift that affects the evolution of the world community'.[31]

If the purpose of theory is to provide description, explanation and prediction, then the scholarship of international politics has been severely challenged by the developments of the 1980s and 1990s. Understandably, it might be argued that theory is constantly confronted in this manner, particularly in studying the tumultuous and constant flow of events which make up the substance of international politics. However, as Michael Cox has argued, recent events have been so profound that they have shattered 'our known political universe', the proper conceptual tools are as yet lacking to make proper sense of them.[32] Moreover, the fact that these events took scholars by surprise has been seen by John Lewis Gaddis as a momumental analytical failure.[33] Gaddis's charge is a damning one and has not passed without reply.[34]

Whatever the merits of his case it has not prevented a proliferation of studies which have sought to explain the end of the Cold War *ex post facto* and to outline the shape of the unfolding post-Cold War international order. Was the end of the Cold War the result of American strength and Soviet weakness, what realism would see as an outcome of a struggle for power in which the more capable US overcame its arch-rival the USSR? Or was it rather, as some pluralists would argue, the result of influences exerted upon the Soviet Union by the multiple channels of international organisations, international law and norms, a spread of ideas to policy-making groups in and around the Soviet leadership? Was it even, as is consistent with globalist analysis, the upshot of an interplay between the USSR's domestic economic predicaments and the increasingly attractive pull of the market and fuller integration with world capitalism? Turning to the debate over the direction of change in the post-Cold War world, here opinion is equally divided. Is this a world characterised by greater instability and threats to peace, one in which the demise of the bipolarity of the Cold War will occasion a more dangerous multipolar configuration of power? Or is it rather a world in which international organisations, liberated from the constraints of the Cold War, can play a more prominent role, tempering conflicts and furthering co-operation? Is it, finally, a world in which the demise of communism makes almost total the globalisation of capital? What is the role of Russia in this post-Cold War world? Is it a state which seeks to maximise and assert its power *à la* realism – a course likely to bring it into competition with its erstwhile adversary the US and its new neighbours in the former USSR? Or is it a state, now freed of communist ideology, more willing to co-operate with the states of the West, with international organisations and with the other successor states?

These questions will be considered in the course of this book. Chapters 1 and 2 provide an overview of the drama that unfolded during the Gorbachev years. In Chapter 1 we shall consider the factors which led the USSR to effect a major reorientation in its foreign policies and thus help bring about an end to the Cold War. In Chapter 2 the multiple crises which resulted in the USSR's disintegration are examined. The remainder of the book is taken up with developments in the post-Soviet period. Chapter 3 provides an introductory review of the foreign policies of Russia and the successor states. Chapters 4, 5 and 6 consider in thematic form specific aspects of these policies, focusing on military and security issues, conflict resolution, and external economic relations. In the Conclusion we shall return to a discussion of the theoretical frameworks outlined above and consider more explicitly their relevance as frames of reference for analysing the place of Russia and the successor states in the post-Cold War order.

In our deliberations we shall attempt to keep sight of several 'interacting trends' in the emerging international landscape. These trends all apply in large measure to the USSR and its successors. They are:

- the end of the Cold War;
- the decline of bipolarity;
- the collapse of communism;
- the rise of new powers;
- the changing map of Europe (including the former Soviet Union);
- the significance (or otherwise) of non-state actors and international organisations;
- revised security challenges;
- the shifting international political economy;
- interdependence.[35]

The former Soviet Union: its inward and outward orientations

In considering the themes outlined in the previous section we shall adopt throughout the book an analytical framework which posits the international politics of the FSU at two distinct, but interacting levels. These are termed the region's 'inward' and 'outward' orientations. The first refers to international politics within the FSU, the latter to the interactions of this region with the wider world. The content of this framework is elaborated more fully in Chapter 3. Here it is worth pausing to consider its broad outlines.

Reference to an 'inward' orientation emphasises the fact that there is something distinctive about international politics within the FSU, something that sets it apart from the manner in which the region interacts with the world outside. The central, defining feature in this regard concerns the obvious fact that Russia and the successor states were all formerly part of the same country, the USSR. Consequently, they are geographically very close and remain bound together by a myriad of political, economic, military and ethnic connections, all legacies of their Soviet past. These states are subject to an interdependence more extensive than anything in their dealings with the wider world. The FSU is criss-crossed by numerous associations of mutual dependence, a situation plain to see in the military and economic relations considered in Chapters 4 and 6 and the civil conflicts of Chapter 5. For the non-Russian states, interdependence largely takes the form of a *vulnerability* to developments in Russia. Many, for instance are open to fluctuations in the price and supply of Russian energy and are dependent upon military assistance provided by their large neighbour. They are vulnerable in the sense that alternatives to their dependence on Russia, such as a recourse to other suppliers or to domestic sources, are few and costly to obtain. For Russia itself, interdependence is more akin to a *sensitivity* to developments in the other successor states.[36] This is most apparent in its concern for the civil order situations in the successor states of the Transcaucasus and Central Asia. The condition of interdependence has been recognised and acted upon by the successor states. One important manifestation of the 'inward orientation' is the numerous attempts at co-operation, many of which have been institutionalised within the framework of the Commonwealth of Independent States (CIS).

A second distinctive feature of the region is the manner in which the shared Soviet past has influenced foreign policy priorities. For Russia, its place at the centre of the USSR means that the process of Soviet dissolution has occasioned mixed, often conflicting emotions.

While able to accept the shedding of communism, many Russians have been less accepting of the break-up of the Union and the loss of the republics. The place of Russia in the 'post-empire' politics of the FSU is the object of fierce debate, as we shall see in Chapter 3. The very fact that the successor states are referred to within Russia as the 'near abroad' is suggestive that this is a region which Russians still consider to be a legitimate sphere of influence. The mirror image of this attitude is a wariness of Russian intentions by the other successor states. The historical legacy of Soviet rule (and in many instances, Russian imperial rule before that) shapes their foreign policies. The fact that the USSR (and the Tsarist empire) was created and expanded through a process of enforced incorporation creates an atmosphere of suspicion in dealings between the successor states and Russia. All of this has severely hampered the development of multilateral co-operation in the form of the Commonwealth of Independent States and has created many instances of bilateral wrangling, of which the strained Russian–Ukrainian relationship is the clearest, but by no means the only, example.

Two contrary trends appear then to be at work in the FSU – an impulse towards co-operation stemming from interdependence and a tendency towards suspicion and disagreement. These trends we shall see at work throughout the current text.

Turning to the 'outward orientation' this is also influenced by the legacy of the Soviet period. Russia, for instance, while it has distanced itself from the ideological and 'messianic' aspects of the Soviet Union's role in world affairs, has nonetheless been anxious to retain much of that country's superpower credentials, its military infrastructure, its seat at the top table in international organisations, and its key role in regional diplomacy. Russia's 'continuer' status has also meant it has taken major responsibility for the multitude of treaty commitments entered into by the USSR. Fulfilment of these, particularly in the security sphere (arms control, disarmament and confidence-building measures) constitutes a major dimension of Russia's relations with the outside world.

The question of status also pertains to the other successor states. Here, the key concern has been to assert an independent identity on the world stage. In doing so they are seeking to overcome one further legacy of the Soviet period. Under Soviet rule, independent pre-existing national identities were stifled by the Soviet authorities. Pre-existing independent states were incorporated into the USSR and experienced decades of 'Russification' (in education, publishing, employment practices and so forth) and Sovietisation (the ideological creation of a Soviet 'nation'). The efficacy of these policies is a moot point, as the resurgence of nationalism in the late Soviet period testifies (see Chapter 2). Nonetheless, several decades in the historical development of nation states were lost as a consequence of their being constituent parts of a larger state. Hence, in a process of 'catching up' many of the successor states have gone to extraordinary lengths to distance themselves from Russia, a country they regard as the possible inheritor of the Soviet mantle of domination. This results in foreign policies that are anxious to expand relations with the outside world, to diversify, and to join international organisations as soon as possible in order to prove and to protect an identity as an independent state.

The outward orientation refers to more than simply the foreign policies of Russia and the successor states *towards* the world beyond the FSU. The term has a second dimension, that is, how the FSU is affected *by* the outside world. In examining this, a whole range of influences are relevant. The role of neighbouring or powerful distant states, the effects of international organisations, international financial institutions and multinational corporations. All of these operate in one context or another within the international politics of the FSU. The latter two are crucial to the economic fortunes of the region; international organisations meanwhile have attempted a key role in conflict mediation; regional powers (Turkey, Japan, China) have been of concern to many of the successor states; the US, finally, has seen the fashioning of a cordial relationship with Yeltsin's Russia and the promotion of stability in the FSU as core planks of its foreign policy.

The outward–inward distinction provides an organising principle for this book. As already noted Chapter 3 fleshes out this division. Chapters 4, 5 and 6 are organised largely with the inward–outward distinction in mind. Chapter 1 is preliminary to understanding the outward orientation of the successor states. Chapter 2 offers material essential to understanding their inward orientation.

Notes

1 The term 'international relations' could, of course, have been used here.

Throughout the text the two terms are used synonymously. On the conflation of these terms, see P. A. Reynolds, *An Introduction to International Relations* (London and New York, Longman, second edition, 1980), p. 10.

2 H. Lasswell, *Politics. Who Gets What, When, How* (Cleveland, Ohio, Meridian, 1958).

3 R. Müllerson, *International Law, Rights and Politics. Developments in Eastern Europe and the CIS* (London, Routledge, 1994), pp. 148–49.

4 P.R. Viotti and M.V. Kauppi, *International Relations Theory. Realism, Pluralism, Globalism* (New York and Toronto, Macmillan, second edition, 1993).

5 C.W. Kegley, Jr and E.R. Wittkopf, *World Politics. Trend and Transformation* (New York, St Martin's Press, fourth edition, 1993), pp. 20–22.

6 H. Morgenthau, *Politics among Nations. The Struggle for Power and Peace* (New York, Alfred A. Knopf, third edition, 1960), p. 39.

7 *Ibid.*, p. 38.

8 *Ibid.*, Chapter 28.

9 M. Wight, *Power Politics* (Harmondsworth, Pelican Books, 1979), p. 102.

10 *Ibid.*, pp. 184–85. The classical realists tended to stress the benefits of multipolarity (three or more states engaging in checks and balances) and held some admiration for the great power diplomacy of nineteenth-century Europe which established a balance between the great powers of France, Britain, Russia and Prussia/Germany. See Viotti and Kauppi, *International Relations Theory*, pp. 48–51.

11 M. Wight, *International Theory. The Three Traditions* (Leicester, Leicester University Press, 1991), pp. 111–14.

12 Morgenthau, *Politics among Nations*, pp. 27–28; Reinhold Niebuhr, *Moral Man in Immoral Society. A Study in Ethics and Politics* (New York, Scribners, 1932), p. 233.

13 J.C. Garnett, 'States, state-centric perspectives, and interdependence', in J. Baylis and N.J. Rengger (eds), *Dilemmas of World Politics. International Issues in a Changing World* (Oxford, Oxford University Press, 1992), p. 66.

14 Viotti and Kauppi, *International Relations Theory*, p. 194.

15 K. Waltz, *Theory of International Politics* (Reading, MA, Addison-Wesley, 1979), pp. 88–93, 105.

16 J.J. Mearsheimer, 'Back to the future: instability in Europe after the Cold War', *International Security*, 15:1 (1990), p. 14; Waltz, *Theory of International Politics*, pp. 102–28, 163–70. (Contrast this with the position of the classical realists outlined in note 10.)

17 Waltz, *Theory of International Politics*, pp. 97, 100, 131, 162, 176–83.

18 This school of thought is also referred to as (neo)liberal institutionalism. See Kegley and Wittkopf, *World Politics*, pp. 30–34.
19 R.O. Keohane and J.S. Nye, *Power and Interdependence. World Politics in Transition* (Boston and Toronto, Little Brown, 1977), pp. 24–29.
20 B. Hocking and M. Smith, *World Politics. An Introduction to International Relations* (New York, Harvester Wheatsheaf, 1990), pp. 74–76.
21 R. Axelrod and R.O. Keohane, 'Achieving co-operation under anarchy: strategies and institutions', *World Politics*, 38:1 (1985), pp. 226–54; H. Milner, 'International theories of co-operation among nations. strengths and weaknesses', *World Politics* 44:3 (1992), pp. 466–96.
22 S. Krasner, 'Structural causes and regime consequences: regimes as intervening variables', *International Organisation*, 36:2 (1982), p. 185. (Regimes have also been employed in neorealist analysis, but here '(r)egime creation and maintenance are a function of the distribution of power and interests among states'. It is the pluralists who remain more convinced of their utility in promoting co-operation. See, S. Krasner, 'Sovereignty, regimes, and human rights', in V. Rittberger (ed.), *Regime Theory and International Relations* (Oxford, Clarendon Press, 1993), pp. 139–40.
23 C.A. Kupchan and C.A. Kupchan, 'Concerts, collective security and the future of Europe', *International Security*, 16:1 (1991), p. 131.
24 Viotti and Kauppi, *International Relations Theory*, pp. 449–50.
25 Two useful collections of essays which contain the framework of his approach are *The Capitalist World Economy* (Cambridge, Cambridge University Press, 1979) and *The Politics of the World Economy* (Cambridge, Cambridge University Press, 1984).
26 Wallerstein, *The Capitalist World Economy*, pp. 18–19; *The Politics of the World Economy*, pp. 16–17.
27 Much of the remainder of the socialist bloc Wallerstein placed in the semi-periphery category. See *The Capitalist World Economy*, pp. 30–35, 115–16, 190–91.
28 C. Brown, 'Development and dependency', in A.J.R. Groom and M. Light (eds), *Contemporary International Relations. A Guide to Theory* (London and New York, Frances Pinter, 1994), pp. 62–64.
29 This refers to the works of scholars such as W.W. Rostow who had foreseen an economic 'take-off' for Third World economies should they emulate the pattern of development of the industrialised nations during their earlier phases of growth. See his *The Stages of Economic Growth. A Non-Communist Manifesto* (Cambridge, Cambridge University Press, 1960).
30 M. Cox, 'Rethinking the end of the Cold War', *Review of International Studies*, 20:2 (1994), p. 187.
31 A. Kozyrev, 'Russia: a chance for survival', *Foreign Affairs*, 71:2 (1992),

p. 1.

32 Cox, 'Rethinking the end of the Cold War', p. 187.

33 J.L. Gaddis, 'International relations theory and the end of the Cold War', *International Security*, 17:3 (1992/93), p. 6. The end of the Cold War is seen as embracing a range of elements, which include the USSR's loss of superpower status and 'an abrupt but peaceful collapse of Moscow's authority both within and beyond the borders of the former Soviet Union'. (see Gaddis, 'International relations theory', p. 18).

34 T. Hopf and J.L. Gaddis, 'Getting the end of the Cold War wrong', *International Security*, 18:2 (1993) pp. 203–6.

35 Adapted from K. Booth, 'Introduction. The interregnum: world politics in transition', in K. Booth (ed), *New Thinking about Strategy and International Security* (London, Harper Collins, 1991), pp. 9–10.

36 On vulnerability and sensitivity interdependence, see Keohane and Nye, *Power and Interdependence*, pp. 12–13.

Recommended reading

K. Booth and S. Smith (eds), *International Relations Theory Today* (Cambridge, Polity Press, 1995).

A.J.R. Groom and M. Light (eds), *Contemporary International Relations: A Guide to Theory* (London and New York, Frances Pinter, 1994).

F. Halliday, *Rethinking International Relations* (Houndsmills, Macmillan, 1994).

P.R. Viotti and M.V. Kauppi, *International Relations Theory. Realism, Pluralism, Globalism* (New York and Toronto, Macmillan, second edition, 1993).

1

Soviet foreign and defence policies during the Gorbachev period

The Soviet Union in the post-war period had every reason to regard itself as a superpower. The Red Army played a heroic and decisive role in defeating Nazi Germany. In the war's immediate aftermath, Moscow established a system of satellite states throughout Eastern Europe, over which it lorded with an ideological, military and economic supremacy. During the 1960s and 1970s it established a strategic parity with the US in nuclear arsenals, broke decisively with its communist rival China and matched the Americans in influence-building throughout the Third World.

This rise to greatness, however, was built on shaky foundations. During the 1970s and 1980s, the Soviet economy proved increasingly unable to sustain Moscow's global ambitions. Moreover, the Soviet Union became embroiled in a series of controversies and hopeless adventures, which brought its foreign policy to an almost complete impasse. Mikhail Gorbachev inherited this unenviable position. His efforts to reform Soviet foreign policy were truly dramatic. Rather than re-establish the USSR's superpower credentials, Gorbachev sought to alter the entire conceptual basis of Soviet foreign policy. No longer would the USSR force respect through threats, leverage or shows of military might. Rather it would cultivate trust, co-operation and harmony. In pursuing this agenda, the USSR became a potential partner, rather than an adversary; a country prepared to divest itself of unwelcome burdens and controversies in order to establish a diminished, but more realistic role for itself.

The Brezhnev legacy

In the USSR the link between domestic decline and foreign policy was plain to see. During the Gorbachev period the parlous condition of the Soviet economy exerted a powerful influence, contributing to an overall improvement in relations with the West, a refashioning of the Soviet defence capability, and a thoroughgoing restructuring of relations with Eastern Europe and the Third World.

This economic crisis had become particularly obvious during the latter years of Leonid Brezhnev's rule (1964–82) and during the short tenures of Yuri Andropov (1982–84) and Konstantin Chernenko (1984–85). Shortly after his election in March 1985 as General Secretary of the Communist Party of the Soviet Union (CPSU), Mikhail Gorbachev was to remark that the situation was so grave by the mid-1980s that any delay in launching a wide-reaching programme of domestic reform would have threatened the Soviet Union with 'serious social, economic and political crises'.[1] Specifically, Gorbachev referred to the appearance, during the latter half of the 1970s, of a 'kind of "braking mechanism" affecting social and economic development'. The roots of this malaise were to be found in an inflexible and outmoded planning mechanism, disincentives to enterprise and technological innovation, low levels of productivity, high levels of waste and the USSR's poor integration into the world economy. These factors contributed to a decline that appeared dramatic even in official Soviet figures. Between the periods 1951–55 and 1981–85, average annual rates of absolute growth in the Soviet economy fell from an impressive 11.4 per cent to a mere 1.9 per cent.[2]

These manifestations of domestic crisis had a clear bearing on the USSR's international position. Gorbachev was well aware of the linkage between economic health and the USSR's continuing vitality as a global power. As he made clear in 1984, '(o)nly an intensive, fast-developing economy can ensure the strengthening of the country's position in the international arena, enabling it to enter the new millennium appropriately as a great and prosperous power'.[3] This predicament of sustaining a world role while experiencing economic decline was felt in a number of areas. Perhaps most seriously, it held important implications for Soviet military status *vis-à-vis* the United States. Since the fall of Soviet leader Nikita Khrushchev in 1964 the Soviet leadership had been prepared to undertake a Herculean effort aimed at achieving and then maintaining a level of rough parity with the US in nuclear forces. This was complemented by the maintenance of a superior level of conventional military forces in the European continent organised within the Warsaw Treaty Organisation (WTO). From the time of the Sino-Soviet split in the early 1960s, a large military presence had also been maintained in the Soviet Far Eastern Theatre.

The emphasis on military power as an instrument of foreign policy resulted in part from what Condoleezza Rice has referred to as the Soviet leadership's suspicion of the international system.[4] Suspicions derived both from painful experience (viz. the invasion by Hitler's armies in 1941), and from an ideological outlook which viewed the world as an arena of conflict between two competing social systems – capitalism (headed by the US) and socialism (headed by the USSR) (see also below, pp. 26–27). Significance was attached to the military build-up for other reasons also. The realisation of military might demonstrated, so it was believed, the USSR's status as a truly global power and added to its claim that it had a justifiable role to play in any issue of international consequence.[5] Moreover, once the military machine had been set in motion, vested interests assured its continued momentum. The priority accorded to military matters meant that the professional military establishment acquired an influential role in national security decision-making.

Whatever the explanation for the military build-up, the resources required to sustain these efforts inevitably imposed a high price upon the Soviet economy. This was evident in the prioritisation of the military sector to the detriment of civilian needs and in a high and rising share of resources devoted to military expenditures. By 1985 the defence budget accounted for 18.4 per cent of Soviet GNP.[6] Given that the US spent an equivalent figure of 6.5 per cent, the long-term inability of the USSR to match American military power at a time of economic slowdown was clear. Moreover, the nuclear modernisation and rearmament programme pursued by the Reagan Administration in the early 1980s, coupled with the fear of an escalation of the arms race into the technologically advanced area of space-based defence systems (symbolised by President Reagan's announcement of the Strategic Defence Initiative [SDI] in 1983) opened up the prospect of further, possibly unsustainable, burdens on the economy. In the absence of improved economic performance, this meant ultimately falling behind American military capacity, thereby undermining the notion of superpower equivalence.

The economic implications of the Soviet Union's unfavourable position in East–West relations was, in turn, accompanied by no less problematic circumstances elsewhere. Ties with communist allies in Eastern Europe, for example, had, since the early 1960s, become an increasing burden. Declining growth rates in the region threatened the political viability of ruling communist regimes, a situation graphically illustrated by the birth of the Solidarity movement in Poland in the early 1980s. In order to minimise the potential destabilising effects, Moscow tolerated domestic economic reform efforts, encouraged lending from Western creditors, and itself provided trade subsidies and generous credits.

A similar situation was also evident in relations with the Third World. The profligacy that had characterised Soviet leader Khrushchev's approach towards this region had been tempered since the late 1960s, resulting in a more rigorous and hard-headed approach to trade and aid relations. Nonetheless, where it was considered politically expedient, Moscow was still prepared to furnish large-scale assistance. In the case of the 'Peoples Democracies' of Cuba, Mongolia and Vietnam this amounted to the equivalent of billions of dollars per annum in the form of economic aid, trade subsidies and military transfers. Lesser, but still huge sums were also funnelled to countries such as India, Syria and Iraq. While these resources proved vital in propping up the economies and defence capacities of Third World allies, little reciprocal benefit was enjoyed by Moscow, as there was little chance of this assistance being repaid.

Economics was not the only source of change. In 1985, the Soviet Union faced a near total impasse in its foreign policies. The blame for this cannot be laid simply at the door of the Kremlin (some account needs to be taken of the assertive nature of the Reagan Administration in accounting for a deterioration in East–West relations). However, as Eduard Shevardnadze and others in the foreign policy establishment were to later suggest, the Soviet Union's predicament was at least partly the consequence of unimaginative and misguided actions on the part of the Brezhnev leadership.[7]

The deadlock in foreign policy was nowhere more evident than in relations with the United States. The gradual warming of ties between the superpowers during the period of *détente* in the 1970s had given way by the early 1980s to an atmosphere of mutual hostility and deep suspicion. The Soviet invasion of Afghanistan in 1979, deadlock over arms control (notably the issue of Soviet- and American-controlled intermediate nuclear forces [INF] deployed in Europe) and the Moscow-backed imposition of martial law in Poland in 1981 led American President Ronald Reagan to refer to the USSR as 'the focus of all evil in the modern world'. While not sharing the American President's apocalyptic anti-communism, the sense of growing disillusionment with Moscow's intentions was shared in West European capitals. Also, and for quite different reasons, the Chinese viewed the Soviet Union with a degree of distrust. At normalisation talks begun in 1982 they raised 'three obstacles' to improved ties: force levels in the Soviet Far East (including Soviet SS-20 INF forces) and in Mongolia, the Soviet troop presence in Afghanistan, and Moscow's support of the Vietnamese presence in Cambodia.[8] Two further matters vexed Beijing: the Soviet use of naval bases in Vietnam and unresolved border issues. Finally, in the Third World, a region which had witnessed Soviet successes in the 1970s, Moscow faced unwelcome dilemmas. The invasion of Afghanistan had turned into a costly and injurious occupation, while clients acquired further afield in Angola, Ethiopia and Mozambique, faced seemingly intractable civil wars, a problem made that much worse by the so-called 'Reagan Doctrine' of American support for anti-Marxist insurgencies.

As we shall explore below, the Gorbachev leadership undertook a bold effort to extricate the Soviet Union from the multiple predicaments it faced in its international position. By the time of his assumption to power in 1985 Gorbachev had come to recognise that many aspects of Soviet foreign policy had failed or had been based on mistaken assumptions. Shevardnadze (Foreign Minister, 1985–90) relates how Gorbachev had concluded – from the moment he heard of the invasion of Afghanistan – that it was a mistaken adventure.[9] Shortly after taking office, Gorbachev himself publicly characterised Soviet foreign policy as 'skidding'.[10] He also made known to military planners his profound disagreement with their assumption that the USSR could fight and win a nuclear war with the US. More generally, those who advised Gorbachev were aware from an early stage the Soviet leader's dissatisfaction with the sorry pass Moscow faced and his determination to change course.[11]

The theoretical support of this reorientation was a set of ideas and concepts known as the 'new political thinking' in foreign policy.

The new political thinking

A focus on the new political thinking suggests that ideas have played an important role in shaping Soviet foreign policy. The new political thinking can be understood as a reaction to a crisis of ideology which had come to afflict Soviet Marxism–Leninism. To understand this it is worth briefly dwelling upon the way in which ideology – and Marxist–Leninist ideology in particular – influenced Soviet foreign policy prior to the Gorbachev period.

The pervasive nature of political education in the Soviet political system and the emphasis within the Communist Party of fealty to the received ideas of key Marxist thinkers (Marx, and Lenin even more so) meant that the Soviet political elite was imbued with a set of shared assumptions. As Coit Blacker has put it, the teachings of Marx and Lenin did not offer a completely reliable guide to Soviet action, but these teachings did 'influence ... the way in which senior Soviet leaders thought about and made sense of the phenomena they observed'. This unavoidably influenced the way they viewed the world and consequently the manner in which foreign policy was formed and implemented. Ideology was more than simply a camouflage for the pursuit of national interests.

Among the most salient ideas of the pre-Gorbachev leadership, Blacker points to the following. First, is the notion of an international system organised on class lines, one divided irreconcilably between socialist and capitalist countries. Here, capitalism was considered the weaker system, ultimately doomed to give way to the higher form of social organisation represented by socialism. Second, is the idea that a war involving the USSR and the West remained a real possibility. The latter conclusion derived from the actual experience of invasion (during the Russian civil war of 1917–20 and the German occupation of World War II), the observation that socialist revolutions occurred following war (as in Russia in 1917 and Eastern Europe in the late 1940s) and the assumption that capitalism was inherently aggressive (it had an imperialist impulse to capture new markets, it was driven by an alliance of big business and military manufacturers and it was prepared to pre-empt the historical inevitability of socialism's triumph through punitive warfare). To this was added the not unreasonable fear that the US's military acquisitions were directed at the USSR.[12]

Ideology can be seen to have influenced Soviet foreign policy in several ways. First, it ruled out certain options. For instance, a permanent reconciliation of interests with capitalism was considered an impossibility. Second, it gave rise to assumptions that entailed costly foreign commitments. Hence, the notion that the international system was defined by the struggle between socialism and capitalism meant the USSR felt it legitimate to rush to the assistance of numerous self-proclaimed socialist regimes in the Third World in order to counter imperialist expansion in the region. Similarly, the idea that the 'correlation of forces' ultimately favoured socialism meant once socialist regimes were established, either in Eastern Europe or the Third World, it was unthinkable that they would revert to a pre-socialist (i.e. capitalist or colonial) status. It was incumbent upon the USSR to support or, in the case of Eastern Europe, to oversee, these regimes in order to ensure their continued survival. Thirdly, Marxist–Leninist concepts often became counter-productive and even self-fulfilling. The view of capitalism as the antithesis of socialism had a deleterious impact on the Soviet economy, isolating it from the world market and the technological revolution sweeping the advanced industrial nations. Similarly, the supposition that capitalism was aggressive and war a possibility led Moscow to arm itself, a move itself considered aggressive in the West, which, in turn, accelerated its own arms build-up. In this sense, ideology reinforced the security dilemma (a concept discussed in Chapter 4, see pp. 210–13).

Ideology then can be seen to have imposed severe limitations on Soviet foreign policy. This alone provided ample reason for a revision of core tenets. In addition, as Stephen Kull has suggested, two fundamental anomalies had taken root within Soviet ideology: the continuing economic vitality of the capitalist system and socialism's inability to confront capitalism in a revolutionary struggle because of the danger of nuclear annihilation. These two developments undermined the philosophical assumption at the heart of Marxist–Leninist ideology, namely that socialism was a superior form of social organisation which would eventually triumph over its capitalist rival. The redundancy of the ideological framework which this implied, necessitated a major process of revision. The new political thinking was the result.[13]

A process of rethinking had, in fact, been in train well before the Gorbachev period. Many ideas which were to figure prominently in the new political thinking had been in circulation in Soviet academic literature since as early as the 1960s and in certain cases were discernible in the public pronouncements of the political leadership prior to 1985. Even in the crucial area of military doctrine the fundamental reassessments of the Gorbachev period were presaged by revisions which can be traced back to the period of Soviet leader Nikita Khrushchev (1953-64). The new political thinking, then, was not entirely 'new'. It is important to note two further qualifications. First, the new political thinking did not go uncontested during the Gorbachev period. A number of its innovations were questioned by higher echelons within the military and by orthodox opinion within the CPSU. Second, while it was noted above that the new political thinking provided a theoretical justification for changes in Soviet foreign policy, in certain cases, its conceptual innovations were to be outdistanced by the rapid unfolding of events. The revolutions in Eastern Europe and German reunification are cases in point.

The new political thinking was, nonetheless, the body of ideas closely associated with Gorbachev's radical reorientation of Soviet foreign policy. The new approach involved the following assumptions:

1 national security cannot be based upon the use or threat of use of nuclear weapons;
2 the Soviet Union should eschew the pursuit of 'absolute security' (obtaining a level of defence as strong as all possible enemies combined) in favour of 'mutual security';
3 security is best ensured by political rather than military means;
4 the combat capabilities of the Soviet armed forces should be based on the concept of 'reasonable sufficiency' – force levels should be adequate for defence but not for attack;
5 military strategy should be based on 'defensive' (i.e. non-provocative) defence;
6 capitalism was no longer to be regarded as inherently militaristic and aggressive, nor as historically doomed; consequently, a permanent *modus vivendi* was required between the capitalist countries and those of the socialist bloc;
7 in an interdependent world 'all-human values' take precedence over class interests;
8 foreign policy should divest its ideological overtones ('deideologisation') and the Soviet Union should have a clearer notion of a specifically 'national interest';

9 the world is multipolar and should not be viewed simply through the bipolar prism of relations with the West.[14]

New thinking in practice: Soviet foreign policy during the Gorbachev period

Objectives of Soviet foreign policy

The Soviet Union's beleaguered international position in the early 1980s, coupled with the tenets of the new political thinking, led to the emergence in the first two years or so of Gorbachev's leadership of fairly clearly defined foreign policy objectives. These may be summarised as:

- an improvement in relations with the major powers, in particular, the US, the countries of Western Europe, and China;
- the pursuit of disarmament and arms control, both at a nuclear and conventional level;
- a more flexible approach towards the countries of Eastern Europe, at this stage, within a continuing Soviet sphere of influence;
- a disentanglement from regional conflicts in the Third World and the pursuit of policies more beneficial to Soviet interests;
- greater involvement in the international economy.

During the Gorbachev period significant progress was registered in all these spheres. Indeed, within the six short years of Gorbachev's rule the alterations in Soviet foreign policy had been so fundamental as to contribute to a profound transformation of the international order. Aspects of this are explored below.

Arms control and disarmament

The touchstone of improvements in East–West relations has historically been progress in controlling the levels, and regulating the use, of armaments, particularly nuclear weapons. The period of *détente*, for example, as well as the Biological Weapons Convention, witnessed the Strategic Arms Limitation Treaties (SALT 1 and 2) and Anti-Ballistic Missile (ABM) Treaty, agreements aimed at stabilising the nuclear relationship. The period after 1985 was similar in this respect; the scale and nature of measures reached, however, was unprecedented. What amounted to a shift from arms *control* to arms *reduction*, promoted by a series of Soviet concessions and unilateral initiatives, illustrates most convincingly the practical pursuit of the postulates of the new political thinking.

Of greatest significance were treaties relating to nuclear arms. The first of these, that concerning intermediate forces, signed in December 1987 at the Washington summit, can properly be regarded as historic. As noted above, the INF issue had proven a severe impediment to improved relations between Moscow and Washington. The incompatibility of Soviet and American positions was swiftly overcome after 1985, in large measure due to a series of concessions offered by Moscow. A linkage the USSR had formerly posited between an INF agreement and accords on longer-range strategic arms and SDI was abandoned. Moscow also dropped its opposition to intrusive verification provisions and the inclusion of SS-20 missiles in the Soviet Far East within the remit of any INF deal. The treaty subsequently concluded was unprecedented in a number of regards. Most importantly, in contrast to previous agreements on nuclear weapons, which had only set ceilings upon future acquisitions, the INF Treaty entailed the actual *elimination* of an entire category of weapon (ground-launched nuclear missiles of a range of 500 to 5,500 km), one in which the USSR held a clear numerical superiority.[15]

While the INF agreement was of great significance, it resulted in an overall reduction of only 3–4 per cent of the nuclear arsenals of the Soviet Union and the US. Real progress in disarmament required reductions in the massive stockpiles of strategic nuclear weapons held by both sides. Furthermore, unlike INF, whose relevance lay in a European theatre, strategic weapons held by the Soviet Union were a direct threat to the American mainland. Reductions in this area would go a considerable way to improving relations with Washington. An agreement was not finally signed until the Moscow summit in July 1991. Its conclusion was aided by Moscow's decision to drop demands regarding SDI and by its readiness to dismantle the phased-array radar at Krasnoyarsk (regarded by the Americans as in breach of the ABM Treaty). In brief, the 1991 START treaty provided for equal ceilings on delivery vehicles (Inter-Continental Ballistic Missiles [ICBM], Submarine-Launched Ballistic Missiles [SLBM] and strategic bombers) and the warheads they were permitted to carry. To meet these limits reductions would be carried out over a seven year period following the treaty's ratification. Because the USSR held a numerical superiority in warheads, it would be required to implement the deeper cuts.

The Gorbachev period also witnessed considerable movement in the sphere of conventional disarmament. While not as newsworthy as the drama of nuclear arms agreements, conventional reductions, nonetheless, merited particular note. Progress on cutting weapons and personnel in this sphere could be calculated to significantly assuage Western anxieties at WTO superiority in Europe. Demilitarisation of the Soviet Far East, similarly, would improve relations with Beijing. Reductions also offered other benefits. Given that the bulk of the Soviet defence budget was apportioned to costs associated with conventional defence, cuts would in the long run help relieve the burden of defence expenditure on the ailing Soviet economy.[16] As some in the Soviet armed forces recognised, this would also have operational spin-offs as the removal of 'dead wood' would help create a smaller, yet more effective military.[17]

These calculations contributed to Soviet involvement in unilateral and multilateral reductions. In a speech to the United Nations in December 1988, Gorbachev announced planned reductions of half a million troops within a two year period. Upon completion in December 1990 this involved the demobilisation of over 150,000 troops in Eastern Europe and nearly 300,000 within the USSR itself.[18] Soviet undertakings, as part of multilateral reductions sanctioned by the 1990 Conventional Forces in Europe (CFE) Treaty, were no less sweeping. The treaty imposed equal limits on WTO and NATO holdings in Europe (in a region roughly between the Atlantic, the Urals and the Caspian sea) in five weapon categories (battle tanks, armoured combat vehicles, attack helicopters, artillery pieces and combat aircraft). Under intra-alliance ceilings arrived at prior to the treaty's signing, each participating country was, in turn, subject to individual limits. The treaty was to be fully implemented by November 1995.

The effects of CFE weighed particularly heavy on the Soviet Union. In fulfilment of the treaty it was required to destroy holdings in four weapons categories. While this would still have left it as Europe's single most powerful military power, it was outgunned by the combined forces of the NATO countries. The demise of the WTO shortly after the signing of CFE (see below, p. 33), meant this disadvantage could not be compensated for by calling on East European armed forces. In addition to the scale of the projected cuts, CFE was significant in other respects. The offensive nature of the weapons covered by the treaty, coupled with Soviet acceptance of separate agreements concerning confidence and security building measures (CSBMs) reached in 1986 and November 1990, eliminated the by now remote possibility of a surprise Soviet attack on Western Europe. This convincingly demonstrated the Soviet Union's shift towards a defensive military posture.

Alongside the pathbreaking achievements of INF, START and CFE, progress was also registered in other areas. A bilateral Soviet–US agreement was reached in 1990 aimed at cutting chemical weapons stockpiles. A comprehensive nuclear test ban treaty remained beyond reach, but this was partly offset by a series of unilateral Soviet moratoriums on nuclear testing. Neither was a formal agreement reached ruling out SDI deployment. This irritant in East–West relations had, however, become something of a non-issue. The US, constrained by funding and research problems and encouraged by the significant improvement in relations with the USSR, had downgraded the SDI programme to a far less ambitious programme announced in January 1991 known as GPALS (global protection against limited strikes). GPALS was meant not as a defence against an increasingly unlikely Soviet strategic strike, but what the Pentagon regarded as the far more realistic threat of missiles launched by accident, by terrorists or by rogue regimes (Iraq, North Korea).[19]

Soviet–East European relations

If changes in Soviet foreign policy on arms issues were dramatic, policy towards Eastern Europe might be described as truly revolutionary. A strategy based on the maintenance of communist rule in the region was replaced by one that tolerated and, in some cases, abetted the removal of communists from power in 1989–90.

This switch did not emerge *ab initio* in 1989. It has been persuasively argued that earlier changes in policy, of which alterations in military thinking and the unilateral troop reductions announced in 1988 were the most obvious, anticipated the transformation of the Soviet Union's traditional relationship with its East European allies.[20] Moscow's objective up until 1989 appears to have been the development of a revitalised alliance system, led by reform communists (pretty much like Gorbachev himself) dedicated to economic modernisation and democratisation. This, it was hoped, would render the East European states economically productive and politically viable and would lighten the burden of Moscow's leadership of the alliance.

This strategy, however, was swiftly undercut during 1989 as moribund leaderships were unexpectedly overthrown throughout the region. That Moscow did not intervene militarily to staunch a process that led to the eventual formation of a series of non-communist governments was the product of a number of factors. Of perhaps greatest importance, changes in military thinking and the warming of East–West relations meant the region was no longer considered of cardinal strategic significance. Even if intervention had been countenanced, the inevitable deterioration of relations with the West, the difficulties of intervening simultaneously in a number of countries throughout the region and the long-term prospect of propping up unpopular communist rule rendered it a practical impossibility.

Following the termination of communist rule Soviet policy pursued what was essentially a course of damage limitation. The continued existence of the WTO was defended as a necessary medium for conducting conventional arms control (i.e. CFE) and as a guarantee against the destabilising effects of a 'Balkanisation' of Eastern Europe. Regardless of Soviet wishes, once the sanction of intervention by Moscow had been removed, the now non-communist members of the WTO demanded an exit from the organisation. Czech and Hungarian requests for full Soviet troop withdrawals, the assertion of full command of national armies and the abandonment of a unified military doctrine undermined the WTO's internal logic and led to its formal disbandment in July 1991. The Council for Mutual Economic Assistance (the economic arm of the Soviet bloc) suffered a similar fate. Moscow, unwilling to subsidise non-communist regimes, introduced a new trading system in January 1991 based on convertible currency settlements and world market prices. This step contributed to a collapse of Soviet trade with the region. In June, the members of CMEA decided to wind up the organisation. Illustrative also of the end of Soviet oversight, new regional organisations of political and economic co-operation were created. The Visegrad and Pentagonal initiatives did not count the USSR as among their members.

Soviet–West European relations

A division of Soviet European policy between East and West is in many respects an artificial one. It made some sense when the continent's demarcation along military, political and economic lines appeared fixed; Soviet policy during the Gorbachev period, however, can only be fully understood in a pan-European framework. This has been alluded to already with regard to shifts in military thinking and theatre-wide disarmament (INF, CFE).[21] Of no less significance was the pursuit of economic co-operation, a greater emphasis on political-security co-operation and a fundamental shift in attitudes towards German unification.

Changes in policy in these areas put flesh on the guiding concept of Soviet policy towards the continent, that of the 'Common European Home'. At its heart was the idea that the peoples of Europe shared a common identity, which highlighted the potential for co-operation between East and West. This, moreover, was not simply a device to exclude the Americans from Europe; in a telling phrase Gorbachev recognised the US as constituting a 'natural part of the European international–political structure'.[22]

These revisions provided a rationale for the pursuit of practical benefits, not least in the economic sphere. A comprehensive trade and co-operation treaty was signed with the European Community (EC) in 1989 (inaugurating a number of assistance programmes). The following year the USSR became a founding member of the European Bank of Reconstruction and Development. Throughout 1990-91, the idea of a large-scale rescue package for the Soviet economy was promoted by EC countries (notably West Germany and France) within the framework of the Group of Seven (G7) industrialised countries. The Soviet Union also sought greater political and security co-operation. It acquired special guest status in the Council of Europe and was a signatory to the 1990 Charter of Paris, which envisaged continent-wide commitments to democracy, free markets and human rights. The ending of communist rule in Eastern Europe led the Soviet Union to see institutions such as the Conference on Security and Co-operation in Europe (CSCE) as the beginnings of a nascent pan-European security framework, which might 'soften the blow' of the WTO's demise by absorbing the East European states and NATO into a single political–security system.[23]

The most far-reaching alteration in Soviet policy was reserved for Germany. Having steadfastly opposed German unification throughout 1989 (despite the collapse of the Berlin Wall), during the second half of 1990 the USSR was party to a number of understandings and agreements, which entailed not only an acce the sanctioning of a united Germany's men respect of the former, the about-face was simply inevitable. By the beginning of 1990, the Socialis from power in the German Democratic Republi accelerating rate of emigration from East to West the political and economic viability of the East appeared in serious doubt. The victory of the pro 'Alliance for Germany' in free elections in the GDR in Ma only to confirm this. Acceptance of NATO membership foll July during a visit by West German Chancellor Helmut Kohl USSR. The *quid pro quo* of Soviet acquiescence was specific ple from Bonn concerning future German force levels, the application special military conditions to the territory of the GDR and German financial assistance for the withdrawal of Soviet troops. In September it was agreed that all Soviet troops would be removed by 1994, assisted by a DM12 billion German aid package. In addition to the influence of these German 'sweeteners' the shift in Soviet policy was conditioned by the wider developments in European security (see CFE and CSCE noted above) and a major revision in NATO strategy announced at the organisation's London Summit in July, all of which helped assuage Soviet fears of an enlarged NATO. The upshot of these developments was the signing in September of the Final Settlement regulating the external aspects of German unification, between the wartime allies and the two Germanys (the Two Plus Four Treaty) and a treaty of Good-Neighbourliness, between Germany and the USSR. These signified, more than any other development, an end to the division of Europe.

Sino-Soviet relations

At the March 1985 CPSU Central Committee at which he took office as General Secretary, Gorbachev expressed his wish for a 'serious improvement of relations with ... China'.[24] The subsequent six years witnessed such a determined effort to promote this course, that by 1991 the 'three obstacles' had been wholly or partially removed and the issue of the disputed border largely settled.

Progress on these issues was first signalled in a speech by Gorbachev in Vladivostok in July 1986 in which he announced the possibility of troop reductions in Mongolia, balanced Soviet and se reductions of ground forces and the imminent withdrawal k regiments from Afghanistan. The 1988 Afghan peace settle- t inaugurated a complete pull-out from that country. The uni- eral Soviet reductions announced by Gorbachev in December 1988 sulted in the demobilisation of some 120,000 troops in the Soviet ar East and 42,000 in Mongolia by December 1990. In March 1990, he USSR and Mongolia agreed to a complete Soviet withdrawal by the end of 1992. In April, an agreement was reached with China on mutual force reductions 'to a minimum corresponding to good-neighbourly relations'. Progress on the third obstacle, that of Cambodia, was also swift. A Vietnamese withdrawal from the country was undertaken during 1988-89, partly in response to Soviet pressure, and during 1990 the USSR and China (along with the three other Permanent Members of the United Nations [UN] Security Council) agreed a peace plan for an internal political settlement.

Relations also moved forward in other areas. The Sino-Soviet summit of May 1989 witnessed a formal normalisation of inter-state relations and the resumption of full links between the Soviet and Chinese communist parties. An agreement demarcating the common border east of Mongolia was signed in May 1991. In the economic field, trade increased fifteen fold between 1982 and 1990 and technological and scientific co-operation, which had been halted in the early 1960s, was resumed. In a notable development, in March 1991 the first ever agreement was reached providing for Chinese economic assistance to the USSR.[25] Finally, in 1990 arms transfers were revived after a thirty-year hiatus with Chinese purchases of Soviet Mi-17 assault helicopters.

Certain strains in relations did, however, remain. Moscow's cautious criticism of the Chinese authorities' crackdown on pro-democracy demonstrators in Tiananmen Square in June 1989 disappointed Beijing, while events in Eastern Europe and political and ideological revisions in the Soviet Union itself were regarded by the Chinese leadership as a betrayal of socialism. These political-ideological differences, however, should not obscure what was, in effect, an almost total turnaround in relations, ending the deep-seated enmity which had prevailed during the Brezhnev period.

Soviet–Third World relations

The Gorbachev period witnessed a thorough-going restructuring of policy towards the developing world, entailing a reversal of the combative approach of the Brezhnev period. Nowhere was this more evident than in Moscow's unwillingness to continue supporting embattled clients embroiled in unwinnable regional conflicts. The dividends it was hoped this would pay in the form of removing sources of conflict with Washington and Beijing contributed (as noted above) to efforts to find a political settlement in Cambodia and a withdrawal of Soviet troops from Afghanistan (where the equally pressing desire to disengage from a war which had cost some 13,000 Soviet lives was also operative). In Africa, the Soviet Union co-operated with the US in framing peace agreements relating to the southwest of the continent in 1988 and 1991. These provided for a Cuban withdrawal from Angola, the initiation of Namibian independence, and an internal political settlement in Angola (including the mutual termination of arms supplies by the USSR and the US to the country's warring parties). In Ethiopia, where US–Soviet co-operation was less successful, Moscow simply abandoned the Mengistu regime to the mercy of its internal opponents, following Addis Ababa's refusal to countenance power sharing.

The most striking example of the Soviet Union's changed approach was policy towards Iraq, following that country's invasion of Kuwait in August 1990. Having failed to persuade Baghdad to withdraw from occupied territories, and unable to condone a flagrant contravention of international law, Moscow endorsed UN Resolution 678 authorising the use of force to eject the aggressor. This amounted to the abandonment of a former ally (Iraq had signed a friendship treaty with the USSR in 1972) and acceptance of UN authorisation of a military operation spearheaded by American forces.

Greater weight was also placed on economic priorities. Continuing a trend already evident prior to 1985, Moscow placed an emphasis in its trade and economic assistance policies upon transactions with the Third World's 'better economic performers' such as India, Egypt and Brazil. Historically, the benefits of this strategy had been undermined by the burdens of costly economic and military assistance to Third World socialist countries, notably Cuba and Vietnam, and unpaid debts owed by long-term clients such as India, Syria and Angola. During 1990-91, this problem was addressed; a major reduction of Moscow's commitments to Havana and Hanoi was pursued, efforts were undertaken to cajole the repayment of debt, many assistance projects were cancelled and the Soviet foreign aid budget was slashed.

These alterations in external economic policies were complemented by a shift of emphasis in Soviet diplomatic activity. Countries previously neglected or ostracised on political grounds were courted owing to their economic potential and regional weight. Tours of Latin America (including Mexico, Brazil, Argentina) and Southeast Asia (including Indonesia, Thailand) were made by Shevardnadze; steps were taken to restore severed relations with Israel and South Africa and full diplomatic relations were established with Saudi Arabia and South Korea. The benefits were often immediate. In early 1991, shortly after the establishment of relations, Seoul pledged loans and project assistance to Moscow worth $3.5 billion.

Finally, as further evidence of Moscow's disengagement from the Third World, a significant diminution of its military presence in the region was undertaken. This reflected not only the reduced strategic significance of the Third World as an arena of East–West competition, but also the implications of a more benign military doctrine and questions of cost, which placed limits on forward missions. Outside the obvious case of Afghanistan, this resulted from the late 1980s in a cutback of 'out-of-area' operations by the Soviet navy and hence the use of support facilities in Vietnam, Cuba and Angola. At the same time, Soviet training missions were either reduced (Vietnam, Angola) or terminated (Mozambique, Ethiopia, Iraq).

Conclusion: the end of the Cold War and the heritage of the Gorbachev period

After Gorbachev's accession to power in March 1985, the Soviet Union pursued a number of innovatory foreign policies, which had a profound impact on its international position. These changes would have important implications following the USSR's demise. Perhaps of greatest importance, the Gorbachev years witnessed a moderation of Moscow's traditional enmity with Washington and its NATO partners and with Beijing. While the latter should not be underestimated, scholars have devoted greatest attention to Moscow's relationship with the West owing to the centrality of the Cold War in post-1945 international politics. With regard to Soviet–American relations, the improvement was more far-reaching than the *détente* of the 1970s. In Soviet eyes *détente* had been premised upon recognition of an equality of status between the superpowers and a continuing ideological competition between East and West. The changes inaugurated in 1985 altered all this. Nuclear and conventional disarmament, the retreat of Soviet power in Eastern Europe and disengagement from the Third World contributed to a qualitative shift in the superpower relationship. Moscow acknowledged a lesser role for itself and accepted that co-operation, rather than simply a more regulated form of competition, was to be the central theme of its relationship with the US.

The moderation of the East–West antagonism and the diminution of Soviet power helped bring the Cold War to an end.[26] The Cold War international system, which had endured throughout the decades after World War II, is usually referred to as a bipolar one. The term 'bipolarity' has a number of different connotations. It can refer to (1) a state of affairs in which states are polarised into two hostile coalitions (those not formally within either bloc are still subject to bloc influence);[27] (2) a condition in which only two states are able to mount a strategy of global deterrence; (3) a system in which power is distributed in such a way that only two states are so powerful that they are able to defend themselves against any combination of other states.[28] These features were evident in the existence of the WTO and NATO, the leading role of the USSR and the US within these alliances and the military strengths, particularly the nuclear capabilities, of the two leading states. During the Gorbachev period this bipolar pattern altered fundamentally. Superpower balance had given way, so it was argued, to a 'unipolar moment' of US global dominance.[29] Here the status of the Soviet Union was demoted to that of a 'post-imperial medium power', one which had abandoned the constant search for equality with the US in favour of a national interest, modestly defined as amounting to nothing more than 'a search for relief from burdens, and for ways of buffering the transition to a diminished world role'.[30] As Table 1.1. makes clear, bipolarity in the sense of bloc opposition ended with the demise of the WTO. Bipolarity in the second and third senses noted above, was called into question by the reduction of Soviet military capabilities and its geostrategic withdrawal from Eastern Europe and the Third World.

Various interpretations have been put forward to explain the reshaping of Soviet foreign policy under Gorbachev. Neorealist

Table 1.1 *The USSR's geostrategic position (1985 and 1991)*

	March 1985	*August 1991*
Strategic nuclear weapons	Parity with US	Parity with US at lower levels
Alliance systems	WTO/CMEA vs. NATO/EC	Disbandment of WTO/CMEA
Conventional forces in Europe	WTO superiority of major weaponry categories over NATO[a]	WTO equivalence with NATO under CFE Treaty limits (Soviet inferiority under intra-WTO limits)
Military personnel in Europe	Marginal NATO advantage overall; WTO advantage in central front	NATO superiority; disbandment of WTO/ unilateral Soviet troop reductions
Forces in Far Eastern theatre	Soviet superiority of major weaponry categories; Chinese manpower advantage	INF reductions; unilateral Soviet troop reductions; bilateral agreement on troop reductions
Forward deployment	Naval facilities in Vietnam, Cuba, Angola, Ethiopia; overseas military training missions; troop presence in Afghanistan	Curtailment of 'out-of-area' operations; abandonment or reduction of use of forward facilities and military training missions; withdrawal from Afghanistan

Note: [a] In four of five categories covered in CFE Treaty.

analysis has viewed the change in terms of a shift in relative capabilities to the USSR's disadvantage. Most importantly, the decline of the Soviet economy, meant the USSR was increasingly incapable of meeting the costs of its presence in the Third World and Eastern Europe and in sustaining its enormous military machine. To lighten itself of these burdens required retrenchment and thus a fundamental reorientation of foreign policy.[31] To make matters worse for Moscow, during much of the 1980s it faced the alarming rhetoric and military build-up of the two Reagan administrations plus the combative Reagan Doctrine in the Third World. Aware of its disadvantage in a revitalised arms race and the costs of toughing it out in a battle of nerves in the Third World, Moscow was forced to negotiate largely on American terms, a victory for Reagan's strategy of 'peace through strength'.[32] A different version of the neorealist explanation argues that retrenchment under Gorbachev was intended to provide the USSR with the breathing space necessary for a revitalisation of its economy. By this view, moves such as the withdrawal from Afghanistan, negotiated arms reductions and the retreat from Eastern Europe would both free up economic resources and create a propitious climate for investment and loans from the West.[33] This would create the economic basis for a later resumption of the USSR's role as a superpower.

These neorealist interpretations are important in pointing out the important influence exerted upon Soviet foreign policy by its declining economic position and straining military capabilities. However, critics have argued that this analysis is both incomplete and that the changes inaugurated by Gorbachev fundamentally contradict many neorealist assumptions concerning the behaviour of states. Neorealism, while recognising retrenchment as a possible response to the decline of a state's power capabilities, fails to account for either the timing or magnitude of retrenchment in the Soviet case. If the distribution of capabilities was the determining factor, surely change would have occurred before 1985. Brezhnev, Andropov and Chernenko all faced economic conditions and military challenges as gloomy as those confronting Gorbachev, but rather than undertake innovation they reacted in an intransigent manner – walking out of negotiations on arms control in 1983 and continuing apace with the USSR's own arms build-up.[34] Thus, for Friedrich Kratochwil, '(t)he rapid changes that occurred since 1989 had hardly anything to do with the changes in Soviet or American capabilities.'[35] Moreover, while the Soviet Union's capabilities could be said to be in *absolute* decline as its economic fortunes worsened, the focus of neorealist interpretations is on *relative* decline. In terms of the American technological lead (as reflected in SDI) this was apparent, but by other measures the USSR was holding up rather well. Its slowing growth rates were comparable to those experienced by Western economies during the 1970s and early 1980s and its military capabilities remained as awesome in the mid-1980s as in previous decades. In the crucial field of nuclear weapons it was more than a match for the US and its NATO allies. Indeed, it was precisely the sense of security provided by nuclear parity that provided Moscow with the confidence to seek reconciliation with the West. Contrary to neorealist thinking then, it was an equivalence of military capabilities rather than the USSR's relative inferiority that explain its behaviour.[36]

Moreover, even if we accept the assumption that the USSR was in relative decline, according to neorealist analysis, states in decline are not expected to retreat in the manner the USSR did after 1989. The withdrawal from the Third World can be understood as retrenchment at the periphery, but in Eastern Europe, Moscow walked away from its principal sphere of influence, one moreover, it was still easily capable of defending militarily. This is entirely at odds with the neorealist assumption that states seek to maximise their power in order to guarantee their security and survival (see p. 6).[37] In addition, under Gorbachev, the process of accommodation involved concessions on Moscow's part that significantly enhanced the relative power of its erstwhile adversaries. In purely military-strategic terms, INF, START, CFE and German unification entailed signifi-cant losses for Moscow, and by the same token, considerable gains for the US and its NATO allies. In this light, the maximisation of power *à la* realism appears inadequate as a description of Moscow's behaviour.[38]

If view of these criticisms of neorealism, how well have alternative perspectives fared in explaining the Soviet shift. Daniel Deudney and John Ikenberry, while partly retaining the neorealist concern with power capabilities, have married this with an analysis of influences usually considered integral to the pluralist approach. They argue that Soviet foreign policy altered because of changes in the USSR's international environment, that relate to things other than simply military or economic resources. In particular, 'cultural, societal, and international-organisational factors ... created opportunities and incentives for greater Soviet integration into the Western system'.[39] Following this line of thought, they emphasise the effect of 'the assimilative and inclusive culture and society of the West', the attractions of business and commodity culture, and the allure of the open and cosmopolitan societies of the West. In addition, international organisations by demonstrating the benefits of co-operative participation helped adapt Soviet behaviour to the 'norms' of these 'functional networks and the broader Western culture that subsumes them'. As Deudney and Ikenberry point out, organisations such as the UN helped to draw 'otherwise antagonistic states into a complex network of transactions', thereby creating mutual interests and helping to moderate differences.[40] This explanation has some value (note, for instance, Gorbachev's faith in the CSCE on p. 34, and the Soviet Union's acceptance of a UN role in Afghanistan, Iraq and Cambodia).

Another approach utilises the concept of 'learning' to explain foreign policy change. This approach explicitly rejects neorealism's focus on power capabilities and its portrayal of the state as a unitary and autonomous actor.[41] Instead it emphasises domestic and transnational political linkages and the importance of the interaction of groups and individual leaders in the formulation of policy. As defined by Jack Levy, learning involves 'a change of beliefs or the degree of confidence in one's beliefs based on the observation and interpretation of experience ... leaders learn lessons from the successes or failures in their foreign policies'.[42] Hence, the ascendancy of the new political thinking under Gorbachev can be interpreted as a response to previous foreign policy mistakes and the international dilemmas the country faced in the mid-1980s. Learning theories do not suggest that Gorbachev was the first Soviet leader to learn but they do suggest that he learnt in a particularly profound manner, thereby triggering a complete reorientation of foreign policy. Why this was so is explained in a number of ways. The generation gap between Gorbachev and Brezhnev *et al.* provides a partial explanation. Gorbachev's formative political experiences occurred in the post-war period and under the relatively reformist leadership of Khrushchev. This was different from Brezhnev, Andropov and Chernenko, whose political outlook was steeled by Stalinism. Yet amongst Gorbachev's contemporaries significant differences were apparent. Age alone, therefore, cannot explain political outlook.[43] Alternatively, others have focused upon the influence of 'epistemic communities' of experts at a transnational level and 'policy entrepreneurs' at a domestic level.[44] Their importance lies in putting new ideas on the agenda, and crucially, in influencing the attitudes of the political leadership. Such communities existed before 1985 and the particular ideas associated with the new political thinking had been in circulation for many years. Hence, this literature also seeks to explain why the purveyors of ideas had such a profound impact upon Gorbachev, more so than any previous Soviet leader, and why he chose to adopt the particular ideas associated with the 'new thinkers' rather than others. Here several salient factors are important: (1) a recognition on the parts of Gorbachev and his close associates, notably Shevardnadze, that Soviet foreign policy had reached an impasse and that the economic and ideological foundations upon which foreign policy was based were failing. Gorbachev and his associates were, therefore, open to new ideas upon their assuming the leadership in 1985;[45] (2) Gorbachev's predisposition to the new political thinking was sharpened by his consultations with those experts who offered the more pertinent solutions to the Soviet Union's foreign policy predicaments. These included liberal scholars within the Soviet academic community (themselves influenced by scholarship and ideas emanating from the West);[46] (3) on taking the helm, Gorbachev's foreign policy amounted to 'learning by doing' – a trial-and-error experimentation or a 'learning from ... behaviour [that] became self-reinforcing and self-amplifying';[47] (4) changes at the domestic political level empowered the purveyors of the new ideas. Political liberalisation permitted greater debate, changes in policy-making advice inserted a greater civilian influence and undermined the military, and greater openness to foreign influences increased the 'access points into the political system' for 'transnational coalitions' of Western and Soviet new thinkers;[48] (5) changes that occurred in the central political institutions (the restaffing of institutions by a dominant political coalition dedicated to change) meant learning could be translated into policy change.[49]

The differing explanations of change under Gorbachev return us to the themes outlined at the beginning of the chapter. Neorealism's focus on power capabilities links in well with the discussion of Soviet economic weakness and military constraints on pp. 21–23, while learning approaches are of relevance in understanding the ascendancy of the new political thinking discussed on pp. 26–29. Consensus among scholars, however, has yet to be reached. Debate on the origins and the impact of Gorbachev's foreign policy revolution is likely to last some time.

The legacy of the foreign policies of the Gorbachev years would loom large in the post-Soviet period. The bedrock of improved East–West relations would have a significant influence on the initial foreign policy priorities of the successor states, as would the legacies bequeathed by Gorbachev in Eastern Europe, the Third World and in regard to China.

Whatever Gorbachev's achievements in foreign affairs, however, these were overshadowed by the radical changes he initiated at home and the collapse of the Soviet system he had striven so hard to preserve. This created an entirely unforeseen rearrangement of the international system as the USSR gave way to fifteen new, independent states. This profound transformation and the evolution of relations between the new states can only be fully understood by considering domestic developments during the Gorbachev period and the events which led to the dissolution of the Soviet Union. These are the subjects of Chapter 2.

Notes

1 M. Gorbachev, *Perestroika. New Thinking for Our Country and the World* (London, Fontana/Collins, 1988), p. 17.
2 D.A. Dyker, *Restructuring the Soviet Economy* (London and New York, Routledge, 1992), p. 42.
3 Quoted in R.G. Kaiser, *Why Gorbachev Happened. His Triumphs and His Failure* (New York, Simon and Schuster, 1991), p. 76.
4 C. Rice, 'The party, the military, and decision authority in the Soviet Union', *World Politics*, 40:1 (1987), p. 80.
5 C.D. Blacker, *Hostage to Revolution. Gorbachev and Soviet Security Policy, 1985–1991* (New York, Council on Foreign Relations Press, 1993), pp. 12–13.
6 D. Steinberg, 'The Soviet defence burden: estimating hidden defence costs', *Soviet Studies*, 44:2 (1992), pp. 262–63.
7 S. Sestanovich, 'Gorbachev's foreign policy: a diplomacy of decline', *Problems of Communism*, 37:1 (1988), pp. 2–4.
8 Between 1979 and 1989 known as Kampuchea. Vietnam had invaded Cambodia in 1978.
9 E. Shevardnadze, *The Future Belongs to Freedom*, trans. C.A. Fitzpatrick (New York, Free Press, 1991), p. 26.
10 Gorbachev, *Perestroika*, p. 135.
11 Gorbachev, interviewed by J.G. Stein and cited in her 'Political learning by doing: Gorbachev as uncommitted thinker and motivated learner', *International Organisation*, 48:2 (1994), pp. 159–60, 175.
12 Blacker, *Hostage to Revolution*, pp. 14–19.
13 S. Kull, *Burying Lenin. The Revolution in Soviet Ideology and Foreign Policy* (Boulder, Westview Press, 1992), p. 17. See also M. Light, *The Soviet Theory of International Relations* (Brighton, Wheatsheaf Books, 1988), p. 326.
14 S.M. Meyer, 'The sources and prospects of Gorbachev's new political thinking on security', *International Security* 13:2 (1988), pp. 124–63;

Gorbachev, *Perestroika*, pp. 135–60.

15 Compliance with the provisions of the treaty was completed in May 1991.

16 In the short term, economic gains would not be forthcoming owing to the costs of dismantlement, demobilisation etc.

17 C. Bluth, *New Thinking in Soviet Military Policy* (London, The Royal Institute of International Affairs/Pinter Publishers, 1990), p. 84.

18 The withdrawal from Eastern Europe went well beyond the 50,000 initially announced in 1988 owing to pressures arising from the break-up of the WTO and German reunification.

19 'GPALS: the bid to save star wars', *New Scientist*, 20 March 1993, p. 32.

20 M. McGwire, *Perestroika and Soviet National Security* (Washington DC, The Brookings Institution, 1991), pp. 355–60.

21 In arms negotiations on INF and conventional forces the framework was always continent-wide, although prior to the Gorbachev period, completely unsuccessful.

22 Cited in N. Malcolm, 'The "common European home" and Soviet European policy', *International Affairs*, 65:4 (1989), p. 667.

23 Kull, *Burying Lenin*, p. 151.

24 Cited in G. Livermore (editor and compiler), *Russian Foreign Policy Today. The Soviet Legacy and Post-Soviet Beginnings* (Columbus, Ohio, The Current Digest, 1992), p. 169.

25 *The Independent*, 16 March 1991.

26 Gorbachev and Bush at the Malta summit in December 1989 declared an end to the Cold War. The Paris Charter adopted at the CSCE summit in November 1990 similarly proclaimed, 'the era of confrontation and division of Europe has ended.' The reader is reminded that the phrase 'the end of the Cold War' has a number of meanings (see p. 12 and Introduction, note 33), including the dissolution of the USSR itself, something not envisaged by either Gorbachev or Bush in 1989.

27 Thus the Third World was subject to superpower rivalry and China was courted by both the USSR and the US.

28 R. H. Wagner, 'What was bipolarity?', *International Organisation*, 47:1 (1993), p. 89.

29 C. Krauthammer, 'The unipolar moment', *Foreign Affairs*, 70:1 (1991). We shall return to this theme in the Conclusion when we consider different views of the post-Cold-War world.

30 S. Sestanovich, 'Inventing the Soviet national interest', in F.J. Fleron *et al.* (eds), *Contemporary Issues in Soviet Foreign Policy. From Brezhnev to Gorbachev* (New York, Aldine de Gruyter, 1991), p. 420.

31 K. Oye, cited in T. Risse-Kappen, 'Ideas do not float freely: transnational coalitions, domestic structures, and the end of the cold war',

International Organisation, 48:2 (1994), p. 189.

32 The relevant literature is summarised in Risse-Kappen, 'Ideas do not float freely', p. 189, and in M. Cox, 'Rethinking the end of the Cold War', *Review of International Studies*, 20:2 (1994), pp. 188–89.

33 For the relevant literature, see R.N. Lebow, 'The long peace, the end of the cold war and the failure of realism', *International Organisation*, 48:2 (1994), pp. 263–64.

34 Risse-Kappen, 'Ideas do not float freely', p. 189; T. Risse-Kappen, 'Did "peace through strength" end the cold war? Lessons from INF', *International Security*, 16:1 (1991), pp. 168–73.

35 F. Kratochwil, 'The embarrassment of changes: neorealism as the science of realpolitik without politics', *Review of International Studies*, 19:1 (1993), pp. 72–73.

36 D. Deudney and G.J. Ikenberry, 'The international sources of Soviet change', *International Security*, 16:3 (1991/92), pp. 95–96, 116–17.

37 Lebow, 'The long peace', pp. 261–62.

38 Risse-Kappen, 'Ideas do not float freely', p. 189; Lebow, 'The long peace', p. 263.

39 Deudney and Ikenberry, 'International sources of Soviet change', p. 106.

40 *Ibid.*, pp. 108–9.

41 J.S. Levy, 'Learning from experience in US and Soviet foreign policy', in M.I. Midlarsky *et al.* (eds), *From Rivalry to Cooperation. Russian and American Perspectives on the Post Cold War Era* (New York, Harper Collins, 1994), pp. 70–71.

42 *Ibid.*, pp. 58, 72.

43 Gorbachev faced opposition, for instance, from those who regarded his foreign policy as capitulation to the West. This was one motivating factor in the launch of the coup of August 1991 (see Chapter 2, p. 68).

44 Risse-Kappen, 'Ideas do not float freely', *passim*; J. Checkel, 'Ideas institutions and the Gorbachev foreign policy revolution', *World Politics*, 45:2 (1993), pp. 271–300, *passim*.

45 Stein, 'Political learning by doing', p.174.

46 Risse-Kappen, 'Ideas do not float freely', pp. 193–94.

47 Stein, 'Political learning by doing', p. 180.

48 Risse-Kappen, 'Ideas do not float freely', pp. 204, 210.

49 Stein, 'Political learning by doing', p. 180.

Recommended reading

M.R. Beschloss and S. Talbott, *At the Highest Levels. The Inside Story of the End of the Cold War* (London, Warner Books, 1993).

C.D. Blacker, *Hostage to Revolution. Gorbachev and Soviet Security Policy,*

1985–1991 (New York, Council on Foreign Relations Press, 1993).
M. MccGwire, *Perestroika and Soviet National Security* (Washington DC, The Brookings Institution, 1991).
R.F. Miller, *Soviet Foreign Policy Today* (London and New York, Unwin Hyman, 1991).

2

The transition: the dissolution of the Soviet Union and the initiation of the post-Soviet order

An understanding of the USSR's demise and of the inter-relations between the successor states requires some consideration of internal developments in the USSR during the Gorbachev period. In this chapter domestic issues are considered, concentrating on themes of greatest significance to the USSR's collapse in 1991 and developments in the post-Soviet period: economic reform, changes affecting the military, the nationalities question and the demise of the Communist Party of the Soviet Union (CPSU). These changes are important also in that they had linkages with the wider world. The Gorbachev leadership's search for greater participation in the international economy and curtailments in defence expenditure were processes which have both affected and been continued by the successor states. This chapter also examines the crucial events of the latter half of 1991: the August coup, the collapse of the USSR, and the formation of the Commonwealth of Independent States.

Economic reform and external economic relations

The Soviet Union's economic stagnation at the time of Gorbachev's coming to power was noted in the previous chapter (pp. 22–23). Attempts to arrest and reverse this decline were a central preoccupation of Gorbachev's domestic policies. Economic reforms took a number of guises. In the first two years of his stewardship, Gorbachev's approach was based on a strategy of 'acceleration' (increasing the productivity of the economy through the greater application of technology) married with an emphasis on discipline and quality control in the workplace. These reforms did little to improve the

USSR's economic predicaments, and consequently, a shift towards more innovative changes was inaugurated after 1986. These later reforms are significant for two reasons: first, they involved steps aimed at introducing full-blooded market principles into an economy that was hitherto almost wholly state-owned and state-planned (1991, for instance, witnessed a partial liberalisation of retail prices and the introduction of a law on denationalisation and privatisation), and second, they opened up the economy more fully to international transactions.

Of no small importance, in regard to the latter, were changes in the operation of foreign trade and measures to encourage external investment. The significance of these measures is obvious when one considers the historically closed nature of the Soviet economy. In 1988, Jerry Hough wrote: '(t)he Soviet Union has permitted no foreign investment; it has imported goods only through a monopolistic ministry of foreign trade; it has not permitted its factory managers to enter the world economy independently with their exports or even given them an incentive system that encourages exports'.[1] True, the USSR had partly broken out of its economic isolation during the 1970s. It imported greater amounts of machinery, consumer goods and foodstuffs and increased its sales of gold and energy on world markets as a means of obtaining hard currency. Nonetheless, total involvement in world trade remained negligible. Of this, trade with the industrialised West was rarely more than a third of Soviet turnover; transactions within the Council for Mutual Economic Assistance (CMEA) accounted for the bulk of transactions. To make matters worse, the countries of the North Atlantic Treaty Organisation (NATO) and Japan, imposed a trade boycott against the USSR through the Co-ordinating Committee for Multilateral Export Control (COCOM), limiting its access to advanced technologies. Economic isolationism had a detrimental impact upon the Soviet economy. The closed domestic market for Soviet products and the absence of any imperative to export removed an important incentive towards either innovation or greater efficiency. The eschewal of foreign investment and know-how, moreover, placed a similar brake on modernisation. Two major reforms attempted to address this situation. The first involved breaking the monopoly of foreign trade enjoyed by central government bodies. The Ministry of Foreign Trade was renamed (becoming the Ministry for Foreign Economic Relations) and reorganised, and the right to engage in trade directly with world markets extended to individual enterprises. The second change was initiated in 1987 with the enactment of legislation on joint ventures, which sanctioned foreign ownership of equity in the USSR. Although investors faced discouraging obstacles to involvement (such as difficulties in the repatriation of profits), this measure did increase the Soviet Union's access to foreign investment.

In response to worsening economic performance, Gorbachev also made a direct appeal to Western countries for assistance. During 1990 and 1991 this call was answered largely in the form of export credits and trade guarantees, and humanitarian aid, notably food, provided by European Community (EC) member countries. In June 1990, the USSR signed an agreement with the US that, subject to approval by the US Senate, would grant it Most-Favoured Nation (MFN) trade status[2] and during 1991 it obtained pledges of credits for the purchase of American grain worth $2.5 billion. The Soviet Union also gained observer status in the General Agreement on Tariffs and Trade (GATT) with an eye to boosting its long-term trade performance. More ambitious assistance, akin to the post-war Marshall Plan, was not forthcoming. A 'Grand Bargain' presented by reformist advisers to Gorbachev that called for $150 billion in trade credits and investments over five years inspired little enthusiasm among the Group of Seven (G7) industrialised countries. Gorbachev's own proposals, presented to the London summit of the G7 in July 1991, for Western forgiveness of Soviet foreign debt and the creation of a $10-12 billion rouble-stabilisation fund met with similar indifference. While the G7's European members lobbied for increased aid, the group as a whole was reluctant to inject substantial funds into an economy that still devoted vast amounts to defence and which was seen to require further moves towards liberalisation and the establishment of a reliable financial and legal infrastructure. The US also took issue at continuing Soviet assistance to Cuba while Japan made large-scale bilateral economic assistance contingent upon a solution to an unresolved territorial dispute over the Kurile Islands. Consequently, Gorbachev left the G7 summit with little of material substance, obtaining only pledges concerning technical assistance, expert advice and a 'special association' with the International Monetary Fund (IMF) and World Bank which stopped short of granting borrowing rights.

For all Gorbachev's reforming efforts, the Soviet economy by 1991 was tottering on the edge of calamity, victim of both the disruptive effects of the reforms themselves and political crisis. In the nine months from January to September industrial output fell by 6.4 per cent in comparison with the same period in 1990, while GNP as a whole declined by a massive 12 per cent. Foreign trade was down 38.1 per cent and in July Soviet foreign debt reportedly reached $70 billion. In the twelve months to September 1991 retail price inflation reached 103 per cent. Finally, a shift away from a unified state budget in 1991, involving the devolution of greater revenue raising powers to the republics, worsened an already yawning budget deficit. In the first six months of 1991 the combined shortfalls of the Union and republican budgets was equivalent to a massive 23.5 per cent of Soviet GNP.[3]

In summary, Gorbachev's reforms altered significantly the manner in which the Soviet economy was organised, but were, ultimately, unsuccessful in stimulating an economic revival. This would leave a painful legacy for the successor states.

Changes in the military

At the time of Gorbachev's accession to power, the Soviet Union faced what Michael MccGwire has labelled a 'triangle of conflicting demands'. National security considerations required the armed forces be able to defend the USSR in the event of war. To be able to do so successfully required access to the most modern weaponry in order to match the systems of potential aggressors. This, in turn, necessitated a vibrant economy capable of innovation and technological advance.[4] The economic reforms detailed in the previous section can be seen as an attempt to address the third point of this triangle. The redefinition of security inherent in the new political thinking and commensurate alterations in foreign policy amounted to a fundamental revision of its apex. In time, it was hoped, these policies would replace the triangle of demands with a virtuous circle, in which the Soviet Union's embrace of its former adversaries would dramatically reduce the defence burden and would facilitate the transfer of resources, personnel and know-how from the privileged defence sector to the civilian economy (a policy known as 'conversion').

The first indication of real progress in this regard was Gorbachev's announcement in January 1989 that defence spending would be cut by 14.2 per cent and weapons production by 19.5 per cent in the 1989–91 period. This, it was hoped, would permit a saving of some 30 billion roubles on the military budget set aside in the 1986–90 five-year economic plan. These targets were largely realised. Official defence spending declined by more than 17 per cent in the three-year period noted by Gorbachev. Cuts in armaments production were dramatic. Output of aircraft declined by 44 per cent, tanks by 52 per cent and strategic missiles by 58 per cent. Smaller, but still significant cuts, were also made in funds allocated to research and development (R and D).[5] These reductions proved essential to compensate for increased budgetary allocations arising from welfare payments (pensions, social security), housing construction and the integration of forces withdrawn from abroad.

Despite these reductions in defence expenditure, by the end of the Gorbachev period the Soviet economy remained highly militarised. In 1991, defence still accounted for an estimated 16.7 per cent of Soviet GNP. This did represent a slight reduction in the period since 1985. However, given the alarming increase in the budget deficit and estimates that the success of economic reform required a figure of only 8 per cent,[6] the urgency of defence reductions had by the early 1990s markedly increased. In this light, the issue of demilitarisation while addressed during the Gorbachev period, was far from resolved.

Alongside economically driven reforms, the military was subject to a series of other reorganisations. Sweeping personnel changes were undertaken, a move calculated to minimise military resistance to Gorbachev's reassessment of Soviet defence and foreign policies. The incumbent Minister of Defence (Sergei Sokolov) and Chief of the General Staff (Sergei Akhromeyev) were removed, in 1987 and 1988 respectively, and replaced by figures of little prior distinction (Dmitri Yazov and Mikhail Moiseyev). At other senior levels the turnover in cadres was so far-reaching that it invited comparisons with Stalin's purge of the Red Army in 1937.[7] Other innovations included a reorganisation of military districts, a pruning of administration, an increase of civilian input in policy formulation, and the removal of certain bodies (e.g. Border Troops, Ministry of Internal Affairs forces, KGB formations) from the armed forces.

The Gorbachev period was significant also in that it witnessed the emergence of widespread dissatisfaction and politicisation within the military. Aspects of this will be considered in sections below in the context of the nationalities issue and the military's position during the August coup. At this point it is worth noting a number of problems: maltreatment of young conscripts, low pay, poor housing, falling morale and draft evasion. These grievances fed into a debate on the role of the military which emerged in the latter Gorbachev years, focusing on issues such as the reduction of the size of forces, the desirability of scrapping conscription in favour of an all-volunteer army and the formation of units on a republican basis. Practical measures to address these matters, however, were few. Increased welfare expenditure has been noted above (p. 53) and this was complemented by experimenting with waged 'contract' recruits within the navy and increasing the stationing of non-Russian recruits within their home republics. Meaningful change, however, appeared to await the introduction of a comprehensive programme of military reform. Blueprints for this were presented by the Ministry of Defence in 1990, but implementation was postponed owing to uncertainties presented by the unresolved nationalities issue.

The nationalities issue

The Gorbachev period, particularly the years after 1988, witnessed an unprecedented upsurge of demands driven by ethnic and nationalist grievances. Separatist aspirations culminated in late 1991 with the attainment of independent statehood by all the Soviet republics.

That the divisive forces of nationalism should have been responsible for the unravelling of the USSR is in some ways understandable given the complexity of the country's ethnic composition. The 1989 Soviet census gave official recognition to one hundred and twenty-eight different nationalities, of which, twenty-two had populations over one million (see Table 2.1). This was complemented by the existence of an equivalent number of separate languages and a religious spectrum embracing varieties of Christian Orthodoxy, Protestantism, Catholicism and both Sunni and Shiite branches of Islam. Overlaying this was a complicated federal structure, composed of fifteen Union republics, five of which were themselves federated. In a comparative perspective it would have been remarkable if this mix did not lead to problems.

Observation of conflicts in Yugoslavia, Nigeria, Lebanon and Sri Lanka suggest the difficulties of maintaining statehood in sectionally divided societies. The USSR was even more heterogeneous –

Table 2.1 *The major Soviet nationalities (1989 census)*

	Population (millions)	*% of total*	*Linguistic group*	*Traditional religion*	*Union republic*
The Slavs					
Russians	145.1	50.8	East Slavic	Russian Orthodox	RSFSR[a]
Ukrainians	44.1	15.5	East Slavic	Russian Orthodox	Ukraine
Belorussians	10.0	3.5	East Slavic	Russian Orthodox	Belorussia[b]
The Balts					
Estonians	1.0	0.4	Finno-Ugrian	Protestant	Estonia
Latvians	1.5	0.5	Baltic	Protestant	Latvia
Lithuanians	3.1	1.1	Baltic	Roman Catholic	Lithuania
The Transcaucasians					
Armenians	4.6	1.6	Indo-European	Armenian–Orthodox	Armenia
Azeris	6.8	2.4	Turkic	Muslim (Shi'a)	Azerbaijan
Georgians	4.0	1.4	Kartvelian	Georgian–Orthodox	Georgia
The Central Asians					
Kazakhs	8.1	2.9	Turkic	Muslim (Sunni)	Kazakhstan
Kyrgiz	2.5	0.9	Turkic	Muslim (Sunni)	Kyrgyzstan
Turkmenians	2.7	1.0	Turkic	Muslim (Sunni)	Turkmenistan
Tajiks	4.2	1.5	Persian	Muslim (Sunni)	Tajikistan
Uzbeks	16.7	5.8	Turkic	Muslim (Sunni)	Uzbekistan
Other					
Moldavians	3.4	1.2	Romance	Romanian–Orthodox	Moldavia[c]

Notes: [a] Russian Soviet Federated Socialist Republic. At the end of 1991, with the USSR's collapse, it became the Russian Federation (Russia, for short). [b] Belorussia became Belarus in September 1991. [c] Moldavia was renamed Moldova in June 1990.

Source: S. White, *Gorbachev and After* (Cambridge, Cambridge University Press, third edition, 1992), p. 147.

its problems were consequently that much greater. Furthermore, the nature of the Soviet political system sustained a latent potential for the assertion of ethnic-based claims. In particular, Soviet federalism had the unintended effect of perpetuating national identities (and in Central Asia, of actually helping to create them). Since the inception of the federal structure in the early 1920s, the organisation of the constituent federal units had been based on conferring representation to national groups. This was, from the Stalin period, overridden by an increasing centralisation involving what was, in effect, direct rule from Moscow. Nonetheless, the existence of Union republics, usually comprised of titular ethnic majorities, enjoying limited cultural and linguistic rights and granted formal, albeit often unobserved, political freedoms created, what Zbigniew Brzezinski has termed, 'institutional vessels ... [that could] be easily filled with nationalist content'.[8] In other words, the Union republics were independent states in embryo.

The oppressive and arbitrary manner of Soviet rule also created latent problems. The deportation of nationalities during the Stalin period, the annexation of territories (Moldavia and the Baltic republics during World War II), the Russification of language, internal migration, the spreading of a Russian diaspora throughout the USSR, a bureaucratic and centralised form of economic planning, a lax attitude towards environmental issues and an arbitrary approach to administrative boundaries generated a series of deep-seated grievances which would prove impossible to pacify.

In light of these factors what is surprising is not the USSR's demise, but that it managed to maintain its existence for so long. True, nationalities' dissent, particularly in the Baltics, was apparent throughout the Brezhnev period. Nonetheless, by comparison with the Gorbachev years, the nationalities were relatively quiescent. This state of affairs was achieved through political and coercive mechanisms aimed at the *management* of the nationalities issue.[9] Such devices included, above all, the protected status of the CPSU. The absence of alternative political parties prevented the mobilisation of nationalist grievances. The hierarchical and centralised organisation of the CPSU itself, coupled with the *nomenklatura* principle of controlled appointment to all important party and government positions, meanwhile gave the central party authorities control and oversight throughout the USSR. The CPSU also had recourse to policies which sought to balance ethnic interests. At its highest levels the party was the preserve of Russians and, to a far lesser degree, other Slavs (i.e. Ukrainians). At the republican level, local interests were allowed considerable leeway, within limits set by Moscow. The republican party first secretary was usually drawn from the titular nationality and, during the latter years of the Brezhnev period, republican leaderships in the Central Asian and the Transcaucasian republics ran their patch relatively unhindered. This style of rule had two effects. Firstly, it helped mute nationalist dissent by encouraging the politically ambitious to direct their energies towards progression within the republican Communist Party. Secondly, it created a form of patron–client relationship wherein republican leaderships, in return for local privileges, acquiesced to the national priorities set by the central CPSU leadership in Moscow and discouraged the articulation of popular, ethnically based demands within their particular republic.

Recourse was also made to the cruder mechanisms of repression provided by the KGB and the armed forces. The harshness of the methods employed varied over time. The terror and mobilisation of military force during the Stalin period gave way to harassment, detention and psychiatric maltreatment of nationalist dissenters under Brezhnev. The end product, however, was similar – the suppression of national sentiment, but the creation of further grievances.

The containment of the national problem, which underlay the *management* approach broke down after 1985 as an unintended consequence of reforms in the political and economic spheres. *Glasnost*, Gorbachev's policy of expanding public debate, gave vent to nationalist feeling throughout most Soviet republics. This took the form both of cultural revival and the voicing of a gamut of grievances, concerned with the iniquities of centralised rule. This process was accompanied by some damning official reassessments of past misdemeanours. To take just one example, the 'secret protocols' of the Nazi–Soviet Pact of 1939, which provided for the annexation of the Baltic states and Moldavia were finally acknowledged by the Kremlin in 1989, a move which served only to highlight the illegitimacy of Soviet rule. Democratisation had an even more dramatic impact. 'Popular fronts' were formed in virtually all republics. In elections to Republican parliaments in 1990 these movements and their allies triumphed in the Baltics, Georgia, Armenia and Moldavia. The introduction of competitive elections meant even communist candidates were forced to take heed of local sentiments, thereby undermining central party control.

The nationalities policies of the Gorbachev period were ultimately unable to stem this tide of rising aspirations. Having witnessed riots in Kazakhstan in 1986 and demonstrations throughout the Baltics in

1987–88, Gorbachev's initial response was to acknowledge that a problem of sorts existed and to urge greater respect for national values. This was followed by a series of worthy declarations adopted by the CPSU in 1988–89. Policy thereafter swung, often inconsistently, between measures aimed at accommodation and devolution and those which reinforced centralisation. The inclusion of republican political leaderships in new central bodies such as the Council of the Federation and the Cabinet of Ministers was offset by the authoritarian implications of a new executive Soviet presidency created in 1990. Similarly, laws on secession, language rights and the delimitation of powers between the republics and the Union passed in 1990, retained for the 'centre' considerable prerogatives. A similar tension existed over attempts to adopt a Union Treaty to replace that of 1922, on which the USSR had been originally founded. Drafts adopted in November 1990 and March 1991 did admit devolved powers, but these were insufficient to satisfy many republics. Indeed, for some, the whole process of negotiating a new federal settlement was by this stage considered superfluous; the Baltic states refused to participate from the start and Armenia, Georgia and Moldavia (now known as Moldova) withdrew at an early stage. A Soviet-wide referendum on the desirability of a reformed Union in March was also boycotted by the authorities in these six republics and received an uncertain endorsement in the majority of the remainder.[10] By April 1991, Gorbachev was forced to recognise the impossibility of dictating a new settlement from the centre. The Novo–Ogarevo agreement reached with nine of the republics that month gave priority to the conclusion of a new Union settlement within three months. This was to be framed with the active participation of the republics.[11] Negotiations on this document resulted in a draft treaty in July on a 'Union of Soviet Sovereign Republics', which guaranteed substantially devolved powers. The treaty was never signed.

Despite all the belated good intentions of Gorbachev and the spirit of compromise evident in the Novo–Ogarevo process, the eighteen months or so prior to the August coup marked a break-down of Soviet nationalities policies and the headlong quest for greater powers by republics. This was apparent in the following ways.

1 By the end of 1990 all fifteen republics had either adopted declarations of 'sovereignty', had set in motion a transition period towards independence (Estonia and Latvia), or had declared the

immediate restoration of independence (Lithuania).

2 A 'war of laws' broke out between the 'centre' and the republics. Sovereignty declarations and amendments to republican constitutions, often granted republican laws precedence over those of the Union, thereby undermining Union prerogatives and disrupting national economic policy.

3 Efforts towards self-government were undertaken, particularly by the six republics outside the Union Treaty negotiations. The Baltic states, for example, withdrew from central political bodies, withheld contributions to the Union budget and began to acquire the trappings of statehood, such as customs services and passports.

In addition, some aspects of the Soviet nationalities crisis served as a prelude to developments in the post-Soviet period.

1 An assertive government emerged in the RSFSR. Prior to 1990, the Russian republic enjoyed a peculiar status. Its geographic, economic and political preponderance within the USSR, patterns of migration into non-Russian republics and the ascendancy of Russian language seemed to suggest that the Union was simply a sphere of Russian influence. Yet ironically, this ascendancy meant a subservient status was accorded to specifically Russian institutions of government, because Union bodies were regarded as the effective manager of Russian affairs. Indeed, in certain regards, the RSFSR entirely lacked its own representation, having no republican Communist Party, security forces, Academy of Sciences or broadcasting authorities.

This political limbo underwent a remarkable transformation during 1990–91 under the leadership of Boris Yeltsin. He tapped into an awakening nationalist sentiment amongst Russians fed by their sense of grievance at Union dominance of Russian affairs and the burden the RSFSR bore as the financial subsidiser of less developed republics of the USSR. Yeltsin, however, was not simply a lightning rod for Russian nationalism. His clash with Gorbachev was also shaped by conflicting attitudes to political and economic reform. The political crises experienced by ruling Communist Parties in Eastern Europe and Yeltsin's first-hand experience of sloth and corruption within the CPSU convinced him of the need for a more radical democratisation of the Soviet political system than the incremental changes favoured by Gorbachev. Similarly, he appreciated far more fully the argument that a shift towards market reform was necessary for economic regeneration. In light of his differences with Gorbachev, Yeltsin's strategy was based on the assumption that necessary reforms could not be obtained from the centre. They would have to be attempted through a revamped Russian government acting alongside the other republics. Yeltsin consequently held a far more reformist attitude towards the Union. Recognising that its continued viability could only be assured through the voluntary efforts of its constituent republics, he viewed the Union's future as a highly decentralised federation in which only a selected few prerogatives would be retained by the central administration.[12]

With the formation of a new Russian government in 1990 headed by Yeltsin as chair of the republic's supreme soviet or parliament, the RSFSR set about asserting its authority. In June, the parliament adopted a Declaration of Sovereignty, and this was followed by measures aimed at strengthening Russian jurisdiction over banking and financial contributions to the Union budget. The RSFSR also initiated its own economic reform programme, having become exasperated with the failures of Gorbachev. These policy innovations inevitably created frictions with Moscow. Worse was to come. In early 1991, Yeltsin began to openly question Moscow's competence to govern. In January he criticised a clampdown by the Soviet authorities in the Baltic republics and openly encroached upon the jurisdiction of the Soviet armed forces by urging Russian conscripts in the region to refrain from armed force.[13] The Baltic crisis, in fact, represented only one facet of an increasingly authoritarian line taken by Gorbachev during the winter of 1990–91 (the executive powers of the presidency were increased, efforts were undertaken to reimpose press censorship, 'workers' committees' were formed to track down food speculation and the powers of the military were increased). In response, Yeltsin called not just for Gorbachev's resignation (grave enough in itself), but for a 'war' against the centre. These demands were retracted once the Soviet leader returned to a reformist course with the Novo–Ogarevo agreement. However, power continued to flow towards the RSFSR. During the first half of 1991, it withheld contributions to the Union budget, set about establishing an independent banking system and, following agreement with Gorbachev in April, was given the go-ahead to establish a republican security organisation outside of the Soviet KGB.

Yeltsin's position was also strengthened by a number of developments within the RSFSR itself. The referendum of March on the future of the Union was supplemented here by an additional question on the desirability of a directly elected republican President. Seventy per cent of those voting favoured the creation of such a post and in June, Yeltsin was elected by a large majority, easily defeating his nearest rival the former Soviet Prime Minister Nikolai Ryzhkov. Emboldened by his new authority, Yeltsin enacted a decree which banned party branches and public movements from government offices and state-owned enterprises within the RSFSR's jurisdiction, a move clearly intended to undermine the CPSU.

2 Nascent foreign policies were pursued by the republics encroaching upon a prerogative jealously guarded by the centre. The RSFSR's growing stature within the USSR during 1990-91 was also felt in its pursuit of a foreign policy independent of the Soviet authorities. This initially served economic purposes. The formation of a Russian Ministry of Foreign Economic Relations and a bank of foreign trade, were intended to encourage direct trade and investment links abroad without having to go through Union administration. The Russian leadership also had a longer-term strategy. It embarked upon a course designed to raise the RSFSR's international profile in an apparent prelude to fully fledged membership of the international community. In October 1990 the hitherto largely symbolic RSFSR Foreign Ministry was revitalised with the appointment of Andrei Kozyrev as Foreign Minister. During the first half of 1991 Yeltsin undertook visits to the European Parliament in Strasbourg (April) and to the US (June), where he affirmed Russia's commitment to the non-proliferation of nuclear and chemical weapons. He also signed Declarations of Friendship and Co-operation with Poland (October 1990), Mongolia (February) and Czechoslovakia (May).

Russia's entry onto the world stage was not met with great enthusiasm by the West. Presidents George Bush and François Mitterrand and Prime Minister John Major, viewed Gorbachev as the guarantor of continued improvements in East–West relations and were reluctant to encourage Yeltsin for fear of undermining the Soviet leader's domestic position. During a visit to the US in June, Yeltsin was informed by the US President of Washington's faith in Gorbachev as the man 'who enabled us to end the Cold War and make Europe whole and free'. However, even the solidly pro-Gorbachev Bush had by mid-1991 begun to recognise the reality of Yeltsin's growing stature. In the same speech he confirmed that relations with the RSFSR and the other republics could be conducted where the new Union Treaty permitted. During the Moscow summit the following month, Bush, having signed the START Treaty with Gorbachev, became the first foreign guest to be received by Yeltsin in the Kremlin offices he now shared with Gorbachev.

Russia was not alone in carving out a role in the international arena. During 1990-91 virtually all the republics took tentative steps towards establishing contacts. Like Russia, these often had an economic rationale. President Nursultan Nazarbaev of Kazakhstan embarked upon trips to the US and Europe in search of investment. His fellow leaders in the other Central Asian republics courted contacts with any and all possible benefactors, including Turkey, Iran and the countries of the Asian–Pacific region.[14] Ukraine's purposes were wider. Breakthroughs occurred in relations with regional neighbours Poland and Hungary. A Treaty of Friendship and Co-operation was signed with the former in October 1990 and President Leonid Kravchuk's visit to Hungary in May 1991 resulted in nine bilateral agreements. The Ukrainian leader also undertook visits to Switzerland and Germany, during which he defended the right of his republic to seek greater powers from the Union.[15]

3 Republican defence postures also emerged. Prior to August 1991, the integrity of the Soviet armed forces was undermined by a number of developments. The first, draft evasion, has been alluded to above (p. 54). During 1990–91, this took on an obvious national dimension as Georgia, Armenia, Moldova and Lithuania declared the Soviet call-up void. Estonia and Latvia introduced alternative forms of military service, and Ukraine prohibited the central authorities from stationing Ukrainian nationals outside its territory. Secondly, local authorities took unilateral actions to curtail the functioning of Soviet military facilities, resulting in a notable case in the virtual cessation of activity at the Semipalatinsk nuclear test range in Kazakhstan. Third, and most seriously from the centre's point of view, a number of republics took steps towards the creation of independent republican militias. This trend was most evident in the Transcaucasus. In Georgia, a National Guard was set up in December 1990, which by mid-1991 numbered some 5,000 persons. In Armenia the military wing of the Armenian Pan-National Movement (the victor of elec-

tions to the republic's parliament in May 1990) developed a 10,000-strong force. Elsewhere, a National Guard was established in Moldova to deal with separatist threats amongst the Russian population in the Trans-Dniester, and in the Baltic republics, small-scale forces akin to Home Guards were inaugurated to defend republican property and patrol borders. Of some significance also, were developments in the RSFSR and Ukraine, militarily the two most important republics in the USSR. Neither took practical measures towards establishing independent forces; however, the right to do so was expressed in Ukraine's declaration of sovereignty of July 1990[16] and in the RSFSR's draft constitution of November.[17]

4 Growing co-ordination was evident between the republics, bypassing the Union authorities. In the course of 1990 and 1991, this involved the conclusion of a plethora of bilateral agreements ranging from accords on cultural co-operation to broad-ranging economic and political-state treaties. The RSFSR, for example, signed agreements with the three Baltic states, which, by recognising the right of each to independence and by containing clauses on issues such as borders, migration and citizenship, approximated relations between sovereign states. A Russian–Ukrainian Treaty on the Principles of Relations signed in November 1990 covered similar issues, in this case going considerably further by calling for co-operation in the areas of defence and security.[18] Multilateral arrangements were also established. In December 1990, officials from the RSFSR, Belorussia, Ukraine and Kazakhstan met with the aim of forging a quadrilateral agreement as an alternative to Gorbachev's projected Union Treaty. In April a second group, comprising the six republics outside the Novo–Ogarevo process agreed to measures to enhance co-operation. Three months later, the five central Asian republics set up an inter-republican consultative council.

5 Inter-ethnic frictions broke out often involving violence. The most intractable and bloody of these was the conflict over the disputed territory of Nagorno–Karabakh between Armenian and Azeri forces. Large-scale violence also erupted in Abkhazia and South Ossetia in Georgia. In the Baltic republics and the Trans–Dniester region of Moldova, ethnic Russian minority populations set up organisations to resist what were perceived as discriminatory language and citizenship laws.[19]

The Communist Party

A defining quality of the pre-Gorbachev political system was the entrenched, ruling position enjoyed by the Communist Party. To summarise briefly, the CPSU monopolised all leading positions of government, channelled the activities of mass organisations such as the trade unions, exercised political oversight of the armed forces and the KGB, and prevented the emergence of political alternatives through a pervasive censorship of the media. This position of political primacy was complemented by what appeared to be impressive organisational strengths. By the mid-1980s the party had a membership of some nineteen million persons, which was subject to a centralised, hierarchical party structure. It would be inaccurate to suggest that this amounted to the 'monolithic' unity claimed by the party leadership. Nonetheless, those divisions which did exist, be these in the form of shifting personal alliances within the leadership or empire-building in republican organisations, were not so serious as to undermine the party's exercise of political leadership in Soviet society. This held important consequences in respect of the viability of the Soviet state, in that the Communist Party was amongst the most powerful centralising influences within the Union (alongside the armed forces), providing an essential, and what seemed an immutable guarantee of the USSR's cohesion.

During the Gorbachev period the political primacy of the CPSU was decisively ended with far-reaching consequences. Its fall was the result of four broad developments. First, the party was an unintentional victim of a programme of democratisation pursued by Gorbachev. Electoral reform and the legalisation of a nascent multi-party politics, while arguably intended as a means of revitalising the CPSU,[20] served in fact only to give formal recognition, and in some cases, political power, to viable alternatives outside it. Moreover, Gorbachev's desire to introduce greater democracy and debate within the party itself, led at the CPSU's twenty-eighth Party Congress in 1990 to the sanctioning of 'platforms', a move which accelerated a debilitating process of faction forming. The formation of these factions reflected a second development: the arousal of controversies arising from policies pursued by the Gorbachev leadership. Economic and nationalities' policies, innovations in foreign relations and revisions to the CPSU party programme (involving an abandonment of Marxism–Leninism in favour of an ill-defined 'humane democratic socialism') all provoked a range of competing opinions around which factions came to be organised. While Gorbachev was criticised by the 'conservatives' for his radicalism, equally important were the opinions of those who felt the Soviet leader's approach was too timid. In this respect, the alienation from Gorbachev was so complete, that individuals felt their interests would be best served outside the party, leading to defections by figures as prominent as Yeltsin and Shevardnadze. Third, the party suffered a massive drop in popularity. This was apparent in opinion poll surveys, a decline in the circulation of the party press and shortfalls in membership dues. The CPSU also suffered a loss of members, amounting to a decline of some four million in the eighteen months to the middle of 1991. Fourth, the party was adversely affected by the nationalities issue. In the face of the tide of rising separatist sentiment, republican Communist Parties in the Baltics, Georgia and Moldova announced their secession from the parent CPSU in an attempt to retain some modicum of local credibility.

The crisis of the CPSU was at an advanced stage by mid-1991. As will be detailed below, this accelerated following the August coup, leaving the party totally emasculated by the end of the year. The party's fall had important consequences. First, because it was one of the foremost centralising influences in the Union, its loss of power was both cause and effect of the break-up of the USSR. Second, the CPSU's decline had an important influence after 1991. During the Soviet period it was the only political organisation that could claim an all-Union presence. New parties and movements established during the Gorbachev period had not succeeded in organising so widely. Many had an explicitly nationalist agenda confined to a particular republic, while even those with broader programmes lacked the finances, skills and membership to match the CPSU's organisational advantages. Hence, in the post-Soviet period, no organisation has had an influence throughout the entire territory of the former USSR. The absence of a forum in which the post-Soviet elites shared membership and held a common loyalty would prove an obstacle to mutual co-operation. Gorbachev's ideological revisions had a similar impact. The discrediting of Marxism–Leninism and Gorbachev's failure to construct a revisionist socialist platform as a popular basis for reform meant the CPSU was no match for movements projecting particularist, nationalist causes. Many of the new leaders in the republics had come to power on the back of such nationalist feeling and were particularly sensitive to their own constituencies. Links with political elites tended to be in service simply of the common cause of opposing the centre; no effort was made to construct a pan-USSR body of reform ideas. Once the centre had disappeared, there was, therefore, no unifying political cause which could act as a form of *esprit de corps* amongst the post-Soviet leaderships.

The August coup

On the morning of 19 August 1991, a self-styled State Committee for the State of Emergency (SCSE) announced it had assumed power in the USSR. Owing, it was claimed, to Gorbachev's poor health, and in accordance with provisions in the Soviet constitution, executive power was transferred to Vice-President Gannadii Yanaev, the SCSE's nominal leader. It soon became apparent that Gorbachev was not ill at all, but subject to house arrest at his holiday home in the Crimea at the Committee's instructions. In fact, the real pretext for the SCSE's actions was not to step in for an unwell President, but, as it claimed in an 'Appeal to the Soviet People', to rescue the country from a 'mortal danger'. The USSR, the SCSE argued, had become 'ungovernable', threatened by 'extremist forces' bent on the 'liquidation' of the country. It was experiencing economic catastrophe, an explosion of crime and had lost much of its international standing.[21] This amounted, in effect, to a wholesale condemnation of the domestic and international policies of the Gorbachev period. The strong representation of the military–industrial complex in the SCSE (see Box 2.1.) and the absence of any overt appeals to ideology in its proclamations, moreover, suggested the overriding concern of the coup was to return 'order' to Soviet society, and in particular to staunch the centrifugal forces brought about by the nationalities issue. Here the significance of the timing of the coup becomes apparent; it was launched the day before the first parties were due to sign the new Union Treaty.

Whatever motives lay behind the coup, its perpetrators proved unable to hold on to power. The members of the SCSE lacked both competence and conviction. In contrast to say the imposition of martial law in Poland in 1981, the Committee failed to take the repressive measures necessary to properly enforce its authority and appeared powerless in the face of the limited resistance that was mounted against it. The plotters were also guilty of errors of judgement, being totally unprepared for even the low levels of opposition which emerged within the KGB and the armed forces.

Box 2.1 The State Committee for the State of Emergency

Oleg Baklanov	First Vice-Chair of the USSR Defence Council
Vladimir Kryuchkov	Chair of the KGB of the USSR
Valentin Pavlov	Prime Minister of the USSR
Boris Pugo	USSR Minister of Internal Affairs
Vasilii Starodubtsev	Chair of the USSR's Peasants' Union
Alexander Tizyakov	President of the Association of State Enterprises
Dmitri Yazov	USSR Minister of Defence
Gennadii Yanaev	Vice-President of the USSR

The role of the armed forces

Almost by definition a *coup d'état* involves military participation: that in the USSR was no different. Although it appears the main impetus for the attempted seizure of power came from within the KGB and the Interior Ministry,[22] the senior leadership within the armed forces was also heavily implicated, including, of course, the Minister of Defence, himself a member of the SCSE.[23]

What motivated these figures can be gleaned from a series of complaints raised in the year or so prior to the coup. Defence Minister Yazov, for example, was particularly aggrieved by the threats to the integrity of the Soviet armed forces posed by rebellious republics. His involvement with the SCSE was in order primarily to reverse the process of separatism within the USSR.[24] Discontent over the nationalities issue was, in fact, widespread within the higher ranks. At a meeting with some 1,100 senior officers in November 1990, Gorbachev was subjected to a series of tirades concerning the prospect of the USSR's dismemberment and was urged to take direct action to prevent this.[25] Voices in the armed forces were also heard on a number of other issues. Cuts in the military budget, defence conversion and the falling standard of living of personnel all impinged directly upon the officer corps. Many senior officers also objected to reform of the CPSU. In 1991 an estimated 70 per cent of the officer corps were members of the Communist Party. What concerned these people was not so much the revisions of ideology undertaken by

Gorbachev, but practical steps towards ending the party's monopoly within the armed forces, which were seen as undermining one of the central mechanisms of unity and discipline. In this connection, greatest concern was directed not towards Gorbachev, but at Boris Yeltsin, who in July had called for the removal of CPSU structures from the military and security forces. The Russian President in fact had no jurisdiction over the Soviet military – it being a Union rather than republican institution. Nonetheless, his demand was taken seriously, provoking a riposte from Yazov, who condemned the move as intended 'to shatter and disperse the Armed Forces'.[26]

Alongside these domestic issues, the military command was also uneasy at aspects of Soviet foreign policy. Gorbachev's acquiescence in the 'loss' of Eastern Europe, for example, was strongly criticised on a number of grounds. It was seen as a betrayal of the lives of Soviet soldiers who had died in World War II, it meant the disappearance of any allies in the region and imposed upon the armed forces a humiliating withdrawal back to a USSR which lacked sufficient housing to accommodate them. Arms agreements and reductions were also the subject of scorn. The CFE Treaty, for instance, was regarded as loaded against the USSR, provoking attempts by the military command to exploit loopholes in the agreement. A further source of military discomfiture – the Soviet stance on the Gulf War – also provoked covert activities. Secret arms deliveries to Baghdad in early 1991, were at odds with Moscow's official adherence to the UN arms boycott of Iraq and Gorbachev's personal efforts to persuade Saddam Hussein of the wisdom of withdrawal from Kuwait. Foreign Minister Shevardnadze's willingness to commit Soviet troops to an American-led UN contingent in the Gulf was fiercely, and successfully, resisted.[27] The Foreign Minister was, in fact, a figure of particular detestation. A campaign of criticism waged by officers, notably military deputies within the Soviet parliament, the Congress of People's Deputies helped provoke his resignation in December 1990.

Sections of the military appeared then to have strong grounds for opposing Gorbachev. The events of the coup, however, made it clear that the armed forces were deeply divided, even at their highest levels. An antipathy to Gorbachev was not always translated into active support for the SCSE. Indeed, it was estimated that only 5 per cent of General Staff personnel took an active role in backing the coup.[28] The most common reaction was passivity. This reflected: (1)

a 'wait-and-see' attitude, awaiting the coup's outcome before deciding who to support; (2) confusion over who actually had acquired power at the centre, often compounded by the absence of direct communications with Moscow and the lack of clear orders from military commands; and (3) a residual loyalty to the established authorities. Once the ineptitude and illegitimacy of the SCSE became apparent, passivity increasingly shifted to opposition. Critically, a minority opposed the Committee from the start. Yevgenii Shaposhnikov the Air Force Commander-in-Chief and Pavel Grachev the commander of Soviet airborne forces, sided with the resistance in Moscow. In Leningrad, General Viktor Samsonov the chief of the local military district, was hesitant but was finally dissuaded from deploying troops in the city by the entreaties of Mayor Anatoly Sobchak. Lower down the chain of command, similar defections occurred. Garrison commanders of at least eleven Russian cities came out against the SCSE. Crucially, they were joined by elements within army divisions deployed in the capital, who took up positions in defence of forces supporting Yeltsin.[29]

The division within the military was the most significant factor in the failure of the coup. An awareness of the possibility of factional battles within the armed forces amongst pro and anti coup supporters appears to have undermined Yazov's resolve and led to a consensus within the Defence Ministry collegium in favour of the withdrawal of troops from Moscow on 21 August.

The role of Boris Yeltsin

Fears of a bloodbath arose not just from possible clashes within the military. Civilian resistance was also an important consideration. Opposition to the coup was, in fact, quite patchy throughout the USSR as a whole. A call by Yeltsin for a general strike received little active support. Demonstrations of defiance did occur in the Baltics and Moldova, but these could be discounted by the SCSE as peripheral to their consolidation of power in the Soviet capital, Moscow, and the USSR's second city, Leningrad. In these two cities, civil resistance did play a major part, ultimately undermining the SCSE's resolve. Mass gatherings in Leningrad's Palace Square and demonstrations outside the 'White House' building (the seat of the Russian parliament) in Moscow confronted the SCSE with the prospect of having to use force in order to impose its rule. The consequent risk of huge civilian casualties was enough to dissuade Yazov from deploying armed units. The crack KGB Alpha Unit, which was given an order to storm the White House, demurred for similar reasons.

That the SCSE ever had to face this predicament owes much to the resolve of Yeltsin. From his redoubt in the White House he condemned the coup as 'illegal', demanded Gorbachev's reinstatement and called for protest demonstrations and a general strike. By such moves the Russian President became a focus of opposition. His actions also contributed to further divisions in the armed forces. Since 1990 Yeltsin's evolution as a figurehead of democracy and Russian nationalism had struck a chord in the military. In the electoral campaign for the Russian Presidency in June 1991, Yeltsin chose shrewdly a hero of the war in Afghanistan, Colonel Alexander Rutskoi as his Vice-Presidential running mate. Moreover, on the campaign trail he made several visits to military bases, articulating a message of Russian national pride. During the coup itself, Yeltsin issued a carefully worded entreaty to the armed forces which contained appeals to both democratic and patriotic sentiment.[30] While the attraction of such populism was confined largely to conscripts and junior officers, it also had some appeal at more senior levels; hence the minority in the upper echelons who actively sided with the Yeltsin camp.

The role of Mikhail Gorbachev

Whereas Yeltsin emerged as the hero of the coup, Gorbachev was fatally compromised by it. Competing conspiracy theories have actually suggested Gorbachev orchestrated the putsch, either as a means of wrecking the new Union Treaty (which would have reduced the status of the Soviet President to that of a figurehead) or, alternatively, as a means of flushing out his conservative opponents in order to return more vigorously to the path of reform. Upon close analysis these scenarios appear rather fanciful.[31] A more convincing argument suggests that Gorbachev *inadvertently* encouraged the coup by his actions in the preceding twelve months. That a majority of the members of the SCSE held leading government posts and positions in executive bodies at the time of the coup was down entirely to Gorbachev.[32] He had, after all, appointed them. Moreover, his authoritarian turn during the winter of 1990–91 (see above p. 60), amounted to a 'creeping coup d'état',[33] which gave the conservatives the impression that the President was not averse to decisive measures. These hopes were dashed by Gorbachev's return to reformism signified by the Novo–Ogarevo agreement of April and negotiations on the Union Treaty. Gorbachev's vacillation led to a deep disillusionment amongst the conservatives. Nonetheless, despite the opening up of a division between the President and his government, the future members of the SCSE remained in their positions. Even an appeal in June by Pavlov (supported by Yazov, Kryuchkov and Pugo) to the Soviet parliament to expand the powers of the Cabinet at the President's expense, did not prompt Gorbachev to undertake any sackings. In this light, Gorbachev's complicity in the coup lay in his unwillingness to neutralise those forces under his own command, which were clearly at odds with him politically. This neglect left the plotters in positions of considerable importance, which they were able to exploit in their quest for power.

The role of the republics

Open defiance of the coup was exhibited by only a minority of republics. Amongst the most forthright were the Baltics, who feared a setback to their aspirations for independence. In Lithuania, President Vytautas Landsbergis called for mass political action to oppose any attempt to overthrow local authority, addressed a message of solidarity to the Russian leadership and called upon Soviet troops based in the republic to desist from encroaching upon the rights of the Lithuanian government. In Latvia and Estonia the situation was complicated by the active support given to the SCSE by organisations close to the large Russian-speaking minorities resident there. Nevertheless, in both cases, the launching of the coup served only to steel the determination of nationalist leaderships. They joined Lithuania in siding with Yeltsin and in condemning the SCSE. In Moldova, where the situation was also rendered problematic by sympathies for the SCSE among part of the Russian populace (in this case, the communist leadership of the Trans–Dniester region), the republic's leadership similarly took a firm stance against the coup, establishing a Security Council charged with defending the republic. In Kyrgyzstan, the liberal President Askar Akaev, took immediate action against the republican, pro-SCSE Communist Party, sacked the head of the Kyrgyz KGB and ordered all local military units to remain in their bases.

Elsewhere, reaction to the coup was far less decisive. Kazakh President Nazarbaev criticised the SCSE as illegal, but appealed for calm, fearful of outbreaks of violence in the republic. In Armenia, caution was also evident. In contrast to the Baltics, where the coup was a catalyst for declarations of independence from the USSR, Armenia was mindful that such moves might provoke strong counter-measures by the Committee. In order not to frustrate what it perceived as an entirely legal path towards independence within the terms of the 1990 Soviet Law on Secession, the Armenian leadership offered criticism of the SCSE, but refrained from calling for active resistance. President Zviad Gamsakhurdia of neighbouring Georgia took a similar line. He too appealed for calm and cut a deal with the head of the Transcaucasus Military District whereby Georgia's National Guard would be disbanded. Only when the coup appeared doomed did he condemn it. In the Ukraine, President Kravchuk initially observed a studious neutrality, apparently awaiting the coup's outcome. Only on 21 August as the coup collapsed, did the Ukrainian leader unequivocally condemn the SCSE. A similar approach was taken by the leadership in Belorussia.

The republican leaderships most compromised were, of course, those which either tacitly or explicitly supported the coup. The President of Tajikistan, Qahhor Mahkamov, allowed the publication of SCSE resolutions, while in Uzbekistan, President Islam Karimov exploited the SCSE's bans on political activity to make arrests of political opponents. In Azerbaijan, finally, President Ayaz Mutalibov openly welcomed the coup, possibly hoping for a tough line by the SCSE on the preservation of the status quo in Nagorno–Karabakh.

The role of the outside world

With an eye to possible international hostility, the SCSE on 20 August issued a message addressed to foreign governments. This justified the Committee's seizure of power and contained assurances that all international commitments entered into by the USSR would be honoured.[34] The merits of this claim were, of course never tested, and in any case appeared dubious given the objections of figures such as Yazov to Gorbachev's foreign policy. More importantly, such appeals carried little weight with those countries which had developed a close working relationship with Moscow.

The coup was particularly worrying for the Bush Administration in the US, where it was felt that the overthrow of Gorbachev would imperil not only the implementation of the CFE agreement and Soviet troop withdrawals from Eastern Europe, but would prevent a ratification of the START agreement signed in July. The continuation of co-operation on regional issues also appeared unlikely, a blow, for instance, to American plans for a peace conference on the Arab–Israeli dispute. Washington, therefore, had a keen interest in Gorbachev's restitution. Bush suggested that normal relations would not be possible so long as the 'illegal coup' remained in effect and took measures such as the suspension of economic assistance in pursuit of 'the restoration of constitutional government in the Soviet Union'. In defiance of the SCSE, a message of support was also relayed to Boris Yeltsin.[35]

Concerns were also voiced in Western Europe. Chancellor Helmut Kohl of Germany mindful of the accord signed with the USSR on the removal of Soviet troops from the former East Germany, called upon the SCSE to respect all international agreements.[36] The British Prime Minister, John Major, meanwhile condemned the SCSE's actions as a 'straight-forward, common or garden, old-fashioned ... hardline and reactionary ... coup', immediately suspended economic assistance and endorsed Yeltsin's appeal for the release of Gorbachev.[37] An emergency meeting of EC Foreign Ministers on 20 August, demanded the re-establishment of constitutional authority and suspended aid worth some $1 billion. A NATO Foreign Ministers' meeting the following day called for Gorbachev's return to power, expressed support for the 'democratically elected leaders' (mentioning Yeltsin by name) and agreed to refrain from any actions which might be construed as recognition of the SCSE.[38]

The coup was also received with concern in Eastern Europe, although here reaction was tempered with caution owing to the region's more exposed position. Polish President, Lech Walesa, while condemning the takeover, called for calm in his country, aware that any disturbance might threaten negotiations on the withdrawal of Soviet troops. In Czechoslovakia, President Vaclav Havel, announced he was reconsidering the transit of Soviet troops returning from Germany through Czech territory and expressed concern at the possibility of an influx of refugees from neighbouring Ukraine. In Budapest, meanwhile, the government aligned itself with the Western position and made preparations for a possible troop mobilisation in the event of threats to Hungarian security. Finally, in

Romania, the official response was one of extreme prudence. Fearful of the spillover of a hardline clampdown in neighbouring Moldova, the Romanian leadership avoided any outright condemnation of the coup and failed to show any support for the resistance of its Moldovan compatriots.

Overall the international reaction to the SCSE's assumption of power was a hostile one, quickly disabusing the plotters of any thoughts they may have held of an even-handed treatment. Indeed, the coup was met with equanimity by only a handful of states. Non-committal responses by China and Cuba reflected a private satisfaction at the incapacity of a Soviet leader with whom they had become increasingly disillusioned. However, such *schadenfreude* was not accompanied by expressions of support for the SCSE, both Beijing and Havana adopting the neutral stance that events in the USSR were a purely internal matter. In fact, active support of the coup was voiced by only a handful of states, amongst them Iraq, Libya and Sudan. The solidarity of these international pariahs served, however, only to undermine further the Committee's credibility.

August–December 1991: things fall apart

On 22 August the coup leaders were placed under arrest, or in the case of Boris Pugo, committed suicide. Gorbachev returned to Moscow on the same day. The Soviet leader's reappearance, however, was far from triumphant. Not only had questions been raised concerning his role in the events of August, but the star of his political rival, Boris Yeltsin, had risen considerably. The ensuing four months, would witness increasingly futile efforts by Gorbachev to patch up the Union Treaty and the sapping of the centre's remaining powers away to the republics, culminating in December in the formal break-up of the USSR.

Decommunisation

The coup plotters during their temporary residence in power made little reference to communist ideology or to a restoration of the 'leading role' of the CPSU. Attracted by the conservative message of the SCSE, the party apparatus and elements of its leadership, nonetheless, played a significant part in support of the coup. All of the Committee were party members and a number of top party officials were implicated in the conspiracy, including Chair of the USSR Supreme Soviet Anatoly Lukyanov, Politburo member Oleg Shenin and Secretary of the Moscow City Party organisation Yuri Prokof'ev. Only on August 21, as the SCSE appeared doomed, did the CPSU Central Committee Secretariat issue a statement, which might be read as a condemnation of the coup.[39]

In the RSFSR, according to an investigation by Russia's chief State Inspector, not a single party committee sided with Yeltsin, two-thirds of them openly supported the SCSE and the remainder awaited events to proclaim their allegiance.[40] Other republics told a similar story. The pro-Moscow branches of republican Communist Parties in the Baltics expressed open solidarity with the coup. In Belorussia, Ukraine and Moldova, the party also sided to varying degrees with the SCSE. In Kyrgyzstan, finally, the party went so far as to conspire with the republican KGB in an attempt to overthrow President Akaev.

Communist involvement in the coup led subsequently to a series of measures, which severely impeded the party's operation throughout the USSR. The lead in this regard was taken in the RSFSR. Yeltsin, mindful also of the political opposition he had faced from the CPSU apparatus (he was sacked from the Politburo in 1987) and from the Russian Communist Party (established in 1990),[41] pursued a vigorous course of action. As the coup crumbled on August 22, he prohibited on Russian territory organised Communist Party activity in the armed forces, the KGB and the police. The following day, the Russian Communist Party was temporarily suspended, and, along with the CPSU as a whole, was formally banned in the RSFSR by a Presidential edict in early November. Decisive action was also taken in other republics, a majority either banning or suspending republican party organisations. Even Gorbachev, the CPSU's General Secretary, was forced to acknowledge the party's shabby performance in the events of August. Upon his return to Moscow, he resigned the party leadership, ordered the nationalisation of Communist Party property, called upon the Central Committee to dissolve itself and extended throughout the USSR Yeltsin's prohibition of party activity in the army and other organs. The USSR Supreme Soviet, meeting at the end of August, suspended the activities of the entire CPSU. By such measures, the political primacy of the CPSU was decisively and irrevocably ended.

The transfer of power to Russia and the other republics

The failure of the August coup served to accelerate the flow of powers towards the RSFSR, which had begun in 1990. At the height of the coup, Yeltsin issued a series of decrees ostensibly aimed at resisting the SCSE, but which involved the concentration of considerable powers in the hands of the Russian authorities. Yeltsin appointed himself commander of Soviet armed forces on Russian territory (a position he retained jointly with Gorbachev after the coup) and placed under his authority 'all USSR bodies of executive power' on the territory of the RSFSR.[42] Following Gorbachev's release, Yeltsin continued to encroach upon Union jurisdiction. Under a decree issued on 22 August, the Russian President sought to wrest control of the economy away from the Union, stipulating that most Union enterprises operating within the RSFSR be transferred to Russian jurisdiction by the end of the year. Yeltsin's assertion of authority did not go entirely unchallenged by Gorbachev. However, even the Soviet President was forced to recognise the new balance of forces and attempted to co-opt, rather than alienate, the Russian leader. An agreement was reached whereby he and Yeltsin would assume each other's responsibilities in the event of an emergency and ministerial changes in late August in the Soviet ministries of the Interior and Defence and in the KGB were made after consultations between the two men.

In the ensuing months, the power of Russia and the other republics continued to rise as the structures of Soviet government were reformed. A Committee charged with running the Soviet economy following the dissolution of the Soviet Cabinet (a body which supported the coup) was not only chaired by the Russian Prime Minister Ivan Silayev, but six of its key ministerial portfolios were given to RSFSR ministers. A State Council made up of the Soviet President and the leaders of the republics became the top all-Union decision-making institution in September. This body decided to commence the closure of some eighty Union ministries with effect from mid-November. An inter-republican initiative, the agreement on an Economic Community, did envisage the survival of economic co-ordination, but even this was torpedoed by Yeltsin's announcement of a programme of radical reform later that month, which would run independently of inter-republican agreements. In November, Yeltsin took further steps to consolidate Russia's economic position, unilaterally assuming control of all oil, gold and diamond resources on RSFSR territory and stripping Union financial institutions of control over exchange rates and money supply. That same month the Russian parliament indicated its intention to take over Gosbank, the Soviet state bank, pending the creation of an inter-republican banking union.

Symptomatic also of the loss of Union powers were developments in foreign policy and defence. At first sight, the August coup appeared to have invigorated Soviet foreign policy. In the month or so following Gorbachev's return a number of initiatives were undertaken. An agreement was reached with the US on the termination of assistance to the warring parties in Afghanistan and Gorbachev announced a withdrawal of the Soviet military presence in Cuba. The Soviet leader (in response to proposals put forward by US President George Bush), also announced projected cuts in nuclear weapons with a range below those covered by the INF Treaty and outlined further reductions in strategic arsenals beyond those mandated by the START agreement. In October, Moscow participated in the Paris Conference on Cambodia, co-chaired with the Americans the Middle East peace conference in Madrid and succeeded in brokering a ceasefire between Serb and Croat forces in Yugoslavia.

That these initiatives reflected the resilience of Union authority, was, however, belied by the greater involvement of the republics in Soviet foreign policy. The appointment of Boris Pankin as Soviet Foreign Minister at the end of August in place of Alexander Bessmertnykh[43] inaugurated a process of institutional reform designed to give the republics a greater input in policy formulation and permit them a measure of diplomatic representation in Soviet embassies and delegations. These measures only partly satisfied the Russian leadership, which demanded a total recasting of the Foreign Ministry's mission to represent republican interests. At a meeting of the State Council in mid-November it was decided that a renamed Ministry of Foreign Affairs (it became the Ministry of External Relations) would take over the responsibilities of the Ministry of Foreign Economic Relations and would, in response to Russian demands, be responsible for both formulating Union policies and for co-ordinating the foreign policies of the republics. Shevardnadze who was appointed to head the new Ministry was aware of a new balance of forces, suggesting upon his return to the post of Soviet Foreign Minister that '(w)ithout Russia, there can be no Union foreign policy'.[44]

The viability of a specifically Union foreign policy was undermined further by initiatives pursued by the RSFSR and other republics, the thrust of which appeared to anticipate the inevitability of the USSR's disappearance as a unified state. In mid-November talks were held with G7 representatives on sharing out and repaying Soviet foreign debt and the RSFSR and three other key republics (Ukraine, Belarus and Kazakhstan) repudiated the right of Soviet authorities to represent their interests in dealings with the IMF, the World Bank and other international institutions. In bilateral matters, the RSFSR asserted its authority over any settlement of the Kurile Islands dispute with Japan. During a visit to Germany in late November, Yeltsin signed a joint declaration, which contained a stipulation that existing treaties between Bonn and the USSR were to be 'applied to the relationship between Germany and Russia', a clause which, in effect, meant assuming responsibility for Soviet troop withdrawals from the former East Germany.[45]

Defence matters also became the subject of the shifting centre-republic balance of influence. Shaposhnikov, promoted to the post of Soviet Defence Minister after the coup, proposed a military reform, which kept intact a unified Soviet conventional armed forces and single, centralised control of nuclear forces, but which also permitted devolved powers to the republics. This, however, did not go far enough. Regarding conventional forces, only the RSFSR, Belarus and the five Central Asian states explicitly supported a single armed forces under a single command structure. The other republics, by contrast, considered the survival of a Soviet defence structure to be only a temporary expedient while powers were devolved to emergent republican organisations. The Baltics demanded a total withdrawal of all Soviet forces, while Azerbaijan and Moldova 'nationalised' all Soviet military property on their territories. Developments in Ukraine were also particularly significant in light of the republic's vast military potential. Following the defeat of the coup, moves were set in motion to create a national defence establishment. On 24 August President Kravchuk endorsed the idea that Soviet forces in Ukraine be placed under the jurisdiction of the republic's parliament. Shortly after, a Minister of Defence was appointed, who in late October unveiled plans for the creation of national forces numbering some 450,000 personnel.

The issue of nuclear weapons' control also illustrates the republics' assertion of authority at this point. In the wake of the coup, considerable confusion arose over these weapons. Statements issued by the leaderships of the four republics in which strategic nuclear weapons were stationed (the RSFSR, Ukraine, Belarus and Kazakhstan) seemed to suggest an imminent usurpation of the Soviet nuclear arsenal's chain of command, which at that point was still headed by President Gorbachev and the General Staff of the Soviet armed forces. The republics lacked *de facto* control. They were, however, determined to acquire *de jure* authority over weapons on their territory. This brought them into conflict not just with the Soviet authorities, but also with the RSFSR.

In Ukraine, where public mistrust of nuclear matters ran deep owing to the Chernobyl nuclear power plant accident in 1986, President Kravchuk announced in late August that he favoured the removal of nuclear weapons. He was 'not worried' if they all ended up in the RSFSR, where it was assumed they would fall under some form of joint, central control.[46] Almost immediately, however, Kiev began to backtrack from this position in response to claims by the Russian leadership. Vice President Rutskoi demanded that the RSFSR have dual control with Gorbachev over the Soviet nuclear arsenal. Yeltsin, meanwhile, advocated the transfer of nuclear weapons in Ukraine and Kazakhstan to the RSFSR and suggested the republic would remain a nuclear power for the foreseeable future in order 'to retain parity with other nations'.[47] In response to these developments, the Ukrainian parliament in early September banned the transfer from Ukraine of arms and military property without the express permission of its government. Kravchuk later declared unequivocally that he was 'against the transfer of nuclear weapons from one republic to another'.[48] It was also made clear by figures in the Ukrainian leadership that non-nuclear status could only be achieved after a process of prolonged negotiation and that in the interim, Ukraine demanded a dual key system, which would allow it an operational veto over the use of weapons on its territory.[49] Kazakhstan and Belarus also sought to dampen Russian ambitions; both disputed the suggestion that nuclear weapons be removed from locations on their territory to the RSFSR. In Kazakhstan's case this represented a complete turnaround in policy. Nazarbaev had formerly championed the cause of Kazakhstan's non-nuclear status owing to concern over the environmental damage caused by nuclear testing at Semipalatinsk.

From Union to Commonwealth

It was suggested above that one of the primary motives of the coup plotters was to block the signing of the Union Treaty, thereby preventing what was viewed as an unacceptable devolution of powers to the republics. The launch and subsequent failure of the coup, however, had precisely the opposite effect. For those republics which had already opted out of negotiations on a revamped Union, the coup illustrated the possibility of a return to power of traditional forces in Moscow and strengthened the determination of local nationalist leaderships to seek outright independence. At the height of the coup, Latvia and Estonia declared their independence (Lithuania had already done so in March 1990). In the following weeks the Baltics won recognition from both the Soviet State Council and were admitted to the United Nations. It was not just the long-standing opponents of Soviet rule, however, who asserted their independence. In Ukraine, President Kravchuk fully embraced a nationalist position in a populist move to keep abreast of an increasingly separatist public mood. Equally opportunistically, a number of Central Asian republics asserted their independence as a means of consolidating existing forms of autocratic rule as communist power crumbled in the centre. By the middle of December all the Soviet republics had declared independence, with the sole exception of the RSFSR.[50]

These declarations ran parallel to efforts to construct a replacement for the aborted Union Treaty. Work resumed in this regard in early September with the adoption by Gorbachev and ten republican leaders of a statement of intent outlining the shape of a future 'Union of Sovereign States' (as opposed to the 'Union of Soviet Sovereign Republics' provisionally agreed in July) as the successor to the USSR. Membership of the 'USS' would be entirely voluntary and co-ordination would be limited to areas specified in future agreements concerning a 'common free economic space' and a 'military-strategic space'.[51] Efforts to construct a new Union settlement on this basis were, however, confounded by a number of apparently irresolvable disputes. Of particular significance was the Russian attitude, for without the RSFSR, any revamped Union was impossible. During the autumn of 1991, the RSFSR took on the role of 'empire saver', calculating that it would be able to dominate a revamped Union in which the centre would be bereft of powers of any consequence. Gorbachev would remain as Soviet President and Commander-in-

Chief of the armed forces, but these would be largely ceremonial positions subordinate, in practice, to Yeltsin and the joint leaders of the other influential republics of Ukraine, Kazakhstan and Belarus.[52] This position, predictably, conflicted with Gorbachev's stance on the nature of the proposed Union. A treaty due to be initialled in late November by seven republics was scuppered after Yeltsin objected to Gorbachev's view that the USS should retain a strong presidency rather than develop into a confederation with greatly devolved powers to the republics.[53] Inter-republican tensions also hampered progress, in particular, controversies arising between the RSFSR and Ukraine. In early September, Kravchuk announced that Ukraine would not participate in talks on the future of the Union until after 1 December (the date of a planned referendum on Ukraine's declaration of independence). Kravchuk did initial the agreement on Economic Community in early November, but political union was increasingly ruled out, owing to fears of Russian dominance. As Kravchuk pithily remarked, Ukraine rejected Yeltsin's assumption that 'Russia should continue to be the centre around which the other planets, called states, will revolve, as if it were the sun'.[54] The Ukrainian leader was conspicuously absent from the aborted initialling ceremony for the USS Union treaty at the end of the month. Just days before the Ukrainian independence referendum, he announced that Ukraine was not even interested in a confederation and that he was withdrawing completely from the talks on the Union. A total of 90.32 per cent of voters in the subsequent referendum voted for independence. In a parallel vote, Kravchuk's presidency was confirmed by a huge majority. Completing the process of Ukrainian separatism, on 5 December the republic's parliament annulled the 1922 Union Treaty, an act which marked its formal exit from the USSR.

Developments in Ukraine were not, however, well received by the RSFSR. Despite its own quest for greater powers, important figures within the RSFSR leadership, including Yeltsin, were reluctant for a variety of historical and cultural reasons to conceive of Ukraine as a state separate from Russia (see Chapter 3, pp. 102–4). The large Russian-speaking minority in the republic and Ukraine's military–strategic potential also raised questions of Russian concern. Consequently, moves towards Ukrainian statehood were met with some perplexity. Ukraine's declaration of independence on 24 August, provoked a statement accredited to Yeltsin's office that the RSFSR reserved the right to review its borders with those republics proclaiming independence.[55] The ensuing controversy was patched up by a joint communiqué which recognised mutual 'state independence' and 'territorial integrity',[56] but Ukrainian doubts remained over Yeltsin's continued insistence on the right to protect ethnic Russians living outside RSFSR borders. The RSFSR became increasingly anxious at the prospect of Ukraine opting out of the new Union. As the Ukrainian independence referendum approached, Yeltsin candidly admitted that he could not imagine a Union without Ukrainian participation and that if Kiev failed to sign the Union treaty, the RSFSR would not sign either.[57]

Following the Ukrainian referendum, Yeltsin abandoned the Union treaty process. He was soon after to claim that the vote, coupled with Ukraine's opposition to the Union idea, threatened 'an escalation of conflicts within the ... USSR' over issues of borders, the development of a Ukrainian army and Ukraine's possession of nuclear weapons. Because Ukraine could not be accommodated within what Yeltsin termed the 'stupid endlessness' of efforts to construct a Union treaty,[58] the Russian leader yielded to the Ukrainian position and agreed to the creation of an association that was far looser than the versions preferred by both himself and by Gorbachev. The result was the Commonwealth of Independent States (CIS) announced on 8 December by the leaders of the three Slav republics of the RSFSR, Ukraine and Belarus. The founding documents of the CIS did, in fact, contain provision for substantial co-ordination in the important areas of economic policy, foreign affairs and the functioning of a 'joint command' over a 'common military–strategic space'. While this might have smacked of the now abandoned Union proposals, the CIS differed significantly in the important respect that, unlike Gorbachev's view of the Union, it was not conceived as enjoying the attributes of statehood. No provision was made for a common citizenship, the subordination of members to central political structures such as a presidency or parliament, or for the CIS to be recognised as a subject of international law. Member countries were to be regarded as the CIS's title made clear, as entirely independent states in their own right.[59]

The establishment of the CIS put paid to efforts to revamp the Union. Article 11 of the Commonwealth's founding agreement prohibited the exercise of Soviet law on the territories of CIS member states and asserted in its preamble that the USSR had ceased to exist both as a 'subject of international law and [as a] geopolitical reality'.[60] These assertions swiftly became self-fulfilling as a majority of other republics sought access to the new organisation. Although wary at what was seen as an exclusive Slav organisation, the five central Asian republics met in mid-December and announced their desire to join the CIS. At a meeting in Alma-Ata (Kazakhstan) on 21 December, the Central Asian republics, along with Moldova, Armenia and Azerbaijan were granted the status of co-founders. Of the former Soviet republics, this left just Georgia and the three Baltic states outside the organisation.

The setting up of the CIS meant the USSR was effectively dissolved. During December all remaining Union ministries (with the exception of the Ministries of Defence and Atomic Power) were taken over by the Russian government and following a lengthy meeting between the Soviet and Russian leaders on the 19th it was agreed that the USSR would formally cease to exist by 1 January. On Christmas Day Gorbachev resigned as Soviet President and Commander-in-Chief of the armed forces. The Soviet parliament voted itself out of existence the next day. The Soviet era had come to a close.

In his valedictory speech as President, Gorbachev outlined the 'work of historical significance' which had been undertaken since 1985: democratic transformation, turning the economy towards the market, opening the USSR up to the world and creating a spirit of trust and respect in relations with foreign countries. He concluded, however, by remarking that he was vacating his post 'with a feeling of anxiety' and warned of the 'grave consequences' of the 'disintegration of the [Soviet] state system'.[61] Developments in the post-Soviet period would only partially allay his fears.

Notes

1 J. Hough, *Opening Up the Soviet Economy* (Washington, DC, The Brookings Institution, 1988), p. 2.

2 The agreement did not come into effect during the Soviet period, but was later applied to Russia . (See Chapter 6, pp. 313–14).

3 J. Tedstrom, 'Economic crisis deepens', *Radio Free Europe/Radio Liberty (RFE/RL) Research Report*, 1:1 (1992), pp. 22–25: A. Åslund, 'The Soviet economy after the coup', *Problems of Communism*,

40:6 (1991), p. 46.

4 M. McCGwire, *Perestroika and Soviet National Security* (Washington, DC, The Brookings Institution, 1991), pp. 241–42.

5 *Ibid.*, pp. 324–25; J. Cooper, *The Soviet Defence Industry. Conversion and Reform* (London, The Royal Institute of International Affairs/Pinter, 1991), pp. 2–3.

6 D.K. Steinberg, 'The Soviet defence burden: estimating hidden defence costs', *Soviet Studies*, 44:2 (1992), pp. 259, 263.

7 W.E. Odom, 'The Soviet military in transition', *Problems of Communism*, 39:3 (1990), p. 58.

8 Z. Brzezinski, 'Post-communist nationalism', *Foreign Affairs*, 68:5 (1989/90), p. 6.

9 S. White, *Gorbachev and After* (Cambridge, Cambridge University Press, third edition, 1992), pp. 152–56; R.J. Hill, 'Managing ethnic conflict', *The Journal of Communist Studies*, 9:1 (1993), p. 65.

10 A turnout of 80 per cent was recorded throughout the USSR, of which 76.4 per cent voted in favour of the official question: 'Do you consider it necessary to preserve the Union of Soviet Socialist Republics as a renewed federation of equal sovereign republics in which the human rights and freedoms of any nationality will be fully guaranteed?' The cumbersome and ambiguous wording of the proposition, coupled with the introduction in some republics of supplementary questions which reflected a striving for greater sovereignty, meant the result of the Union referendum was open to question. See White, *Gorbachev and After*, p. 180.

11 The agreement became known as 'nine-plus-one' after the nine republics and the Soviet President who signed it. The six republics who demurred were those who had already opted out of negotiations: the three Baltic republics, Armenia, Georgia and Moldova.

12 J. Morrison, *Boris Yeltsin. From Bolshevik to Democrat* (London, Penguin Books, 1991), pp. 120, 156.

13 *Current Digest of the Soviet Press (CDSP)*, 43:2 (1991), p. 2.

14 B. Brown, 'Central Asia emerges on the world stage', *RFE/RL Research Report*, 1:1 (1992), pp. 52–56.

15 M. Smith, *The Eastern Giants. Russia, Ukraine and European Security* (London, The Royal United Services Institute, 1992), pp. 13–17.

16 Reprinted in C.F. Furtado, Jr and A. Chandler (eds), *Perestroika in the Soviet Republics. Documents on the National Question* (Boulder, Westview Press, 1992), p. 240.

17 *Argumenty i fakty*, No.47, 1990, p. 7.

18 *CDSP*, 42:47 (1990), pp. 21–22.

19 The conflicts over Nagorno–Karabakh, in Georgia and in the Trans–Dniester are considered in detail in Chapter 5.

20 See N. Robinson, 'Gorbachev and the place of the party in Soviet reform', *Soviet Studies*, 44:3 (1992), pp. 423–43.
21 *CDSP*, 43:33 (1991), pp. 4–5.
22 J.W.R. Lepingwell, 'Soviet civil–military relations and the August coup', *World Politics*, 44:4 (1992), p. 562.
23 S. Foye, 'Leading plotters in the armed forces', *RFE/RL Report on the USSR*, 3:36 (1991), pp. 12–15.
24 Morrison, *Boris Yeltsin*, pp. 203, 279; *CDSP*, 43:34 (1991), pp. 31–32.
25 M. Sixsmith, *Moscow Coup. The Death of the Soviet System* (London, Simon and Schuster, 1991), pp. 96–97.
26 Lepingwell, 'Soviet civil–military relations', p. 558.
27 Sixsmith, *Moscow Coup*, p. 87.
28 S. Miller, 'The Soviet coup the benefits of breakdown', *Orbis*, 36:1 (1992), p. 73.
29 S. Foye, 'A lesson in ineptitude: military-backed coup crumbles', *RFE/RL Report on the USSR*, 3:35 (1991), p. 7; J.B. Dunlop, *The Rise of Russia and the Fall of the Soviet Empire* (Princeton, New Jersey, Princeton University Press, 1993), pp. 247–50.
30 *CDSP*, 43:33 (1991), p. 8.
31 Sixsmith, *Moscow coup*, pp. 151–53.
32 At the time of the coup, four members of the SCSE were in the Cabinet, five were in the Security Council and four in the Defence Council.
33 M. Malia, 'The August revolution', *The New York Review of Books*, 26 September 1991, p. 24.
34 *CDSP*, 43:33 (1991), p. 6.
35 *The Guardian*, 21 August 1991, p. 1.
36 *The Independent*, 20 August 1991, p. 6.
37 *The Guardian*, 20 August 1991, p. 7 and 21 August 1991, p. 1.
38 *Keesing's Record of World Events*, August 1991, p. 38370.
39 *CDSP*, 43:34 (1991), p. 7.
40 R. Sakwa, 'A cleansing storm: the August coup and the triumph of perestroika', *The Journal of Communist Studies*, 9:1 (1993), p. 138.
41 The party's leader Ivan Polozkov, had stood against Yeltsin in elections to the Chair of Russia's standing parliament, the Supreme Soviet, the previous month. During a session of the full parliament, the Russian Congress of Peoples' Deputies, in March–April 1991, deputies allied to the Russian Communist Party, had attempted to censure Yeltsin and block his plan for an extension of the powers of the Russian Presidency.
42 *CDSP*, 43:33 (1991), pp. 7–8.
43 Bessmertnykh had replaced Shevardnadze in January 1991. He played a small role in support of the coup and was removed from his position at the end of August.
44 *CDSP*, 43:47 (1991), p. 12.

45 British Broadcasting Corporation, Summary of World Broadcasts, SU/1237 A1/7–9, 23 November 1991.
46 B. Nahaylo, 'The shaping of Ukrainian attitudes towards nuclear arms', *RFE/RL Research Report*, 2:8 (1993), p. 24.
47 *Ibid*., p. 25.
48 *Ibid*., p. 27.
49 *Ibid*., pp. 27–28.
50 The Russian position reflected its desire to assume the status of the 'continuing' state of the USSR (see Chapter 3, pp. 108–9)
51 *Soviet Weekly*, 5 September 1991, p. 2.
52 Dunlop, *The Rise of Russia*, pp. 266–67.
53 A. Sheehy, 'The Union treaty: a further setback', *RFE/RL Report on the USSR*, 3:49 (1991), p. 2.
54 *CDSP*, 42:47 (1991), p. 8.
55 *CDSP*, 43:35 (1991), p. 15.
56 *The Independent*, 30 August 1991, p. 8.
57 *RFE/RL Report on the USSR*, 3:49 (1991), pp. 27–28.
58 *CDSP*, 43:50 (1991), pp. 11–12.
59 For documents signed on 8 December see *Agreements on the Creation of the Commonwealth of Independent States Signed in December 1991/January 1992* (London, Russian Information Agency/Novosti, January 1992), pp. 1–8.
60 *Ibid*., pp. 1, 4.
61 *CDSP*, 43:52 (1991), pp. 1,3.

Recommended reading

A. Dallin and G.W. Lapidus (eds), *The Soviet System. From Crisis to Collapse* (Boulder, Westview Press, revised edition, 1995).

R. Sakwa, *Gorbachev and His Reforms, 1985–1990* (New York, Phillip Allen, 1990).

G.B. Smith, *Soviet Politics. Struggling with Change* (Houndsmills, Macmillan, second edition, 1992).

R. Walker, *Six Years That Shook the World* (Manchester and New York, Manchester University Press, 1993).

S. White, *Gorbachev and After* (Cambridge, Cambridge University Press, third edition, 1992).

3

The former Soviet Union: its inward and outward orientations

In this chapter we elaborate more fully upon the analytical framework laid down in the Introduction by placing the foreign policies of the successor states within the context of the former Soviet Union's (FSU) 'inward' and 'outward' orientations. In addition, we touch upon many of the general themes of international politics also outlined in the Introduction:

- The realist concern with power, status and self-help, and the competing pluralist view of the utility of co-operation can be examined with reference to the strength of regional co-operation in the FSU. Have the successor states been able to construct a viable mechanism of co-operation that can contribute to regional stability? How have they viewed such co-operation – as a desirable end in itself or simply as a temporary and self-serving expedient? These questions are considered here in terms of the viability of the Commonwealth of Independent States (CIS) and other mediums of co-operation within the FSU. Russia's relations with the so-called 'near abroad' and the manner in which Moscow is perceived by the other successor states also tells us a lot about the potential for harmony or discord in the region. We shall also pursue these themes in greater detail in subsequent chapters when considering specific forms of co-operation and conflict within the FSU.
- Such issues are also germane in the wider international context. How have the successor states set about establishing themselves beyond the old Soviet borders? What have been their foreign policy priorities? What has been their attitude towards co-operation with regional powers? More specifically, what has been the

role of Russia, the largest and diplomatically most important of the successor states? Again in this chapter we provide a partial answer to these questions, in anticipation of a more detailed consideration in Chapters 4, 5 and 6.

The dissolution of the USSR and the subsequent emergence of the successor states, entailed what was described in the Introduction as a 'tectonic shift' in the 'world's political landscape'. In many respects this transformation could be seen as all to the good, representing the dawn of freedom for the nationalities long suppressed under the Soviet system, and a decisive shift towards democratisation and the development of market economies.[1] The security implications of the transformation were also of fundamental significance. The retreat of Soviet power from Western and Eastern Europe, already much advanced during the Gorbachev period, was given further impetus by the USSR's collapse. Russia, the largest of the successor states, lacked both the inclination and ability to return to an interventionist strategy. Indeed, at this point, Russia faced severe practical difficulties. A truncated military capability stemming from the break-up of the Soviet armed forces plus political, social and economic divisions within Russia itself, severely undermined the army's ability to mount large-scale operations. Furthermore, Russia was geographically isolated from the continent by a two-tier buffer zone. The first tier, a post-communist Eastern Europe presented a formidable obstacle to any Russian offensive against the countries of the North Atlantic Treaty Organisation (NATO), while the independent former western Soviet republics (Ukraine, Moldova, Belarus and the Baltic states) formed a second tier which provided a similar security cushion for the East European states.[2]

Alongside what were regarded as the welcome consequences of the Soviet break-up, observers also noted a number of more alarming possibilities. On the territory of the FSU a 'geostrategic hole' had appeared in which nuclear proliferation, squabbles over the spoils of the Red Army and localised conflicts threatened to erupt into inter-state wars between the successor states.[3] At the end of 1991, the underlying dynamics of these rivalries were seen to lie in a number of areas: (1) a Soviet-wide process of economic disintegration and tensions over the distribution of Soviet property;[4] (2) potent nationalism, which was deliberately cultivated to create a sense of post-Soviet identity, and which rendered the elites in the successor states extremely sensitive to perceived encroachments, particularly by Russia;[5] (3) political instability and crises of governance, which made democratic consolidation extremely uncertain and increased the likelihood of 'strong men' being granted the reins of leadership.[6]

These instabilities held implications beyond the FSU, not least owing to problems arising from the disintegration of Soviet conventional and nuclear arsenals and the risk of conflicts spilling beyond the old borders of the USSR.[7] In addition, the danger was also seen that the partnership which the West had enjoyed with Moscow during the Gorbachev era would not be so assured in regard to the new Russia under Boris Yeltsin.[8] This problem was compounded by the uncertainties of having to deal diplomatically with the plethora of new states which had emerged from the USSR, integrating them into international organisations and winning their adherence to the numerous treaty commitments of the USSR. A further source of flux concerned the opening up of the former USSR to the politics of nearby regions and to the influence and interests of neighbouring states. Turkey, Iran, Afghanistan, Pakistan, Romania, Poland and China might look upon the successor states as presenting opportunities for influence building, a situation which threatened not only regional competition, but, more ominously, conflict with Russia.[9] A final problem was the threat of economic collapse leading to a feared upsurge in East–West migration.

The inward orientation: the CIS and Russia's relations with the 'near abroad'

The one organisation which could claim some authority in dealing with the problems of the USSR's disintegration was, of course, the Commonwealth of Independent States (CIS). At the time of its foundation, at least seven important tasks confronted the Commonwealth:

1. working out the legal issues relating to state succession owing to the replacement of the USSR by fifteen sovereign states;
2. managing the Soviet nuclear legacy;
3. maintaining the conventional armed forces of the USSR in some guise and providing a managed transition to national armies;

4 dividing up rights and responsibilities concerning the assets (i.e. properties overseas and debts owed *to* the USSR) and liabilities (i.e. debts owed *by* the USSR);
5 dealing with the legacy of close economic interdependence amongst the former Soviet republics;
6 establishing principles concerning issues of borders and minorities;
7 resolving armed conflicts on the territory of the FSU.

As the following chapters will illustrate, the CIS and its member states have been severely tested in all these areas. Degrees of both military and economic co-operation have been maintained, but at levels somewhat less marked than those originally envisaged in the Commonwealth's founding documents. The CIS has also proven a deficient mechanism in dealing with the various bloody crises which have unfolded in the FSU and has not been able to co-ordinate foreign policy amongst its members. After a particularly disappointing initial year, the CIS did experience during 1993–94 some consolidation in its membership and organisational structures. It has remained, however, beset by a number of weaknesses which have rendered its long-term viability a matter of some uncertainty.

Whether the CIS will emerge as a mechanism of long-term integration amongst the post-Soviet states rather than simply a means of managing their civilised separation from the bonds of the Soviet period depends on a host of factors: membership; institutionalisation and decision-making abilities; the differing conceptions of the organisation amongst its member states; and the development of bilateral ties and sub-groups. We shall consider these in turn.

Membership

Since the creation of the CIS, membership of the organisation has fluctuated. Not once has it embraced all fifteen of the successor states. In 1992, the original CIS club of eleven was reduced to ten following the refusal of the Azeri parliament to ratify the membership entered into by former First Secretary of the Azeri Communist Party, Ayaz Mutalibov. In August the following year, the Moldovan parliament failed to muster the absolute majority required to ratify membership. By the time of the CIS summit in April 1994, economic crisis and the effects of war had, however, compelled these two countries to rejoin. Georgia, a country which had consistently distanced itself from the CIS during 1992–93 signed up in December 1993 for similar reasons. This consolidation in the ranks of the CIS has, however been offset by the fact that the three Baltic states have remained steadfastly outside the organisation. The legacies of the Soviet period, which created a necessity for co-operation in other successor states, have been viewed in the Baltics as totally inimical to national independence, a stalking horse for Russian influence and an obstacle to greater integration with their European neighbours.

Institutionalisation and decision-making

At the time of its formation, the CIS was rather short of the institutions necessary to carry out its ambitious designs. The founding documents drawn up in December 1991 and statements of leaders of the successor states envisaged the following co-ordinating structures: (1) the Council of Heads of States; (2) the Council of Heads of Government; (3) 'working and auxiliary bodies' to be created at the behest of the two Councils; (4) Ministerial Committees to co-ordinate activity in areas such as defence and foreign policy; (5) a Joint Command of the CIS armed forces.[10] By the time the heads of state met in October 1994, the institutions of the CIS had undergone considerable expansion. At this juncture, the Commonwealth had the appearance of Box 3.1.

Box 3.1 Commonwealth of Independent States: Charter and institutions (as of October 1994)

The CIS Charter

Initially endorsed in March 1993. According to the Preamble and Section I of the Charter, the CIS is a voluntary association of sovereign states that is not itself a state and does not enjoy supranational powers. Its aims include political and economic co-operation; upholding generally recognised principles and norms of international law; ensuring international peace and security and promoting the free association and movement of citizens of member states within the Commonwealth. Relations between CIS members are governed by mutual respect for sovereignty, inviolability of state frontiers, non-use of force or the threat of force, non-interference in one another's affairs and mutual assistance. Joint activity is to be accomplished through 'common co-ordinating institutions'. Membership of the CIS requires ratification of the Charter; as of January 1994, the date on which it entered into force, seven states had completed ratification, namely, Armenia, Belarus, Kazakhstan, Kyrgyzstan, Russia, Tajikistan and Uzbekistan.

Council of Heads of State
According to agreements reached in December 1991 this is the 'highest body' in the Commonwealth. It is comprised of the Presidents of member states who convene in summit meetings at least twice a year. According to the Charter, it 'discusses and decides fundamental questions connected with the activity of member states' .

Council of Heads of Government
Made up of CIS states' Prime Ministers, this is described in the Charter as responsible for co-ordinating 'the co-operation of the organs of executive power in the economic, social and other spheres of their joint interests'. It meets at least four times a year.

Councils of Ministers of Defence and Foreign Affairs
The former was established in February 1992, the latter in September 1993.

Co-ordinating–Consultative Committee
This body was set up at the CIS summit in Moscow in May 1993. In the Charter the Committee is described as the 'standing executive and co-ordinating agency' of the CIS, responsible for implementing the decisions of the Councils of Heads of State and Government and drawing up proposals for co-operation. It is assisted by an Executive Secretariat and Executive Secretary.

Economic Court
Agreed in principle in July 1992 to rule on breaches of contract obligations and disruptions in deliveries between enterprises in CIS states. The Ashgabat summit of the CIS in December 1993 adopted a resolution on 'organisational-financial aspects' of the Court as a step towards its operationalisation.

Interstate Bank
Agreed in principle in January 1993 and formally constituted in December 1993. The Bank was set up to facilitate interstate financial transactions. The Interstate Bank is chaired by the head of the Central Bank of Russia.

Interstate Economic Committee (IEC)
This was formally constituted at the meeting of the CIS Heads of State in October 1994. It is comprised of a Presidium of Deputy Prime Ministers that meets every two to three months and a standing Collegium of delegates from CIS member states. At the time of its foundation Russia suggested the IEC assume executive functions (thus making it the first supranational body within the CIS). This was resisted by a majority of CIS states. Dmitrii Ryrikov, foreign policy adviser to the Russian President, suggested in October 1994 that the IEC is concerned with 'research, preparation of documents for meetings of heads of states and governments, and *recommendations* to CIS member states. Later on, and to *the degree agreed upon by the (CIS) states*, the IEC will also perform executive functions' (emphases added).

Staff for Co-ordinating CIS Military Co-operation
This is the successor organ to the CIS Joint Forces High Command which was formally abolished in December 1993. It is subordinate to the CIS Council of Defence Ministers and its membership is comprised of military representatives drawn from the signatory states to the CIS Collective Security Treaty (as of April 1994, Armenia, Azerbaijan Belarus, Georgia, Kazakhstan, Kyrgyzstan, Russia, Tajikistan and Uzbekistan).

Council for Collective Security
This is an organ not mentioned in the Charter. It is headed by a General Secretary and is made up of the CIS Collective Security Treaty signatories. It oversees military/security co-operation within the framework of the Treaty and has close organisational links with the Staff for Co-ordinating Military Co-operation and the CIS Council of Defence Ministers.

Council of the CIS Border–Troop Commanders
Set up in July 1992. In the absence of permanently constituted CIS Border Troops, this provides a forum for consultations between the chiefs of the border guards of individual CIS member states.

Organs of Sectoral Co-operation
Agreements have been reached for the creation of specialised agencies in fields such as: space research, ecology, power engineering, railway transport, science and technology, standardisation, and customs services.

CIS Interstate Court
This was proposed at the CIS Minsk summit of January 1993 to adjudicate on disputes concerning minorities and state boundaries.

Inter-parliamentary Assembly
Established March 1992. The Assembly is a consultative body made up of delegations from the legislatures of CIS member states. It has no decision-making function, but its recommendations are submitted to the Councils of Heads of State and Government for consideration.

For further detail of the workings of these bodies see Chapters 4, 5 and 6.

The impressive collection of institutions shown in Box 3.1 is a clear asset if CIS co-operation is to move forward. In practice, however, these bodies have been hamstrung by a number of inherent limitations. Decision-making in the CIS has occurred in an unwieldy manner. Decisions of the Councils of Heads of State and Government, for instance, have relied on consensus and have been subject to an 'interested party' principle, whereby a state can opt out of provisions with which it disagrees. This has led to a situation in which support for most CIS documents has been far from unanimous. It has also given rise to a differentiated membership within the Commonwealth. A first group of states comprising Armenia, Belarus, Kazakhstan, Kyrgyzstan, Russia, Tajikistan and Uzbekistan, has favoured close co-operation within the CIS and has signed most CIS agreements. As of January 1994, the seven members of this core group were party to the CIS Treaty on Collective Security (for a discussion of this important document see Chapter 4, pp. 167–68, 193) and had ratified the CIS Charter. A second group, consisting of Azerbaijan, Moldova, Turkmenistan and Ukraine, has either opposed the creation of co-ordinating structures or has entered into them half-heartedly. The members of this group have signed only a minority of CIS agreements. Only Azerbaijan has signed the Collective Security Treaty.

A further obstacle to effective co-ordination within the CIS has been the lack of any mechanism for enforcing compliance with its agreements. Decisions taken within the institutions of the Commonwealth are not legally binding even upon those members which have agreed to them. As the Charter points out, the CIS does not enjoy supranational powers. In cases such as the Interstate Economic Committee, where executive functions have been mooted, these have been to little effect (see Box 3.1). Some agreements do have a legal standing by virtue of being international treaties requiring ratification by national parliaments (this applies, for instance, to the Agreement on the Creation of the CIS, the CIS Collective Security Treaty and the Treaty on Economic Union). Once signed by individual heads of state or government and subsequently ratified, there is no guarantee, however, that their provisions will be carried out and no machinery for punishing non-fulfilment. In sum, Kazakh President Nursultan Nazarbaev suggested in October 1994 that 452 agreements had been signed within the framework of the CIS, but most remained unimplemented. In his view the CIS amounted to nothing more than a discussion club.[11]

CIS effectiveness has also been impaired by the political legacy of the USSR. Even those most committed to the Commonwealth have been sensitive to anything which smacks of the old Soviet 'centre' and which impinges upon newly acquired national sovereignty. The CIS when created at the end of 1991 was, after all, conceived as a mechanism of separation from the USSR, not as a means of restoring a unified inter-republican personality. Its purpose is not akin to the international integration carried out by organisations such as the European Community (EC) (since November 1993 known as the European Union [EU]), which involves the voluntary transfer of functions carried out by national governments to larger political units. The CIS has created institutional machinery *among* states, but there is no desire to erect decision-making machinery *above* states capable of making and enforcing obligatory decisions. In this sense, the CIS is an 'intergovernmental' rather than a 'supranational' body. It is, as its name makes clear, a *commonwealth*, not a *confederation*.

Conflicting conceptions of the CIS amongst its members

The differentiated membership of the CIS reflects, ultimately, disagreement on the role the organisation should fulfil. To the extent that the members of the CIS were thrown together more by historical accident than conscious political design, it should come as no surprise that they have held divergent views on the desirability of long-term co-operation. The contrast with the EC, an organisation carefully crafted through incremental enlargement and deliberative and prolonged effort, is again marked. In Europe several background conditions have promoted integration: high levels of economic interdependence; shared political and economic values amongst elites; a common identity of foreign policy goals; the existence of an external threat; and a balance of influence among member states.[12] Within the CIS, only the first of these has operated to any significant degree. The detailed analysis of Chapters 4, 5 and 6 will bear this out. Throughout this chapter we will also refer to these conditions. At this stage, a brief overview of members' views of the CIS provides an indication of the attitudinal obstacles to integration.

In some cases, notably Moldova and Georgia, participation in the CIS has been a consequence of Russian coercion applied during moments of economic and political crisis.[13] This provides a poor basis for co-operation within the CIS framework and these states remain suspicious of the organisation. Elsewhere membership has been viewed on strictly instrumental grounds. Armenia, for instance, calculated upon joining that membership might win it support from CIS member states in its conflict with Azerbaijan. In the case of

Belarus, signing up to the CIS reflected an exposed position within the collapsing USSR. The new state was dependent upon economic transactions with other republics, had a high concentration of Soviet military facilities on its territory and was acutely aware of the need to maintain good relations with Russia, its giant eastern neighbour. During the Gorbachev period this dependency had led Belarus, under the guidance of parliamentary Chair (i.e. President) Stanislau Shushkevich, and Prime Minister Vyacheslau Kebich, to give firm and consistent support to Gorbachev's Union schemes.[14] At the end of 1991 as Gorbachev's Union ran out of steam, Shushkevich threw in his lot with Russia and Ukraine and helped hatch the CIS. The weakness of Belarus at this point was accentuated by the fact that it lacked any prior experience of independence. Its history has been one of incorporation into the empires of others: the Grand Duchy of Lithuania, the Polish–Lithuanian Commonwealth, Prussia, Tsarist Russia and latterly, the USSR.[15] With the collapse of the latter, Belarus was consequently a ship 'without a compass' – a state which lacked historical orientation for its newly acquired independence and one whose titular population had a weak sense of national identity. In this uncharted ocean, the CIS offered a means of navigation, preserving for Belarus the close link with Russia and, it was hoped, the military and economic benefits of Russian patronage.[16]

A similar situation pertained in Central Asia. In the words of one scholar, independence had come to the states of this region in the form of an 'unsolicited gift'.[17] Prior to Soviet rule, Central Asia had been subjected to incorporation in the Mongol, Timuride and, from the eighteenth century onwards, the Tsarist empires. The indigenous populations of the region shared a common ethnic origin (Turkic, with the exception of the Iranian-rooted 'Tajiks') and a common religion (Islam).[18] Specific national identities, however, were poorly established. The formation of nascent nation-states began, in effect, with the creation, by fiat, of the Soviet Central Asian republics during the 1920s and 1930s; a 'National Delimitation' which was carried out largely on the basis of linguistic distinctions. The establishment of administrative boundaries and the designation of an official 'nationality' to the inhabitants of the new republics helped shape national identities, but these were often weakly defined, without political focus and subject to cross-cutting cleavages along the lines of clan and regional loyalties. Nationalism's lack of political salience in Central Asia meant popular-front style organisations were slow to develop during the Gorbachev period. In the referendum of March 1991 on the future of the Union, the five Central Asian republics returned votes of over 90 per cent in favour of the USSR's preservation. The ruling elites thus had little to gain by appealing to a nationalist constituency. This fact, coupled with Central Asia's acute economic dependence on Moscow, meant the leaderships of these republics were the most ardent supporters of Gorbachev's New Union Treaty and lagged far behind the Baltic and Transcaucasian republics in seeking greater powers from Moscow.

This accommodationist stance was upset by the August coup and the creation of the CIS. Central Asia was now presented with a *fait accompli*. Independence was unavoidable. Yet the republics wanted to preserve the economic benefits the region had enjoyed in the Soviet context. This, more than anything else, compelled them to throw in their lot with the CIS. Other factors also played a part. The Central Asian republics lacked even nascent national military structures, were home to large Russian minority populations (which amounted to 21.5 per cent and 37 per cent of the total population in Kyrgyzstan and Kazakhstan respectively); and hoped that the CIS (for which, read Russia) would guarantee security in the region in the face of a destabilising war in Tajikistan.[19] With the exception of Turkmenistan (which had no common frontier with Tajikistan and which was well-endowed with energy resources) independent Central Asia has subsequently championed the CIS. Kazakhstan's President Nursultan Nazarbaev, in particular, has emerged as a most outspoken advocate of CIS co-ordination. He is an admirer of the EC/EU, and favours the eventual creation of a form of confederation (he has dubbed this a 'Eurasian Union') in which sovereign powers would be delegated to 'interstate co-ordinating bodies', with the power to enforce CIS initiatives.[20]

For Russia, policy towards the CIS has overlapped with its approach towards the so-called 'near abroad', a geographical area comprising all the former republics of the USSR. The emergence of this region following the disintegration of the USSR required a profound political and psychological adjustment on the part of the Russian population and its political leadership. Already disoriented by the loss of the 'outer' empire in Eastern Europe, Russia was now forced to contemplate the loss of its 'internal' empire closer to home.[21] Yeltsin had, of course, contributed to this process; the construction of a power base within the RSFSR at the expense of Soviet leader

Gorbachev had hastened the USSR's demise. However, alongside this trend, Yeltsin and his associates were mindful of preserving Russian influence in the space occupied by the collapsing USSR.[22] Nowhere was this imperialist mindset more obvious than in the hurried efforts to create the CIS in order to keep Ukraine within a Russian orbit. The assumption of the position of the USSR's 'continuing' state, and acquisition of former Union assets at this juncture, also testified to a somewhat inegalitarian view of Russia's status amongst the new states (see below, pp. 108–9).

In the year following the creation of the CIS, Yeltsin was keen to assure the other successor states that Russia had broken with its imperial traditions.[23] Yet, it soon became clear that many in the Russian leadership were reluctant to consider their having a legitimacy separate from Russia. The view, rooted in centuries of Russian influence-building and presumed political, economic and cultural ascendancy, that Russia had a valid right of interference, was extremely difficult to surrender.[24] It was buttressed by a number of more concrete contemporary concerns. Armed conflicts and political instability in Central Asia and the Transcaucasus threatened to spill over into Russia in the form of a flood of refugees. Porous borders meant the risk of gun and narcotics smuggling. Russia also desired access to former Soviet military and economic infrastructure and was keen to protect the rights and privileges of the estimated twenty-five million ethnic Russians resident in its newly independent neighbour states.[25]

However, while the assumption of supremacy was pervasive in Russian political circles, agreement was absent on just how far Russia should go in projecting its influence. During 1992 an unresolved debate raged within Russia on this theme. The failure to arrive at a consensus seemingly prevented the adoption of an activist policy towards the region. A lack of attention also sprang from Yeltsin and Foreign Minister Andrei Kozyrev's preoccupation with forging a relationship with the West (see below, pp. 121–22) and from an overly relaxed attitude towards the successor states. Russia's leaders simply assumed that the new states would be unable to resist the gravitational pull of Russian military and economic influence and would naturally orientate themselves to Moscow. In this scheme of things, the CIS was viewed as an alluring mechanism. It would develop of its own accord as a consequence of interdependence among its member states and would come to entrench in institutional form Russia's status as *primus inter pares* in the FSU.[26] This, in turn, would be complemented by the development of democracy and market reforms in the near abroad, which, Kozyrev argued, would promote Russia's economic interests and guarantee the rights of ethnic Russians.[27]

This *laissez-faire* approach soon proved mistaken. That democracy and markets would become easily rooted in the FSU proved little more than wishful thinking. Moreover, trends towards military, civil and economic disintegration within the FSU continued apace during 1992 (see Chapters 4, 5 and 6) belying the assumption that the CIS would evolve into a viable co-ordinating mechanism. The Commonwealth proved unable to deal with a series of bitter disputes between Russia and Ukraine over military assets and economic policies and even less able to contain the clutch of civil wars which raged in the Transcaucasus and Central Asia. Finally, Russia's poor attention to developing its own co-ordinated institutions (a department for dealing with the CIS member states was established within the Russian Foreign Ministry in March 1992, but began to function only gradually) led to incoherence in policy and a damaging competition for influence among policy actors. Both the Russian parliament and the military tended to take a more assertive line than Kozyrev's Foreign Ministry (which had been formally charged in April 1992 with developing a unified policy line towards CIS member states). Indeed, during 1992, Kozyrev became an object of almost universal vilification, criticised by parliamentary deputies, Vice-President Alexander Rutskoi, and the Russian Security Council alike for his neglect of the near abroad.[28]

A shift in the Foreign Ministry's position began to emerge in the latter half of 1992. In a telling analysis Fedor Shelov-Kovedyaev, the deputy foreign minister appointed to oversee policy towards the near abroad, argued that Russia's passivity in the region had resulted in a loss of influence and had stunted the development of the CIS. This posed severe problems for Russia. An inattention to the region, coupled with the retreat from Eastern Europe, threatened the creation of a 'double *cordon sanitaire*' isolating it from Western Europe. The failure to properly address the issues of conflict resolution in the FSU, moreover, had created a problem closer to home as unresolved regional wars threatened to spread into the Russian hinterland and undermine the multinational Russian Federation.

Shelov-Kovedyaev's recipe for alleviating these difficulties was a more dynamic policy, in which Russian-led co-ordination in the near abroad would be promoted through a greater activism in regard to the CIS.[29] His arguments seem to have had some influence on Yeltsin. The political imperative of countering nationalist voices in the Russian parliament, also had its effect. During late 1992, the President sanctioned a shift in Russian priorities. As this policy unfolded during 1993-94, several strands were discernible. At a rhetorical level, Russia adopted a more insistent tone regarding its claims to the near abroad. Russia's 'Foreign Policy Concept', adopted by the Security Council and signed by Yeltsin in the spring of 1993, gave greater attention to relations with the region and called for 'the maximum possible degree of integration of the former Soviet republics'.[30] Even the otherwise liberal Kozyrev was infected by this. By early 1994 an implicit 'Kozyrev doctrine' had emerged based around the argument that '(t)he countries of the CIS and the Baltics ... [constitute] a region where the vital interests of Russia are concentrated ... We should not withdraw from those regions which have been the sphere of Russia's interests for centuries'.[31] In tandem, the Russian leadership insisted upon the long-term viability of the CIS. Yeltsin, in his address to the CIS summit in Minsk in April 1993, berated those who saw the Commonwealth's role as simply 'a mechanism for a civilised divorce' of the former Soviet republics. Instead, he outlined its potential as a means of putting forward joint positions on foreign policy, promoting economic co-operation, dealing with conflict situations (notably through peacekeeping operations) and guaranteeing CIS-wide human rights (for which, read the rights of ethnic Russians). To further these aims he called for the strengthening of CIS institutions and swift accession to the organisation's Charter.[32] Russia has subsequently spearheaded the development of the CIS Economic Union, promoted military co-operation through the mechanism of the CIS Collective Security Treaty and sought to win formal recognition of the CIS as an international organisation in order to further Russia's peacekeeping role and military presence in the near abroad. In January 1994, Russia finally created a Ministry for Co-operation with CIS States; the following November a Deputy Prime Minister in charge of CIS Affairs was appointed.

Russia's return to the CIS has undoubtedly boosted the organisation's prospects. However, the fact that the development of the CIS has increasingly entrenched Russian dominance within the FSU has only aggravated the concerns of those successor states who view the

Commonwealth with suspicion. For small, vulnerable states such as Georgia, Azerbaijan and Moldova, Russian assertiveness is something that can only be watched with resignation. Ukraine's position, however, is different. It had, alongside Russia, been the driving force in the creation of the CIS and, moreover, was better equipped to resist Russian encroachment.

Ukraine's attitude towards the CIS has been qualified since the organisation's inception. President Kravchuk, in an interview in December 1991, argued that the Commonwealth should be carefully monitored 'so that no one tries to stand above anyone else ... If there is any attempt to do this, the Commonwealth will fall apart, because Ukraine will never agree to be subordinated to anyone'. Fearful of any attempt to resurrect the old Soviet 'centre' in a new guise Kravchuk opposed the development of CIS co-ordinating structures and viewed the organisation simply as a transitional mechanism – 'a committee to liquidate the old structures'.[33] Kravchuk's replacement in July 1994 by his erstwhile Prime Minister, Leonid Kuchma, suggested change might be in the offing, owing, so it was believed, to the latter's pro-Russian sympathies.[34] But following his inauguration, Kuchma has behaved in much the same way as his predecessor, resisting any moves designed to extend CIS competence. Ukraine refused to sign five of the ten documents presented at the CIS Heads of State meeting in October 1994 and acceded to the others (e.g. on the creation of the Interstate Economic Committee) with the proviso that it would be guided in their implementation 'by the current legislation of Ukraine'.[35]

Ukraine's jealous guarding of its newly acquired independence springs from a number of sources. First, it is potentially a giant among the successor states, enjoying huge economic possibilities, and a population and territory approximating that of France. Secondly, the peculiarities of Ukrainian nationalism are important. Ukrainian national consciousness might appear at first sight somewhat stunted. It had been undermined by decades of Russification during the Soviet period. Moreover, experience of independence prior to Soviet rule lacked contemporary resonance, being either too long ago (as in the case of Kievan-Rus' from the ninth to the fourteenth centuries and rule by the Cossack *hetmen* from the mid-eighteenth to the mid-nineteenth centuries) or too short lived (as in the case of the Ukrainian National Republic which briefly existed during the Russian civil war of 1917–21).[36] This historical development was a poor basis for an affirmative Ukrainian nationalism. However, a striving for independence has fed instead off a sharp sense of grievance at being the victims of rule by Moscow. Under Tsarist rule, Ukraine experienced the affliction of serfdom and the suppression of its education system and language. The Soviet period had even more harmful consequences. The victims of the famine which accompanied Stalin's enforced collectivisation of agriculture in the early 1930s could be counted in their millions. The longer-term incorporation of Ukraine into the Soviet planning system, meanwhile was seen to have impaired, rather than enhanced, economic well-being.[37] These grievances were exploited by Kravchuk in his political journey from communist to Ukrainian nationalist, and fired the growing mood in favour of independence during 1990-91. In the post-Soviet period, they have led Ukraine to adopt a cautious attitude towards organisations such as the CIS which could potentially perpetuate external interference.

The feared source of such meddling has, of course, been post-Soviet Russia. Ukraine is well aware that the concept of Ukrainian statehood has historically been rejected in Russia. Mainstream Russian thought has long held the opinion that Ukrainians are, ethnically, culturally and linguistically, a part of the Russian nation. This 'Ukrainian complex' is based on common Slavic and orthodox identities and the historical origins of Russia in Kievan Rus'. During the Soviet period, when Russians tended to regard the entire Soviet Union as their domain, Ukraine occupied a distinctive position as the core of the Union alongside the RSFSR.[38] Yeltsin's desire to preserve the Russian–Ukrainian relationship through the CIS reflected precisely this assumption of Russia and Ukraine's inseparability. Formally, Russia did, at least, recognise the legal reality of Ukrainian independence[39] and Yeltsin has publicly and repeatedly eschewed any territorial claims on the country. Others within Russia's political class, however, have proven less able to accept Ukraine's new status. Deputy Prime Minister Mikhail Poltoranin suggested in mid-1992 that the former Soviet republics had 'fallen ill with independence' and predicted that in three to four years 'the dust will settle' and 'Russia, Ukraine, and a number of other republics ... will be something single'.[40] Alexander Rutskoi, Russian Vice-President throughout 1992, has argued, in a similar vein, that the borders bequeathed by the break-up of the USSR were artificial and that 'Russia' was comprised of territories beyond the current Russian Federation.[41]

The one territory Rutskoi had in mind above all others was the

Crimea. The status of this southern Ukrainian peninsula encapsulates in a nutshell the problematic historical legacies bequeathed to post-Soviet Moscow and Kiev. At least three factors have served to make the question of Crimea particularly troublesome.[42] First, it had formerly been Russian territory. The Crimea was seized from Turkish suzerainty in 1772 and formally annexed to Russia in 1783. Later, under Soviet rule, the Crimean Oblast formed part of the RSFSR. It was transferred to the Soviet Ukraine in 1954 on the three-hundredth anniversary of the Pereyaslav agreement which had united Ukraine with Tsarist Russia in 1654. A resolution of the Russian parliament in May 1992 questioned the legality of the transfer. A further motion in July of the following year, meanwhile, accorded the Crimean port city of Sevastopol, 'Russian federal status'. Rutskoi in an address to Cossack organisations in August 1992 was characteristically blunt, suggesting that '(t)he Crimea was Russian, it's covered with Russian blood, and it must be Russian'.[43]

A second problem is Crimea's ethnic Russian majority. Several regions in Ukraine have large numbers of Russian inhabitants (Luhans'k, Donets'k, the Donbass and Odessa) but only in the Crimea do they outnumber the Ukrainian population. This has not only buttressed Russian territorial claims, but has presented Kiev with the additional problem of accommodating a domestic constituency itself agitating for Crimea's return to Russia. The strength of local Russian feeling can be gauged from a series a votes taken in the Crimea during the first half of 1994. In January, the first ever Presidential elections in the Crimea returned Yuri Meshkov, a Russian nationalist, who in his campaign had spoken in favour of Crimea's reunification with Russia. Two months later, Meshkov's Russia Bloc won a landslide victory in elections to the Crimean parliament. A non-binding plebiscite carried out at the same time produced a large vote in favour of increasing Crimea's already extensive autonomy and seeking closer links with Russia. In May, the parliament passed a series of constitutional amendments that raised Crimea's status from a region of Ukraine to an equal partner with Kiev, one which would negotiate relations on the basis of bilateral treaties. The changes also gave the Crimean authorities the right to raise their own militia and to establish Crimean citizenship.

A final issue is the link between the status of the Crimea and the division of the Soviet Black Sea Fleet, a tortuous and complex issue which has involved Ukraine and Russia in a seemingly endless process of argument and negotiation (see Chapter 4, pp. 183–88).

Bilateralisation and localisation

Relations among the successor states have been marked by the development of bilateral ties and localised co-operation. Such developments, not in themselves at odds with the existence of the CIS,[44] have nevertheless implied a diminishing role for multilateral institutions and, in some cases, a lack of appreciation for the long-term potential of the CIS as a body of comprehensive co-operation. Take, for example, the case of Turkmenistan. It has regarded bilateral relations, from the outset, as the preferred means of conducting its affairs with the other successor states. It has seen such ties as a more useful method of maximising the benefits to be had from selling energy to other states within the CIS and of furthering relations with Russia, its potential military partner.[45] Ukraine and Belarus have also developed bilateral links with Russia, albeit with differing purposes. In Belarus a powerful lobby led by Prime Minister Vyacheslau Kebich and Foreign Minister Pyotr Krauchanka has argued in favour of an intimate economic and defence alignment with Russia. The leader of the dominant parliamentary group, the Popular Movement of Belarus (PMB), has gone further. The PMB's leader Syarhei Haydukevich suggested in August 1993, that the country's economic woes were the result of the break-up of the USSR and could only be rectified by the restoration of Belarus within a Russian state.[46] In Ukraine, opinion has been more uniformly opposed to such close links. Nonetheless, both Kravchuk and Kuchma have recognised the necessity of dealing directly with Moscow, in order to preserve beneficial economic ties and to deal expeditiously with contentious military and economic issues.

Bilateral links have been developed by all the successor states, creating a dense network of agreements, understandings, economic ties and so on. Over issues such as mutual recognition of borders, minority rights, military co-operation and free trade regimes, these are often seen as a more binding and fruitful method of conducting interstate affairs than operating via the cumbersome and uncertain machinery of the CIS. Russia's preponderant military and economic position among the successor states has meant the majority of bilateral ties have centred on Moscow. By early 1994 Russia had signed wide-ranging friendship and co-operation treaties with seven CIS member states.[47] Coupled with the multitude of more specific agreements concerning military and economic co-operation, these treaties have effectively supplanted the authority of the CIS. For Russia, bilateralism offers numerous benefits that cannot be obtained within the CIS. It allows a differentiated approach to the countries around Russia on the basis of their degree of vulnerability to economic and military leverage, their geostrategic significance and the size of their ethnic Russian population. Such criteria offer a more direct means of pursuing Russia's interests in conflict resolution, military presence and economic advantage, than the multilateral equivalence offered by relations conducted solely through the Commonwealth.

Alongside bilateralisation, the weakness of the CIS has also been evident in a process of *localisation* involving the development of close ties by sub-groups of states within the FSU. The Baltic states, for instance, resolved at an early stage that mutual ties were a preferred alternative to the Commonwealth. They have since co-operated through frameworks such as the Baltic Free Trade Zone and the 'common visa space'. They have also co-ordinated their diplomatic positions on issues such as the removal of Russian troops. Amongst the membership of the CIS itself, localisation has occurred in two forms. First, the formation of sub-groups on the basis of CIS agreements (illustrated by a *de facto* Russian–Central Asian axis amongst the core membership of the CIS); and second the creation of co-operative arrangements outside of the CIS framework. The clearest case of the latter has been co-ordination within Central Asia.

Central Asia had been moving in this direction well before the fragmentation of the USSR. The presidents of the then five Union republics met in June 1990 to discuss the concept of a confederation and in August of the following year set up a consultative council to co-ordinate economic policy. Co-operation was given a further impetus by the creation of the CIS. The initiative to form the Commonwealth by the three Slavic states was met initially with consternation by the Central Asian republics, who were insulted by the lack of consultation and the arrogant presumption on the part of Russia, Ukraine and Belarus to effectively wind up the USSR. Although the Central Asian states were soon after admitted as CIS co-founders, the prospect of their being cast adrift from the wealthier former Soviet republics had been raised. This strengthened their resolve to develop mutual ties in order to increase their collective influence and to seek alliances independent of the Slavic states. In May 1993 all five

Central Asian states agreed to the formation of a Central Asian Regional Union. A year later, Kazakhstan, Kyrgyzstan and Uzbekistan took practical steps towards the realisation of this body with the signing of agreements on the creation of a Central Asian Bank for Co-operation and Development and inter-state committees for defence and foreign affairs.

The Central Asian case, while illustrating the allure of localisation, has also revealed its limitations. This, however, has not been to the benefit of the CIS, but has rather added to the trend towards bilateral relations with Russia. Co-ordination in Central Asia has been hindered by local rivalries. Uzbekistan the most populous and the most central in location has regarded itself as the natural leader of Central Asia. This has not been well received by the other states of the region. Kazakhstan has an equally valid claim in this regard owing to its nuclear inheritance, vast size and proximity to Russia. Nazarbaev's distinctive position on the CIS and his international profile on nuclear weapons issues (see Chapter 4.) seem confirmation of his country's ability to carve out a pre-eminent position. The domestic political circumstances of the Central Asian leaderships have also differed. Turkmenistan and Uzbekistan entered independence under the stewardship of former republican Communist Party first secretaries, who set about imposing stern authoritarian rule under the pretext of thwarting Islamic fundamentalism. Kazakhstan, whose President Nazarbaev had also held the office of first secretary, was more tolerant of political life, but has not been averse to electoral manipulation to bolster his authority.[48] Tajikistan, meanwhile has experienced civil war and anarchy. Only Kyrgyzstan, under the leadership of President Askar Akaev, has developed a democratic state in embryo.

The outward orientation: the successor states and the wider world

Internationalisation

In the wake of the August coup the West hoped that the Soviet state in some form would survive. This was not just the result of some premature nostalgia for Gorbachev's historic role in ending the Cold War. It was as much a hedge against the unsettling effects a Soviet collapse would have on matters such as disarmament, debt repayment and regional stability. Recognising the independence of the

Baltic states was one thing, but accommodating a further twelve new states and coping with the withdrawal of the USSR from the international diplomatic circuit was quite another. During the autumn of 1991, however, the latter scenario became increasingly likely as Gorbachev struggled with little success to keep the USSR together. Fearing the worse, the Bush Administration outlined criteria for recognition of the republics' independence. These included: respect for human rights and democratic process, due regard for borders, and adherence to international law and to the principles outlined in the Helsinki Final Act and Charter of Paris of the Conference on Security and Co-operation in Europe (CSCE). Similar guidelines were issued by the EC.[49] Western nations, however, did not want to either hasten or legitimise the break-up of the USSR and awaited the resignation of Gorbachev before welcoming the former republics into the community of states. Once Gorbachev stood down, the diplomatic floodgates opened. The Baltics, who had already won recognition as independent states in September, were now joined by the other former republics; within a matter of days, most had been granted diplomatic recognition by the US, Canada, Japan, the member countries of the EC and China. By the end of March 1992 all bar Georgia had entered the United Nations (UN) and the CSCE as member states.[50]

The process of recognition conferred upon the successor states the sovereign statehood they had previously lacked as constituent parts of the USSR. The legal tidiness of this process was seemingly matched by the manner in which the former republics themselves executed the transference of sovereignty away from the former USSR. Two major issues stood out in this regard.[51] First, the question of borders. This matter was dealt with in CIS founding agreements, which recognised the administrative borders of the Soviet republics as the inviolable frontiers of the successor states, a move which denied the legitimacy of any territorial claims amongst the member states of the CIS.[52] A second issue concerned the legal obligations and rights of the defunct USSR. Who would assume the multitude of treaty and other responsibilities of the former state and take its important seat in international organisations? A precedent in this matter had been set by the Baltic states. By claiming a restoration of their pre-war independence rather than asserting secession from the Union, these countries did not consider themselves 'successor' states to the USSR in international law and, therefore, did not seek to claim any of its rights or obligations (for instance, the payment and servicing of Soviet debts). The member states of the CIS, by contrast adopted the opposite position, pledging in the Commonwealth's founding agreements to fulfil all the USSR's international commitments.[53] This step conferred upon the CIS members the position of successor states. The apparent egalitarianism of this common status was, however, belied by Russia's emergence as *primus inter pares*. The CIS heads of state recognised Russia's continuation of the Soviet Union's membership of the UN (including its permanent seat in the Security Council) and other international organisations.[54] This position was welcomed by the international community, who saw it as a method of alleviating some of the uncertainty over the Soviet treaty and other obligations.[55]

Russia's status as the continuing state of the USSR had three significant consequences. First, unlike the other former Soviet republics, it was not obliged to submit formal applications for membership to international bodies in which the USSR had participated. (A caveat here concerns Belarus and Ukraine – see below, p. 109). Second, continuation, from a legal position, bestowed upon Russia all the treaty obligations and other international commitments of the USSR. Notwithstanding the assumption of these duties by all the CIS members in their founding agreements, Russia's standing as the continuing state of the USSR implied that Soviet responsibilities would impinge unequally and that only Russia had the capability to ensure the widest implementation of treaties and other obligations entered into by the USSR.[56] Finally, Russia's privileged status furnished a quasi-legal gloss to the unilateral acquisition of Soviet assets. Here, the Russian position rested on a legal technicality. The fact that Russia alone among the former republics had not declared independence, meant only it remained in the Union when the USSR was dissolved. In this sense, what belonged to the USSR perforce belonged to Russia.[57] Making good this interpretation, during December 1991, Yeltsin had issued decrees asserting Russian control over the Soviet Ministry of External Relations (and thus, all Soviet embassies and consulates abroad), the USSR Foreign Intelligence Agency and the Soviet bank for foreign economic affairs (and thus, Soviet foreign-currency accounts). This had been met with some consternation by the other former republics. A majority (Ukraine was an exception), had been prepared to accept the notion of Russia as the USSR's continuing state on the basis of two calculations: first, that Russia provided the most credible voice for representing their collective interests in diplomatic fora; and second, that Russia could assume the position of party of last resort in fulfilling the international commitments of the now defunct USSR. The spirit of trust implicit in these assumptions was clearly contradicted by Russia's unilateral exploitation of its elevated status. This created a bitter legacy, and seemed to confirm for Ukraine the case against Russia's assumption of Soviet responsibilities.

The former republics, then, did not enter the international community as equals.The legal tag of continuing state attached to Russia reflected the perception of Russia's dominant position both by a number of the states of the FSU and by the wider international community. Indeed, as will become apparent in the following three chapters, Western policy towards the FSU has been essentially Russocentric. This reflects the simple fact that by almost any criteria, Russia is leagues ahead of the other former republics in terms of its capabilities. It thus has the greatest potential to pursue foreign policies of consequence to the wider world. The military, geostrategic and economic dimensions of this will be taken up in the remainder of the book. At this point, it is worth noting that Russia has enjoyed a number of organisational advantages stemming from its acquisition of Soviet assets. Russia's takeover of the Soviet Ministry of External Affairs, for instance, expanded in one fell swoop the size of the Russian Foreign Ministry from some 270 persons to 3,000. By contrast, in the other successor states a deficit of both experience and institutions existed in the realm of foreign affairs. All were handicapped by Russia's acquisition of embassies and consulates abroad, forcing them into ad hoc sharing arrangements with Russia or an expensive search for new premises.[58] Estonia, Latvia and Lithuania were able to use premises abroad retained by Baltic exile legations, but they still had to build up a diplomatic corps and find the funds to open new embassies. Ukraine and Belarus enjoyed the anomalous position of having been allowed a diplomatic identity by the USSR, which had seen them enter the UN as founding members in 1945, join several other inter-governmental organisations (Ukraine, for instance, was a member of the International Labour Organisation and the International Atomic Energy Agency) and sign countless agreements, treaties and conventions. These international activities, however, had been closely supervised by the Soviet government, had not embraced state-to-state relations with foreign countries and had resulted in a diplomatic corps too small to deal with the demands of full independence. Ukraine entered the post-Soviet period with the best developed institutions among the former republics (other than Russia), but still at a level inadequate for an independent state. Belarus, meanwhile, had a Foreign Ministry of just thirty diplomatic personnel. The remaining successor states had even smaller pools from which to draw.

Regionalisation

This lack of experience and preparation, it has been argued, meant that, with the exception of Russia, the foreign policies of the successor states have a poorly developed conceptual base.[59] An absence of consensus on national priorities and fragile political institutions in the successor states have compounded this problem. In functioning democracies, the norm is for foreign policy prerogatives to be exercised by the executive with oversight being carried out by the legislature on the basis of a clear, constitutionally defined division of powers. The Baltics, Armenia, Ukraine and Belarus have approximated this model, albeit imperfectly (resulting, as we shall see, in deadlock on certain matters) while in Central Asia, the executive has enjoyed a clear ascendancy. In other cases (Georgia, Tajikistan, Azerbaijan) decision-making has been disrupted, often to the point of anarchy, by civil wars.

The foreign policies of the successor states have not, however, been entirely rudderless. With independence, priorities emerged quickly by force of circumstance. Defining relations within the CIS and with Russia and obtaining international recognition have already been touched on above. Equally important aims relating to national security, conflict resolution and external economic relations form the subject matter of later chapters. At this point, it is worth exploring the immediate influences exerted by geographic location and ethnic/cultural/religious inclinations, which have drawn the successor states into patterns of *regionalisation* involving the cultivation of ties with geographically adjacent countries outside the FSU and the setting of regional priorities in relations with the outside world.[60] In this connection four distinct groups have emerged: (1) the Baltic states – Estonia, Latvia and Lithuania, who have considered themselves part of the European mainstream and whose leanings have been towards Scandinavia and Germany; (2) Ukraine, Belarus and

Moldova, who have also aspired to greater involvement in European structures, but whose geography has dictated a close attention to Eastern Europe; (3) the Transcaucasian states of Armenia, Azerbaijan and Georgia whose fortunes have been severely affected by war and who have been the object of Iranian and Turkish attention; (4) the Central Asian states of Kazakhstan, Kyrgyzstan, Tajikistan, Turkmenistan and Uzbekistan, whose location has placed them amidst the concerns of China, Pakistan and India, has exposed them to the destabilising influence of Afghanistan and has rendered them vulnerable to the regional ambitions of Iran and Turkey; (5) Russia, finally, is a separate case. By virtue of its geographic enormity it has had no clear direction in which to travel and has had to strike a balance between competing regional demands. We shall consider these five groups in turn.

1 In certain respects Estonia, Latvia and Lithuania have much in common with some of the other successor states in their orientation towards the outside world: the desire to diversify relations in order to mitigate Russian influence, a limited experience of independence in the modern era (a brief independence was enjoyed between 1920 and 1940), a legacy of disputed borders and minority issues (notably between Poland and Lithuania) and a strong inclination towards closer involvement with Western Europe.

The differences, however, have been equally important. First, among the successor states, Estonia, Latvia and Lithuania are the strongest contenders for entering the European mainstream. Even though Russia has maintained an influential economic and geostrategic pull on the Baltics, the pronouncements of the post-independence leaderships have indicated a strong desire to reorientate towards the West. At independence, several options existed: Baltic–EC/EU relations; Baltic–Nordic relations; relations with the other Baltic Sea countries; and Baltic–US relations. With the exception of the latter, all entailed a focus on the European democracies.[61] In this, the Baltics are advantaged by favourable perceptions in the West itself, where they have benefited from their status as a bulwark of resistance to Soviet communism. The forced incorporation of the Baltics into the USSR under the terms of the 1939 Nazi–Soviet pact was not recognised by a majority of Western states. During the Soviet period extensive links were maintained with Western capitals and Baltic diplomatic representatives continued to be accredited in the UK, the

US, Canada and Australia. Under Gorbachev, the Baltic states were the leading lights in the struggle for national independence.

A second difference consists in the fact that the Baltics are, in relative terms, economically well developed and are amongst the more enthusiastic supporters in the FSU of building free-market economies. They have consequently viewed full membership of the EC/EU as a realistic objective and have seen entry into financial institutions such as the European Bank for Reconstruction and Development (EBRD), the International Monetary Fund (IMF) and the World Bank, as a path towards this end. In Lithuania's case, bilateral ties with Germany have also been seen as offering potential economic rewards, while all three Baltic states have set great store by relations with the developed economies of the Nordic region. Geographic location has made such ties with Denmark, Sweden and Finland a matter of priority. Linguistic and cultural affinities have also been important, facilitating, for instance, strong links between Estonia and Finland.

Thirdly, Estonia, Latvia and Lithuania are unique among the post-Soviet states in that they have remained outside the CIS. This step has been intended to distance them from Russian influence, but equally, it has been one designed to keep their European orientation untarnished.

2 The geographic location of Ukraine, Moldova and Belarus places these states on the eastern periphery of Eastern Europe. Of the three, Ukraine is the most significant in terms of size and population. It is the largest and potentially the most powerful country between Germany and Russia. Ukraine also has the most diverse borders. On its western and south-western flanks it faces Poland, Slovakia, Hungary and Romania. It is also a maritime country; the Black and Azov Seas lie to the south. This position has several consequences for Ukraine: the need for a merchant and naval fleet, a desire for cordial relations with Turkey (which straddles the straits at the Dardanelles, the only route in and out of the Black Sea) and an interest in stability in the Balkans. Belarus and Moldova, by contrast, are landlocked states, buttressing Poland and Romania, respectively, on their western flanks. This has given them a strong vested interest in cordial relations with their non-FSU neighbours in order to ensure reliable transportation routes and access to the sea.

The dictates of geography mean that close attention has been paid to relations with Eastern Europe. This region, as noted in Chapter 2 (pp. 61–62) was a major focus of the republican foreign policies of the late Gorbachev period. Following independence, the leaderships in Ukraine, Belarus and Moldova considered it imperative to continue this course. All three were determined to normalise relations, aware of the intertwined histories of the countries of the region and the possibility of a resurgence of border disputes and political controversies over the rights of ethnic minorities. In cultivating Eastern Europe, Ukraine was poised to become the trailblazer. It shared with the countries of the region a common cultural inheritance stemming from incorporation in the Polish–Lithuanian Commonwealth and the Habsburg Empire, an economic interdependence cultivated by the Council for Mutual Economic Assistance (CMEA), military compatibilities fostered by the Warsaw Treaty Organisation (WTO), and perhaps above all, a mutual suspicion of Russia. Co-operative arrangements with the countries of the 'Visegrad Group' (Poland, Hungary, the Czech Republic and Slovakia) offered a possible long-term alternative to the CIS, and Poland, not Russia, was seen as Ukraine's major partner in the future.[62] Moldova, which was also keen to distance itself from Moscow, was much more restricted in its options. Its geographic isolation and limited economic potential made it an unenticing proposition for the Visegrad countries. Its neighbour and potential partner, Romania, meanwhile, harboured territorial ambitions, was amongst the least developed and politically stable countries in the entire region and was, to boot, a source of friction in Moldova's troubled relations with its Russian minority population (see Chapter 5, pp. 237–41).

Eastern Europe, for all its attractions, has not offered the successor states a route towards economic regeneration or meaningful security guarantees. Indeed, the East European countries have shared with the FSU a condition of economic flux and uncertain security. In this light, Ukraine, Belarus and Moldova have, for pragmatic reasons, looked to Russia, on the one hand, and Western Europe and the US, on the other, as partners capable of offering military and economic guarantees. This has, however, posed a fundamental dilemma: how to cultivate favourable relations with the West without upsetting Moscow? The delicacy of this situation has been particularly evident in Belarus. President Shushkevich's strategy of neutrality, a course designed to balance the Western and Russian poles, alienated him from the Belarus parliament. This body, dominated by a conservative majority of former communists, has favoured close relations with Russia and made an issue of Shushkevich's refusal to sign the CIS Collective Security Treaty (he was finally persuaded to do so in January 1994). This contributed to his removal from office in January 1994. The following July, Alexander Lukashenko, a figure more pro-Russian in outlook, was the victor in Belarus's first Presidential elections.

Ukraine and Moldova displayed a clearer desire for involvement with the West European countries and the US. As will become evident in the following chapters, involvement with institutions such as the EC, the EBRD, the IMF, the World Bank, NATO and the CSCE reflect these priorities, as does Ukraine's security dialogue with the US. Ukraine has also sought to cultivate bilateral relations with important European countries, notably Germany and Austria, and with countries containing significant Ukrainian communities, such as Canada, in an effort to promote economic growth.

Ties with Western Europe have meant keeping a distance from Russia in more ways than one. They required the successor states to affirm at an early stage their 'European' identity. For Ukraine, in particular, the notion of Europe contains important symbolic connotations. It is a means of distancing the country from the 'Eurasian' character of Russia. Moreover, while Ukrainians cannot claim to be fully fledged members of the West, they can stake out a pivotal role in Europe as the frontier of two worlds. Posing as a bridge between European 'civilisation' and the imperialist tradition of Russia offers to Kiev an important status as a reconciling force between East and West.[63]

3 The Transcaucasus has historically been an 'interface between two worlds', a region in which Christian and Islamic cultures meet.[64] Armenia and Georgia are predominantly Christian, and Azerbaijan, Islamic. The three countries are also a patchwork of ethnic complexity, a situation which has helped provoke warfare throughout the region: Armenia and Azerbaijan have been at war over the enclave of Nagorno-Karabakh and Georgia has been torn apart by secessionist struggles (see Chapter 5). These conflicts have had calamitous effects in the post-Soviet period and have limited foreign policy options. Geopolitical position has also imposed restrictions. Azerbaijan, Armenia and Georgia are all isolated from major searoutes; Armenia is totally landlocked. The Transcaucasus region is

also bounded by three influential neighbours: Russia, Turkey and Iran. Developing a preference in relations with one of these three or, alternatively, striking a balance between them, is a major preoccupation of foreign policy.

In Azerbaijan, independence found the country under the leadership of the former Republican Communist Party first secretary, Ayaz Mutalibov. He had strongly supported the Union, but when this was seen to be no longer viable, threw in his lot with the CIS and cultivated close relations with Russia. At the same time, when asked to state a preference between an orientation towards Turkey, Russia or Iran, he opted for Turkey, arguing that this was the more 'European' of the three.[65] The balance sought by Mutalibov was upset somewhat by his successor as President Abulfaz Elchibey, leader of the Azerbaijan Popular Front (AzPF). His assumption to power in June 1992 did not disrupt a steady development of relations with Russia, but did mark a sharp turn towards Turkey. Elchibey and his party made no secret of their pan-Turkic sympathies. Equally, they were scornful of the regime in Iran. Tehran was condemned for its maltreatment of the Azerbaijani population in northern Iran and the AzPF's programme called for 'the ethnic unity of Azerbaijanis living on both sides of the [Iranian] border'.[66] Elchibey was himself removed as President, a year later, to be replaced by another former communist first secretary, Gaider Aliev. This move heralded a further shift in Azeri foreign policy, this time involving a greater emphasis on Russia, a cooling of relations with Turkey and a marked improvement in ties with Iran.

Armenian foreign policy has laboured under the historical legacy of painful relations with Turkey, stemming from the organised slaughter of ethnic Armenians within the Ottoman Empire during World War I and the loss of Armenian territory as a consequence of the Turkish–Armenian wars of 1917–20. The programme of the Armenian Pan-National Movement (which was the largest party in the parliament elected in 1990) demanded UN recognition of the Armenian massacre as an act of genocide and international acceptance of its 'historical and legal right' to lost Armenian territory.[67] Armenia has viewed Russia as a possible source of support for its territorial claims. During the post-Soviet period, Armenia has warmed to Turkey slightly, partly out of a desire to expand economic ties. In November 1992, agreement was reportedly reached on the dropping of claims concerning genocide and border revisions.[68]

Relations, however, have remained far from cordial. A fundamental strain has existed over Turkish sympathies towards Azerbaijan's stance on Nagorno–Karabakh. Little compensation for frictions in the relationship with Turkey have been offered by the cultivation of Iran; this would scupper the prospects of economic co-operation with the West, and Tehran, in any case, has not favoured Christian Armenia over Islamic Azerbaijan.

Georgia has faced similar dilemmas to Armenia. It initially sought to balance Russian influence by developing ties with its Turkish and Iranian neighbours. Both these states, moreover, were seen as potential economic partners. Georgia has also cultivated ties with Tel Aviv, benefiting from the channel of contact provided by the sizeable Georgian Jewish population in Israel. 'Suitcase trading' in Israeli produce has provided an economic lifeline in food produce and consumer goods, and Abkhazian rebels in west Georgia have accused Israel of sending arms to the Georgian government. Close bilateral ties have also been forged with Bulgaria and Georgia has been a keen participant in the Black Sea Economic Co-operation project. In the final analysis, however, Georgia's foreign policy in the post-Soviet period has been geared to seeking solutions to its civil conflicts, a priority which has resulted in an increasing reliance on Russia. Until these conflicts are settled the full benefits of regional diversification are likely to remain elusive.

4 The outward orientation of the Central Asian states has been determined by geography, political and economic weakness, and socio-cultural diversity.

'Central' is an appropriate designation for this part of the FSU. All five of the successor states are essentially landlocked. The Caspian Sea, an inland waterway, does provide a maritime route to the Transcaucasus and Iran, but the major trading lanes of the world's oceans are several hundred miles distant. The dictates of geography are also apparent in the long and multiple borders of the region. Three of the Central Asian states – Kazakhstan (the largest of the successor states after Russia and larger than all of Western Europe), Tajikistan and Kyrgyzstan – abut upon China. Tajikistan, Turkmenistan and Uzbekistan share frontiers with the troubled country of Afghanistan, and one, Turkmenistan, lies alongside Iran. Further to the south, lie India and Pakistan, and to the south-west, Iraq, Turkey and the Gulf states. The location of the Central Asian states amidst this array of regional powers exposes them to a host of influences: regional competitions for hegemony amongst neighbouring states; the knock-on effects of local wars, notably that in Afghanistan; border disputes, particularly with China; and the attractions of competing forms of Islam amongst sections of their populations. The potency of these forces has been compounded by economic underdevelopment, military vulnerabilities and, in the case of Tajikistan, religious and cultural links with Iran and Afghanistan.

In the midst of this uncertain environment, the Central Asian states resolved at an early stage to consolidate relations with Russia and the CIS and to seek a degree of localised co-operation (see above, pp. 105–6). In their relations with the outside world, a major foreign policy priority has been to secure investment and technical assistance from any source on offer. During 1992 this led to applications for membership of financial institutions such as the World Bank, the IMF and the EBRD, and a close attention to cementing bilateral relations with the US and European countries.[69] Flying in the face of economic and geopolitical logic, Kazakh President Nazarbaev has even gone so far as to voice a desire for his country's eventual membership of the EU.[70] Central Asian leaders have also recognised the potential benefits of regional economic links: trade with China, investment from Japan, South Korea and the Gulf, and transport and communications links with their southerly neighbours (see Chapter 6). A second priority has been to consolidate territorial integrity. All have had an interest in limiting the effects of the civil war in Afghanistan and have been keen to resolve outstanding border issues with China (see Chapter 5, pp. 235–37, 253–54).

In the West (and to some degree, also in Russia), discussion of Central Asia has been informed by perceptions of the region's susceptibility to competing models of development. In this light, two stark alternatives have been posited. First, there is Islamic fundamentalism as espoused by Iran, a model seen as anathema to Western and Russian interests. Second, is the secular model represented by Turkey, one in which Islam coexists with democracy, free markets and an openness to contacts with the West.[71] Leaving aside for now the question of whether Iran or Turkey aspire to regional influence,[72] it is worth noting that the Central Asian states themselves have been cautious about courting these potential patrons. True, during the nationalist revival of the Gorbachev period, Islam and ideas of Turkish identity (or in the Tajik case, Iranian) had been revived. Following independence, Central Asian leaders have also enthusiastically cultivated relations with both Turkey and Iran and have adopted Islamic symbols as a means of cultivating domestic popularity. Of the two models, the Turkish has been the more popular owing to its secularism and Western orientation. As the President of Uzbekistan has spelled out: 'I say unambiguously that the Turkish path of development is more acceptable to us ... as a secular civilised path of societal development. We must work out our own path of development, relying on Turkey's experience.'[73] A secular state has been the only realistic option for the leaders of countries such as Kazakhstan and Kyrgyzstan with large Russian minorities. Moreover, all the leaders of the region have been traumatised by the war in Tajikistan, a conflict with diverse roots, but one which they see as the result of an attempt to introduce an Islamic government by force.[74]

Even the Turkish model, however, has its limitations. To the degree that it has been associated with notions of pan-Turkism, it has been rejected as contrary to the consolidation of national independence. Relations with Turkey have been seen as desirable, but not on the basis of subservience to a potential regional leader. Moreover, the achievements of Turkey have been seen as less than impressive. What Central Asian leaders have found when visiting Turkey is a country beset by inflation and unemployment, and mired down in a war against its native Kurdish population. Their impression of Ankara as subservient to the West also has little to offer Central Asia, which alongside favourable ties with the West has a huge stake in close relations with Russia.[75] It should also be remembered that for all their nationalist credentials the ruling elites in Central Asia received their political education through the particularly venal and self-serving Communist Parties of the Soviet Central Asian republics. The instinctive dislike of political pluralism this engendered has been strengthened by the allegedly divisive influence of religion and overt nationalism. In Uzbekistan and Turkmenistan, in particular, this has resulted in the continuation of a pattern of rule almost pre-Gorbachev in its absence of democratic norms, involving the suppression of nationalist and religious organisations. In this light, the preferred model among some Central Asian elites is that exemplified by countries to the east – China, Indonesia, Singapore and South Korea – where economic success has been accompanied by political authoritarianism, guaranteeing a measure of prosperity, a high level of civil order and the political longevity of the ruling authorities.[76] In Kyrgyzstan, by contrast, a somewhat different model has been favoured, guided by the more democratic inclinations of President Akaev (a leader with a less pronounced communist past).[77] In order to balance the two 'great neighbours' of Russia and China and to boost economic fortunes, Akaev has preferred the Swiss model of permanent neutrality and financial openness.[78]

It is also significant that, with the exception of Turkmenistan, all the Central Asian states have been amenable to the development of ties with Israel, a trend which illustrates clearly the weakness of a specifically Islamic direction in foreign policy. While these states have been wary of being drawn into the Arab–Israeli dispute and have remained suspicious of Israel's motives (namely its desire to counter the influence of Arab and Gulf states in the region) Central Asian leaders have 'perceived [... Israel] as being something of a model of new state economic development'. Israel's success in developing agriculture and irrigation systems in climatic conditions similar to those of parts of Central Asia has resulted in the cultivation of significant commercial ties.[79]

5 Russian foreign policy beyond the FSU is quite different from that of the other successor states. According to Alexei Arbatov, a Russian specialist on international relations, the frame of reference for Russian foreign policy in the post-Soviet period consists of four main 'realities'.[80]

The first is the USSR's disintegration. Out of the ruins, Russia has emerged as the largest and most powerful of the successor states. With a population of 147 million and a land mass comprising over three-quarters of the former USSR, Russia dwarfs all its new neighbours. It alone is the largest country on earth. Russia can, therefore, realistically be termed a 'multiregional' power.[81] Its huge expanse means it abuts a number of regions (North and Eastern Europe, the Far East/Asian–Pacific region, Asia Minor and the Indian subcontinent) bringing it into direct contact with a host of influential states (Poland, Japan, China, India, Turkey and Iran). The Soviet collapse is also germane to Russian foreign policy, in that Russia has laid claim to the superpower status formerly enjoyed by the USSR. The validity of this claim rests partly on Russia's practical inheritance. It acquired the diplomatic machinery of the USSR, the standing of continuing state, and, as will be explored in Chapters 4 and 6, much of the Soviet Union's formidable military might and economic resources. Yeltsin has also stressed other Russian credentials. In a speech to the Russian parliament in 1992 he suggested that 'Russia is rightfully a great power by virtue of its history, its place in the world and its material and spiritual potential.'[82] In essence, this claim entailed a sleight of hand, conflating Russian achievement with that of the USSR. The Soviet victory in World War II, for instance, has been portrayed by Yeltsin as the result of the sacrifice of 'the Soviet, the Russian soldier ... without [whom] ... the fate of the world could have been quite different'. Just as Soviet leaders used the triumph over Nazism as a justification for the USSR's special position in Europe and its status as a great power, so Yeltsin has put forward a similar pretext with regard to Russia.[83]

The second reality is that of the deep economic and social crisis with which Russia entered the post-Soviet period. The severe economic downturn of the Gorbachev era carried over with the change of regime. Falling production, rising inflation and unemployment, a yawning budget deficit and growing foreign indebtedness held important implications for decisions in the realms of foreign policy and defence. How, for instance, would Russia conduct itself in relations with international economic institutions and potential bilateral partners? How might trade be expanded? How might foreign investment be increased? What would be the fate of the defence budget in a period of austerity?

Russia's third reality also reflects a problem formerly experienced by Gorbachev, namely a state of flux in the decision-making structures of foreign policy. This state of affairs has partly resulted from the administrative transition from Soviet to Russian structures. But, in addition, the problem stems from the difficulty of arriving at a consensus on foreign policy priorities. During 1992–93, divisions were as marked in attitudes towards the wider world as they were concerning policy towards the 'near abroad' (analysed above, pp. 97–100). Below the level of President, bureaucratic 'turf-battles' broke out between the Ministries of Foreign Affairs and Defence, the Parliament, Vice-President and the Presidential apparatus (notably the Security Council) over the formulation and implementation of foreign policy.[84] This resulted in a drift in Russia's overall foreign policy direction and, more specifically, in inconsistencies on divisive issues such as policy towards Japan and Yugoslavia and on disarmament and security issues.

The fourth reality with which Russia has had to contend is a changed international environment. The rise of Russia from the ashes of the USSR is, of course, itself part of this fundamental alteration in the international system. This, however, is only part of a broader pattern of change. The end of the bipolarity of the Cold War (of which the USSR's demise was part) has, according to Arbatov, not been replaced by American global hegemony. Rather, it has strengthened the long-standing trend towards multipolarity, a phenomenon which Gorbachev had earlier attempted to come to terms with in the new political thinking and of which Kozyrev has a fairly sophisticated understanding.[85] In addition to the US, and to a lesser degree, Russia itself, the main actors in this multipolar world are Western Europe, China, Japan, and a number of regional powers in the Third World (Brazil, India, South Korea etc.). A multipolar world is a more complex one, involving multilateral diplomacy, a growing role for organisations such as the UN and the ever more present dangers of regional conflicts, weapons proliferation, and ecological and humanitarian disaster.

In the face of these new realities Arbatov argues that Russian foreign policy in the 1990s has to address four main problems.[86] The first has been analysed in the previous section: Russia's relations with the other successor states. A second challenge has been to formulate a policy to deal with regional conflicts on the periphery of the FSU. Open hostilities in Afghanistan and the Balkans and potential conflicts in Eastern Europe, the Indian subcontinent, the Far East and the Asian Pacific region all hold implications for Russia (as we shall explore in Chapter 5). Third, and closely related, Russia has to deal with regional powers at a time when its own relative economic, military and political weaknesses might allow them to expand their influence in the trouble spots of the FSU. Lastly, the Soviet Union bequeathed to Russia a number of responsibilities in areas of a global significance, notably disarmament and arms control and the activities of the UN Security Council. Setting priorities, however, has been problematic. As already suggested, Russia's approach to the world beyond the FSU has been a matter of some disagreement. Only at the end of 1993 was something approaching a consensus achieved between the main policy-making actors. By this point, Russian foreign policy looked quite different from the time of its initial inception at the end of 1991.

During the first six months or so of 1992, Russian foreign policy was dominated by what has been dubbed the 'Atlanticist' or 'Westernist' orientation. This tendency was personified by Kozyrev and was sympathetically treated by Yeltsin. It had much in common with the ideas of the Gorbachev era, leading one commentator to call it 'new political thinking plus'.[87] Like the new political thinking, the 'Atlanticist' approach was driven, to an important degree, by economic factors. As Yeltsin explained in February 1992, two tasks were central to foreign policy: to secure Russia's entry into the 'civilised community' of states and 'to enlist maximum support for our efforts to transform Russia'.[88] To these ends, it was essential Russia cultivate the West. Correct relations with the near abroad might have been germane to national security, but only the West had the wherewithal to offer Russia meaningful assistance and contribute to future economic prosperity. Moreover, as the Russian President was to later explain: 'Russia's independent foreign policy started with the West. It started with the United States, and we believe that this was justified. We had to lay the foundation – that is, to prepare a detailed treaty on the global reduction and elimination of strategic nuclear weapons, on the basis of which it would be easier, afterward, to build relations with any country, be it in the West or East, Europe or Asia.'[89] Co-operation was also viewed as a means of affirming Russia's great power status. In rejecting the messianism of Tsarist imperialism and Soviet communism, status was to be judged not in terms of Moscow's ability to stand up to the West but in its readiness to join it in a commitment to the common values of democracy, market economics and respect for human rights. In this light, the countries of the West were no longer to be regarded as adversaries, but, rather, as 'natural allies' of Russia.[90] In practical terms, the Atlanticist line found realisation in a flurry of diplomatic visits by Yeltsin and Kozyrev to Western capitals, negotiations on a successor treaty to START and involvement in international co-ordination of economic assistance.[91]

Russia's preoccupation with the West soon came in for criticism. As noted above (pp. 98–99), the neglect of the near abroad formed one plank of the attack. In addition, influential figures in Russia were scornful of the initial Yeltsin/Kozyrev line on a number of grounds. An early and trenchant critique was provided by Sergei Stankevich. An adviser to Yeltsin, he outlined a position known as 'Eurasianism'. Stankevich conceded that an attention to the West had a strong economic rationale, but warned that this entailed an underestimation of the importance of Russia's 'Eastern Orientation'. Russia was after all geographically separated from Europe by a string of new states, had its own Turkic and Islamic populations, which demanded harmonious relations with countries in Asia, and faced in the Transcaucasus an 'arc of crisis', which was being keenly watched by Turkey, Iran and Saudi Arabia. Moreover, Russia's geographic embrace of both the European and Asian continents and its 'strength as a unique historical–cultural alloy of Slavic and Turkic, Orthodox and Muslim elements' impelled it towards a unique mission. Russia, he argued, ought to be a 'country that takes in West and East, North and South' in pursuit of 'a multilateral dialogue of cultures, civilisations and states'. Stankevich thus sought a balance between East and West in Russian foreign policy. He also advocated a policy which would play to Russia's strengths rather than its weaknesses. Instead of tying itself economically to the West, Russia should seek self-sufficiency through the development of its own resources and the tightening of co-operation with the other CIS member states.[92]

Variations on Stankevich's position were offered by other influential politicians. Vladimir Lukin, Russian Ambassador to the US, for instance, emphasised not the centrality of the cordial Russian–US relationship, but rather a 'new encirclement' created by unresolved tensions with Japan and China and Russia's proximity to trouble spots in places such as the Korean peninsula. To deal with these challenges, Lukin, like Stankevich, advocated a mission for Russia; in this case, to 'become a guarantor of stability throughout the Eurasian heartland', first and foremost through the cultivation of the near abroad, and secondly through building close relations with important neighbours such as China and India.[93] This, moreover, offered economic benefits. Rather than relying on what could prove ephemeral assistance from the Group of Seven (G7) countries, it was necessary, he argued, to exploit the potential of relations with more compatible economic partners in China, the Third World and Eastern Europe. Even more critical were the positions taken by Alexander Rutskoi, the Vice President, and his political ally, Ruslan Khasbulatov, Speaker of the Russian Parliament. Although their major bone of contention lay with Russian policy in the near abroad, their ire was also turned towards Kozyrev's pro-Westernism. Rutskoi, for instance, berated the West's prescriptions for Russian economic reform as designed to 'destroy the scientific and technical potential that has been created in Russia'. He was equally dismissive of a close relationship in the field of security. The 'military doctrine' of the US was seen as essentially antithetical to Russian interests. It was necessary, therefore, that the Russian armed forces maintain their defence capability, a stance which implicitly ruled out further East–West disarmament.[94]

The divide between these influential positions initially appeared so wide as to be unbridgeable. However, by the end of 1993 the dissonance which had characterised the foreign policy debate had been replaced by a tentative consensus amongst Russia's political elite. The policies around which this consensus was built marked a distinct shift from the ascendant Atlanticism of 1992. The 'new Russian foreign policy' consisted of a tougher line towards the near abroad (see above, pp. 99–100), an end to the preoccupation with the West, the staking out of Eastern Europe as a Russian sphere of influence, a more questioning attitude towards the intentions of the NATO powers, and a less flexible posture in areas of diplomatic and economic co-operation with the West. The route Russia travelled to reach this juncture will be charted in detail in the following chapters.[95] At this point it is worth noting some of the broad contributory factors. First, the perception arose that Russia, rather than being treated as an equal by the West, was in fact increasingly playing second fiddle to it. Moreover, Kozyrev's Atlanticism had been based partly on the assumption that the pursuit of Western prescriptions would witness Russia's swift transformation into a prosperous, democratic and stable country. When this failed to happen the fascination with the West soon evaporated. The disillusionment with the West increased the appeal of elements of the Eurasian agenda, both as these applied to the increasingly unstable near abroad and to the major neighbouring powers. The redirection of foreign policy also served important political functions, and might be seen as both cause and effect of the desire of the agencies involved in its formulation to reach accommodation. With the Russian parliament largely tamed by the adoption of a new Russian constitution at the end of 1993 (achieved after the forcible dissolution of the old Russian parliament and the arrests of Rutskoi and Khasbulatov)[96] the new policy amounted to a *rapprochement* between Yeltsin and those institutions that retained a significant influence, notably, the Ministries of Defence and Foreign Affairs and the Security Council. All recognised that division had resulted in a foreign policy, which was by turns erratic, prevaricating and indecisive. Consensus was required, in order to return to reliability and effectiveness, and thereby ensure Russia's continued influence abroad.[97] That this matched more closely the agenda of the military reflected the debt Yeltsin held for the crucial support it had given to the President's struggle with the Russian parliament in 1993.

Conclusion: the foreign policies of new states

A substantial body of literature exists on the nature of foreign policy, its goals, the sources of influence that underlie these goals and the instruments used to pursue them. If we take the goals of foreign policy, Kal Holsti has identified four common 'purposes' pursued by states: security, autonomy, (economic) welfare, and status or prestige.[98] Amongst new states (such as those in the FSU), more so than established ones, these objectives appear immediate and pressing. Physical insecurities, for example, are more acute for new entrants into the international system. The (neo)realist's concern with the imperative of survival in a hostile international environment, noted in the introductory chapter, seems especially pertinent in this regard. Since they may want for the military means of defence, new states are particularly exposed to external threats and consequently are especially distrustful of the motives of their neighbours.[99] These consequences of the anarchic international system provide, however, only a partial picture of the catalogue of the challenges facing new states. As Caroline Thomas has observed with regard to the new states of the Third World, physical threats outside the boundary of the state tend to be secondary to those which arise internally, most viciously in the form of civil war.[100] True, in the Third World interstate wars have also proliferated – Iraq's battles with Iran and latterly Kuwait are recent examples. However, a brief perusal of the war zones of Nigeria, Somalia, Angola, Liberia, Mozambique, Chad, Nicaragua and Yemen seems to bear out Thomas's claim. Her observation, as we shall discover in Chapter 5, is also largely true of those new states of the FSU that have experienced warfare.

Security may be promoted in several ways. Guarding against external dangers may call forth a number of responses, of which building up military capabilities is the obvious, but not the only method. States may also seek reassurances from, and co-operation with, other states; they may enter into formal alliances; and they may place their faith in the mechanisms of international organisations and international law. Similarly, dealing with internal threats may require more than military muscle – political dialogue and external mediation are often called for.

Security is closely linked to the desire for autonomy – 'the ability to formulate and carry out domestic and external policies in terms of a government's own priorities ... the capacity to withstand influence, coercion or rule by others'.[101] As Holsti points out, this is a relative concept. At one extreme, the absolute crushing of autonomy arises when a state is invaded, occupied and annexed. Yet more commonly, it is undermined in less cataclysmic ways: through vulnerability to international economic forces and a reliance on an external economic and/or military patron. One symbolic bulwark against these pressures is the notion of sovereignty. The acquisition of sovereign statehood confers upon states both a formal autonomy (the 'eligibility [of a state] to participate in international relations in ... [its] own right' and the right to be protected against the interference in its internal affairs by another state) and an equality of status (a sovereign status 'which is the same as that of all [other] members of the international society').[102] Yet for all its promise, sovereignty itself does not offer a reliable guarantee of autonomy. States, in a formal sense, may be equal, but they are distinctly unequal in terms of their capabilities; and autonomy is more susceptible to compromise when a state's capabilities are weak. This explains why new states have an urgent desire to acquire the instruments which will further their military and economic integrity: national armies, an independent currency, a national bank and so on. Ultimately, these are incapable of totally withstanding the pressures exerted by superior military force (either directly or through veiled threats) or economic interdependence, but they do illustrate 'the obvious desire of all governments to retain some room for manoeuvre ... however large or small it can be in practice'.[103] In the post-Soviet context, Chapters 4 and 6 will bear out this observation.

New states also have a particular concern with status. To the degree that sovereign statehood affords some protection, states will seek continuously to confirm this independent identity through the elaboration of a distinctive and meaningful foreign policy and through participation in international organisations. Peter Calvocoressi has suggested that by such actions, new states 'prove their worth' and obtain 'the respect of the international society into which they have graduated'.[104] For W.C. McWilliams, foreign policy activity helps fulfil 'the desire for dignity, the yearning to "matter"'. This becomes, moreover, an especially powerful drive if a state feels its dignity is being demeaned by a condition of economic or military weakness.[105]

Taking arguments regarding status one step further, the old-fashioned realist would claim that for some states a particular form of status is desired, one that confers deference and respect amongst fellow states. In short, prestige is sought. For Morgenthau, prestige is the means by which power is demonstrated; for Wight, it is 'the influence derived from power'.[106] The usefulness of this concept in explaining the foreign policies of new states may appear exaggerated at first sight. The craving for prestige, after all, often follows from an awareness of some glorious past. Hence, for example, the British government's acquisition and retention of a nuclear capability, and its prominent role in important international bodies such as the UN Security Council, the G7 and NATO, accords it a prestige that provides compensation for its relinquishment of empire. The situation among new states is quite different. Almost by definition, a recent glorious past does not exist for these states owing to their former position as subjects of empire (or in the case of the successor states, subordinate republics within the USSR). Furthermore, new states upon independence assume a fairly lowly position in the diplomatic pecking order and the circumstances of their birth rarely confer the capabilities which might generate deference or respect in others. The exception is, of course, Russia, which has assumed the continuing status of the USSR and has acquired many of its capabilities.[107] Aware of the opportunities afforded by this inheritance, its political elite has explicitly voiced a desire that Russia perform the role of a great power and that it consciously exercise influence throughout its near abroad.

The goals of foreign policy are affected by a number of influences that have been touched upon in the references to the capabilities of states in the above paragraphs and in our discussion of approaches to international politics in the Introduction. Here we noted that the (neo)realist's concern with the constraints of anarchy and his/her view of the state as a unitary and rational actor have been challenged by the pluralist perspective which accords considerable significance to opportunities for international co-operation and domestic decision-making processes. In this light, in ascertaining foreign policy objectives it is of benefit to have some understanding of domestic political conditions. Influential approaches in this regard have focused on the bureaucratic politics of foreign policy decision-making (the competition between various agencies of government in formulating foreign policy) or on organisational process (the incremental and conservative nature of decision-making in large bureaucracies). These models do, however, have their limitations. They apply well to foreign policy making in advanced societies possessing a complex array of government agencies and a large and well-trained army of bureaucrats (it has, therefore, some applicability in the Russian case, given its inheritance of much of the vast machinery of Soviet government). They are of far less relevance in new states where bureaucracies are small[108] and where the executive, and its personification in a national leader, tends to be pre-eminent within the state machinery (two features commonplace in the successor states). In such cases foreign policy-making tends to be a 'personal much more than an institutional process'.[109]

The degree of ascendancy of the leader also, of course, has much to do with the nature of the political system as a whole. In a democracy, it is argued, foreign policy is likely to be the outcome of a diverse set of influences. Pressure groups, public opinion and the mass media are all engaged in seeking to affect policies and in balancing the dominance of powerful groups such as the military, industrial conglomerates and the higher reaches of government bureaucracy. Other moderating influences include elections, which ensure that popular preferences are weighed in governmental decision-making and that leaders are brought to book for ineptitude, and the institutional division of powers, which hold the executive in check. In authoritarian systems by contrast, the preferences of leaders are less restrained by these democratic devices and foreign policy tends to be the jealously guarded prerogative of a small elite. This may have potentially damaging consequences. An unchallenged leader, sated in ambition in the domestic sphere, may attempt to translate his/her power into international achievements. This often results in quests for regional influence, and in certain cases, in intervention in the domestic affairs of neighbouring states. Even when the ambitions of the leader are circumscribed by limited capabilities, an active profile may still be sought, with detrimental consequences for domestic populations forced to suffer the direction of scarce resources into inflated militaries and fruitless overseas adventures.[110]

The importance of democratic government, moreover, can be seen in its purportedly peaceable character. An influential proposition in international relations literature has it that democracies almost never fight each other in war. Michael Doyle, for one, has suggested that the key to this lies in the observations made by Immanuel Kant as far back as the late eighteenth century. Democracies ('republics'), so Kant argued, are inherently less warlike than authoritarian regimes (autocratic monarchies in Kant's time). There are three reasons for this: the accountability of leaders to a public which has to bear the human cost of warfare restrains government from waging war; states united by common principles have a mutual respect for one another; and trade between free economies creates a commercial incentive to peace.[111] The auxiliary propositions that follow from this argument are: that war more commonly occurs between authoritarian regimes; democracies only go to war when forced to do so by the aggression of dictators; democracies are prone to engage with one another in alliances; and the spread of democracy will mean the enlargement of a zone of peace or 'pacific union'.[112]

Turning more specifically to the domestic political conditions within the successor states. All these states face similar problems arising from the end of Soviet rule: the creation of new political and administrative institutions, new constitutional frameworks and the accommodation of ethnic and regional demands for greater autonomy.[113] The political responses of the successor states to these common challenges of transition have by no means been uniform (see Table 3.1). At one extreme, political development in Azerbaijan, Georgia and Tajikistan has been stunted by warfare (the roots of which are detailed in Chapter 5), accentuating tendencies towards acute political fragmentation and ineffective authoritarian rule and severely constraining foreign policy options. A second pattern, a more stable authoritarianism has been apparent in Uzbekistan and Turkmenistan. Here foreign policy priorities (Uzbekistan's regional ambitions and Turkmenistan's semi-detached attitude towards the CIS) have been closely associated with the preferences of Presidents Niyazov and Karimov respectively. Similarly, in Kazakhstan, subject to a perhaps 'softer' version of authoritarian rule, foreign policy remains the unchallenged prerogative of President Nazarbaev.

A somewhat different pattern has been observable in Russia, Ukraine, Belarus and Armenia. These states have sounder democratic credentials, but have experienced protracted tussles between President (in the Belarus case, the Chair of the parliament) and legislature. This, as we have seen above, has hampered foreign policy formulation in Belarus and Russia. In the case of the former, the initiative lay with the parliament owing to the absence of a constitutionally separate executive. The adoption of a new constitution in March 1994 and the election of an executive President in July shifted the balance somewhat, although parliament retains important prerogatives. In Russia, President Yeltsin's victory over the Russian parliament in late 1993, means foreign policy has more than ever become the preserve of the executive. In Chapter 4, the impact of parliamentary pressure will be noticeable in Ukrainian nuclear weapons policy and in Chapter 5 in Armenian policy towards Nagorno–Karabakh.

Table 3.1 *Civil and political rights in the successor states (CIVIC scores)*

	1991	*1992*	*1993*
Russia	6.7	5.8	5.8
Ukraine	6.7	6.7	5.0
Belarus	5.0	5.8	4.2
Uzbekistan	2.5	1.7	0.0
Kazakhstan	4.2	3.3	3.3
Georgia	2.5	4.2	3.3
Azerbaijan	3.3	3.3	1.7
Moldova	4.2	3.3	3.3
Kyrgyzstan	4.2	6.7	5.0
Tajikistan	3.3	2.5	0.0
Armenia	3.3	5.8	5.8
Turkmenistan	2.5	0.8	0.0
Lithuania	7.5	7.5	8.3
Latvia	7.5	6.7	6.7
Estonia	7.5	6.7	6.7

Note: CIVIC scores refer to state respect for civil and political rights; this is taken as a measurement of democratic performance. A higher score reflects a stronger state commitment to the protection of civil and political rights.

Source: J-E. Lane and S. Ersson, *Comparative Politics. An Introduction and New Approach* (Cambridge, Polity Press, 1994), p. 226.

The clearest democratic pattern has taken root in the Baltic states. None can yet be regarded as consolidated democracies, however, in all cases important steps have been taken towards securing democratic transition. Estonia, Latvia and Lithuania all enjoyed during 1992–93 the free and peaceful election of new parliaments. Moreover, according to Darrell Slider, all three have made 'significant progress' in building democratic institutions (party systems and legislatures) and in avoiding 'political gridlock'.[114] In foreign policy terms, the Baltic states' leaning towards the Nordic countries and the countries of the EU seems a natural corollary of their democratic orientation. Finally, it is worth highlighting Kyrgyzstan, a country, which in comparison with the other Central Asian states, has progressed relatively well towards democratic governance. However, in this case, the foreign policy impact of nascent democracy is more difficult to gauge. A foreign policy eschewing an overt Islamic bent is not solely reducible to secular democratic government (authoritarian Uzbekistan and Turkmenistan have followed a similar course). Moreover. Kyrgyzstan's geographic position ensures that, whether democratic or not, it pay close attention to developing relations with neighbouring states such as China. Yet as Ian Pryde has suggested, 'Kyrgyzstan's ultimate aim politically is ... a state more European than Asian'. Hence, Akaev's admiration of Switzerland and his openness to Western-oriented financial and economic institutions.[115]

Political diversity amongst the successor states has several consequences. Firstly, the absence of a set of shared norms that might bind co-operation throughout the FSU has a debilitating influence on integration, a situation most clearly evident in the problems which have faced the CIS. Secondly, the wide variety of different agendas amongst governments suggests that co-operation in specific areas is likely to be problematic. Thirdly, as well as influencing inter-relations within the FSU, political diversity reinforces the patterns of regionalisation apparent in the outward orientation. The fragility of democracy in the FSU, similarly, has certain implications. The prospect of a 'pacific union' both within the FSU and between the successor states and the Western democracies, depends, in the logic of the Kantian argument, on the spread and consolidation of democracy. Moreover, internal peace within the successor states is more likely to be furthered if democratic mechanisms of conflict resolution and group bargaining are able to evolve.

In posing these issues we are anticipating more detailed treatment in subsequent chapters. We turn first to a consideration of defence and security issues.

Notes

1 Z. Brzezinski, 'The Cold War and its aftermath', *Foreign Affairs*, 71:4 (1992), p. 33; P. M. E. Volten, 'Security dimensions of imperial collapse', *Problems of Communism*, 41:1–2 (1992), p. 140.
2 C. Bluth, 'Russia and European security', *The World Today* (April 1994), p. 76.
3 S. Karaganov, 'Russia I: a Moscow view on the West's role', *The World Today* (July 1992), p. 122.
4 *Ibid.*; R. Levgold, 'Foreign policy', in T.J. Colton and R. Levgold (eds), *After the Soviet Union. From Empire to Nations* (London and New York, W.W. Norton, 1992), pp. 158–59.
5 *Ibid.*, pp. 159–60.
6 A.J. Motyl, 'Russian hegemony and non-Russian insecurity: foreign policy dilemmas of the USSR's successor states', *The Harriman Institute Forum*, 5:4 (1991), pp. 1–11.
7 G. Wettig, 'Developments in the former USSR and European security', *Aussenpolitik*, 43:3 (1992), pp. 233–34.
8 W.W. Newmann, 'History accelerates: the diplomacy of cooperation and fragmentation', in J.E. Goodby and B. Morel (eds), *The Limited Partnership. Building a Russian–US Security Community* (Oxford, Oxford University Press/SIPRI, 1993), p. 49.
9 *Ibid.*, p. 51; Levgold, 'Foreign policy', pp. 165–66.
10 *Agreements on the Creation of the Commonwealth of Independent States Signed in December 1991/January 1992* (London, Russian Information Agency/Novosti, 1992), pp. 17–20. (Hereafter *Founding Agreements*).
11 British Broadcasting Corporation, Summary of World Broadcasts (BBC, SWB), SU/2134 A/6, 24 October 1994.
12 W.S. Jones, *The Logic of International Relations* (New York, Harper Collins, seventh edition, 1991), pp. 606–8.
13 Moldova, having initially confined its role in the CIS to the economic sphere, was forced to adopt a more committed stance following the imposition by Russia in August 1993 of prohibitive customs duties and excise taxes on Moldovan agricultural produce. The circumstances of Georgian entry are noted on p. 273, note 19.
14 This was also true of the wider population in Belarus. In the Soviet–wide referendum of March 1991 on the preservation of the Union, 83 per cent of those who voted in the republic were in favour

of the Union's continuation.

15 J. Zaprudnik, *Belarus. At a Crossroads in History* (Boulder, Colorado, Westview Press, 1993), Chapters 1 and 2.

16 K. Mihailisko, 'Belorussia: setting sail without a compass', *Radio Free Europe/Radio Liberty (RFE/RL) Research Report*, 1:1 (1992), pp. 39–41.

17 A. Hyman, 'Moving out of Moscow's orbit: the outlook for Central Asia', *International Affairs* 69:2 (1993), p. 295.

18 S. Akiner, *Central Asia. New Arc of Crisis?* (London, The Royal United Services Institute for Defence Studies, 1993), pp. 5–7.

19 The war in Tajikistan is covered in detail in Chapter 5.

20 *Izvestiya*, 15 September 1992, pp. 1, 3 and 5 June 1993, p. 5.

21 P. Reddaway, 'Russia on the brink?', *The New York Review of Books*, 28 January 1993, pp. 30–32.

22 V. Tolz, 'The burden of the imperial legacy', *RFE/RL Research Report*, 2:20 (1993), pp. 41–43.

23 Yeltsin's New Year message for 1993 claimed that 'The imperial period in Russia's history has ended.' BBC, SWB, SU/1576 C1/1, 1 January 1993.

24 J. Lough, 'Defining Russia's relations with neighboring states', *RFE/RL Research Report*, 2:20 (1993), p. 53.

25 B.D. Porter and C.R. Saivetz, 'The once and future empire: Russia and the "near abroad"', *The Washington Quarterly*, 17:3 (1994), pp. 77–80.

26 Lough, 'Defining Russia's relations', p. 54; J. Lough, 'The place of the "near abroad" in Russian foreign policy', *RFE/RL Research Report*, 2:11 (1993), p. 25.

27 *The Economist*, 18 September 1993, pp. 41–42.

28 The Security Council is an influential advisory body attached to the office of the President.

29 Lough, 'Defining Russia's relations', pp. 55–56.

30 *Current Digest of the Post-Soviet Press (CDSP)*, 45:17 (1993), pp. 13–15.

31 Kozyrev cited in *Moscow News*, 24 January 1994, p. 2.

32 Foreign Broadcasting Information Service (FBIS), SOV-93-073, 19 April 1993, pp. 3–5.

33 R. Solchanyk, 'Kravchuk defines Ukrainian–CIS relations', *RFE/RL Research Report*, 1:11 (1992), p. 9.

34 D. Arel and A. Wilson, 'Ukraine under Kuchma: back to "Eurasia?"', *RFE/RL Research Report*, 3:32 (1994), p. 1.

35 BBC, SWB, SU/2134 A/6, 24 October 1994.

36 Robert Conquest cited in 'Unruly child: a survey of Ukraine', *The Economist*, 7 May 1994, p. 13.

37 B. Krawchenko, 'Ukraine: the politics of independence', in I. Bremmer and R. Taras (eds), *Nations and Politics in the Soviet Successor States* (Cambridge, Cambridge University Press, 1993), p. 84.
38 R. Solchanyk, 'Russia, Ukraine, and the imperial legacy', *Post-Soviet Affairs*, 9:4 (1993), pp. 340–41.
39 Recognition was granted on 3 December 1991.
40 *RFE/RL Research Report*, 1:26 (1992), pp. 74–75.
41 Tolz, 'The burden of the imperial legacy', p. 44.
42 Solchanyk, 'Russia, Ukraine', pp. 358–62.
43 *RFE/RL Research Report*, 1:33 (1992), p. 74.
44 Article 5 of the CIS Charter states that both multilateral and bilateral agreements form 'the legal basis of interstate relations within the framework of the Commonwealth'.
45 B. Brown, 'Turkmenistan asserts itself', *RFE/RL Research Report*, 1:43 (1992), p. 29. Turkmenistan's economic and military relations are considered in Chapters 4 and 6.
46 U. Markus, 'Belarus a "weak link" in Eastern Europe?', *RFE/RL Research Report*, 2:49 (1993), p. 21.
47 In chronological order, such treaties have been signed with Armenia (December 1991), Kazakhstan (May 1992), Uzbekistan (May 1992), Kyrgystan (June 1992), Turkmenistan (July 1992), Tajikistan (November 1993) and Georgia (February 1994). During 1994 negotiations were underway on similar treaties with Belarus and Ukraine.
48 In elections to the Kazakh parliament in 1994, 42 of the legislature's 177 seats were allocated on the basis of a 'Presidential list'.
49 Newmann, 'History accelerates', pp. 42, 47; *Keesing's Record of World Events*, December 1991, p. 38656.
50 Georgia was the last to join the CSCE in late March; it did not enter the UN until the end of July. Its belated entry into these bodies was a consequence of its pariah status under the leadership of Zviad Gamsakhurdia (see Chapter 5, p. 230).
51 R. Müllerson, 'The continuity and succession of states, by reference to the former USSR and Yugoslavia', *International and Comparative Law Quarterly*, 42:3 (1993), pp. 473–93.
52 The Baltic states and Georgia were not party to these agreements. Given the manipulation of Baltic borders during the period of Soviet rule this might be seen as a significant omission in the Baltic cases. On border issues see Chapter 5.
53 *Founding Agreements*, pp. 4, 16.
54 *Ibid.*, p. 12.
55 UK Prime Minister John Major in a letter to Boris Yeltsin stated that Her Majesty's Government recognised 'the continuity of statehood between Russia and the former USSR', *The Independent*, 24 Decem-

ber 1991.

56 This was later explicitly recognised by the CIS members themselves, who in a memorandum of July 1992 suggested that the degree of participation in treaties entered into by the USSR should be decided upon according to whether these affected individual successor states. See Müllerson, 'The continuity and succession of states', p. 477.

57 A.J. Motyl, *Dilemmas of Independence. Ukraine after Totalitarianism* (New York, Council on Foreign Relations, 1993), p. 107.

58 A Treaty on Succession to the USSR's Debt and Assets signed in early December 1991 by eight of the then Soviet republics just days before the formation of the CIS did lay down their respective shares in debts and assets of the USSR (Russia would be responsible for 61.34 per cent and Ukraine 16.37 per cent), on the basis of size of population, national income, and trade turnover. A CIS agreement signed in late December also suggested that each CIS state 'has the right to an appropriate, fair and ascertained share of the property of the former Soviet Union abroad'. In practice, these agreements did not prevent Russia's acquisition of overseas properties. Just days after the CIS agreement, Vitaly Churkin, a Russian Foreign Ministry representative, asserted that Soviet embassies and consulates abroad have 'become Russian and the flag of the Russian Federation has been raised over them'. He did concede, however, that the cost for the successor states of establishing representation abroad meant Russia would be prepared to represent their interests if agreement could be reached (*Izvestiya*, 4 January 1992, p. 3). Later efforts within the CIS framework failed to resolve this question and furthered Russian acquisition. In July 1992 a CIS agreement was reached that reiterated the division agreed in early December 1991. However, a CIS Commission to deal with issues of state succession was suspended in October by the CIS heads of state, who resolved that matters of debt and assets of the USSR should be decided on a bilateral basis. This resulted in a series of deals that revolved around the so-called 'zero-option', by which Russia assumed the share of former Soviet debt obligations of individual successor states, who in return dropped claims to former Soviet property abroad. On these matters see, R. Müllerson, *International Law, Rights and Politics. Developments in Eastern Europe and the CIS* (London and New York, Routledge, 1994), pp. 143–44 and B. Vibe Christensen, *The Russian Federation in Transition. External Developments* (IMF Occasional Papers, III, February 1994), p. 24. See also Chapter 6, pp. 306–8.

59 Levgold, 'Foreign policy', p. 155.

60 Motyl, 'Russian hegemony and non-Russian insecurity', p. 6.

61 P. Vares and M. Haab, 'The Baltic states: *quo vadis*?', in R. Cowen

Karp (ed.), *Central and Eastern Europe. The Challenge of Transition* (Oxford, Oxford University Press/Sipri, 1993), p. 285.
62 Motyl, *Dilemmas of Independence*, p. 124.
63 *Ibid.*, p. 89.
64 O. Alexandrova, 'Geostrategic reconstructuring in the former USSR', *Aussenpolitik*, 43:4 (1992), p. 328.
65 *Moscow News*, 1–8 March 1992, p. 14.
66 Reprinted in C. Furtado, Jr and J. Chandler (eds), *Perestroika in the Soviet Republics. Documents on the National Question* (Boulder: Westview Press, 1992), p. 461.
67 *Ibid.*, p. 441.
68 E. Fuller, 'The thorny path to an Armenian–Turkish rapprochement', *RFE/RL Research Report*, 2:12 (1993), p. 48.
69 B. Brown, 'Central Asia's diplomatic debut', *RFE/RL Research Report*, 1:10 (1992), p. 21.
70 *RFE/RL Research Report*, 1:11 (1992), p. 69.
71 Levgold, 'Foreign policy', p. 166; *Moscow News*, 23 February–1 March 1992, p. 14.
72 The depth of Iranian and Turkish commitment to these objectives is discussed in Chapter 5, within the context of the war in Nagorno–Karabakh, an area admittedly outside Central Asia, but one in which similar arguments of influence-building have been applied.
73 Quoted in A. Ehteshami and E.C. Murphy, 'The non-Arab Middle East states and the Caucasian/Central Asian Republics: Iran and Israel', *International Relations*, 12:1 (1994), p. 91.
74 M. Brill Olcott, 'Central Asia's Islamic awakening', *Current History*, 93:582 (1994), p.153. (The war is discussed in Chapter 5.)
75 Akiner, *Central Asia*, p. 57.
76 *Ibid.*; C. Cavanaugh, 'Uzbekistan looks south and east for role models', *RFE/RL Research Report*, 1:40 (1992), pp. 11–14.
77 Although a former secretary for ideology, Akaev, unlike fellow Central Asian leaders, was not a republican Communist Party first secretary under Soviet rule.
78 I. Pryde, 'Kyrgyzstan: secularism vs. Islam', *The World Today*, (November 1992), pp. 210–11.
79 Ehteshami and Murphy, 'The non-Arab Middle East States ... Iran and Israel', pp. 96–101.
80 A. Arbatov, 'Russia's foreign policy alternatives', *International Security*, 18:2 (1993), pp. 6–8.
81 V.P. Lukin, 'Russia and its interests', in S. Sestanovich (ed.), *Rethinking Russia's National Interests* (Washington, DC, Centre for Strategic and International Studies, 1994), p. 109.
82 *Diplomaticheskii vestnik*, 8 (1992), pp. 4–5.

83 J.W.R. Lepingwell, 'The Soviet legacy and Russian foreign policy', *RFE/RL Research Report*, 3:23 (1994), p. 2.
84 S. Crow, *The Making of Foreign Policy in Russia under Yeltsin* (Munich/Washington, DC, RFE/RL Research Institute, 1993).
85 A. Kozyrev, 'The lagging partnership', *Foreign Affairs*, 73:3 (1994), p. 63.
86 Arbatov, 'Russia's foreign policy alternatives', p. 26.
87 J. Checkel, 'Russian foreign policy: back to the future?', *RFE/RL Research Report*, 1:41 (1992), p. 18.
88 *Diplomaticheskii vestnik*, 4–5 (1992), p. 70.
89 Cited in S. Crow, 'Why has Russian foreign policy changed?', *RFE/RL Research Report*, 3:18 (1994), pp. 1–2.
90 A. Kozyrev, *Izvestiya*, 2 January 1992, p. 3.
91 These are all covered in the following chapters. For an overview of Russian foreign policy in 1992, see H. Timmermann, 'Russian Foreign Policy under Yeltsin: Priority for Integration into the "Community of Civilized States"', *The Journal of Communist Studies*, 8:4 (1992), pp. 163–85.
92 *CDSP*, 44:13 (1992), pp. 1–3.
93 V.P. Lukin, 'Our security predicament', *Foreign Policy*, 88 (1992); *Nezavisimaya gazeta*, 19 August and 10 September 1992.
94 *CDSP*, 44:6 (1992), pp. 6–9.
95 Two signposts along this route were the 'Foreign Policy Concept' adopted in the spring of 1993 and the new military doctrine approved in the autumn. The former is mentioned in the section on Russia's relations with the near abroad; the military doctrine is discussed in Chapter 4. On their significance in the context of Russia's foreign policy shift see N. Malcolm, 'The new Russian foreign policy', *The World Today* (February 1994), p. 31.
96 The new Russian parliament, the Federal Assembly, has also been ill-disposed towards Yeltsin. One of the largest factions elected to the parliament's lower chamber, the State Duma, was the ultra-nationalist Liberal Democratic Party led by Vladimir Zhirinovsky. Zhirinovsky has advocated the restoration of the Tsarist empire and a Russian expansion through the Indian subcontinent in order to gain access to warm water ports. The new constitution adopted in December 1993 did, however, strip the new parliament of many powers formerly enjoyed by its predecessor, the Russian Congress of Peoples Deputies, thus rendering its interventions much less significant.
97 For a discussion of the shift in Russian foreign policy see, Crow, 'Why has Russian foreign policy changed?', pp. 1–6; Malcolm, 'The new Russian foreign policy', pp. 28–32.
98 K.J. Holsti, *International Politics. A Framework for Analysis* (London,

Prentice-Hall, sixth edition, 1992), Chapter 4.

99 P. Calvocoressi, *World Order and New States* (London, Chatto and Windus, 1962), p. 34; S. Harden (ed.), *Small is Dangerous. Micro States in a Macro World* (London, Frances Pinter, 1985), pp. 2, 5.

100 C. Thomas, 'New directions in thinking about security in the Third World', in K. Booth (ed.), *New Thinking about Strategy and Security* (London, Harper Collins, 1991), p. 267.

101 Holsti, *International Politics*, p. 96.

102 R.H. Jackson, 'Continuity and change in the states system', in R.H. Jackson and A. James (eds), *States in a Changing World. A Contemporary Analysis*, (Oxford, Clarendon Press, 1993), p. 347.

103 R.H. Jackson and A. James, 'The character of independent statehood', in Jackson and James (eds), *States in A Changing World*, pp. 10–11.

104 Calvocoressi, *World Order and New States*, p. 34.

105 W.C. McWilliams, 'Political development and foreign policy', in R. Butwell (ed.), *Foreign Policy and the Developing Nation* (Lexington, University of Kentucky Press, 1969), p. 19.

106 H.J. Morgenthau, *Politics among Nations. The Struggle for Power and Peace* (New York, Alfred A. Knopf, third edition, 1960), pp. 39, 72–73; M. Wight, *Power Politics* (Harmondsworth, Pelican Books, 1979), p. 29.

107 In the context of this current section, the caveat could be entered that because Russia is the continuing state of the USSR and has a pre-history in the period prior to 1917 it ought not be regarded as a 'new' state at all.

108 B. Korany, 'The take-off of Third World studies? The case of foreign policy', *World Politics*, 35:2 (1983), p. 477.

109 C. Clapham, *Third World Politics. An Introduction* (London, Croom Helm, 1985), p. 124.

110 C.W. Kegley, Jr and E.R. Wittkopf, *World Politics. Trend and Transformation* (New York, St Martin's Press, fourth edition, 1993), pp. 64–66; M. Smith, 'Comparing foreign policies: problems, processes and performance', in M. Clarke and B. White (eds), *Understanding Foreign Policy. The Foreign Policy System Approach* (London, Edward Elgar, 1989).

111 M.W. Doyle, 'Liberalism and world politics', *American Political Science Review*, 80:4 (1986); R. Cohen, 'Pacific unions: a reappraisal of the theory that "democracies do not go to war with each other"', *Review of International Studies*, 20:3 (1994), p. 209.

112 Kegley and Wittkopf, *World Politics*, pp. 66–67; Cohen, 'Pacific unions', p. 209.

113 D. Slider, 'Politics outside Russia', in S. White *et al.* (eds), *Develop-*

ments on Russian and Post-Soviet Politics (Houndsmills, Macmillan, third edition, 1994), p. 267.

114 Slider, 'Politics outside Russia', p. 270.

115 Pryde, 'Kyrgyzstan: secularism versus Islam', p. 211.

Recommended reading

T.J. Colton and R. Levgold (eds), *After the Soviet Union. From Empire to Nations* (London and New York, W.W. Norton, 1992)

K. Dawisha and B. Parrott, *Russia and the New States of Eurasia* (Cambridge, Cambridge University Press, 1994).

Eastern Europe and the Commonwealth of Independent States (yearly, London, Europa Publications).

The International Politics of Eurasia (3 volumes, New York, M.E. Sharpe, 1994)

D.T. Twinning, *Guide to the Republics of the Former Soviet Union* (Westport, Connecticut/London, Greenwood Press, 1993).

4

Defence and security in the former Soviet Union

Gorbachev's anxiety at the collapse of the USSR (see Chapter 2, p. 83) was felt partly because of the uncertain future of the Soviet military arsenal, particularly its nuclear weapons. With hindsight, the former President's worries appear well founded. Relations among the successor states have been plagued by controversies over a range of issues relating to the military assets of the former Soviet armed forces. All the successor states have had to face the daunting challenge of constructing national defence establishments, in some cases almost from scratch. Simultaneously, they have had to define new security priorities and military orientations, not only with each other, but also with the outside world. The Commonwealth of Independent States (CIS), has provided, on paper, a framework within which these issues could be tackled. Its potential has, however, been far from realised.

In this chapter we will explore the evolution of a number of military and security issues pertaining to the successor states and interested states beyond. These are divided into four sections dealing with nuclear weapons, conventional armed forces, case studies of disagreement and military alliances. We will conclude with a discussion of the national security problem, national security strategies and the notion of the security dilemma.

Controversies over nuclear forces

The potential dangers of Soviet collapse were nowhere more evident than in the area of nuclear weapons. The fate of thousands of nuclear warheads was a problem which, in late 1991, exercised the minds both of the founding fathers of the CIS and leaders in the West. How would command and control be exercised over these weapons? Would the USSR's break-up lead to a proliferation of nuclear powers within the old Soviet borders, posing the risk of local nuclear conflicts? Could the relaxation of command and control result in the leakage of technology and know-how to countries beyond the FSU? How would the successor states be incorporated within existing nuclear arms treaties?

Resolution of these questions has proven especially troublesome, giving rise to a profound rift within the CIS and sustaining deep anxieties amongst Western governments.

The nuclear legacy of the USSR

At the end of 1991, an estimated 24,500 nuclear warheads were scattered throughout the USSR. The weapons of which they were part were of two broad types: strategic and tactical.[1] First, strategic nuclear weapons. These were located in four former republics: Belarus, Kazakhstan, Russia and Ukraine. Those in Russia accounted for some 72 per cent of the total, taking the form of intercontinental ballistic missiles (ICBMs), submarine-launched ballistic missiles (SLBMs) and weapons deployed on heavy bombers. Russia's share marked it out as the pre-eminent military power within the CIS and of sufficient weight to assume from the Soviet Union the mantle of a nuclear superpower in its own right. Outside Russia, Ukraine possessed the largest inventory. While only 14 per cent of Soviet strategic weapons were located on its territory, these still constituted a substantial force, larger, in fact, than the combined nuclear arsenals of France and the United Kingdom. Kazakhstan's share was only slightly smaller and the country was an important site for the SS-18 missile, the largest Soviet ICBM. Belarus, finally, accounted for less than one per cent of strategic forces, these being made up entirely of the mobile, single warhead SS-25 (see Table 4.1). Alongside the weapons themselves, it is important to note that the infrastructure which had supported the Soviet nuclear deterrent lay partly outside Russian borders. This included early-warning radar systems situated in Kazakhstan, Belarus, Latvia and Azerbaijan; the USSR's major location for nuclear testing at Semipalatinsk in Kazakhstan (albeit shut down since the end of August 1991); and two of the largest missile production facilities (for the SS-18 and SS-24 ICBMs) located in Ukraine.[2]

Table 4.1 *Disposition of strategic nuclear weapons in the USSR (end of 1991)*[a]

Republic	*Sites or bases*	*Launchers*	*Warheads*	*(%)*
Russia				
ICBM(SS-11, 13, 17, 18, 19, 24, 25)	24	1,064	4,278	
Heavy Bombers[b]	4	122	367	
SLBM	2	940	2,804	
Sub-total warheads			7,449	(72)
Ukraine				
ICBM (SS-19, 24)	2	176	1,240	
Heavy Bombers	2	101	168	
Sub-total warheads			1,408	(14)
Kazakhstan				
ICBM (SS-18)	2	104	1,040	
Heavy Bombers	1	40	320	
Sub-total warheads			1,360	(13)
Belarus				
ICBM (SS-25)	2	54[c]	54[c]	(Under 1)
Sub-total warheads			54	
Total ICBM	28	1,398	6,612	
Total Heavy Bombers	7	263	855	
Total SLBM	2	940	2,804	
Total warheads			10,271	(100)

Notes: [a] ICBM – intercontinental ballistic missile; SLBM – submarine launched ballistic missile. [b] Heavy bombers main inventory is air-launched cruise missiles. [c] Belarus Deputy Foreign Minister, A. Stytchev, later put this at 81.

Source: W. Walker, 'Nuclear weapons and the former Soviet republics', *International Affairs*, 68:2 (1992), p. 258.

As for tactical nuclear weapons (short-range missiles, artillery warheads, 'atomic mines' etc.) these had been more widely dispersed, although a process of relocation had been in train before the USSR's dissolution. Outside of Kazakhstan, their deployment in Central Asia was negligible. In addition, since 1989, the nationalities crisis had led to the removal of these weapons from the Baltics, the warring republics of Armenia and Azerbaijan and the conflict-prone Moldova. Nuclear weaponry stationed with Soviet forces abroad (in Eastern Europe and the former East Germany) had also been withdrawn in the period 1989-91. By the end of 1991, therefore, tactical nuclear forces were concentrated in the same four republics as were home to the strategic arsenal, the majority being located in Russia.

Nuclear issues and the formation of the Commonwealth of Independent States

As described in Chapter 2 (pp. 78–79), the months leading to the creation of the CIS were marked by controversy over nuclear arms issues. Agreements reached among members of the Commonwealth during December 1991 addressed these matters by putting forward a number of compromises which sought to satisfy Russian desires for nuclear pre-eminence, while retaining for the three other republics in which nuclear weapons were located an involvement in the command structure.

The initial breakthrough occurred at the founding summit of the CIS in early December, at which it was agreed that 'single control' be exercised over nuclear weapons.[3] This short phrase, however, raised as many questions as it answered. At this point, authority over nuclear matters still rested with Gorbachev and not with CIS structures (not until the Soviet President's resignation on the 25th were the nuclear launch codes formally handed over to Yeltsin). Moreover, what single control meant in practice was far from clear, and could only be partial, given Kazakhstan's exclusion from the CIS at this juncture. The significance of this omission was brought home by Kazakhstan President Nursultan Nazarbaev's continuing insistence that his country would retain nuclear weapons as long as Russia did.

The Alma–Ata summit of the CIS on the 21st went some way to tackling these issues. As well as expanding the Commonwealth's membership (to include Kazakhstan), the meeting witnessed the adoption of an 'Agreement on Joint Measures Regarding Nuclear

Arms', which affirmed the desire of CIS member states to 'jointly work out nuclear policy' and called for the removal by July 1992 of tactical nuclear weapons to 'central [i.e. Russian] pre-plant sites for dismantling ... under joint supervision'. This was intended both as a means of reducing the dangers of proliferation and seemingly of proceeding with the implementation of Gorbachev's pledge of October 1991 concerning reductions in tactical weapons (see Chapter 2, p. 77). Other important provisions were also agreed. These, however, were again either vague or incomplete. It was intended that 'all nuclear weapons' in Belarus and Ukraine be 'eliminated' and that these two would accede to the 1968 Non-Proliferation Treaty (NPT) as non-nuclear weapon states (the practical effect of which would be the relinquishing of any claim to ownership of nuclear weapons within their territories). In the interim, decisions on the use of nuclear weapons there would be taken by the Russian President 'on agreement with the heads of state, signatories to this agreement'.[4] These phrases were clearly ambiguous, leaving open, for example, the question of how any disagreement over the use of weapons in Belarus and Ukraine would be resolved and suggesting only by implication the decision-making procedure for a launch of weapons located in Russia itself. Moreover, the position of Kazakhstan remained anomalous. The agreement was silent on that country's future (non)nuclear status and on the control of strategic missiles located there.

At the CIS summit held in Minsk on 30th December the situation was only partly clarified. An 'Agreement on Strategic Forces' foresaw the creation of a 'Joint Command of the Strategic Forces', which would maintain 'a single command of nuclear ... weapons of the former USSR' (a geographic remit which included all the CIS states, thereby clarifying the situation regarding Kazakhstan and Russia). The decision on the use of weapons was again granted to the Russian President, although he was obliged to 'co-ordinate' his actions with the heads of Belarus, Kazakhstan and Ukraine and, in addition, to 'consult' with the other member states of the Commonwealth. (While not stipulated in the agreements, central operational control over nuclear weapons, as well as lying with Yeltsin, was also vested with Marshal Evgeny Shaposhnikov, the Soviet Union's last Defence Minister, who was appointed interim Commander-in-Chief of CIS joint armed forces at Alma–Ata.) CIS member states also pledged to honour the international treaties entered into by the USSR and to follow a 'co-ordinated policy' of disarmament and arms control. Reference to the elimination of strategic weapons was again confined to those in Belarus and Ukraine. Weapons in the latter, it was pointed out, would be 'dismantled by the end of 1994'.[5] Uncertainties remained, not least concerning the removal of weapons in Kazakhstan and the exact arrangements for implementing nuclear arms agreements (i.e. START) entered into by the Soviet Union. Nonetheless, in the space of a few short weeks, the infant CIS had succeeded, on paper at least, to pick up the single nuclear control system from the dying USSR. Whether the vague provisions agreed upon in December would be equal to the complex task of managing a vast nuclear arsenal remained to be seen.

From the formation of the CIS to the Lisbon Protocol

Many of the issues left unresolved at the end of 1991 were brought into stark relief during the first few months of the Commonwealth's existence as a series of disputes concerning nuclear issues wracked the organisation. The first of these related to the relocation of tactical weapons. This matter appeared straightforward under the agreements of December 1991. The deadline of July 1992 for their removal to Russia was completed by early May, two months ahead of schedule. The transfer from Kazakhstan and Belarus occurred without a hitch. Ukraine, however, did present problems. Here, the transfer was temporarily halted, owing, according to the Ukrainian President Leonid Kravchuk, to a lack of assurances that warheads were actually being disassembled in Russia and not added to the Russian arsenal. A resolution by the Ukrainian parliament called for international monitoring, a position rejected both by Russia and Western countries. A compromise was reached in mid-April allowing Ukrainian verification of dismantlement, and as a result the transfer of weapons was resumed.[6]

The disagreement over tactical weapons, while successfully resolved, illustrated the potentially disruptive effects of intra-CIS disputes on the management of the former Soviet nuclear arsenal. In regard to strategic nuclear weapons, where the accords of December 1991 were more ambiguous, the likelihood of controversy was that much greater. An initial problem during 1992 was the go-it-alone position of Kazakhstan. This was a source of concern to Russia and the North Atlantic Treaty Organisation (NATO), both of whom were anxious to prevent a proliferation of nuclear powers in the wake of the USSR's disintegration and wanted a firm commitment from Kazakhstan to a future non-nuclear defence policy. Statements by the Kazakh leadership in early 1992, however, offered a contradictory picture of its intentions. A pledge in mid-January to join the NPT as a non-nuclear weapons state was offset by suggestions made soon after that it would retain strategic weapons for up to fifteen years and would accede to the NPT, in the words of Nazarbaev, as a 'republic on which nuclear weapons are temporarily located'. This was a status not, in fact, catered for within the treaty's provisions.[7]

Problems were also posed by a Ukrainian demand that it be considered a party to the START treaty. In some respects this seemed a reasonable request. It was consistent first, with the agreements creating the CIS in which all its members pledged to honour the former USSR's treaty commitments, and second, with a provision contained in the 'Agreement on Joint Measures Regarding Nuclear Arms' that START be submitted for ratification to the parliaments of Belarus, Kazakhstan, Russia and Ukraine. In other respects, the Ukrainian position appeared at odds with the broad objectives of CIS agreements. To accept that Ukraine (and for that matter, Kazakhstan or Belarus) were parties to START could be taken to mean that weapons on their territory, while under joint CIS command, were actually owned by these countries, or at least, were under their jurisdiction. This amounted, in effect, to admitting that they were formally nuclear weapons states, thereby obstructing progress on the NPT. Ukraine's demands inevitably brought it into conflict with Russia. Its stance in early 1992 (one largely supported by Washington) was that START ought to remain a bilateral treaty, which Russia, as the USSR's continuing state, should be the bilateral party to along with the US. This would confer upon it responsibility for implementing the treaty throughout the non-Russian FSU and by implication grant it ownership of weapons located there.[8]

Controversies arising from START were compounded by other disputes relating to strategic nuclear weapons. In response to disarmament proposals in this area floated by Yeltsin in January 1992, Ukraine and Kazakhstan complained that Russia lacked a proper mandate for its actions. These forces were under joint CIS command and the CIS states had not consented to further arms reductions. Perhaps more seriously, Ukraine itself took a number of steps that undermined joint command and control. Although not seeking to subvert existing operational control (i.e. the ability to transmit launch orders), which ultimately rested with Yeltsin and CIS Commander-in-Chief Shaposhnikov, Kiev did set about instituting a procedure whereby the exercise of this Russian/CIS prerogative might be physically blocked, an action designed to give practical effect to the implicit political veto contained in the Alma–Ata and Minsk agreements. Moreover, the Ukrainian Ministry of Defence asserted in April what it termed 'administrative control' over strategic nuclear forces, defined to include the subordination to itself of all the personnel, financial, logistical and supply facilities of these forces on its territory.

The various strands of the strategic nuclear weapons debate converged during May. Visits by Presidents Kravchuk and Nazarbaev to Washington elicited pledges by the US to allocate to Ukraine and Kazakhstan part of a $400 million sum authorised by Congress in November 1991 (under legislation sponsored by Senators Sam Nunn and Richard Lugar) to assist disarmament efforts in the then Soviet Union. As a further incentive to disarmament, the US made clear it would honour its minimal security commitment to non-nuclear states threatened with nuclear attack.[9] Nazarbaev was also reassured by developments within the CIS itself, notably the Treaty on Collective Security signed at the Tashkent summit in the middle of the month (see below, p. 167), which was supplemented by a Russian guarantee to extend a nuclear umbrella over Kazakhstan and the treaty's other signatories.

At the end of May at a meeting between the leaders of Belarus, Kazakhstan, Russia, Ukraine and the US the 'Lisbon Protocol' to START was signed. It recognised all four of the successor states as parties to the treaty along with the US, required these four to work out amongst themselves arrangements 'as are required to implement the Treaty's limits and restrictions', and included pledges by Ukraine, Kazakhstan and Belarus to sign the NPT as non-nuclear weapons states 'in the shortest possible time'. The signatories also undertook to ratify the Protocol alongside the START treaty itself, after which the latter would finally enter into force. The Protocol was supplemented by a number of legally binding commitments on the part of the three non-Russian successor states contained in letters addressed to President George Bush. In these, each country committed itself to the complete elimination of all nuclear weapons on their territories within the seven-year implementation period of

START.[10] This was a crucial stipulation, in that it strengthened the pledges concerning the NPT and closed a loophole by which the START treaty's numerical limits could conceivably be fulfilled within the FSU without the full removal of strategic nuclear arms from Ukraine, Kazakhstan and Belarus.[11]

In short, the Lisbon documents were an important advance on the CIS agreements of December 1991. Uncertainties and differences of interpretation did nonetheless remain. In the first place, the Protocol's provision that nuclear weapons be 'maintained under the safe, secure, and reliable control of a single unified authority' while commensurate with CIS agreements, left as a hostage to fortune the question of who actually 'owned' the weapons. It was hard to make a case for CIS ownership, given this was not a state. Russian ownership, the most practical alternative, was also not clear cut. In a note circulated to NATO members after the Lisbon meeting Kiev claimed that it had 'voluntarily renounced the right to possess nuclear weapons', but reserved a right of entitlement by virtue of Ukraine's status as an 'equal successor state' of the former USSR.[12] A second issue concerned the disposal of nuclear weapons in the non-Russian states. What, for example, would be the fate of strategic nuclear *warheads*? Ukraine, Kazakhstan and Belarus, lacking facilities and expertise for their disassembly, would logically be expected to transfer them to Russia, as they had already done with tactical warheads. Ukraine, as it had already illustrated over tactical nuclear warheads, was, however, distrustful of such a procedure. Indeed, Kravchuk's letter accompanying the Lisbon Protocol alluded to a possible alternative in the form of 'the elimination of nuclear weapons in Ukraine ... under reliable international control', an ambiguous phrase, which might be read as calling for international assistance in dealing with the warheads in Ukraine *in situ*. Controversy also surrounded *missiles*. Kazakhstan and Ukraine let it be known that they would like to retain some of the land-based missiles on their territories after the removal of their warheads for use as launch vehicles for commercial satellites. This position, while consistent with denuclearisation and START[13] proved unacceptable to Russia. In a statement issued at Lisbon, Foreign Minister Andrei Kozyrev stated that Moscow proceeded from the assumption that at the end of the seven-year START implementation period no nuclear warheads or 'strategic nuclear delivery vehicles' would remain on the territory of the non-Russian states. The Russian statement contained further points of contention.

It outlined an expectation that the accession of Belarus, Kazakhstan and Ukraine to the NPT would occur 'not later than the entry into force of the START treaty' and laid down the proviso that progress on this matter would be taken into account before Russia exchanged the instruments of ratification for START. Finally, Kozyrev's statement reiterated the target date of 1994 for Ukrainian denuclearisation originally specified in the Minsk agreement on strategic forces, thereby contradicting the seven-year period outlined in Kravchuk's letter to Bush.[14]

From the Lisbon Protocol to START-2

The Lisbon meeting, then, only went part of the way towards a resolution of the nuclear weapons issue. Throughout the remainder of 1992 controversies continued to arise. In August, for example, the initialling of a Russian–American agreement concerning the sale of enriched uranium extracted from warheads of the former Soviet nuclear arsenal raised strong Ukrainian objections. Kiev, now convinced of the financial value of the warheads on its territory began to demand that it be compensated for the fissile material they contained and backed this claim by affirming its right of ownership over all locally based strategic nuclear forces.[15] (In this regard, the Ukrainian position was entirely distinct from that of Belarus, which accepted Russian ownership of nuclear weapons on its territory, and Kazakhstan, which had not forwarded a claim). In one sign of flexibility, Ukraine was now prepared to concede that the disassembly of warheads would be 'best' conducted at existing facilities in Russia. However, the likelihood of troubled negotiations with Moscow over remuneration appeared to rule out progress on the NPT and on denuclearisation via START.[16] During late 1992, Kiev's position on these issues hardened. Complaints were voiced in the Ukrainian parliament and government at what was considered a lack of material compensation for denuclearisation and insufficient security assurances. President Bush in December did offer $175 million worth of Nunn–-Lugar money, provided Kiev ratify START and accede to the NPT.[17] This sum fell far short of Ukrainian demands that it might need up to $1.5 billion. In such a climate, it seemed unlikely that START, submitted for the consideration of the Ukrainian parliament that month, would be ratified with any speed.

The control of nuclear weapons also continued to cause controversy. During the course of the year, Ukraine took further steps towards 'administrative control' and claimed in December 1992 that it possessed the capability to physically block launch orders for nuclear weapons in the country.[18] Its position on this matter ran counter to an increasing acceptance within the CIS of the need for direct Russian control. The ground for this had been laid in May with the creation of a Russian Defence Ministry (see below, p. 174), which quickly asserted its own version of 'administrative control' of nuclear forces within Russia via its own Strategic Forces. This created a confusing dual command over nuclear weapons, involving a commander of CIS Strategic Forces subordinate to CIS Commander-in-Chief Shaposhnikov, and a commander of Russian Strategic Forces responsible to a Russian Defence Minister. Russian dominance within this untidy dual structure raised the question of whether a specifically CIS role was, in fact, still necessary. The assumption by Russia of immediate operational control of nuclear weapons throughout the entire FSU had been advocated by its Defence Minister, Pavel Grachev, since shortly after the signing of the Lisbon Protocol. In the ensuing months, this view, significantly, was supported by Shaposhnikov (who saw it as the best means of ensuring unified control and implementation of START), and the leadership of Belarus. Kazakhstan's position was unclear, but only Ukraine rejected Russian control out of hand, suggesting at the October CIS summit in Bishkek (Kyrgyzstan) that it preferred Shaposhnikov (whom it still regarded as representative of a separate CIS authority) over the Russian Defence Minister in the nuclear chain of command.

By the end of 1992, then, slow progress had been registered on issues relating to strategic nuclear arms. The signing of a successor agreement to START in January 1993 did not, therefore, occur in particularly auspicious circumstances. Under START-2, Russia and the US pledged to implement cuts in strategic warheads of up to 70 per cent of the Russian and American arsenals by the year 2003 (or the year 2000, should the US provide financial assistance for Russia to meet the treaty's requirements). This represented a further large cut beyond the levels established by the original START agreement (hereafter, START-1) (see Table 4.2.). As well as the depth of the proposed cuts, their spread was also significant. The treaty foresaw a total prohibition of multiple-warhead ICBMs, a stipulation which would have a profound impact on forces within the FSU where some

Table 4.2 *START-1 and START-2 limits by warhead*[a]

Launch vehicle	*Warhead inventories as stated in the memorandum to START-1*		*START-1 limits (USSR[CIS]–USA)*	*START-2 limits (Russia–USA)*
	Warheads			
	(USSR)	*(USA)*		
ICBM	6,642	2,450	[b]	
(of which multiple warhead)	(5,988)	(2,000)	[b]	(0)
SLBM	2,804	5,760		1,750
(ICBM + SLBM)	9,446	8,210	4,900	
Heavy bombers	855	2,353	[c]	
Total	10,301	10,563	6,000	3,000–3,500

Note: [a] If a column is blank it indicates the absence of any specified limit for that category applicable to both parties. [b] A sub-limit of 1,100 was placed on the mobile Soviet ICBMs (SS-24 and the single warhead SS-25) and of 1,540 on Soviet 'heavy' ICBMs (the SS-18). [c] A sub-limit of 1,500 warheads was stipulated for American heavy bombers carrying air-launched cruise missiles.

Sources: The Military Balance, 1991–1992 (London, The International Institute of Strategic Studies/Brassey's, 1991), pp. 216–20; T. Bernauer *et al.*, 'Strategic arms control and the NPT: status and implementation', in G. Allison *et al.* (eds), *Co-operative Denuclearisation. From Pledges to Deeds* (Cambridge, MA, Centre for Science and International Affairs, Harvard University, 1993), pp. 60–61; O. Sokolov and Yu. Klyukin, 'Starting off for a secure future', *International Affairs*, (Moscow), March 1993, pp. 6–8; 'Text of START II Treaty', Foreign Broadcast Information Service: SOV-93-001, 4 January 1993, esp. p. 3; G.L. Schulte, 'NATO's nuclear forces in a changing world', *NATO Review* (February 1993), p. 18.

60 per cent of warheads were accounted for in this manner (as opposed to 18 per cent in the US). Limits on warheads deployed on SLBMs, meanwhile, would fall heaviest on the US, which had enjoyed a traditional advantage in this category.[19] From the Russian point of view, START-2, if implemented, would lower what had become economically unsustainable strategic-nuclear force levels,

would increase strategic stability by reducing mutual capabilities to launch a decisive first strike, and ultimately would transform the Russian–US military–strategic relationship into one based on mutual trust rather than deterrence.[20]

The two START Treaties were intimately connected. In that START-2 was a bilateral Russian–American treaty, its provisions in a strict sense applied only to those FSU nuclear forces based in Russia. However, both Moscow and Washington had signed START-2 on the assumption that it would only come into force after Belarus, Kazakhstan and Ukraine had ratified its precursor and acceded to the NPT. In effect, this would permit the carrying out of START-2 in parallel with the denuclearisation of the non-Russian states under START-1.

When START-2 was signed, however none of these countries had fulfilled their undertakings concerning the NPT and only Kazakhstan had completed the process of START-1 ratification.[21] One obstacle was quickly removed with the Belarusian parliament's ratification in February of both treaties along with the Lisbon Protocol. (In a further significant gesture the parliament approved in December the removal of all nuclear arms to Russia by the end of 1994). Typically, however, the Ukrainian position remained the major hurdle, casting a long shadow over future progress towards disarmament.

START 2 to the Massandra Agreements

At the beginning of 1993, ratification of START-1 and the NPT was made conditional by Ukraine on a settlement of what were by now long-standing issues. These included, the provision of security guarantees from the nuclear powers (including Russia); compensation for nuclear weapons materials (including a Russian assurance that plutonium and uranium in them belonged to Kiev); financial assistance in carrying out disarmament (to pay for the separation of warheads from missiles and the destruction of missiles and silos in Ukraine); and control over the non-use of weapons while they remained located in Ukraine.

The familiarity of these issues, however, provided no guarantee of their quick resolution. Only with regard to security guarantees was any real headway discernible, and even here success was limited. During the first half of 1993, all five nuclear powers (Russia, the US, France, the UK and China) offered to come to Ukraine's assistance in the event of a nuclear threat.[22] Kiev, with an eye to Russia, regarded these assurances as insufficient. It demanded that guarantees be directed also towards the threatened use of conventional force, the use of economic and political coercion and should, moreover, encompass an explicit recognition of its territorial integrity. Russia, for its part, suggested that any guarantee could only come into force after Ukraine's ratification of START-1 and accession to the NPT, a stance hard to square with Kiev's position that such guarantees were required *before* it take up the two treaties.

The standoff on this issue was matched by increasingly acrimonious disputes over control and ownership. In January, a Russian proposal that it assume direct control over nuclear forces was rejected by Ukraine (Kiev on this occasion was backed by Kazakhstan; the Belarus position was supportive of Moscow – President Shushkevich indicated after the meeting that nuclear forces in his country had been transferred to Russian jurisdiction). Ukraine's continuing efforts at strengthening 'administrative control', meanwhile, were met by accusations from the Russian Defence Minister that it had failed to properly maintain strategic nuclear weapons, a situation which threatened a 'second Chernobyl'.[23] On the question of ownership, a draft agreement drawn up by the Russian government in July did concede compensation to Ukraine in the form of reactor fuel derived from enriched uranium extracted from warheads, but refrained from explicitly recognising a right to Ukrainian ownership of nuclear weapons.

The dispute between Moscow and Kiev came to a head during the summer of 1993. A meeting of CIS Defence Ministers announced in mid-June the abolition of the CIS Joint Forces High Command in favour of a slimmed down CIS Staff, a move that had important consequences for nuclear control. Shortly prior to the dissolution of the High Command, its Commander-in-Chief Shaposhnikov, had been appointed Secretary of the Russian Security Council, an executive body overseen by Yeltsin. Shaposhnikov's move from a military to a civilian position did not initially appear to mean a relinquishing of his pivotal role in the operational control of nuclear weapons. There were no indications, moreover, that a role in nuclear matters would be assumed by Viktor Samsonov, the newly-appointed chief of the CIS Staff. This meant that the two figures at the top of the nuclear chain of command (Yeltsin, to recap, was the other) were within the Russian leadership. The political veto open to other CIS leaders under the terms of the December 1991 Alma–Ata and Minsk agreements remained *de jure*; however, this detracted little from the fact that *de facto* operational control now lay clearly with Russia. Any lingering doubts on this score were dispelled later that month when Shaposhnikov transferred his launch authorisation codes to Russian Defence Minister Grachev.

The strengthening of the Russian position led to counter-measures in Ukraine. Its parliament in April rejected a draft military doctrine which referred to Ukraine's future non-nuclear status, and in July it declared ownership of all locally-based nuclear warheads. Kravchuk, too, moved towards an endorsement of a Ukrainian nuclear future. Prompted by the abolition of CIS control, he announced Ukraine's intention to retain forty-six SS-24 ICBMs (carrying 460 warheads) even after the implementation of START-1 and the Lisbon Protocol, claiming that the agreements did not obligate the destruction of these weapons.[24] This amounted to a wholesale abandonment of Ukraine's non-nuclear pledges and threatened to derail the entire START process. Even the dismantling of SS-19s which began in Ukraine in July did little to alter the generally despondent mood. Ukraine made clear, that in keeping with its ownership declaration, the removed warheads would not be transferred to Russia, until it had received satisfactory guarantees of financial compensation.

An attempt to break out of the nuclear impasse was made at a Yeltsin–Kravchuk summit at Massandra in the Crimea the following September. The agreements that resulted from the meeting appeared to mark a significant breakthrough. Crucially, they provided for the transfer of nuclear warheads to Russia, in return for which Kiev would be supplied with nuclear fuel. The deal was dependent on progress on START-1; the transfer of warheads would be completed two years after Ukraine had ratified the treaty. Confusion, however, was soon apparent. Russia argued that the Massandra agreements covered all warheads in Ukraine, while Kiev suggested that they applied only to those warheads it felt were covered by Kravchuk's recent reinterpretation of START-1. On the rocks of these differences, the agreements foundered. After accusing the Ukrainian side of deception, for trying to change an agreement to meet its interpretation, Russia annulled the most important protocol, that concerning warhead withdrawal, in late September.

The Trilateral Statement and after

Nuclear issues between Moscow and Kiev in the remaining months of 1993 remained problematic. On the positive side, an agreement was reached in October on Russian servicing of warheads and later that month two were transferred to Russia for repair. These developments were, however, overshadowed by more controversial matters relating to actions of the Ukrainian parliament. The first of these, the adoption of a document outlining Ukraine's military doctrine, again failed to clearly commit Ukraine to a non-nuclear defence. The document did allude to a non-nuclear status for Ukraine, but the elimination of nuclear weapons was made prisoner to 'appropriate actions' and 'reliable security guarantees' on the part of other nuclear states (i.e. including Russia).[25] Similar qualifications were apparent over START-1. In November, the Ukrainian parliament finally ratified the Treaty (along with the Lisbon Protocol), almost a full year after it had been submitted for consideration. This seemingly momentous occasion, however, was cause for little celebration in Moscow or Washington. Point one of the resolution on ratification reaffirmed Ukraine's right of ownership of nuclear weapons; point two renounced Ukraine's commitment under the Lisbon Protocol to accede to the NPT as a non-nuclear weapons state; point three asserted administrative control over nuclear weapons. In addition, the final exchange of the instruments of ratification by Ukraine was made conditional on long-standing demands concerning financial assistance, compensation (including a new demand that it be recompensed for fissile material from tactical warheads sent to Russia in 1992) and security guarantees, plus an interpretation of START-1 that would result in a destruction of only forty-two per cent of the warheads in Ukraine.[26] The reaction to the resolution was immediate and damning. Russia threatened to withdraw from the recently agreed weapons maintenance arrangements and to impose economic sanctions to compel Ukraine into altering its position. The US was equally forceful, warning Kiev that economic aid and membership of NATO's 'Partnership for Peace' programme would be jeopardised unless it moved on the nuclear disarmament issue.

The furore over START-1 ratification was the nadir of Ukraine's troubled nuclear relationship. The severity of Russian and American outrage, coupled with mounting evidence that warheads on Ukrainian soil were unstable, pushed Kravchuk into a sudden *volte face*. During December Washington revived the diplomatic role it had undertaken in the weeks leading up to the Lisbon protocol in 1992, resulting in January 1994 in the 'Trilateral Statement on Ukrainian Nuclear Weapons'. This set out procedures for the removal of arms to Russia under conditions which answered some of Kiev's long-standing concerns. It was to receive the equivalent of $1 billion in nuclear fuel from Russia in return for the warheads and a minimum of $175 million of American Nunn–Lugar money to assist with the dismantling of nuclear forces. Security guarantees were also offered (these would come into effect once Ukraine acceded to the NPT and START-1 had entered into force), including pledges by Russia and the US to refrain from threats to Ukraine's territorial integrity, to desist from the use of nuclear weapons against it and to assist Kiev through the UN Security Council in the event of an actual or threatened nuclear attack. While nuclear weapons remained in Ukraine, Russia would provide for their safety and upkeep. The Statement was also highly satisfactory for the Russians and Americans. Ukraine reiterated its pledge to join the NPT as a non-nuclear weapons state (and only when this was done would the security guarantees become operative), to transfer *all* warheads to Russia within seven years from the initiation of START-1, and seemingly dropped its claim for compensation for tactical nuclear weapons (the issue was not mentioned in the agreement). Furthermore, a specific timetable was laid down for the initiation of the agreement: within ten months of its signing at least 200 warheads were to be sent to Russia and all Ukraine's SS-24s were to be deactivated. In return, Kiev would receive, simultaneously, nuclear fuel deliveries from Russia financed by a $60 million advance payment by the US under the terms of a Russian–American agreement signed in February 1993 on the purchase of uranium extracted from nuclear warheads.[27]

Uncertainties remained, notably the attitude of the Ukrainian parliament. While the Trilateral Statement did not require parliamentary ratification, its clauses did depend on Ukraine moderating its positions on START-1 and the NPT, actions which required parliamentary approval. The parliament's reconsideration of START-1 in February proved to be decisive. In response to Kravchuk's argument that the Trilateral Statement answered Ukrainian concerns, warnings of warhead deterioration and promises of American aid, the parliament removed the conditions it had attached to ratification of

START-1 the previous November. This paved the way for an increase in American aid for weapons dismantling announced during a visit by Kravchuk to Washington the following month. Shortly after, the first batch of Ukrainian warheads was transferred to Russia. In May, Russia and Ukraine reached agreement whereby all nuclear warheads would be withdrawn from Ukraine within three to four years. During late 1994, Ukraine completed its policy turn-around. In November its parliament agreed to accede to the NPT. At the summit of the Conference on Security and Co-operation in Europe (CSCE) in Budapest the following month, along with Belarus and Kazakhstan, it formally signed the document, receiving in return a codification of the security guarantees laid down in the Trilateral Statement.[28] By this point some 360 warheads had already been transferred to Russia for dismantling.

Progress towards denuclearisation was even more clear cut outside Ukraine. In Belarus, thirty-four of the eighty-one single-warhead SS-25s situated there had been returned to Russia by January 1994 (where they were redeployed rather than destroyed). Agreement had also been reached on compensation. A Belarus minister announced later that month that his country would be free of nuclear weapons by the end of 1996. In Kazakhstan, matters were a little more vexed owing to a claim for $1 billion for compensation (Kazakhstan appeared to be basing its claim on the figure agreed for Ukraine under the Trilateral Statement). This did not, however, prove an impediment to progress on related issues. In December 1993 the Kazakh parliament voted to accede to the NPT as a non-nuclear weapons state. Visiting US Vice-President Al Gore thereupon signed an agreement with Nazarbaev providing for $84 million to be spent on nuclear weapons safety and the dismantling of silos. In February 1994 it was reported that all the strategic bombers in Kazakhstan had been removed to Russia along with all but twelve ICBMs. Yeltsin and Nazarbaev signed an agreement in March that placed remaining nuclear forces in Kazakhstan under Russian jurisdiction and provided for the removal to Russia of all warheads within fourteen months.

By such moves, Russia itself was encouraged to undertake disarmament. In May 1994 it was announced that 302 launchers in Russia had been destroyed under START-1. A 'Joint Statement on Strategic Stability and Nuclear Safety' signed at the Yeltsin–Clinton summit in September outlined an accelerated implementation of START-2 once that treaty took effect (it still awaited ratification by the Russian parliament) and held out the prospect of future negotiations to reduce remaining nuclear stockpiles.

Motives for retaining and relinquishing nuclear weapons

The tortuous saga of nuclear weapons in the FSU raises important questions relating to the very purpose of these weapons of mass destruction. During the Cold War, their purpose appeared clear, creating a so-called 'balance of terror' between the USSR and the US. From a strategic point of view a nuclear attack was an essentially pointless and indeed suicidal undertaking. A strike on one's enemy would inflict wholesale and irrevocable destruction, but, in response, would invite an equally devastating counter-attack upon one's own territory. This state of affairs – tellingly labelled 'mutually assured destruction' (MAD) – meant the costs of an attack were so high as to rule out the calculated use of nuclear weapons. The superpowers, therefore, had a compelling reason to exercise a degree of restraint in their relations in order to avoid moments of crisis where direct conflict was possible, which, through a process of escalation, might have resulted in a nuclear exchange. The degree of stability in superpower behaviour to which nuclear weapons contributed, was, however, offset by certain costs: the vast economic resources which were required to achieve and sustain a credible deterrent, the entrenched logic of 'arms racing' by which one side felt the necessity to continually outdo or to at least match the military–technological achievements of its adversary, and the threat of accidental use arising from misperception or technical faults. A desire to minimise these costs, while retaining the logic of restraint (at a far lower, but still effective level of forces), was intrinsic to the new political thinking and provided the impetus for the nuclear disarmament measures (INF and START-1) of the Gorbachev period.

In the post-Soviet period, the possession of nuclear weapons has, in many respects, advanced for Russia similar purposes to those it served for the USSR. Even though the potential for conflict with the West might have fundamentally diminished, so long as the US and other NATO powers have continued to retain a nuclear potential a residual desire for deterrence has remained. Measures such as the START-2 Treaty simply indicate a belief both in Moscow and Washington that this can be achieved with shrinking nuclear arsenals. Calculations regarding China have also been germane. Beijing has remained untouched by nuclear disarmament and possesses a formidable inventory. Although a *rapprochement* has occurred in relations with Beijing (see below, p. 201), Russia's nuclear capability has remained a weapon of last resort should conflict resurface over matters such as the common border, and offers a guarantee against Chinese expansionism (in view of Beijing's occupation of Tibet in 1950 and its failed invasion of Vietnam in 1979). Russia has also sought to retain nuclear weapons as an insurance against the rise of new nuclear powers. The diminished threat from the US and China has directed Russian attention towards Third World regimes such as Pakistan, North Korea and Iraq. A Russian Intelligence Service report published in 1993 identified nuclear proliferation as a threat to Russia's vital interests and deemed unacceptable the emergence of nuclear powers along Russia's periphery.[29] Such a statement was, of course, equally applicable to Ukraine. As we shall explore below, the operational utility of weapons in Ukraine has been dubious at best, but their mere presence there has posed a theoretical threat to the survival of Russia. The albeit remote contingency of a nuclear exchange with Ukraine has clearly influenced Russian military thinking. The 'Basic Provisions of the Military Doctrine of the Russian Federation' adopted by the Security Council in November 1993, significantly dropped the Soviet no-first use pledge and permitted a first strike, in certain circumstances, against other nuclear states and non-signatories of the NPT.[30] Moreover, amongst what were termed 'direct military threat(s)' to Russia was included 'the actions of other countries that impede the functioning of Russia's systems of safeguarding strategic nuclear forces'.[31] This was a clear allusion to Kiev.

Finally, nuclear weapons offer prestige. Russia's membership of the exclusive club of nuclear powers has been a guarantee not just of the survival of the historical superpower relationship with the US, but also of its reputation as a world power. Nuclear weapons by this view act as a means of generating deference and respect in the international community at a time when by other indicators (economic prowess, political stability) Russia has been the object of sympathy rather than envy.

If the logic of nuclear possession and deterrence still has a relevance in the case of Russia, has it also applied to the other successor states which inherited nuclear weapons? Arguably, Ukraine and

Kazakhstan have had fairly sound strategic reasons for wishing to retain their nuclear windfalls. Kazakhstan, for example, has been in dispute with its nuclear neighbour, China, over border issues and is home to a large, concentrated Russian population in its northern regions that might form the basis for future Russian territorial claims. Its close proximity to countries with nuclear ambitions in South Asia (India, Pakistan) and the Middle East (Iraq, Iran), has also given it an incentive to secure a nuclear umbrella. Kiev meanwhile has been concerned at the prospect of a return to some form of expansionist dictatorship in Moscow committed to the 'reunification' of Russian with Ukraine.[32] That Kiev cannot rely on its own conventional forces (which are never likely to be a match for Russia) or on a concrete security guarantee from the US, moreover, has increased the allure of the nuclear option.[33]

However, as we have detailed above, both Ukraine and Kazakhstan eventually came round to a realisation that nuclear weapons were an impractical means of furthering security. The logic of deterrence applies only where a country has a credible force and this is appreciated by a potential adversary. Yet in Ukraine and Kazakhstan such credibility has been absent. Neither could be said to have controlled the weapons on their territory other than in the negative sense claimed by Kiev of being able to block orders transmitted from Moscow. The positive ability to initiate a launch has, it seems, been absent and probably unobtainable. Ukraine, which possessed a body of expertise by virtue of its past role in the Soviet nuclear defence industry, would have encountered insurmountable technical difficulties had it sought to access the complex procedure necessary for launch authorisation, missile guidance and the retargeting of those nuclear weapons on its territory. The fact that many of them, despite Ukraine's assumption of 'administrative control', have been guarded by troops whose loyalty to Kiev could not be guaranteed has only added to these problems. The alternative strategy of inserting new enabling devices has been equally problematic, and would have required the dismantling and reassembly of warheads possibly equipped with disabling and self-destruct mechanisms. Even in the unlikely event that nuclear weapons could be made operative, problems would have remained in the form of maintenance, crucial facilities for which are located only in Russia (e.g. heavy water reactors for the production of tritium, the replenishment of which is essential to keep warheads functional). By the same token, creating weapons from scratch would have been an even more formidable undertaking. It is beyond the economic capabilities of all the successor states but Russia. Moreover, even though Ukraine and Kazakhstan benefited from a fortuitous nuclear inheritance and both are blessed with supplies of natural uranium, all existing facilities for fissile material production and the design, construction and refurbishment of nuclear warheads are located in Russia.[34]

Given the difficulties in retaining a credible nuclear force, why did Ukraine and Kazakhstan delay the removal of these weapons from their territories? On the one hand, it has been suggested that the mere possession of nuclear weapons, even at a dubious operational level, acts as an effective deterrent because a potential aggressor can never be sure that the risk of nuclear retaliation is completely absent. The Ukrainian leadership in particular may well have been driven by such considerations for a time, hence its equivocal stance on nuclear retention up until the Trilateral Statement. Another way of explaining Ukraine and Kazakhstan's stance is to regard their nuclear status not as a permanently desired state of affairs, however, but as a temporary position designed to give prominence to their security concerns, and thereby extract the maximally beneficial terms for relinquishing their arsenals. So long as these states possessed even a theoretical deterrent, they provoked the attention of the international community and in particular the established nuclear powers, from whom concessions could be negotiated. Hence, the demands for security guarantees and financial assistance. In this sense there is a strong incentive to seek maximum short-term gains, for once the weapons in question are relinquished there is every likelihood that Western attention will swiftly evaporate and Russian attitudes will be divested of any desire towards accommodation.[35]

Both these strategies, however, have contained inherent pitfalls, which became all too evident on the case of Ukraine. Here the retention of nuclear weapons served to infuriate both Moscow and Washington, locking Kiev into a classic 'security dilemma' (a concept discussed below, pp. 210–13). Russia has viewed Ukraine's ambiguous nuclear stance as threatening and this steeled its resolve during 1992–93 to abandon CIS collective mechanisms in favour of unilateral command of the former Soviet nuclear arsenal. Nuclear weapons, therefore, rather than adding to Ukraine's security, served only to undermine it. The nuclear issue followed a similarly circular path in regard to the US. On the one hand, the Americans have been perceived by Ukraine as the potential purveyors of security and financial guarantees. Yet on the other, Washington's persistent efforts to persuade Ukraine to forgo its nuclear weapons, cultivated the impression, certainly among conservatives in the Ukrainian parliament, that the Americans were in fact pro-Russian or themselves a threat to Ukrainian interests.[36] Such an attitude, in turn, only served to alienate the White House. Moreover, Kiev's stuttering progress towards denuclearisation meant it courted the risk of being looked upon as a nuclear pariah rather than a co-operative disarmer. Holding out for security assurances through allusions to nuclear retention became self-defeating as the US already reluctant to extend a comprehensive guarantee became even more indisposed in view of what it regarded as Kiev's increasingly unpredictable and maverick conduct.

In short, the retention of nuclear arms outside Russia has been operationally problematic, of dubious strategic value and politically costly. Having exhausted any short-term benefits flowing from their possession, by the end of 1993 Belarus, Kazakhstan and Ukraine had begun to execute, with varying degrees of enthusiasm, their surrender to Russia.

The nuclear problem: an overview

The fate of nuclear weapons within the FSU presented during 1992–93 a seemingly intractable problem. By the end of 1994, however, significant progress had been made towards its resolution. All tactical nuclear weapons had been moved to Russia in 1992 and during 1994 progress was evident also on the removal of strategic weapons. By this point Belarus, Kazakhstan and Ukraine had ratified START-1 (and the linked Lisbon Protocol) and had acceded to the NPT as non-nuclear weapon states. This relocation was to Russia's benefit.The issue of nuclear weapons control also evolved in its favour. The political veto inherent in the Alma–Ata and Minsk agreements of December 1991 was from the start a fig leaf in view of the operational control which had been vested with Yeltsin and the CIS Commander-in-Chief, Shaposhnikov. The abolition of the CIS High Command in mid-1993 strengthened *de facto* Russian control. Some resistance was offered by Ukraine's assertion of administrative control and the claim by that country to have set up the means to block launch orders for nuclear weapons on its territory.

This, however, had never amounted to an ability to launch the weapons and was, in any case, rendered meaningless once the physical removal of weapons to Russia had begun.

The resolution of the nuclear issue was not a success for the CIS as such (its mechanisms for settling the issue had proven incomplete and by mid-1993 had been rendered useless) but rather a victory for Russian leverage and American diplomacy. Indeed, the role of Washington was crucial. It was a signatory to the two START agreements, the major sponsor of economic assistance to facilitate disarmament in the FSU and a prospective guarantor of the security of Belarus, Kazakhstan and Ukraine. Throughout 1992-94 its position had largely accorded with that of Russia, supporting swift denuclearisation in the non-Russian FSU and placing pressure on Ukraine in particular to meet its commitments to START-1 and the NPT. American diplomacy clearly had an influence as testified by the Lisbon Protocol and the Trilateral Statement.

Upheaval in conventional armed forces

The break-up of the USSR posed fundamental questions not only with regard to nuclear weapons. The future of the massive conventional arsenal and armed personnel of the Soviet armed forces was also rendered uncertain. Would these remain under some form of unified or co-operative structure, or would the attainment of independence by the Soviet republics open the way to the development of fully fledged national armed forces? If the latter course was pursued, how would military property be shared out? What, moreover, would be the fate of former Soviet units in the successor states? The break-up of the USSR also had profound implications for non-nuclear arms control, and, in particular, the CFE Treaty. Was the agreement still applicable and, if so, how would the arms limits placed on the USSR be divided up?

Conventional armed forces of the Soviet Union

Shortly prior to the collapse of the USSR, the active personnel of the Soviet armed forces numbered some three and a half million, backed by over five million reservists. This was, in short, the world's largest military force. The USSR also possessed an immense arsenal of conventional weaponry, which matched or exceeded that of the other major military powers (see Table 4.3).

Table 4.3 *Conventional armed forces of the USSR and others (mid 1991)*

Category	*USSR*	*China*	*USA*	*Total NATO*
Active Personnel	3,400,000	3,030,000	2,029,600	5,013,750
Battle Tanks	55,210	7,500–8,000	16,345	35,201
Artillery	65,030	14,500+	6,899	25,929
Fighter Aircraft	7,540	4,500	4,893	9,857
Submarines	317	94	121	254
Destroyers	29	19	49	105

Source: Figures derived from *The Military Balance, 1991–1992* (London, The International Institute of Strategic Studies/Brassey's, 1991), pp. 19–29, 36–45, 51–79, 150–53.

At the end of 1991, conventional armed forces were dispersed throughout the FSU. The strategic importance of the region west of the Ural mountains (that facing Europe), meant a large proportion of weaponry was concentrated in just three of the successor states – Russia, Ukraine and Belarus. The long border the USSR had shared with China accounted for large deployments of forces in Russia's Far East and, to a lesser extent, in Kazakhstan (see Table 4.4).

Alongside the weapons themselves, the bulk of arms production and related facilities was located in Russia. At the end of 1991 between 70 and 80 per cent of the Soviet defence industry was located on Russian territory. This included all plants for producing and storing chemical weapons, most final assembly plants and shipyards and almost 90 per cent of all military research and development facilities. Despite this concentration, certain sensitive military locations did lie outside Russia. Ukraine, for example, was a major producer of non-nuclear missiles and the T-64 tank. It also accounted for a number of large shipyards, which significantly were the sole producers of the Soviet Navy's aircraft carriers and the *Slava* class of guided missile cruiser. Kazakhstan contained the largest number of weapons test sites (five out of twelve, some of which were linked to nuclear arms). Belarus, finally, was an important centre for military-related electronic components. The Soviet Union's conven-

Table 4.4 *Location of Soviet conventional weaponry and military personnel at time of USSR's dissolution (all figures are estimates)*

	Tanks	*Armoured combat vehicles*	*Artillery pieces*	*Helicopters*	*Fighter aircraft*	*Personnel*
Armenia	258	641	357	7	0	20,000
Azerbaijan	391	1,285	463	24	124	66,000
Belarus	2,263	2,776	1,384	82	650	170K
Latvia	138	100	82	23	183	51,000
Lithuania	455	2,074	408	0	46	43,000
Estonia	184	201	29	10	153	24.5K[a]
Georgia	850	1,054	363	48	245	30,000
Russia	50K[b]	33,500	15,500	1,215	3,685[b]	2 M
Ukraine	6,404	6,394	3,052	285	1,431	720K
Moldova	155	400	248	0	0	30,000
Central Asia[c]	4,000	10,100	3,200	170	220	150K
Abroad[d]	5,081	9,167	4,228	432	1,029	385K[e]
Total	70,179	67,692	29,314	2,296	7,766	3.7M

Notes: [a] Personnel figures for Baltics do not include those serving in Baltic Fleet, which numbered some 87,000. [b] Figure based on Russian force level in mid 1992. [c] Includes Kazakhstan, Turkmenia, Tajikistan, Kyrgyzstan and Uzbekistan. [d] Weaponry held by Soviet forces in Germany and Poland. [e] 338,000 (Germany i.e. former GDR); 35,000 (Poland); 6,000 (Cuba); 3,000 (Mongolia), 2,800 (Vietnam). Contingents of advisers also present in Afghanistan, Algeria, Angola, Congo–Brazzaville, India, Cambodia, Laos, Libya, Mali, Mozambique, Nicaragua, Peru, Syria, Yemen.

Sources: The Economist, 21 March 1992, p. 63; *The Military Balance, 1991–1992* (London, The International Institute of Strategic Studies/Brassey's, 1991), pp. 45, 61, 92; D.L. Clarke, 'Former Soviet armed forces in the Baltic states', *Radio Free Europe/Radio Liberty (RFE/RL) Research Report*, 1:16 (1992), p. 45; D.L. Clarke, 'Implementing the CFE Treaty', *RFE/RL Research Report*, 1:23 (1992), p. 51; J. Dean *et al.* 'CFE and beyond: the future of conventional arms control', *International Security*, 17:1 (1992), p. 120; *SIPRI Yearbook 1992. World Armaments and Disarmament* (Oxford, Oxford University Press/Sipri, 1992), p. 347; S. Foye, 'Civilian–military tension in Ukraine', *RFE/RL Research Report*, 2:25 (1993), p. 62.

tional military capability had also involved an integrated air defence/early warning system (some of which depended on facilities outside Russia) and was capped by a large number of bases. Of these, the greatest potential for trouble lay in connection with naval forces – two of the USSR's four Fleets (the Baltic and Black Sea) being located at bases in more than one republic.[37]

The failure to set up CIS joint forces

The integration of armed forces and military infrastructure in the FSU appeared good reason to preserve a unified military. This was the opinion of the Soviet armed forces' senior command and the leaderships of Russia and the militarily underdeveloped Central Asian republics. However, at the time of the formation of the CIS, the integrity of the Soviet armed forces had already been placed under severe strain by the efforts of some republics to establish independent defence postures (see Chapter 2, pp. 62–63). Efforts to preserve military co-ordination subsequently proved extremely difficult.

Two key documents were agreed at the CIS Minsk summit in December 1991. These provided for first joint CIS 'strategic forces', defined sufficiently broadly to include (in addition to the nuclear Strategic Missile Force) the former Soviet Air Force, Navy, Air Defence and Paratroops, and second, joint general-purpose forces and border troops.[38] Yet, in laying down principles for co-operation, these documents also contained significant concessions to national aspirations. In deference to the insistence of Ukraine, Azerbaijan and Moldova, the latter of the two accords affirmed in its very first article the 'legitimate right' of CIS member states 'to create their own armed forces'. This separatist sentiment was eventually to win the day. During the next six months a number of further agreements were concluded, but with the exception of an accord on peacekeeping forces, these usually failed to attract more than a minority of signatures amongst CIS members.

By the time of the CIS Tashkent summit in May, the prospects for military co-operation appeared uncertain at best. By this point, a majority of CIS member states, including Russia, had announced their intention to create independent armed forces and/or defence organs. This development scuppered the last hopes for the creation of standing joint general-purpose forces and effectively narrowed the definition of 'strategic forces' to strategic nuclear weapons and their support facilities, thereby excluding conventional forces altogether. The Treaty on Collective Security agreed at the summit should be understood in this context. Leaving aside the fact that it was signed initially by just six states (Armenia, Kazakhstan, Kyrgyzstan, Russia, Tajikistan and Uzbekistan), its provisions for mutual defence assistance could, in the absence of a CIS joint force, only be implemented by national forces. In recognition of the underdevelopment of joint conventional forces the CIS High Command was reorganised in mid-1992 to perform essentially two functions: the oversight of nuclear weapons and the organisation of peacekeeping forces. In July the post of Commander of CIS General Purpose Forces was abolished.

In the subsequent twelve months, little further progress was made. Proposals that sought the subordination of national forces to an alliance structure modelled on the lines of NATO, or a minimalist solution whereby a joint force would only be constituted in time of war, came to nothing. A CIS Border Force, similarly, failed to take shape as former Soviet units either came under Russian jurisdiction, were replaced by new national commands or became subject to joint Russian–local arrangements. Formerly unified early-warning, air defence and space defence systems also experienced severe disruption owing to their 'privatisation' by the successor states. In a sweeping indictment in June 1993, CIS Commander-in-Chief Shaposhnikov conceded that joint armed forces did not exist at present, nor would they be likely to in the near future. The decision of CIS Defence Ministers that month to wind up the CIS Joint Forces High Command, effectively signalled the end of any desire to do so and reflected the precedence now given to national armies.[39]

CIS military co-operation thereafter became confined to those states which had signed the CIS Collective Security Treaty, a group which, with the signatures of Belarus, Georgia and Azerbaijan during the winter of 1993–94, expanded to nine members. In organisational terms, a fairly elaborate structure was developed to further joint efforts – a CIS Council of Defence Ministers, a CIS Collective Security Council and a Staff for Co-ordinating CIS Military Co-operation (which formally replaced the High Command in December 1993). In practice, however, co-operation within this adapted framework proved equally problematic. Interviewed in February 1994, the Chief of the Staff for Co-ordinating CIS Military Co-operation Victor Samsonov bemoaned the absence of common operational planning, training, and joint command and control systems. In fact, CIS efforts by this point reflected less an attempt to retain something of the comprehensiveness of the former Soviet armed forces than the development of a framework for Russian-led operations. This is a point clearly illustrated by one of this military sub-group's major undertakings – a Russian-dominated peacekeeping force in Tajikistan[40] – and by Grachev's advocacy of a CIS Defence Union, a mechanism that would allow a reintegration of military infrastructure in the successor states for the purpose of providing Russia with a form of forward defence. Moreover, the fact that Ukraine (along with other CIS member states Turkmenistan and Moldova) remained outside the Treaty meant the absence of the FSU's second largest military power from co-operative arrangements.

National armed forces[41]

Following the dissolution of the USSR, the development of nationally based armed formations has been apparent in all of the successor states. Yet for all the determination to create such forces, with the exeptions of Russia and possibly Ukraine, they are far from adequate to meet national defence tasks, confronting the successor states with the need to forge alliances and seek external assistance. The scale of development has differed depending on a host of factors: the nature of the military inheritance, perception of external threat and the national symbolism attached to raising armed forces. In Tajikistan, Georgia, Moldova and Azerbaijan, military development has also been adversely affected by ongoing civil war and political infighting.

Several patterns have been evident in the formation of national armed forces. A first pattern is exemplified by the Baltic states. Here, military development has been entirely outside the CIS framework and armies have had to be constructed almost from scratch owing to the pillage of *matériel* by departing former Soviet personnel. These states also face the daunting task of guarding against a Russian threat. In this light, their small-scale local forces, while totally inadequate to the task, do serve the important symbolic function of demonstrating resolve, a posture designed to win them friends in their quest for a joint defence system with Western states.

While the Baltic states have seen their future in an orientation away from their Russian neighbour, a large number of other successor states have sought compensation for military vulnerabilities in tight co-operation with Moscow. This reflects not simply a calculation that this is the best way to stave off a Russian threat, but has also been directed towards other possible threats, both internal and external. This second pattern has been most in evidence in Central Asia and Armenia (and latterly Georgia), where underdeveloped military potential and the presence *in situ* of former Soviet units has impelled these successor states towards co-operation within the CIS (via the Collective Security Treaty) and towards bilateral arrangements with Russia. The benefits of co-operation have perhaps been best exemplified by the case of Tajikistan, where not just joint CIS efforts, but also Russian assistance, has helped prop up central government against opposition forces. Under the terms of the Russian–Tajikistan Friendship Treaty signed in May 1993, former Soviet troops under Russian command were to remain until the Tajik government had formed its own border guard. By August a 15,000-strong Russian force was guarding the Tajik–Afghan border against infiltration by *Mujahidin*-backed Tajik rebels located in north Afghanistan. Similarly, in Georgia, where co-operation with Russia had initially been shunned, the perilous military position of the administration headed by former Soviet Foreign Minister Eduard Shevardnadze, led to a reversal of policy and the framing of an alliance with Russia. In February 1993 agreement was reached on the stationing of Russian troops in order to guard rail and shipping lines and on the positioning of Russian border guards along the Georgian–Turkish frontier. The Friendship Treaty signed in February 1994 along with related military agreements went even further, providing for comprehensive Russian assistance in the formation of a Georgian national army. In return, Russia was granted until the end of 1995 continued use of the three military bases in the country it had inherited from the former Soviet armed forces.

A third pattern has been evident in the cases of Moldova and Azerbaijan, states which have resisted Russian assistance despite their own internal conflicts. During 1992 they were fearful of Russian dominance of projected joint forces and they resolved at an early stage to create their own national armed forces. Progress in this regard, however, has been limited. The first Moldovan army battalions formed in May 1992 were equipped only with light artillery and armoured personnel carriers, the lion's share of *matériel* being held by the former Soviet Fourteenth Army whose loyalties lay with a separatist Russian minority (which itself had organised a Republican

Guard of some 7–8,000) in the Trans–Dniester region. In Azerbaijan meanwhile the situation has been complicated, first by the conflict over Nagorno–Karabakh, which erupted into a full-scale war with Armenia during 1992, and second, by political in-fighting within the Azeri side. These two factors operated to form a vicious circle throughout 1992-94 as political rivalries impeded the development of unified and motivated armed forces, a situation which, in turn, did little to prevent a string of military defeats at the hands of ethnic Armenian forces. Moreover, even though Azerbaijan fared well from the re-allocation of former Soviet military property on its territory (see below, p. 191), a lack of trained personnel has meant this has not been put to good use. The gravity of Azerbaijan's predicament finally persuaded it to accede to the CIS Collective Security Treaty (see above, p. 167) as a means of accessing Russian assistance.

Belarus and Ukraine illustrate a fourth pattern of military development. In these cases, fortuitous inheritances from the Soviet period (see table 4.4.) have resulted in inflated military structures ill suited to national defence requirements. Both have also had to deal with the sensitive issue of relations with Russia and the large concentrations of Russian personnel within their putative national forces. Of the two, military development has taken the most determined course in Ukraine. This stance springs from fears of a Russian threat, and of historical observation (that Ukrainian independence during 1917–20 did not survive has been seen as stemming from the demobilisation of the Tsarist imperial army by the Ukrainian People's Republic, an act which rendered it defenceless in the face of a takeover by the Bolsheviks in 1920).[42] The basis of Ukrainian forces had been laid in the months following the August coup (see Chapter 2, p. 78). Their creation in earnest began in December 1991. Emboldened by the massive yes vote in the referendum on independence, the Ukrainian parliament passed on the 6th, laws on the Armed Forces and Defence, which provided a legal framework for the emerging defence system. The inauguration of the CIS in the days that followed did nothing to dampen Ukrainian ardour. Decrees signed on the 12th by President Kravchuk subordinated all conventional forces in Ukraine to himself as newly appointed commander-in-chief and placed the three former Soviet military districts in the country under Kiev's command.

The practical realisation of a Ukrainian force, however, appeared at this stage to be far from certain. By relying on the resubordination of the former Soviet armed forces within its territory, Ukraine had to confront the ticklish problem that these units had a large Russian component, whose loyalty to a new command could not be guaranteed. At the end of 1991, it was estimated that ethnic Russians accounted for some 44 per cent of personnel, compared to the 40 per cent who were Ukrainian.[43] The method chosen to deal with this problem was the introduction of a new oath of loyalty to the Ukrainian state. With the exception of the Black Sea Fleet, adherence to the oath spread rapidly, and had been taken up by some 450,000 personnel by early April.[44] A pledge of allegiance was in itself, however a fairly superficial indicator of loyalty. Many Russians who took it up were swayed in their judgement by material incentives and a perception in early 1992 that prospects for a unified CIS force remained good. In the event of conflict with Russian forces, the likelihood of such personnel submitting themselves to battle was, therefore, extremely dim. To compensate for this problem, a shakeup of the officer corps was also pursued involving the promotion of ethnic Ukrainians to posts vacated by sacked or demoted Russians.

In parallel with these moves, Ukraine has undertaken a series of steps directed towards long-term military restructuring. Its inherited military capability was not only incompatible with certain categories of the renegotiated CFE Treaty but was financially unsustainable. From the time of their inception, Ukrainian armed forces were thus subject to various plans of reduction. A reduced force of some 200–220,000 was envisaged by the end of the century. Implementing this reduction has proven less than straightforward. It has been hindered by the cost of demobilisation and the process of repatriating up to 320,000 Ukrainian officers serving elsewhere in the FSU or in Eastern Europe. Restructuring has also been necessitated by the fact that at the end of 1991 forces in Ukraine reflected the military planning needs of the USSR. This could be seen, for example, in relation to production and supply. The disintegration in early 1992 of links between Ukrainian defence establishments and those elsewhere in the FSU (notably Russia) resulted in a sharp fall in arms output. Similarly, the operation of the Air Force on Ukrainian territory was disrupted by its near total dependence on spare parts supplied by Russia. The pattern of force deployments also posed problems for Kiev. These were concentrated overwhelmingly in the country's western regions (facing Eastern Europe); bases, radar and aerial defences on the border with Russia were almost entirely absent.

In the two years following independence, Ukraine made some progress towards the reform of its armed forces. During 1992 legislation was passed which undercut the legacy of the Soviet period. The system of military education was revamped, while the three military districts inherited by Ukraine were reorganised into two operational commands – western and southern. Neither of these appeared to fully address the issue of Ukraine's border with Russia, in that they simply entrenched the layout of existing forces. However, calculations concerning Russia were not without influence. A military reorganisation in early 1993 aimed at increasing the mobility and responsiveness of troops in the southern command could be read as answering concerns over territorial claims to the Crimea voiced in the Russian parliament. As for the force structure itself, a 'concept for defence' drawn up in December 1991, outlined the creation of three service branches: ground forces (supplemented by a national guard and border troops), the air force (including air-defence) and the navy. As of mid-1994 only the latter had not been fully realised, in this case, owing to the Black Sea Fleet dispute.

As for Belarus, it too resolved from an early stage to set about the formation of an independent defence establishment. In January 1992 its newly appointed Minister for Defence announced that Belarus intended to set up its own army on the basis of former Soviet military contingents. Following negotiations with the CIS High Command, it was agreed that Belarus would take over land forces, air defence and 90 per cent of fighter–bomber aviation in the country. This strategy was, however, replete with problems owing to the Soviet legacies of heavy militarisation and a problematic ethnic balance amongst its service personnel (approximately half of its officer corps was Russian, more than one-fifth Ukrainian and just one-fifth of local origin). In tackling these issues, Belarus introduced in 1992 a new military oath, which was taken up by some 100,000 personnel by year end. More fundamentally, a comprehensive restructuring of its newly acquired forces was set in motion. Under the guidance of Defence Minister Pavel Kozlouski, a draft military doctrine was formulated during the course of 1992 which called for a reduction in personnel and the abandonment of a defence posture based on tank formations in favour of more mobile mechanised brigades. Progress on the latter was slow owing to drastic cutbacks in the military budget, but demobilisation proceeded apace, despite huge social costs presented by rehousing. The armed forces were reduced to just over 100,000 by late 1992 and a further reduction to just 87,000 was envisaged by late 1993.

While sharing similar problems and following a line of independent military development, Ukraine and Belarus have differed in their degree of co-operation with Russia/CIS. Belarus has been far more pragmatic in this regard. The decision taken by the parliament in April 1993 to seek entry to the CIS Collective Security Treaty appears to have been partly motivated by charges Russia was demanding of non-signatories for officer training and by a desire to rescue the ailing Belarusian arms industry. In March the following year a comprehensive military agreement was signed with Russia, providing for joint training, the maintenance of a joint air-defence system and co-operation in arms development and export. Belarus has also been sensitive to possible conflicts of interest with Russia. The Belarus oath of allegiance was far less restrictive than that administered in Ukraine (avoiding any stipulation concerning citizenship). In July 1992 the 30,000 troops supporting strategic nuclear weapons and air force equipment were placed under Russian jurisdiction, and a timetable adopted permitting their withdrawal over a lengthy seven-year period.

A final and unique pattern is evident in the case of Russia. Here, the alacrity with which armed forces were formed in some successor states was not initially evident. This reflected an assumption among the Yeltsin leadership that CIS military structures would prove to be viable and would come to encompass the bulk of former Soviet forces. Within these structures, Russia – as the major source of funding, personnel, defence production and research – would play a predominant role. Support for CIS joint forces had a further rationale. They would allow of a Russian-led military presence outside Russia's new borders and grant Moscow some scope to influence military policy making in the successor states.[45] The fact that the CIS High Command had been created on the basis of the defunct Soviet High Command/Ministry of Defence, themselves preserves of Russian interests, strengthened Yeltsin's confidence in the wisdom of joint forces.

Developments in the first quarter of 1992, however, quickly disabused the Russian leadership of its initial optimism. The trend towards national armies, associated problems in constructing CIS forces and the failure to agree upon a joint military budget increasingly compelled Russia towards a more independent course. The opening up of a clear conflict of interest with Ukraine at this point (over nuclear issues and the division of the Black Sea Fleet), moreover, pointed towards the impossibility of the co-existence of two potential rival military powers within a single structure. Political considerations also coloured the judgement of the Russian leadership. Yeltsin was well aware of the strong military feeling (expressed, for example, at a stormy meeting of an All-Army Officers' Assembly held in the Kremlin in mid-January) in favour of retaining united armed forces. Yeltsin had won military support for the CIS in December 1991 precisely on the grounds that this organisation promised a guarantee of such unity. When this failed to materialise, the creation of a Russian command remained the next best option, as this would allow Moscow to exercise a direct claim over the bulk of the USSR's military inheritance, thereby preserving a semblance of the former Soviet armed forces. The move towards a Russian force, moreover, could also have been calculated to help Yeltsin's troubled relations with a parliament, which had during 1992 led the way in urging the formation of a Russian Ministry of Defence.

The Russian leadership set about the creation of its own armed forces in the spring of 1992.[46] Exploiting its status as the USSR's continuing state, Russia placed former Soviet forces outside the FSU (in Germany, Poland, Mongolia and Cuba) under its jurisdiction in March. It also took over personnel within former Soviet borders. In the Baltics these passed to Russian command in January and in the spring control was extended to troops in the Transcaucasus Military District (the Soviet Seventh Army in Armenia, the Fourth Army in Azerbaijan and the Thirty-Fourth Army Corps in Georgia) and the Fourteenth Army situated in the Trans–Dniester region of Moldova. These were initially to remain under CIS command pending the formal establishment of a Russian Defence Ministry. On March 16th a Presidential decree affirmed an intention to create a Defence Ministry. A further decree published the same day appointed Yeltsin Supreme Commander-in-Chief of Russian forces. The Russian Ministry of Defence and senior command was recruited during the summer largely from officers serving in the CIS High Command. In May Yeltsin appointed Army General Pavel Grachev – an Afghan veteran, keen proponent of military reform and supporter of the Yeltsin cause during the events of August 1991 – as Defence Minister. Russian Border troops under the jurisdiction of the Russian Security Ministry were formed in June. In October the process of military formation was rounded off with the signing by the President of a Law on Defence outlining the structure and organising principles of the Russian armed forces. In sum, these actions amounted to a usurpation of projected CIS joint forces. This was confirmed not just by symbolic acts such as the raising of the Russian ensign in the Northern, Pacific and Baltic Fleets, but by comments of the CIS command itself. Shaposhnikov suggested in July 1992 that some 80 per cent of the former Soviet air force, navy and air defence infrastructure now belonged to Russia.[47]

The acquisition of these forces confronted Moscow with the major task of reorienting a force structured for Soviet needs. Soviet troops had been poised primarily for engagement with either NATO forces in Europe or with those of China along the long common border. Such threats had largely dissipated during the Gorbachev period. For Russia, these traditional concerns were replaced by major challenges which arose as a consequence of the break-up of the USSR. Given the obvious point that Russia's borders did not accord with those of the USSR, a need arose to rethink the territorial organisation of defence. This involved not just a mooted redrawing of military districts, but also the reinforcement of the important Moscow and Leningrad (St Petersburg) Military Districts, which, with the independence of the Baltics, Ukraine and Belarus to their west and south, had assumed the status of 'frontline' regions.

Furthermore, with the formation of new states on the basis of the former Soviet republics, the 'near abroad' became an important calculation in defence planning (see also the discussion in Chapter 3, pp. 97–100). A draft of Russia's military doctrine published in May 1992, and statements by military officials offered two important assertions in this regard. First, that Russia had a duty to protect the estimated twenty-five million ethnic Russians living outside Russian borders and second, that the most credible threat to security was posed by instability and local conflicts to the south of the country.[48] This latter point was apparently borne out by Russia's military presence in Tajikistan. The war which erupted with some ferocity there during 1992 was viewed by Russia as presaging a wave of turmoil throughout Central Asia, fomented by Islamic fundamentalism abetted by Afghanistan and Iran.[49] This not only threatened the security of the large Russian minority populations in the region, but presented an unwelcome prospect of the spread of arms and drug trafficking to Russia itself.[50] In the Transcaucasus, meanwhile, the conflicts in Georgia and that in Nagorno–Karabakh were unsettling owing to fears of knock-on effects within Russia itself (see Chapter 5, p. 225). In response, forces in Russia's North Caucasus Military District were substantially strengthened by the redeployment of equipment and personnel withdrawn from the Baltics and Germany. Russia also formulated plans which demoted the emphasis on tank-heavy land forces tailored for a major war in Europe in favour of peacekeeping and mobile units to guard against conflicts on or near Russia's borders.

Russia was also keen to preserve the use of military facilities in the near abroad, guaranteed access to which had been lost once joint CIS forces proved untenable. These were perceived, in certain cases as essential to carry out Russian strategic tasks, particularly in areas of air and naval defence (hence, as we shall see below, the interest in the Black Sea Fleet and the Baltic states). The protection of ethnic Russians and the stabilisation of local conflicts was also seen as better served by a Russian military presence in the states in question. To this end, Russian generals argued in favour of a strategy which emulated the American approach of supporting a network of bases in neighbouring states.[51] As of September 1994, Russia still maintained troops in every former Soviet republic bar the Baltic states and Azerbaijan, and of the CIS states, only Azerbaijan and Moldova guarded their external frontiers without Russian assistance.

Overarching the entire debate on the future of the Russian armed forces has been the question of financing and resources. In a similar vein to changes introduced during the Gorbachev period, the Russian leadership has sought reductions in the burden of defence as a long-term solution to gross imbalances in the domestic economy. In the post-Soviet period the dwindling need for a huge standing conscript army has resulted in plans for drastic reductions in the size of the active armed forces. The 2.8 million active personnel inherited by Russia from the former Soviet armed forces was to be cut under the Law on Defence to 1.5 million by as early as the end of 1995. Alterations in the quantity and quality of personnel, however, have presented a whole catalogue of problems. In the first place, before the financial benefits of a smaller military can be reaped huge financial costs have to be borne for the rehousing, retraining and social provision (i.e. pension payments) for the hundreds of thousands of demobilised service personnel. Huge potential costs have also been presented by other aspects of military reform. Programmes of weapon modernisation, begun prior to 1991, involving the introduction of 'smart' weapons, the deployment of new command and control systems and the necessary research and development all require large and ongoing outlays. Moreover, Russia has also had to compensate for the loss of up-to-date Soviet weaponry located in Ukraine and Belarus. Hence, even though the Russian military as a shrinking force and as a subject of the CFE Treaty is expected to reduce its stocks of weapons in absolute terms, the need for qualitative improvements has continued to exert significant demands on procurement. Plans to shift to a more professional army are similarly costly, requiring improved salaries, better service conditions and advanced training. Disarmament and troop withdrawals have also presented daunting financial challenges. These combined costs are outlined in Table 4.5.

Table 4.5 *Major Russian military reform programmes to the year 2000 (billion roubles: 1992 prices)*

Troop withdrawals	346
Extra personnel payments per annum	59
Dismantling and storage of nuclear-powered submarines	100
Destruction of strategic nuclear weapons	23
Destruction of tactical nuclear weapons	150
Destruction of chemical weapons	90
Destruction of conventional weapons	5

Source: K. Sorokin, 'The creation of Russian armed forces', *Brassey's Defence Yearbook 1993* (London and New York, Brassey's, 1993), p. 149.

Russia's ability to pursue this military restructuring has been undermined by a deepening economic crisis. Huge budget deficits have had a far-reaching impact on military expenditure. In 1991, Russian military spending amounted to 6.7 per cent of its GNP.[52] Defence budgets in 1992, 1993 and 1994 amounted to 6.5, 5.5 and 6.0 per cent of GDP in respective years. Controlling the defence budget at a time of upward pressures on spending has been achieved primarily through paring down procurement and research and development.[53] This is a politically more acceptable option than the alternative of reining in expenditure on personnel. Cuts in procurement were so savage in 1992 as to be compared to the demilitarisation which occurred in Europe and the USA in the immediate post-war era.[54] A modest increase in 1993 did little to revise this picture. By the summer of 1994, procurement had, according to the Defence Ministry, fallen by as much as 80 per cent since 1991.[55]

Strategic reorientation, organisational restructuring and curtailments in funding and supply suggest that the morale, preparedness and operational efficiency of Russian forces has been in decline. Evidence for this is not hard to find. First, while it was noted above that material provision for service personnel has been protected for political reasons, the basic conditions for conscripts remain – as in the Soviet period – fundamentally unattractive, provoking widespread drug abuse, alcoholism, suicide and draft evasion. Conditions for officers and the increasing number of contract soldiers are somewhat better, but in many cases still short of comfortable. While salaries have been raised repeatedly in an attempt to keep pace with inflation, a decline in living standards has nonetheless occurred. Coupled with the prospect for many of demobilisation to an uncertain future in civilian life, this has had an appreciable effect on morale, encouraging many officers to seek compensation in the form of criminal activities, such as pilferage, extortion and illegal arms sales. The effectiveness of the Russian armed forces has also been placed in question by fiscal restraints on combat training and patrols. Air force pilots were, during 1993, restricted to an average of only 23-50 hours flight time a year (well below the minimum 120 hours necessary, according to NATO estimates, to retain effectiveness). The navy has been largely confined to port, while the army, in the opinion of none other than the Commander-in-Chief of ground forces, Vladimir Semenov, in 1993 undertook 'no combat training, in the old sense'.[56]

Case studies of disagreement

To summarise the preceding section, the rapid collapse of the USSR resulted in the disintegration of the formerly monolithic and powerful Soviet armed forces. Attempting to reorganise these forces through the medium of the CIS has proven a largely fruitless endeavour. The Commonwealth has been unable to reach agreement on a workable set of co-operative military arrangements. The failure of multilateral co-operation has been paralleled by a trend towards independent defence postures and, in some cases, bilateral arrangements with Russia.

As will become apparent in this section, the development of national defence postures has by no means been free of conflict. In the Baltic states – the first case study considered here – it has led to a bitter controversy with Russia over the removal of unwanted troops and military installations. Raising national defence has also fuelled arguments over the spoils of the former Soviet armed forces, an issue examined here in relation to the naval forces of the Black Sea Fleet. The final case study in this section also touches upon this theme, and, in addition, considers an important external consequence of military disintegration, the entry of the successor states into the international non-nuclear arms control regime.

Troops in the Baltic states

The independence of the Baltic states in September 1991 removed any legal basis for the Soviet military presence in the region. Troops of the USSR were, in a legal sense, now to be regarded as truly a 'foreign' force. Demands that Soviet and later Russian forces be withdrawn were an obvious corollary of the desire of the Baltics to fully reclaim their national sovereignty. The poor behaviour of locally stationed troops (the flouting of transport and customs regulations, harassment of national militias and undertaking unnotified manoeuvres) only strengthened this feeling. The removal of the military presence was also calculated to have certain immediate and practical benefits. It would help allay the fears of foreign investors concerned at the military's destabilising influence, staunch a major source of environmental pollution, and facilitate the psychological adjustment required of civilian Russian minorities to their new status as citizens of foreign countries rather than the beneficiaries of Russian colonisation.[57]

The Soviet Union and latterly Russia have proven less than accommodating towards Baltic demands. One reason for this stance lies in the extensive military facilities of the region. At the end of 1991, these included air defence and fighter/bomber air bases and garrisons for motorised rifle, tank and airborne divisions. As for the Baltic Fleet it was actually headquartered at a Russian port, Baltiisk, and enjoyed major facilities at a second Russian base at Kronstadt. These locations on Russian territory were, nonetheless, considered strategically vulnerable. Baltiisk, situated in the enclave of Kaliningrad is cut off from the rest of Russia (being bordered by Lithuania and Poland), while Kronstadt, owing to its position in the narrow Gulf of Finland, is icebound in winter and easily blockaded (as occurred in both World Wars). The Fleet consequently was forced to rely upon a range of important support facilities in the Baltic states.

A standoff over the issue of military withdrawal developed immediately upon the achievement of Baltic independence. Flushed by their political triumph, the leaders of the three states demanded at a joint meeting in October, the commencement of a troop departure. The Lithuanian leader, Vytautas Landsbergis, went so far as to call for the total evacuation of troops from his country by the end of the year. In response, Shaposhnikov, in his capacity as then USSR Minister of Defence, suggested that a wind-down could only begin after the task of transferring troops from Germany and Poland had been completed, and not, therefore, before 1994.

Russia's assumption of responsibility for the Baltic military presence did little initially to resolve this impasse. Although the Russian leadership had been a firm advocate of the Baltic cause during the Gorbachev period and had criticised the antics of Soviet troops in the region, once it laid claim to these forces, it adopted a particularly forthright stance in seeking to delay their removal. This about-face reflected the fact that it was now Russia that had to face the logistical difficulties and financial and social consequences of evacuation. Yet aware also of the untenability in international law of seeking to maintain abroad an unwanted military presence, the most comfortable option was to accept the principle of withdrawal, but to raise sufficient preconditions in order to win time and possibly concessions from the Baltic leaders. Less tangible factors also played a part in Russian doggedness. The new leadership in Moscow, for all its earlier opposition to the Union designs of Gorbachev and promotion of republican independence, was simply unable to take seriously the idea that three small nations overshadowed by the enormity of Russia had any claim to determine its military priorities. Sergei Stankevich, a Presidential Councillor to Yeltsin, complained with apparent hurt pride, that Russia was not a defeated nation and would not be ordered about.[58]

Negotiations took a tortuous course during 1992-94. Throughout, the Baltic states remained wedded to the basic demand that a withdrawal be carried out with good speed. The strength of their resolve was illustrated by a number of unilateral moves. The Estonian and Latvian Parliaments nationalised military installations within their borders and in June 1992, a referendum in Lithuania indicated that 91 per cent of voters desired an unconditional troop withdrawal by year end with Russia being obliged to pay compensation for damage the Soviet military had caused since 1940. The Baltics also proved adroit in seeking international support for their cause. The US, the CSCE and the UN General Assembly, amongst others, all demanded a Russian departure.

The Russian position, however, was equally uncompromising. It not only rejected the demand for compensation (on the grounds that it was not responsible for the past misdemeanours of the USSR) but during the course of 1992 outlined at least eight other conditions which would have to be met. Even then a withdrawal would only be possible by the end of 1994 at the earliest.[59] Its preconditions included military requirements such as a guaranteed right of transit to Kaliningrad and the right of temporary access to naval installations while the relocation of the Baltic Fleet to Baltiisk and Kronstadt was in progress. Russia also sought assistance in ameliorating social and financial costs. It demanded, for example, help in constructing housing for departing troops, compensation for vacated land and property, and social security guarantees for officers who had retired in the Baltic states. The requirement that the Baltics drop any territorial claims, meanwhile, was made with an eye to sealing off the issue of Soviet transfers of Estonian and Latvian lands to the RSFSR after the Second World War. The final and perhaps most controversial stipulation concerned alterations to citizenship laws which were seen to discriminate against Russian speakers. This raised the familiar theme of protecting Russian minorities in the new neighbouring states – a matter that was particularly sensitive in Estonia and Latvia where 30 per cent and 34 per cent, respectively, of the population was made up of Russians. Indeed, what Yeltsin referred to as his profound concern over 'numerous infringements of the rights of Russian-speakers' provided the occasion for a very public suspension of troop departures in October 1992.[60] The issue reached a head in the summer of 1993. In Latvia, elections found hundreds of thousands of local Russians barred from voting. In Estonia a controversial law on aliens passed by the parliament resulted in accusations from Moscow that a policy of 'ethnic cleansing' was being implemented.[61] Criticism of the law by the CSCE and the Council of Europe, the intervention of the Estonian President and the amendment of the legislation came too late to prevent yet another call by Yeltsin that withdrawals were not possible so long as human rights were being violated.

The apparently irreconcilable Baltic and Russian positions did not, in fact, prevent a winding down of the military presence (see Table 4.6), at first without a legal framework and latterly on the basis of schedules agreed with Russia. In Lithuania, an agreement on a complete withdrawal by the end of August 1993 was met on schedule. Russian-Latvian agreements signed in April 1994, provided for a complete Russian withdrawal by the end of August of that year in return for temporary Russian access to the ballistic-missile, early-warning radar base at Skrunda. In Estonia, a timetable for withdrawal was agreed in July 1994, providing also for a complete pull-out by the end of August.

Table 4.6 *The withdrawal of Soviet/Russian troops from the Baltic states*

	Estonia	*Latvia*	*Lithuania*
August 1991	36,000		
December 1991		51,300	
January 1992			34,500
February 1992	26,000		
August 1992	12,000	28,000	21,000
December 1992	9,000		
January 1993		27,000	10,000
March 1993	7,600		
April 1993		23,000	
July 1993			7,500
September 1993			0[a]
May 1994	3,000	12,000	
September 1994	0[b]	0[c]	

Notes: [a] the last Russian troops left on 31 August 1993. [b] the last Russian troops left on 31 August 1994. [c] the last Russian troops left on 31 August 1994. (600 specialists remain to staff the radar base in Skrunda. A reported 1,115 decommissioned officers still resident in Latvia as of September 1994).

Sources: RFE/RL Research Report, RFE/RL News Briefs and *RFE/RL Daily Report* various issues; *The Independent*, 10 July 1993, p. 1; *The Economist*, 21 May 1994, p. 53.

While Russia found the loss of its strategic presence hard to stomach, it accepted this as a *fait accompli*. Its diplomatic hardline, as noted above, was designed only to delay, and not to prevent, a withdrawal. Russia derived small, but concrete benefits from this strategy. It succeeded in publicising the predicament of Russian minorities, won pledges of small-scale assistance in the construction of housing, resisted any linkage to the issue of territorial adjustments and postponed consideration of claims to compensation (even for damage inflicted in the short period since 1991, for which it could legitimately be held responsible). That demilitarisation should have progressed more swiftly in Lithuania, meanwhile, was to be explained by the far smaller Russian population there (standing at 9.4 per cent), the absence of any territorial demands and the fact that with the election of the former communist leader Algirdas Brazauskas as President in November 1992, it placed greatest emphasis on good relations with Russia.

The Black Sea Fleet

Of the USSR's four Fleets, only the Black Sea Fleet (BSF) has given rise to rival claims of ownership. The Pacific and Northern Fleets had come under Russian control following the creation of Russian armed forces. Even the Baltic Fleet, which could have been a potential source of dispute, was left to Russian jurisdiction in the absence of any claims by the Baltic states. By contrast, rights to the BSF were asserted by all three successor states in which the Fleet had been anchored during the Soviet period.

Of these claims that of Georgia proved the least difficult to resolve. Its case, laid out in a decree of November 1991 'nationalising' Soviet naval forces deployed on its territory, did give rise to some initial problems. Naval appointees nominated by the Georgian authorities in early 1992 were unable to take up their posts on board ships in local ports owing to the protests of existing officers there. These incidents did not, however, prevent the reaching of an agreement with Russia in May by which naval bases at Poti, Batumi and Ochamchire, plus the small number of vessels located there, were to be placed under Georgian control.

Reconciling the contending positions of Ukraine and Russia has proven significantly more troublesome, leading to a squabble whose complexity and seeming insolubility has rivalled the argument over nuclear weapons. The Ukrainian position on this issue was staked out in parallel with its moves towards the creation of national armed forces. Having displayed a rather cautious attitude towards the future of the Fleet in the autumn of 1991, Kiev took a more forthright stance once the matter of Soviet military assets became a central concern of the newly formed CIS. Displaying a boldness that served only to provoke outrage in Russia and the CIS High Command, the Ukrainian Ministry of Defence in January 1992 effectively laid claim to the bulk of the Fleet. In early April, Kravchuk appointed a naval Commander and issued a decree that threatened to create parallel command structures to those then exercised by the CIS Naval Command.

The Ukrainian leadership considered it had an irrefutable case in favour of its jurisdiction over the Fleet. It rejected, for example, the Russian assertion that the Fleet's origins under Peter and Catherine the Greats gave Moscow a historical claim by pointing to the Fleet's precursor in the form of the naval force of the Ukrainian Cossack Host. While such arguments might have been viewed as historical hair-splitting, Kiev could also point to the fact that the headquarters (Sevastopol) and the bulk of the Fleet's shore-support lay within its borders in the Crimean peninsula.[62] This territorial argument, furthermore, was backed by a geostrategic one, which averred to Ukraine's need to patrol its extensive coastline and its interest in maintaining open sea lanes for commercial shipping to and from the Mediterranean.[63] To these basic positions were added arguments relating more immediately to the consequences of the break of the USSR. Kiev, while renouncing any claim to the Baltic, Northern and Pacific Fleets and parts of the BSF stationed outside Ukraine, did nonetheless claim that during the Soviet period it had made an important contribution to overall naval development. This, according to Defence Minister Konstantin Morozov, entitled it to 16–17 per cent of the total naval forces of the Soviet Union. It was plain that such figures were being used to justify taking over the lion's share of the BSF, which in total had made up only 8–10 per cent of the Soviet Union's naval capacity.

Ukraine's stance on the BSF has brought it into direct conflict with both the CIS High Command and Russia. The argument with the former has boiled down to competing interpretations over what were to be considered 'strategic' forces. The catch-all definition included in the Minsk agreement of December 1991 clearly specified 'the

Navy' of the FSU as falling within the jurisdiction of the CIS (see above, p. 166) and, therefore, appeared to preclude national control by CIS member states. Kiev, however, applied a narrower definition, which regarded 'strategic' forces as simply those which carried nuclear weapons.[64] Given the BSF does not carry SLBMs, this led Ukraine to suggest in early 1992 that once tactical weapons had been removed, it could take possession of the entire Fleet.[65] Having revised his own formulation of what constituted CIS strategic forces, commander Shaposhnikov was later to implicitly acknowledge the Ukrainian position on the status of the BSF (see below). He and his colleagues remained opposed, however, to granting Ukraine all but a small share of the BSF, considering the portion demanded by Kiev far in excess of both its financial capabilities and modest defence needs.

CIS control over the BSF was initially supported by Russia, albeit with some ambivalence. Yeltsin's apparently conflicting suggestions that the Fleet had to be placed under joint CIS command yet 'was, is and will be Russia's'[66] simply reflected the reality of Russian ascendancy within the Commonwealth. Hence, in early 1992, when the CIS still appeared a credible vehicle of managing the FSU's military legacy, Russia's response to Ukrainian claims was to assert the right of Russian jurisdiction in order to guarantee the subordination of the Fleet to the CIS command. However, once, Russia had determined upon forming its own armed forces, it unashamedly asserted its claim to the assets of the BSF as the basis of a specifically Russian, rather than CIS fleet. Shaposhnikov's announcement in late May that the BSF did not, in fact, make up CIS strategic forces, moreover, effectively removed the fleet from Commonwealth concerns and rendered it, thereafter an object of straightforward competition between Moscow and Kiev.

Russia's claim to the BSF is based on a mix of historical and practical concerns. The origins of the Fleet in Russia's distant past have already been alluded to. To this has been added an assumption that as the primary contributor to military might during the Soviet period, Russia has a legitimate interest in the military spoils of the USSR. The ethnic balance of the Fleet's personnel provide further substance to Moscow's case, in that the officer corps is dominated by Russians, who have displayed a marked reluctance to swear loyalty to Ukraine. As well as securing the Fleet, Russia has been equally concerned with obtaining ownership and/or access to shore facilities.

According to Rear Admiral Ivan Semenov deputy chief of the Russian Navy Main Staff operations directorate, as of January 1993 more than 90 per cent of the BSF's base facilities were located in Ukraine, the loss of which would require the wholesale construction of new units in Russia's Krasnodar region at huge expense over a period of twelve to fifteen years.[67] Their loss, moreover, has been made harder to bear by the fact that the Crimea region, where most facilities are based, is populated largely by ethnic Russians. The logistical and political impracticalities of relocation led Moscow at one point to stake a claim of ownership (later moderated to a request for a leasehold) to Fleet headquarters at Sevastopol – a demand rejected outright by Ukraine as an infringement of its sovereignty and territorial integrity.

While the positions of Kiev and Moscow over the BSF have been diametrically opposed, both have nonetheless recognised the necessity of attempting to reach agreement through negotiation. A failure to resolve the Fleet's future has served the interests of neither side. It has created uncertainties over financing, encouraged indiscipline resulting on occasion in violence between Ukrainian and Russian fleet personnel, and has undermined the operational effectiveness of the Fleet as a whole owing to poor relations between Ukrainian and Russian officers. Moreover, the obvious fact that neither side has been prepared to voluntarily relinquish a claim to the BSF has made negotiations an unavoidable necessity.

These talks, not surprisingly, have proven extremely difficult. Greatest progress has been registered only when Yeltsin and Kravchuk felt the need to intervene personally. At meetings of the two Presidents, interim agreements on the fate of the BSF have been reached on five separate occasions (see Box 4.1).

Box 4.1 Russian-Ukrainian Agreements on the Black Sea Fleet

Dagomys, June 1992

- agreement in principle 'to create a Russian Navy and a Ukrainian Navy in the Black Sea on the basis of the Black Sea Fleet'; details to be worked out in subsequent talks;
- joint financing in the interim.

Yalta, August 1992

- during a transition period lasting until the end of 1995 the Fleet to be removed from CIS command and placed under a joint command appointed by and subordinate to the Presidents of Russia and Ukraine;
- after 1995 fleet to be divided;
- during the transition period both sides to use the existing shore-support facilities, with a future system of support to be fixed in a separate agreement;
- recruitment to the Fleet to be carried out equally by conscription;
- service personnel permitted to swear allegiance to their own state.

Moscow, June 1993

- division of the Fleet on an equal basis to begin September 1993 and be completed by the end of 1995; details to be worked out by a special commission;
- this division, in fact, to proceed only after a separate agreement on 'the conditions of basing the Russian Navy on Ukrainian territory' has been concluded; this will fix the terms of Russian access to shore facilities;
- financing in interim to be joint; details again subject to a separate accord.

Massandra, September 1993

- Ukraine to surrender its share of the BSF and allow Russia to lease the port of Sevastopol; in return Russia would write off debts owed by Kiev for energy imports.

Moscow, April 1994

- division of the Fleet on an equal basis; Ukraine to sell part of its share to Russia or to give it up in exchange for debt forgiveness;
- Russian and Ukrainian vessels to be based separately;
- details to be worked out in subsequent agreement.

At face value, these agreements did signal progress. They laid down important principles in respect of the BSF's future and demonstrated compromise on both sides. Under the agreement of June 1993, Moscow conceded that Ukraine deserved half of the Fleet. Kiev, for its part, not only accepted a right of Russian access to Ukrainian ports, but by agreeing to the BSF's equal division seemed to be trimming its claim to the bulk of the Fleet.

Despite this flexibility, success has been far from assured. The agreements have not only met with opposition amongst the bulk of officers, who prefer a united fleet under Russian command, but seemingly require ratification by the two national parliaments, both of whom view the issue of the BSF as linked to the wider issue of the status of the Crimea. The agreements have also been open to conflicting interpretations. That at Massandra, which Yeltsin regarded as sealing the fate of the Fleet, was immediately disavowed by Kravchuk, who accorded it simply the status of a Russian proposal. The inadequacies of the agreements are also evident in their deferral of important issues to future, more detailed, accords. These have failed to materialise. The final agreement cited above, for instance, fell apart once the Russian and Ukrainian Defence Ministers were faced with working out the detailed division of the Fleet and the allocation of basing rights.

The CFE Treaty

At the time of the collapse of the USSR four major, non-nuclear, arms control measures were in the process of being negotiated. During 1992 talks on all four were completed. The 1992 Vienna Document on Confidence and Security-Building Measures (CSBMs) applied to all the successor states (bar Georgia which did not participate in the final stage of negotiations). Accession to the Document proved relatively straightforward. Its provisions are voluntary rather than binding and it does not impose any actual limitations on military capabilities. The second measure, the Treaty on Open Skies, is also concerned with military openness (in this case, surveillance by reconnaissance flights, to be used *inter alia* to monitor compliance with arms control agreements). The fact that by the end of 1992 only five successor states (Russia, Belarus, Georgia, Kyrgyzstan and Ukraine) had signed, reflected less an antipathy to the treaty's provisions than to its complexity and cost. Negotiations on the third, the Chemical Weapons Convention (banning the development, production, stockpiling and use of such weapons) were completed in September 1992. Within six months it had been signed by ten successor states, including most importantly, Russia, the site of the former Soviet armed forces' chemical weapons complex. Finally, the CFE-1A Agreement on military personnel levels within the Atlantic-to-the Urals (ATTU) region did occasion some difficulties. Even so, none of the eight successor states involved in the talks disagreed with the actual purpose of the agreement. Its ceilings have not involved any requirement to undertake deep cuts. Not only is it a voluntary agreement, but in all cases personnel limits exceed or equal actual holdings (or in the Ukrainian case were consistent with future planned reductions). Those problems which have arisen stem not from objections to personnel levels, but from delays in fixing limits in Armenia, Azerbaijan, Georgia and Moldova owing to conflicts there. This was resolved during 1994, when Armenia became the last successor state to declare its personnel limit (see Table 4.7).

Table 4.7 *Military personnel holdings of the successor states in the ATTU area and limits under the CFE-1A Agreement*

	Holding	*Limit*	
Armenia	32,682	32,682	
Azerbaijan	56,000	70,000	
Belarus	92,664	100,000	
Georgia	[a]	40,000	
Kazakhstan	N/A	0	(in area of application)
Moldova	11,123	20,000	
Russia	1,110,578	1,450,000	(in area of application)
Ukraine	495,156	450,000	

Note: [a] As of December 1993 Georgia had not notified its holding.

Source: The Military Balance 1994/1995 (London, The International Institute of Strategic Studies/Brassey's, 1994), pp. 263, 267.

The greatest difficulties in the field of conventional arms control have, in fact, been posed by the 1990 CFE Treaty (see Chapter 1, p 31). The break-up of the USSR just one year after the treaty's conclusion presented the obvious question of whether its provisions still held any relevance. Scrapping the agreement and renegotiating it from scratch, however, proved a far less attractive option than seeking to divide up the USSR's entitlements amongst the successor states. While this offered direct benefits to the treaty's other signatories in that their holdings would remain unaltered, it promised to open up potentially insuperable conflicts of interest between the claimants to former Soviet military assets. A series of complex technical issues would also have to be resolved. Sub-zonal ceilings within the USSR, for example, were hardly coincident with the frontiers of the successor states, while the overall zone of application (the ATTU region) placed Kazakhstan part in and part out of the treaty's geographical remit.[68] Moreover, a decision taken by the Baltic states in October 1991 to dissociate themselves from the CFE obligations of the USSR, while hardly likely to upset the European military balance, created a worrying precedent of unilateral withdrawal from the treaty's provisions.

These issues formed the backdrop to a series of negotiations held during the first half of 1992 amongst the successor states (excluding the Baltics) that fell within the ATTU region. Russia initially attempted to assume sole responsibility for the treaty's implementation in the former Soviet zone of application. A generous interpretation of this move would suggest that Russia hoped the treaty could be implemented via the single medium of the projected CIS joint forces (this would still have created problems with then non-member Georgia), thereby avoiding the need for national ceilings. A less charitable view, however, suggests Moscow was attempting to determine military levels in the other successor states. In any case, its proposal came to nothing in the face of opposition both amongst the successor states themselves and from other CFE signatories. Instead it was agreed that all eight states were to be regarded as parties to the treaty. The major bone of contention thereafter was the formula by which national equipment ceilings were to be devised – a necessity in view of the diminishing likelihood of CIS joint forces. General Konstantin Kobets, adviser on Defence to Yeltsin, for example, proposed a solution in February based on population size, length of borders and total area of the state. This was advantageous to Russia and was clearly aimed at redressing the concentration of deployments in Ukraine and Belarus. The prospects of implementing such a formula, however, appeared remote given that the non-Russian states wanted to appropriate most of the former Soviet *matériel* on their territories.

These differences were largely overcome in the 'Tashkent Document' signed at the CIS summit in May. This divided the USSR's original entitlements under the CFE Treaty into national ceilings amongst the FSU states within the ATTU region, while retaining the sub-zonal limits of the original treaty.[69] National ceilings were to be largely proportionate to the geographic dispersal of Soviet weaponry at the end of 1991 and thus permitted reduced, but still high concentrations within both Belarus and Ukraine. Soviet forces in Germany, Poland and the Baltics were to be counted against the Russian allocation, while the anomalous position of Kazakhstan was dispensed with by placing no limit on its national forces but requiring the demilitarisation of that small area of its territory within the ATTU region.[70] Under the terms of the Document, Russia emerged as a clear loser, liable to implement significant reductions in all five weapon categories (see Table 4.8.).

The conclusion of the Tashkent Document was, at first sight, a significant achievement, particularly when compared to the acrimony that surrounded other military issues in the FSU. Perhaps the reason for progress was simply the fact that CFE-related ceilings accorded with military developments (the formation of national armies, defence cutbacks propelled by economic considerations) occurring, in any case, within the FSU. In this sense, even Russia could be consoled by the fact that the relatively high ceilings accorded to Belarus and Ukraine outstripped these countries' economic capabilities and were unlikely to reflect long-term active force levels.

The Tashkent Document was not the end of the matter, however. Moldova, for example, has presented a problem in that its national ceiling had been based upon the holdings of the former Soviet Fourteenth Army in the country. Only a portion of this, however, has been accessible to the Moldovan authorities, much being held by the Fourteenth Army forces under Russian jurisdiction within the Trans–Dniester region. In the Transcaucasus, where Russia exercised jurisdiction over the former Soviet armed forces, a further agreement was required in late May 1992 between Moscow, Armenia, Azerbaijan and Georgia on the partitioning and transfer of former Soviet equipment (to compensate these states for arsenals well below CFE-permitted ceilings). This agreement however, proved difficult to implement owing to Russia's subsequent reluctance to hand over weapons to all three countries given the conflicts waging in or between them. Unilateral seizures of equipment resulted, which, in the case of Azerbaijan, led to the accumulation of ground equipment well in excess of its CFE limits.

Table 4.8 *Successor states declared treaty-limited equipment (TLE) holdings in the ATTU region in August 1992 and CFE/Tashkent Document ceilings to be reached by November 1995*[a]

	Battle tanks	Armoured combat vehicles	Artillery pieces	Attack heli-copters	Fighter aircraft
Armenia[b]					
August. 1992[c]	77	189	160	13	3
November 1995	220	220	285	50	100
Azerbaijan[b]					
August 1992	134	113	126	9	15
November 1995	220	220	285	50	100
Belarus					
August 1992	3,457	3,824	1,562	76	335
November 1995	1,800	2,600	1,615	80	260
Georgia[b]					
August 1992	77	28	0	0	0
November 1995	220	220	285	50	100
Moldova					
August 1992	0	98	108	0	30
November 1995	210	210	250	50	50
Russia[d]					
August 1992	9,338	19,399	8,326	1,005	4,624
November 1995	6,400	11,480	6,415	890	3,450
Ukraine					
August 1992	6,128	6,703	3,591	271	1,648
November 1995	4,080	5,050	4,040	330	1,090
Total August 1992	19,211	30,354	13,873	1,374	6,655
Total by November 1995	13,150	20,000	13,175	1,500	5,150

Notes: [a] The CFE Treaty officially entered into force in November 1992. Its ceilings must be complied with by November 1995. [b] 'Holdings' refers to equipment which had been brought under national control by August 1992. As these states acquired more former Soviet assets, holdings expanded putting them over CFE/Tashkent limits (see the case of Azerbaijan above).

[c] Figures for December 1992. [d] Includes TLE held by Russian forces in Poland, Germany and the Baltic states.

Source: SIPRI Yearbook 1993. World Armaments and Disarmament (Oxford, Oxford University Press/Sipri, 1993), pp. 602, 609.

Alliances and security interests

Within the FSU, a military alliance formally exists in the form of the CIS Collective Security Treaty. The Treaty provides that signatories 'will not enter into military alliances or participate in any groupings of states or in actions directed against another participating state' (Article 1). Article 2 provides for 'joint consultations' in the event of 'the emergence of a threat to the security, territorial integrity, and sovereignty of several participating states'. Article 4 sanctions military assistance by all the participating states should one of their number be subject to an act of aggression. Articles 5 and 7 envisage a degree of military integration – 'the co-ordination and support of joint activities' and the 'functioning of installations in the collective security system'.[71]

As a functioning military alliance, the Collective Security Treaty, however, has severe limitations. As noted above, not all CIS member-states have signed up (as of December 1994, Ukraine, Moldova and Turkmenistan remained outside) and multilateral military co-ordination has been fraught with difficulties. Moreover, to the degree that an alliance rests on a common appreciation of an external threat, the CIS has been hamstrung by the absence of any such shared perspective. Many CIS states have viewed Russia, rather than any external power, as their dominant source of concern and – as the example of Ukrainian–Russian dispute illustrates – have been so deeply divided over issues of security as to render a voluntary co-operative alliance impossible. The absurdities of the Collective Security Treaty have been nowhere more apparent than in the Armenian–Azeri conflict over Nagorno–Karabakh, where two ostensible allies under the treaty have been engaged in open war.

The presence within the FSU of competition alongside levels of co-operation and interdependence means the states of the region (and specifically those grouped together within the CIS) might be regarded less as an alliance and more as a *security complex*. In such a system, states, by virtue of geographic proximity, regard one another as their primary security concerns, whether or not this be in terms of 'amity' or 'enmity'. However, even this more flexible concept does not fully capture the nature of relationships enveloping the FSU, for while a security complex tends to be 'inward-looking', and weak in its interactions with neighbours, the successor states have, to varying degrees, cultivated relations with outsiders.[72] Russia's status as *primus inter pares* and claimant to a sizeable proportion of the USSR's military potential means it has a clear interest in maintaining bilateral relations of a security nature, particularly with the US (noted already in the case of nuclear disarmament). The European locations of Russia, Ukraine and Belarus mean a concern for arrangements involving Eastern Europe. The attentions of the Transcaucasian and Central Asian states have been towards states such as Iran, Turkey and Afghanistan. The Baltic states which had expressed no interest in the CIS from the start, meanwhile, have naturally sought provisions entirely distinct from the Commonwealth.

Russia

The collapse of the Warsaw Treaty Organisation (WTO) and later the USSR, has confronted Russia with an acute sense of isolation. Not only does it face a security vacuum on its western flank and a series of localised conflicts along its southern borders (the Transcaucasus, Tajikistan, Afghanistan), but nowhere along its extensive periphery can it point to countries that might be regarded as actual or even potential allies. Indeed, in most cases such countries have more cause for complaint than comfort. This applies whether one looks west from Moscow (the Baltics, Poland), east (China, Japan) or south (Ukraine, Turkey, Iran). Russia's close relations within the CIS with Belarus and certain Central Asian states offer scant consolation.

Russia's isolation would, of course, be complete should it face a hostile Western Alliance. As we saw in Chapter 1, however, the qualitative improvements in East–West relations during the Gorbachev years had reduced almost to zero the likelihood of confrontation across Europe's former divide and created the beginnings of a strong partnership between the West and the USSR. In the post-Soviet period this has in many respects continued. The practical expression of a Russian–Western axis has already been detailed above in regard to progress on both nuclear and conventional disarmament. The dismantling of the arsenals of the Cold War has, moreover, been accompanied by military developments within the NATO countries which bear equal testimony to the changed strategic climate. The stabilisation of defence expenditures, the scaling down of the US and Canadian presence in Europe, America's withdrawal from military bases around the globe and the emergence of war-planning scenarios and foreign policy concepts under the Clinton Administration concerned with regional conflicts in the Third World rather than a residual Russian threat, bear testimony to an increasingly benign Western Alliance.

Opportunities for security co-operation with the West were eagerly seized by the Yeltsin leadership at the time of the USSR's dissolution. Indeed, in the euphoric weeks at the end of 1991, Yeltsin even went so far as to claim that Moscow might one day join NATO.[73] While this ambition soon disappeared from view, the institutionalisation of co-operation was nonetheless achieved through Russian membership of the North Atlantic Co-operation Council (NACC), established in December 1991 as a consultative forum embracing the NATO countries, the former East European members of the WTO and the successor states. Further evidence that Russia no longer considered itself an adversary of the West could be seen in a series of headline initiatives in the military sphere during 1992. These ranged from assurances by Yeltsin that the CIS/Russian nuclear arsenal had been retargeted away from the US, to an interest in co-operation with the US in developing strategic defences to guard against ballistic missile attacks mounted from the Third World. During 1993–94 co-operation with the US and other NATO powers continued at a more mundane, but not insignificant level, a visit by Defence Minister Grachev to Washington in September 1993, for example, yielded agreement on measures such as officer exchanges and mooted joint exercises. Twelve months later a Russian–American peacekeeping exercise was conducted in the southern Urals.

Yet for all this apparent cordiality, the impression was nonetheless evident during 1993–94 that a distinct tempering of the initial enthusiasm had occurred. This shift was part of the turn to a more assertive Russian foreign policy examined in the previous chapter. While important elements of the improved relationship have been preserved (for instance, progress on the START process), Moscow has dug in its heels on other matters, notably the CFE Treaty[74] and the issue considered her, NATO enlargement in Eastern Europe.

The prospect of the Atlantic Alliance extending its membership eastwards is in fact a rather dim one. Despite applications for membership by a number of East European states, NATO (with the exception of Germany) has been reluctant to welcome new members for fear of complicating decision-making, undermining membership cohesion and becoming embroiled in Yugoslav-style conflicts. Its calculations regarding Russia have also been germane. At a military planning level, carrying out the mutual defence provisions of the North Atlantic Treaty seems an extremely risky undertaking in the albeit unlikely event that the East European states are attacked by Russia. Western capitals have also not wanted to encroach upon regions of traditional Russian interest. In the short term, such reasoning has been guided by a need to deny military hardliners and ultra-nationalists in Russia reason to challenge the more moderate foreign policies personified by Yeltsin and Kozyrev.[75]

NATO's caution has in some respects been justified. Although the Soviet/Russian military has been exposed to both Gorbachev's new political thinking and the early, pro-Western slant of the Yeltsin leadership, the view of NATO as an adversary has remained ingrained within its higher echelons. As for Yeltsin himself, he seems to have been swayed by competing desires: a wish to overcome the legacy of Soviet oversight in Eastern Europe, a lingering sense of the region as a Russian sphere of influence, and a desire to appease the Russian military establishment. The Russian leader has consequently displayed an ambivalent attitude towards the role of the Western Alliance in Eastern Europe. Statements during a tour of the region in August 1993 that Russia would not object to Polish or Czech applications for NATO membership were flatly contradicted by a letter to the governments of the US, the UK, France and Germany, a month later.

Yeltsin's *volte-face* on this issue coincided with his suppression of the Russian parliament, an act which required the support of the military. At this point, more than any other, Yeltsin was mindful of the need to avoid alienating his generals by open support for NATO expansion. Short-term expediency, however, has not been the only influence. A lingering concern remains as to NATO's purpose. Kozyrev has argued that the survival of the Atlantic Alliance presupposes the existence of an adversary, and by opening up NATO to Eastern Europe, this clearly suggests that the supposed enemy is

Russia.[76] A report by the Russian Foreign Intelligence Service released in late 1993 made an even more cogent case against enlargement. While the report conceded that NATO had no intention of establishing a staging ground for strikes against Russia, the movement of NATO's area of responsibility into 'direct proximity' with Russia would have profound implications. The Russian armed forces would be compelled to revise their 'defensive concepts' and operational plans, redeploy major troop contingents and reassign military theatres, all of which would be extremely costly and would add to the already massive disruption occurring within the military.[77] Russian concerns have also been linked to the recurring theme of isolation. East European membership of NATO would leave Russia outside a security organisation which effectively embraces the entire European continent. More worringly, the inclusion of Eastern Europe could act as a catalyst to claims for membership by the Baltic states and even Ukraine.[78] To pre-empt such scenarios, Yeltsin suggested in late 1993 that the East Europeans should enter NATO only if Russia did. Given this was unlikely, Kozyrev implied Russia's isolation could be overcome if, rather than extending NATO, existing pan-European organisations (notably the CSCE and NACC) were empowered to provide 'watertight guarantees of security'.[79] These bodies already involved Russia, the other successor states and Eastern Europe, and their transformation would be a process over which Russia could exercise a decisive influence, something it was clearly unable to do within NATO.

The arguments over NATO enlargement experienced a new twist following NATO's Brussels summit in January 1994. At this gathering, the Alliance formally outlined the 'Partnership for Peace' (PFP) initiative. This represented a carefully crafted programme that aimed to solve NATO's three-way dilemma of offering something concrete to the East Europeans, meeting Russia's concerns, and overcoming its own anxieties at the organisational difficulties of embracing new members.[80] PFP was open to all members then in the CSCE. It offered greater military co-operation (planning, training, budgetary transparency etc.) with the Alliance and consultations in the event of attack. It also accepted in principle that the membership of NATO itself would eventually expand. PFP, however, offered neither a specific timetable for such enlargement nor concrete security guarantees.

By deferring the issue of full NATO membership, PFP appeared to partially answer Russian objections. Moscow, subsequently, voiced no opposition to the East European or successor states joining the programme. During 1994 it did, however, make its own entry the subject of prolonged diplomatic wrangling. One demand raised by Russia was for a special status within PFP, which would distinguish it from other members. That Russia, a nuclear power and the site of Europe's largest conventional armed force, should be treated as an equal of countries like Albania or tiny Estonia was considered an affront to its 'greatness'.[81] NATO, however, was reluctant to accord Moscow a privileged status, out of deference to the concerns of Eastern Europe and Ukraine. Following intense negotiations a compromise was reached. Moscow signed the PFP framework agreement in June, making it the eleventh successor state to do so. In return, NATO offered a series of sweeteners. In a joint document Russia's 'weight and responsibility as a major European, world and nuclear power' was recognised and a 'broad and in-depth dialogue' was proposed on security issues. In practical terms, these measures amounted to very little. Moscow was not offered any formal consultative mechanism within PFP and its preference for the development of the CSCE and NACC was effectively ignored.[82] Nonetheless, the symbolic value of the protocol should not be underestimated. It granted to Russia an implicit recognition of the great power status it so craved and offered the possibility at least of greater dialogue on sensitive issues such as the war in Yugoslavia where an absence of consultation had proven a source of friction (see Chapter 5, p. 266).

Further progress on PFP, however, remained hostage to the enlargement issue. Russia, which had been due to formally enter the PFP programme on 1 December 1994 with the presentation of an implementation document, announced that day that it was deferring its participation. Kozyrev in making public this decision, argued that NATO was unduly hastening an extension of its full membership, rather than developing the potentialities of the more acceptable PFP programme. Kozyrev's statement was directed specifically at the communiqué of a recent meeting of NATO foreign ministers held earlier in the day that had mentioned an acceptance in principle of enlargement. Yet for all Kozyrev's displeasure, the NATO document also made plain, however, that no extension of Alliance membership was imminent. It again laid down no timetable for accession and deferred negotiations until after the completion of a major NATO study on the consequences of enlargement. In this light, Kozyrev's real target was probably the US, whose Democratic President, Bill Clinton, had taken a more forthright stance on NATO expansion following Republican victories in Congressional elections in November. Harsh words were also heard from Yeltsin. At the CSCE summit in early December he spelled out by now familiar themes: Moscow objected to an extension of 'NATO's responsibility up to the frontiers of Russia' and preferred the development of existing pan-European bodies such as the CSCE as a co-ordinating security structure. Yeltsin married this with a more emphatic sign of displeasure, suggesting that NATO enlargement by 'sowing the seeds of distrust' threatened to plunge Europe into a 'cold peace'.[83]

Whatever the hopes and fears voiced concerning arrangements for Eastern Europe, the fact remained that the passing of the WTO had not resulted in the institutionalisation of an alternative collective security structure. PFP offered the East Europeans a link with NATO and the distant prospect of full membership, but did not grant a clear assurance of their security. In this sense, the region faced a 'security vacuum' which gave the East European countries a clear incentive to balance their desires for greater co-operation with the West with a sensitivity towards Russia. This, moreover, coincided with a Russian desire to place its relations with the East European countries on a stable basis. Although the break-up of the USSR had placed Russia at some remove from the former members of the WTO, the region still represented what Kozyrev termed 'an area of interest for Russia'.[84] This stemmed from the long history of Soviet and indeed Imperial Russian attention to the region, the prevalence of potential instabilities there occasioned by resurgent ethnic identities and, perhaps most importantly, a fear that neglect of Europe's eastern part would increase Russia's isolation from the continent as a whole and relegate it to the role of an Asian rather than a European power. The issue of NATO enlargement simply increased the urgency of Russian policy.

East European entreaties towards NATO illustrated that a Russian-led alliance system in the region was a clear non-starter. Indeed, hopes expressed at the end of 1991 that these states might join the CIS proved singularly ill-founded. The alternative for Russia was to fashion bilateral security links. At one level, these could be found in the clauses of treaties on friendship and co-operation. Stock references to respect for territorial integrity, non-interference and the peaceful resolution of disputes contained in that signed with Poland in May 1992 might have been dismissed as empty phrases were it not for the fact that Poland was the only former WTO state with a land border with Russia (along the heavily militarised region of Kaliningrad). In the case of Bulgaria, a similar treaty signed in August also had far-reaching implications, containing in its text non-aggression clauses and provision for consultations to avert threats to peace in Europe and the Black Sea region.

Other mutual concerns remained as a legacy of the WTO. The delicate nature of these issues was most evident in the case of Poland, which at the end of 1991 was home to at least 30,000 former Soviet troops and was the major transit route for returning troops from the former East Germany. Russia had undertaken a near-total withdrawal from Poland by September 1993. A small mission remained to oversee the retreat from Germany, and this too was rendered superfluous once the German operation was completed in August 1994. While the troop issue was a major bone of contention (numerous disputes arose with Warsaw over claims for compensation and the financing of the withdrawal), elsewhere clear opportunities existed for co-operation. The Soviet and East European armies had, through the medium of the WTO, been effectively integrated, and this paved the way for continuing Russian military assistance, whether this be the training of Bulgarian and Hungarian officers in Russian military academies or debt for arms swaps as in the case of Hungary's receipt of MiG-29 fighter aircraft.

Russia inherited from the USSR a number of security and military concerns further afield. The process of military disengagement from the Third World pursued by the Gorbachev leadership has been largely completed under Yeltsin. In May 1992, military advisers departed from Vietnam and in December the last Russian troops withdrew from Mongolia. In Vietnam, Russia retained access to the Cam Ranh naval base, but its warships became less and less frequent visitors, reflecting a scaling down of activities by the Pacific Fleet. In November 1992 Yeltsin made a pledge to cease military aid and arms supplies to North Korea and signalled that Russia, as the inheritor of Soviet treaty commitments, was willing to revise security commitments contained in the 1961 Treaty of Friendship and Co-operation.[85] This was geared not just to improving relations with South Korea (a potential economic partner) but was the result of concern at the North's apparent desire to construct a nuclear arsenal. Cuba also fell victim to Russian retrenchment. Arms sales were reduced to the supply of spare parts and all but a few of the large former Soviet military contingent returned home under an agreement setting 1 July 1993 as a deadline for withdrawal. By this date the only remaining presence was at the intelligence-gathering facility near Havana used to track US communications. Once part of the infrastructure of East–West confrontation, this facility, according to Russian officials, would now be used to monitor START implementation and provide backup to proposed Russian–US co-operation in anti-missile defence.[86]

Strategic relations with China have developed along the lines of *rapprochement* mapped out during the Gorbachev years. Yeltsin's visit to Beijing in December 1992, for example, was the occasion for agreement on force reductions along the Sino-Russian border and a joint communiqué containing non-aggression pledges. A year later a military co-operation accord was reached providing for a large increase in the exchange of officers. An agreement signed during a visit to Moscow by the Chinese President Jiang Zemin, in September 1994, provided for the detargeting of nuclear missiles against one another. Points of contention have remained. Russia has been concerned at Chinese nuclear testing, while Beijing has been unhappy at the redeployment of CFE-limited equipment to Russia's Far East Military District.

The non-Russian states

For many of the successor states, security considerations have been principally related to Russia (whether as potential ally or adversary). In the case of Belarus this has largely been to the exclusion of other security relations. Here an official stance of neutrality has been largely offset by what has amounted to a *de facto* military alliance with Moscow. Ukraine, by contrast, has sought to offset its relationship with Moscow by means of external links. Its options in this regard, however, have been severely circumscribed. Russia's sensitivities over Western encroachment apply equally to Ukraine as they do to Eastern Europe. Hence the best that could be realistically hoped for in Kiev has been the strengthening of existing arrangements (CSCE, NACC, PFP) even though these bodies have not offered comprehensive security guarantees. A parallel strategy has been to deepen co-operation with neighbours closer to home in Eastern Europe. This has offered a number of potential benefits, not least fostering good relations throughout the region, thereby denying a future, potentially resurgent, Russia the opportunity to intervene in, say, Poland or in Ukraine itself, in the cause of restoring stability to the region.[87] It is in this light that Kiev's interest in the Visegrad group of nations and its proposals for a 'zone of stability and security in the Central and Eastern European region' should be understood. As Kravchuk explained whilst on a visit to Hungary in the spring of 1993, such a group, embracing the Baltic states, Ukraine, Belarus, Moldova and the countries of Eastern Europe, could promote military co-operation, avert the prospect of conflicts arising over territorial claims, provide a regional supplement to the CSCE and a framework for co-operation with NATO.[88] However, the fact that the idea was swiftly criticised by Russia as an attempt to build around it a *cordon sanitaire*, demonstrated all too clearly the nature of Ukraine's predicament.

Improving relations with Eastern Europe have also relieved Ukraine of its own sources of conflict with countries in the region. Kiev has been sensitive not only to the matter of a disputed border with Romania, (a dormant territorial issue has also existed between itself and Poland) and the status of a Ukrainian minority in Poland's eastern borderlands (and by the same token the treatment of Polish, Hungarian, Bulgarian and Romanian minorities in Ukraine) but also to suspicions regarding its new-found status as one of Europe's largest military powers. Consequently Ukraine has sought to cement bilateral co-operation, particularly with Poland and Hungary. In the case of Poland, a programme of military co-operation was agreed as early as January 1992. A Friendship Treaty signed in May recognised the inviolability of borders and provided for regular security consultations. The 1991 Ukrainian–Hungarian Friendship Treaty, meanwhile was ratified by the parliament in Kiev in May 1993. It too renounced any border changes. Several military co-operation agreements have also been reached, while Ukraine's treatment of the Hungarian minority in the Transcarpathian region, has been described by Budapest as a model of tolerance.[89]

Turning to Moldova and the Baltic states, here a sense of strategic vulnerability has been keenly felt owing to the presence of Russian troops and large Russian minority populations. The response in the Baltics' case has been an overtly pro-Western orientation. They have been the beneficiaries of military assistance provided by the countries of the Nordic Council (Denmark, Finland, Iceland,

Norway and Sweden) and both Nordic and NATO countries agreed in September 1994 to assist in the formation of a joint Baltic 'peace-keeping battalion'. The Baltics have also forged a relationship with the Western European Union (the embryonic defence arm of the European Union), joining as 'associate partners' in May 1994. These links, however, have been poor substitutes for the avowed aim of full NATO membership. If membership has been problematic for countries in Eastern Europe out of the West's concern for Russian sensibilities, how more so for the Baltics. That these states are considered militarily indefensible in view of their proximity to Russia, moreover, simply provides a tactical justification for denying the defensive guarantees of entry into the Alliance.

The two remaining regions of the FSU – the Transcaucasus and Central Asia – contain states whose desire for security has in a very real sense been the most acute, given the incidence of conflicts there. Azerbaijan's losses at the hands of Armenian-backed Karabakh forces, for instance, have led it to propose the creation of a defence pact with Ankara. For reasons explored in Chapter 5 (pp.226–29), however, it has been unable to elicit much in the way of a material response from Turkey or, indeed, Iran – neighbouring states with sympathies towards the Azeri cause. The effects of war in Tajikistan meanwhile, have rippled throughout neighbouring Central Asian states, provoking fears amongst secular leaderships of the spread of radical Islamic influence. As noted above this has impelled them towards the security mechanisms of the CIS (Turkmenistan excepted) and close defence co-ordination with Russia. The Tajik conflict has illustrated a larger issue, namely the Central Asian states' confluent position in Asia and their consequent potential for destabilisation. While the ambitions of regional powers towards the successor states has often been overstated, the long history of Iranian and Pakistani interference in Afghanistan does suggest a degree of assertiveness on the part of Central Asia's southern neighbours. China has also been an object of concern. Kazakhstan, Kyrgyzstan and Tajikistan have shared anxieties over the border with China and in Kazakhstan Chinese immigration has aroused popular fears of an alleged plan to annex part of the country.[90] In search of stability and security in the region, the obvious course for Central Asian leaders has been to maintain close military links with Russia. Exceptions to this pattern, such as Turkish training of Turkmenistan officers, have been of marginal significance. Similarly, while all five states of the region have gained entry into NACC and the CSCE and as of July 1994 all but Tajikistan had joined PFP, these bodies do not offer practical security guarantees nor, given their essentially Eurocentric focus, much in the way of a viable forum for Central Asia's security interests.

Conclusion

The national security problem

Security is widely considered to be the paramount goal of foreign policy. In the absence of security, the very survival of the state (and the nation it often embodies) cannot be guaranteed. In the main, discussions of security in international politics have tended to focus upon *national security*, taken to mean the pursuit of strategies designed to guard against external invasion and attack. This traditional usage concentrates on military threats, neglecting other possible challenges to security arising from economic, environmental, epidemiological and political problems. For many scholars these non-military aspects of security are of growing importance. Many have pointed out that in an increasingly interdependent world, the military issue falls lower down on the agenda of national policy-makers. Governments are as concerned with guaranteed supplies of energy, trade balances and other factors that contribute to national prosperity as they are with the threats posed by potential military aggressors.[91] However, while the state's security environment is far more complex than a simple focus on military threats would suggest, it remains the case that the military factor remains a central preoccupation. Barry Buzan posits that 'security ... is affected by factors in five major sectors', of which four (the political, economic, societal and environmental) are outside of traditional military concerns. Yet, as he puts it, '(m)ilitary threats occupy a special category precisely because they involve the use of force'. Because force can wreak damage more drastic and swift than any other type of threat, military security is accorded a disproportionate emphasis, and this remains the case even if threats in other sectors appear to pose a greater or more immediate danger.[92]

National security policies

Responses to the national security problem can take a variety of forms. Here we will consider the relevance to the successor states of four common security policies. These are: isolation; self-reliance; neutrality and non-alignment; and finally, alliance strategies.[93]

Karl Deutsch has suggested that *isolation* proves effective as a means of security to the degree that it removes a state from sources of disagreement with its potential adversaries. By reducing contacts, the occasion for quarrels will be minimised and war avoided.[94] Isolation might be appealing in that it precludes the need for large military forces and allows the state to direct its energies towards developing agencies of internal security. Amongst the successor states, isolationism has not been viewed as an attractive option. Such a strategy is at odds with the desire for status amongst new states outlined in Chapter 3 (pp.126–27) and their urgent need for external economic assistance, both of which require an active engagement with the outside world. Moreover, the mutual dependencies of the successor states render isolationism a difficult and perhaps dangerous strategy to adopt. In the presence of a large regional power such as Russia, isolation would be no guarantee against interference and might, in fact encourage it, if withdrawal was taken as a sign of passivity. Furthermore, the record of states employing such strategies has not been good. First, isolationism tends to breed paranoia, an often xenophobic distrust of the outside world. This, in turn, provokes suspicion amongst others. The example of North Korea illustrates this point well. Second, no matter how far a country withdraws from the world, this does not remove it from the calculations of others, who will soon find reason to bother it. Such was the fate of Japan, when coerced in the latter part of the nineteenth century to open up to American commercial activities, and of Bhutan once it became an object of Chinese–Indian ambitions in the 1950s.[95] Isolationism, amongst the Central Asian states (where geography might make this a possible course of action) would not diminish Russia's interests in the region.

A second strategy, one of complete *self-reliance*, is perhaps the most complete expression of the condition of anarchy in the international system. Here the state seeks to counter military threats simply by strengthening its own military capabilities. The merits of the approach lie in its apparent certainties. The state concerned need not rely on what it might consider the dubious guarantees of security provided by membership of an alliance. Nor need it make sophisticated judgements about the intentions of other states given all are regarded with suspicion. Any potential threat, whatever its source, will be guarded against by military capabilities that are able to keep all adversaries at bay.[96] States pursuing this course in its pure form are few in number. Communist China and the apartheid regime in South Africa are two rare examples. The concept of 'absolute security' pursued by the USSR prior to the Gorbachev period also approximates this model. Why this course of action should be so rare boils down to the fact that only great powers with command of massive resources can pursue it with any hope of success. In fact, even they are inclined to distribute the load of their own defence via alliance arrangements (viz. the USSR's membership of the WTO and the US's role in NATO). Similarly, Russia, which alone among the successor states has the resources to strive for self-sufficiency, has felt the need to seek allies and strategic access through the CIS Collective Security Treaty and numerous bilateral arrangements.

Turning to *neutrality* and *non-alignment* these are strategies by which a state may seek to insulate itself from the conflicts of others. The latter of these terms has a very specific meaning, referring to the principle by which Third World states avoided formal military commitments to either of the superpowers during the period of the Cold War. Neutrality is similar, being characterised by non-involvement in disputes involving other states, an eschewal of military alliances and the prohibition of the use of one's own territory by others for military purposes. It is a state of affairs that has been used to describe the stance of a group of countries in Europe in the post-war period – Finland, Sweden, Switzerland, Ireland, Austria – who have remained outside NATO and, while it existed, the WTO. Amongst the successor states, neutrality/non-alignment has been rendered difficult by the peculiarities of their military inheritance, which has meant both a Russian presence *in situ* and/or a dependence on Russian military assistance. Despite this, neutrality may hold a certain attraction as a means of affirming an independence *vis-à-vis* Russia. Such a stance was championed by Belarus President Shushkevich prior to his removal from office. Although this was not a position wholly shared by the Belarus parliament (see pp. 113–14), it too has attempted to keep Belarus's options open. In April 1993 it authorised accession to the CIS Collective Security Treaty with the proviso that

Belarusian troops could not be sent outside the country. To a degree, neutrality also describes the position of Ukraine and Moldova, CIS member states which have tried to distance themselves from CIS military provisions and from military links to Russia. Yet true neutralism/non-alignment would require equal alacrity in avoiding a military relationship with the West. Ukraine's dogged search for security guarantees from the US, and (along with Moldova) involvement in NACC and PFP suggest that this has not entirely been the case.

While both isolation and non-alignment/neutrality decrease the chances of involvement in the wars of others, these strategies provide little comfort when a state is threatened or attacked. For this very reason, many states prefer a strategy of military *alliance*. According to Glen Snyder, alliance membership promotes security by reducing the probability of attack (deterrence) and providing greater strength should an attack occur (defence).[97] For Kegley and Wittkopf, alliances 'adhere to realism's first rule of statecraft: to increase military capabilities'; in this case, by acquiring allies rather than acquiring arms.[98] For many of the successor states recourse has been made to Russian military assistance or to a theoretical security guarantee through the mutual security clause of the CIS Collective Security Treaty. This illustrates the attractions of alliance strategies for many of the less well endowed Central Asian states and the turbulent states in the Transcaucasus. Given the military interconnectedness arising from the Soviet military legacy, alliance has been a short step to take. In this sense, it is a function of the FSU's 'inward orientation'. Only in the case of the Baltic states has a full-blooded military alliance with the West been considered a firm (if somewhat distant) objective.

Aside from the exceptional circumstances among the successor states, do more general theories shed any light on their alliance strategies? In recent years the conditions that give rise to and sustain alliances have been the subject of growing attention, particularly amongst neorealists. Stephen Walt, for example, has proposed a comprehensive theory of 'balance of threat', which seeks to augment Kenneth Waltz's focus on power capabilities and balance of power politics as determining factors in alliance patterns. For Walt the level of threat a state faces depends not just on the distribution of power capabilities in the international system but also on further factors that include geographic proximity to a likely adversary, and the offensive capabilities and offensive intentions of the presumed enemy. According to Walt, the most common pattern of alliance formation is 'balancing' – allying with states 'in opposition to the principal source of danger'. The alternative pattern of 'bandwagoning' – allying with the state that poses the major threat – is much less common. Balancing is viewed as advantageous both because it is the 'alignment that preserves most of a state's freedom of action' (bandwagoning, by contrast, involves subordination to the threatening power) and because it is the surest way to counter the expansionist aspirations of a regional power.[99]

Applying Walt's analysis to the successor states, a good case could be made that balancing is the dominant pattern. The Central Asian states, for instance, have joined in an alliance with Russia via the CIS in order to balance the threat posed by China and destabilisation emanating from Islamic forces in Tajikistan and Afghanistan. Armenia has balanced a perceived Turkish threat in a similar manner. In these cases joining with Russia is not considered bandwagoning because Russia is not regarded as the primary threat. Where it is, the general pattern has been one of balancing against Russia. Hence, attempts by the Baltic states and Ukraine to solicit support from Western powers and military organisations such as NATO and the WEU.

Walt's analysis, however, only goes so far in the FSU. In some cases it is difficult to identify a clear pattern. Is Belarus bandwagoning (allying with Russia the most powerful potential threat) or is it balancing (joining with Russia against a possible future Polish threat)? Does it, in fact, regard either of these as threats? An influential lobby in Belarus has sought alliance with Russia simply for reasons of political and national affinity. In other cases it is difficult to apply Walt's analysis at all. In the cases of Georgia and Azerbaijan Walt's preoccupation with external threats is to a large degree irrelevant because of the predominance of internal threat assessments in determining alliance preferences. True, both states have faced external threats – Georgia has at various times accused Russia of military intervention and Azerbaijan has endured an undeclared war with Armenia – but their major problems are domestic. Georgia's belated accession to the CIS Collective Security Treaty and its Friendship Treaty with Russia were largely responses to its perilous civil war. Similarly, Azerbaijan's accession to the Treaty was prompted by its own war of secession in Nagorno–Karabakh, a conflict which while aggravated by Armenian interference, is as much a civil as an inter-state war (see Chapter 5).

The neorealist focus on external factors then cannot account for alliance preferences when internal conditions are also of significance. One attempt to bring internal factors into an explanation of alignment has been provided by Stephen David's theory of 'omnibalancing'. This argues that where the primary threat to the political survival of leaders is domestic in origin, two possible alliance patterns follow. States will ally with whatever 'outside power is most likely to do what is necessary to keep them in power' or they will ally in a manner aimed at appeasing an external threat, allowing them to concentrate on 'the more immediate and dangerous [domestic opponents]'.[100] While David's work is directed at explaining alignments in the Third World, it also rings true for those successor states enduring civil war. Georgia and Tajikistan for instance, have both sought Russian military aid to deal with their internal conflicts. Georgia, moreover, has turned towards alliance with Russia in order to neutralise a fraught relationship and to minimise the likelihood of Russian meddling on behalf of its secessionist opponents. This allows it to more effectively target its energies on the domestic threat.

Another explanation that focuses on internal factors looks at 'ideological solidarity'. This suggests states will ally if their rulers share core political beliefs. Here the emphasis is on alliance *with* states rather than alliance against states. This explanation only holds up best in cases of liberal democracies and hardly at all in cases of socialist alliances. NATO, an alliance of liberal democracies, has demonstrated a durability far greater than the socialist alliance of the now defunct WTO or the short-lived Sino-Soviet axis of the 1950s.[101] This may have something to do with the Kantian notion of the 'pacific union' noted in Chapter 3. Applying ideological solidarity to the successor state does shed some light on the desire of the nascent democracies in the Baltic region to ally with the West, but does not get us very far in analysing the CIS Collective Security Treaty. Its signatories are not bound by a common set of political values, being a diverse group politically (see again Chapter 3).

Both omnibalancing and ideological solidarity are, in fact, modifications of neorealism.[102] One explanation that departs entirely from the realist approach in considering alignment is learning theory. This emphasises the beliefs of governing elites as determining influences. A recent proponent of this approach, Dan Reiter, has suggested that '(w)hereas realism proposes that states ally in response to changes in the level of external threat ... learning theory ... proposes that states make alliance policy in accordance with lessons drawn from formative historical experiences'.[103] Amongst the successor states, this approach has some relevance, although its limitations might be seen in the fact that similar historical experiences can lead to quite different lessons being drawn. The absence of Ukraine and Moldova, amongst the CIS states from the Collective Security Treaty, and the absence of the Baltics from the CIS altogether, can be seen as a consequence of painful historical experiences at the hands of Imperial Russia and the USSR. Yet the states of the Transcaucasus, who have had a similar ordeal, have followed a different course of action. They have seemingly 'learnt' that for good or ill some form of alliance with Russia is unavoidable. Better to accept this than to resist and court disaster.

The security dilemma

The strategies outlined above bear directly upon the security dilemma, one of the quintessential concerns of international politics and a core idea in realist thinking. The security dilemma is a particularly troublesome and often perverse consequence of efforts to deal with the national security problem. John Herz describes it in the following way:

> (g)roups and individuals ... must be, and usually are, concerned about their security from being attacked, subjected, dominated, or annihilated by other groups and individuals. Striving to attain security from such attack, they are driven to acquire more and more power in order to escape the impact of the power of others.This, in turn, renders the others more insecure and compels them to prepare for the worst. Since none can ever feel entirely secure in such a world of competing units, power competition ensues, and the vicious circle of security and power accumulation is on.[104]

Applying the concept of the security dilemma to the FSU, Barry Posen suggests a situation of 'emerging anarchy' amongst the successor states owing to the disappearance of Soviet (central) power. In this situation he argues, the security dilemma is accentuated by three factors. The first of these – 'the indistinguishability of offence and defence' – arises because groups will tend to regard the military postures of others as offensive. This follows from the fact that the military equipment inherited from the collapsed predecessor state may be rudimentary – more suited to offence than defence; and because a warped reading of history will tend towards a prejudicial view of others. The second factor – 'the superiority of offensive over defensive action' – refers mainly to the existence of an 'offence-dominant world' when empires collapse. In other words, the existence of intermingled populations can lead to fears of rapid offensive actions by a state in preventive wars to protect stranded ethnic islands outside its new borders. The final factor concerns 'windows of vulnerability and opportunity'. In this case, insecurities arise as a consequence of the scramble for resources (military *matériel* included). The new states that obtain a position of superiority may expect to retain this position in the long term. If, however, they expect others to catch up this may provide an incentive to maximise gains while the advantage lasts. Incentives exist, therefore, for 'preventive expropriation' by one state towards another. Inevitably, this renders the weaker state highly suspicious of its stronger neighbours.[105]

Another scholar of the security dilemma is Robert Jervis. His ideas while forming the basis of Posen's pessimistic analysis, can also be deployed to reach rather more sanguine conclusions. Jervis has suggested that the security dilemma need not be axiomatic in an international system characterised by anarchy.[106] The degree to which it operates is influenced by 'whether offensive weapons and strategies can be distinguished from defensive ones, and whether the offence is more apparent than the defence'.[107] Mutual security is possible when weapons and policies aimed at security do not provide a capability to attack and are perceived as such by others. In such situations a state's actions are considered purely defensive and thus, according to Jervis 'the basic postulate of the security dilemma no longer applies. A state can increase its own security without decreasing that of others. A differentiation between offensive and defensive stances comes close to abolishing [the security dilemma]'.[108]

Distinguishing between the offence and the defence amongst the successor states seems particularly crucial in the case of nuclear weapons. Ukraine's (and to a lesser degree Kazakhstan's) ambiguous position on nuclear retention was perceived as destabilising both by Russia and the other nuclear powers, notably the US. A nuclear capability did little to enhance Ukrainian security and much to undermine it given the suspicions it aroused, particularly in Moscow where the defensive nature of Ukraine's nuclear weapons could not be distinguished from their offensive possibilities. By contrast, Belarus's clear signal that it intended to divest itself of its nuclear windfall raised no fears in Moscow and helped it consolidate a close strategic relationship with Russia. Turning to conventional arms, distinguishing the offensive and defensive seems particularly difficult in those cases where a successor state has inherited a large military capability. Here Ukraine and Belarus are relevant owing to their disproportionately large conventional arsenals and in the case of the former, a determination to hold on to a proportion of the BSF arguably more than adequate to meet its strategic-maritime needs. This inflated military capability has created concerns not only in Russia but also amongst East European states and NATO members. A second pattern of conventional armament has been evident in the Transcaucasus. Here the security dilemma has been particularly virulent among states of the region and their neighbours (Turkey and Iran) owing to the insecurities aroused by the scramble for former Soviet *matériel*. By contrast, in Central Asia and the Baltic region the security dilemma holds hardly at all; the defensive is superior to the offensive as a consequence of the undeveloped military potentials of states in the region.

As for Russia, to what degree has it been confronted by the security dilemma? Within the FSU, the sheer superiority of its military capabilities over and above those of the other successor states suggests that it cannot but be perceived as a potential aggressor. The offensive is clearly dominant over the defensive. This perception is reinforced by a judgement on the part of the non-Russian states of Moscow's desire to influence events in the near abroad and to retain a military presence there. The degree to which these perceptions undermine Russia's own military security is a moot point. It has certainly impeded military co-operation within the CIS framework and has utterly ruled out a military alliance with Ukraine, both of which can be regarded to Russia's disadvantage. Similarly, it has encouraged some of the successor states, notably the Baltics to increasingly view their security interests as lying in closer association with Western bodies (NATO, the Western European Union) and, in the case of Ukraine, in some arrangement with Eastern Europe. These developments again are to Russia's detriment. Yet, in other respects, the anticipated security problems have not been fully realised. The Central Asian states for instance have not been prompted into seeking external alliances or building up large military capabilities directed against Russia. Quite the reverse has happened, in fact, since they rely on Russian assistance for their own security. Even Kazakhstan poses little danger, having begun the surrender of its nuclear weapons and having realised the military uselessness of these weapons in any conflict with Russia.

As to Russia's relations with outside powers, its inheritance of much of the Soviet conventional and nuclear capabilities means its position is analogous to that of the USSR. Gorbachev appreciated early on the nature of security dilemma, hence the rejection of the concept of 'absolute security' and the concern with notions of defensive defence and so on. National security policy under Yeltsin seems to share many of these assumptions.[109] While post-Soviet Russia lacks a strategic formulation as sophisticated as the new political thinking, Russia's practical pursuit of START-1 and 2, CFE and CFE-1A and its interest in NACC, CSCE and, less enthusiastically, PFP suggest a recognition that its own security can be best improved by mutual measures with the Western powers. This co-operation has not removed the security dilemma (Russia's nuclear capability and vast conventional arsenal still arouses strong concern in NATO) but Yeltsin, like Gorbachev, has certainly moderated it. In the case of relations with China the security dilemma also remains. Measures to encourage mutual security have been taken, but nothing commensurate with the demilitarisation in relations with the West has been achieved.

Notes

1 A third category, intermediate nuclear forces, had been taken out of service under the terms of the 1987 INF Treaty.
2 W. Walker, 'Nuclear weapons and the former Soviet republics', *International Affairs*, 68:2 (1992), pp. 257–58, 261.
3 *Agreements on the Creation of the Commonwealth of Independent States Signed in December 1991/January 1992* (London, Russian Information Agency/Novosti, January 1992), p. 3. (Hereafter *Founding Agreements*.)
4 *Ibid*., pp. 14–15.
5 *Ibid*., p. 22. The agreement on strategic forces entered into force the moment it was signed. For this reason its legal status was superior to

the Alma–Ata agreement, which required ratification by all parties.

6 J.W.R. Lepingwell, 'Ukraine, Russia and the control of nuclear weapons', *Radio Free Europe /Radio Liberty (RFE/RL) Research Report*, 2:8 (1993), pp. 7–8.

7 *The Arms Control Reporter* (1992), pp. 611.B.725 and 611.B.733.

8 I.H. Daalder and T. Terriff, 'Nuclear arms control: finishing the Cold War agenda', *Arms Control*, 14:1 (1993), pp. 8–9.

9 This actually amounted to very little. It appears to have been the standard commitment contained in United Nations Security Council Resolution (UNSCR) 255 of June 1968, which obliges the permanent members of the Security Council (i.e. the nuclear-weapons states of China, France, the United Kingdom, the US and the then USSR) to act immediately 'in accordance with their obligations under the United Nations Charter' in the event of a nuclear attack or threat of such attack against a non-nuclear weapon state. See, E. Bailey, 'The NPT and security guarantees', in D. Howlett and J. Simpson (eds), *Nuclear Non-Proliferation. A Reference Handbook* (Harlow, Essex, Longman, 1992), p. 52.

10 *Arms Control Today* (June 1992), pp. 34–37.

11 T. Bernauer *et al.*, 'Strategic arms control and the NPT: status and implementation', in G. Allison *et al.* (eds), *Co-operative Denuclearisation. From Pledges to Deeds* (Cambridge, MA, Centre for Science and International Affairs, Harvard University, 1993), pp. 31–32.

12 Cited in K. Mihalisko, 'Security issues in Ukraine and Belarus', in R. Cowen Karp (ed.), *Central and Eastern Europe. The Challenge of Transition* (Oxford, Oxford University Press/Sipri, 1993), p. 243.

13 START required the destruction only of missile silos, submarine tubes and strategic bombers; see Bernauer *et al.*, 'Strategic arms control', p. 29.

14 *Diplomaticheskii vestnik*, 12 (1992), p. 51.

15 Statement of the Ukrainian Mission to the UN dated 12 November 1992, cited in Lepingwell, 'Ukraine, Russia and the control of nuclear weapons', p. 14.

16 *Ibid.*, pp. 13–15.

17 In deference to Ukraine, the US also initially refused to sign the agreement on American purchases of enriched uranium from Russia until Kiev was guaranteed a portion of the proceeds. The agreement Concerning the Disposition of Highly Enriched Uranium Extracted from Nuclear Weapons was finally signed in February 1993 and committed the US to purchase 500 metric tonnes of uranium over twenty years. The process was not to begin until arrangements had been agreed between Russia and the three other nuclear successor states on the division of the proceeds. In October 1992 the US also allocated a fur-

ther $400 million to assist disarmament efforts in the FSU, bringing the total to $800 million.

18 T. Kuzio, 'Nuclear weapons and military policy in independent Ukraine', *The Harriman Institute Forum*, 6:9 (1993), p. 11.

19 Foreign Broadcast Information Service: FBIS -SOV-93-001, 4 January 1993, pp. 2–13.

20 K.E. Sorokin, 'Russia after the crisis: the nuclear strategy debate', *Orbis*, 38:1 (1994), pp. 28–29.

21 The Kazakh parliament ratified START-1, along with the Lisbon Protocol, in July 1992. As for Russia, its Parliament ratified START-1 in November 1992. Although Russia inherited the USSR's treaty obligations, this step was necessary because the old Soviet legislature had not ratified the treaty.

22 The exact details were not made public pending START-1 ratification, but appeared to be the standard security guarantee refered to in note 9. See, *RFE/RL News Briefs*, 1–4 June 1993, p. 11.

23 *Izvestiya*, 2 April 1993.

24 Under START-1 a sub-limit of 1,100 was placed on warheads carried by mobile ICBMs (SS-24, SS-25), necessitating a reduction of at least 160 of the 1,260 held by then Soviet forces. Technically, the 1,100 limit could be met by reductions in the 300 single-warhead SS-25 (over two-thirds of which were located in Russia, the remainder in Belarus).

25 U. Markus, 'Recent defense developments in Ukraine', *RFE/RL Research Report*, 3:4 (1994), p. 29.

26 'The Ukrainian parliament's resolution on START-1 ratification', *RFE/RL Research Report*, 3:4 (1994), p. 9.

27 The Trilateral Statement is reprinted in, *SIPRI Yearbook 1994. World Armaments and Disarmament* (Oxford, Oxford University Press/Sipri, 1994), pp. 677–78. The Russian–American uranium agreement is described in note 17.

28 In the documents signed in Budapest the US, Russia and the United Kingdom extended security guarantees to Ukraine. France and China, the other two nuclear powers, had issued similar guarantees shortly before the summit.

29 Sorokin, 'Russia after the crisis', pp. 25, 31.

30 *Current Digest of the Post-Soviet Press (CDSP)*, 45:44 (1993), p. 11; Lepingwell, 'Ukraine, Russia and the control of nuclear weapons', p. 24.

31 *CDSP*, 45:46 (1993), p. 12.

32 The good showing of the ultra-nationalist Liberal Democratic Party in the Russian parliamentary elections of December 1993 prompted one Ukrainian deputy to announce 'Maybe now the world will under-

stand why Ukraine should keep its nuclear weapons'. Cited in *The Guardian*, 14 December 1993, p. 13.

33 J.J. Mearsheimer, 'The case for a Ukrainian nuclear deterrent', *Foreign Affairs*, 72:3 (1993), p. 56.

34 P. van Ham, *Ukraine, Russia and European Security: Implications for Western Policy* (Paris, Institute for Security Studies, Western European Union, Chaillot Papers 13, 1994), pp. 19–21; C. Bluth, 'What do you do with a nuclear arsenal?', *New Scientist*, 18 July 1992, p. 27.

35 This stance is redolent of what R.J. Art refers to as 'swaggering'. This is one function of military power, whereby military might is utilised to enhance a state's stature in the eyes of others in order that its interests are taken more seriously into account. See his, 'To what ends military power?', *International Security*, 4:4 (1980), p. 11.

36 *The Christian Science Monitor*, 14–20 May 1993, p. 7.

37 The other two fleets were the Northern and Pacific; these were headquartered and serviced at Russian ports.

38 *Founding Agreements*, pp. 21, 24.

39 S. Foye, 'End of CIS command heralds new Russian defense policy?', *RFE/RL Research Report*, 2:27 (1993), p. 48.

40 An agreement reached at the CIS Summit in January 1993, committed Russia, Uzbekistan, Kazakhstan and Kyrgyzstan to dispatch 500 troops each to secure the Tajik–Afghan border. Under an agreement the following September, these four states plus Tajikistan decided to set up a coalition force under the command of a Russian Colonel–General, Boris Pyankov. By the end of 1993 this numbered some 6,500 personnel, of whom 5,500 were drawn from the Russian 201st Motorised Infantry Division. (The summit of CIS heads of state in October 1994 extended the mandate of the CIS force until the end of June 1995.)

41 Detail in this section is drawn largely from *RFE/RL Research Report*, 2:25 (1993), special on 'Post-Soviet armies', and R. Allison, *Military Forces in the Soviet Successor States* (London, The International Institute of Strategic Studies/Brassey's, Adelphi Paper 280, 1993).

42 Kuzio, 'Nuclear weapons', p. 6.

43 S. Foye, 'The Ukrainian armed forces: problems and prospects', *RFE/RL Research Report*, 1:26 (1992), p. 58.

44 The oath did not apply to troops guarding nuclear weapons.

45 S.M. Meyer, 'The military', in T.J. Colton and R. Levgold (eds), *After the Soviet Union. From Empire to Nations* (New York and London, W.W. Norton, 1992), pp. 125–26.

46 The detail which follows owes much to R. Woff, *Commonwealth High Command and National Defence Forces* (Sandhurst, Soviet Studies Research Centre, May 1992), pp. 8–12; and J.W.R. Lepingwell,

'Restructuring the Russian military', *RFE/RL Research Report*, 2:25 (1993).

47 *RFE/RL Research Report*, 1:30 (1992), p. 57.

48 S. McMichael, 'Russia's new military doctrine', *RFE/RL Research Report*, 1:40 (1992), pp. 45–50.

49 Defence Minister Grachev cited in *RFE/RL News Briefs*, 8–12 February 1993, p. 8, and Yeltsin's comments cited in *CDSP*, 45:21 (1993), p. 16.

50 See the comments of First Deputy Minister of Foreign Affairs Anatoly Adamishin, in *Moscow News*, 13 June 1993, p. 1.

51 *The Observer*, 17 October 1993, p. 17; *The Washington Post*, 3 February 1994, p. A21.

52 This was comprised largely of the Russian contribution to the Soviet defence budget.

53 Owing to the ambiguities of the official figures it is difficult to calculate accurately whether a real fall or rise in defence expenditure has occurred. According to the International Institute of Strategic Studies '(s)ince 1992 ... Russian defence budgets have been effectively static in real terms with perhaps a small increase in 1994'. *The Military Balance, 1994/1995* (London, International Institute of Strategic Studies/Brassey's, 1994), pp. 282–85.

54 S. Deger, 'World military expenditure', in *SIPRI Yearbook 1993. World Armaments and Disarmament* (Oxford, Oxford University Press/Sipri, 1993), p. 360.

55 *RFE/RL Daily Report*, 22 August 1994.

56 *The Economist*, 28 August 1993, p. 19.

57 R.J. Krickus, 'Latvia's "Russian question"', *RFE/RL Research Report*, 2:18 (1993), p. 31.

58 *The Observer*, 22 November 1992, p. 19.

59 D. Bungs, 'Progress on withdrawal from the Baltic states', *RFE/RL Research Report*, 2:25, 1993, p. 52.

60 *The Independent*, 31 October 1992, p. 12.

61 *Keesing's Record of World Events*, June 1993, p. 39524.

62 D. Clarke, 'The saga of the Black Sea Fleet', *RFE/RL Research Report*, 1:4 (1992), p. 46.

63 Sir James Eberle, 'Russia and Ukraine: what to do with the Black Sea Fleet?', *The World Today* (August/September 1992), p. 159.

64 *Izvestiya*, 4 January 1992, p. 1.

65 D.L. Clarke, 'The battle for the Black Sea Fleet', *RFE/RL Research Report*, 1:5 (1992), p. 55. (The BSF was declared nuclear free in early May.)

66 *Izvestiya*, 9 January 1992, p. 5; *The Guardian*, 10 January 1992, p. 1.

67 FBIS-SOV-93-003, 6 January 1993, p. 5.

68 It should be made clear that the ATTU region does not include Russian territory east of the Urals and hence CFE and CFE 1A provisions exclude Russian weaponry and personnel deployed in Russia's Siberian, Transbaikal and Far Eastern military districts, which includes the still substantial forces directed against China.

69 *The Military Balance, 1992–1993* (London, The International Institute of Strategic Studies/Brassey's, 1992), pp. 237–41.

70 The Tashkent Document is reprinted in *SIPRI Yearbook 1993*, pp. 671–77.

71 'Treaty on CIS Collective Security', reprinted in *RFE/RL Research Report*, 2:25 (1993), pp. 4–5.

72 On the term *security complex*, see B. Buzan, *People, States and Fear. An Agenda for International Security Studies in the Post-Cold War Era* (New York, Harvester Wheatsheaf, second edition, 1991), pp. 186–94.

73 British Broadcasting Corporation, Summary of World Broadcasts, SU/1262 A1/1, 23 December 1991.

74 Russia met its equipment reduction obligations under Phase I of the treaty. By mid-November 1993 it had eliminated from use 804 tanks, 2,368 armoured combat vehicles, 173 artillery pieces, 25 attack helicopters and 324 fighter aircraft. Thereafter, Russian compliance has been linked to the so-called 'flank issue', involving a demand on the part of Moscow for a revision of zonal sublimits to allow greater deployments of treaty-limited equipment in the 'northern' and 'southern' flanks of the CFE Treaty's zone of application. The southern flank is considered especially significant as it includes the unstable Transcaucasus and Russia's own north Caucasus region. The military operation in Chechnya launched in December 1994 placed Russia well above the zonal sublimit. This, coupled with Russian deployments in Georgia and Armenia (which count against Russian limits) mean that without a revision of the treaty (something the NATO countries have been reluctant to endorse) Russia will be in breach of the CFE flank limit by the final implementation date of November 1995. (For details see *SPIRI Yearbook 1994*, pp. 568–72 and D.L. Clarke, 'Uncomfortable partners', *Transition*, 1:2 (1995), p. 31.)

75 R.D. Asmus *et al.*, 'Building a new NATO', *Foreign Affairs*, 72:4 (1993), pp. 28–40.

76 S. Crow, 'Russian views on an eastward expansion of NATO', *RFE/RL Research Report*, 2:41 (1993), p. 22; *CDSP*, 46:8 (1994), p. 13.

77 *CDSP*, 45:47 (1993), p. 12.

78 A. Pushkov, 'Russia and the West: an endangered relationship?', *NATO Review*, (February 1994), p. 22. All three Baltic states had made clear their intention to join NATO. Lithuania made a formal application for membership in January 1994.

79 *Moscow News*, 24 September 1993, p. 5.
80 M. Mihalka, 'Squaring the circle: NATO's offer to the east', *RFE/RL Research Report*, 3:12 (1994), p. 1.
81 *The Observer*, 24 April 1994, p. 16 and 22 May 1994, p. 19 (citing Yeltsin). See also Chapter 3 for Russia's notion of its great power status.
82 M. Mihalisko, 'European–Russian security and NATO's partnership for peace', *RFE/RL Research Report*, 3:33 (1994), pp. 44–45.
83 *The Guardian*, 6 December 1994, p. 20.
84 Cited in Crow, 'Russian views on eastward expansion', p. 23.
85 The 1961 Treaty had obligated the USSR to come to the rescue of North Korea in the event of aggression.
86 *RFE/RL Research Report*, 1:46 (1992), p. 48.
87 I.J. Brzezinski, 'Polish–Ukrainian relations: Europe's neglected strategic axis', *Survival*, 35:3 (1993), p. 27.
88 *RFE/RL News Briefs*, 26–30 April 1993, p. 17 and 3–7 May 1993, p. 10.
89 A.A. Reisch, 'Hungarian–Ukrainian relations continue to develop', *RFE/RL Research Report*, 2:16 (1993), pp. 22–27.
90 B. Brown, 'Central Asia: The economic crisis deepens', *RFE/RL Research Report*, 3:1 (1994), p. 62.
91 B. Hocking and M. Smith, *World Politics. An Introduction to International Relations* (New York: Harvester Wheatsheaf, 1990), pp. 127–28.
92 Buzan, *People, States and Fear*, pp. 117–18.
93 Adapted from K. Holsti, *International Politics. A Framework for Analysis* (London, Prentice-Hall, sixth edition, 1990), pp. 86–95.
94 K.W. Deutsch, *The Analysis of International Relations* (Englewood Cliffs, Prentice-Hall, second edition, 1978), p. 194.
95 Holsti, *International Politics*, pp. 86–87.
96 *Ibid.*, p. 87; Buzan, *Peoples, States and Fear*, pp. 331–33.
97 G.H. Snyder, 'Alliance theory: a neorealist first cut', *Journal of International Affairs*, 44:1 (1990), p. 110.
98 C.W. Kegley and E.R. Wittkopf, *World Politics. Trend and Transformation* (St Martin's Press, New York, fourth edition, 1993), pp. 466–67.
99 S.M. Walt, 'Alliance formation and the balance of world power', *International Organisation*, 39:4 (1985), pp. 3–43.
100 S.R. David, 'Explaining Third World alignment', *World Politics*, 43:2 (1991), pp. 235–36.
101 Walt, 'Alliance formation', pp. 18–21.
102 David, 'Explaining Third World alignment', pp. 236–37 and Walt, 'Alliance formation', pp. 18–21, 24–27.

103 D. Reiter, 'Learning, realism, and alliances: the weight of the shadow of the past', *World Politics*, 46:4 (1994), p. 490.
104 J. Herz, 'Idealist internationalism and the security dilemma', *World Politics*, 2:2 (1950), p. 157.
105 B.R. Posen, 'The security dilemma and ethnic conflict', *Survival*, 35:1 (1993), pp. 29–35.
106 R. Jervis, 'Security regimes', *International Organisation*, 36:2 (1982), p. 362.
107 R. Jervis, 'From balance to concert: a study of international security co-operation', *World Politics*, 38:1 (1988), p. 62.
108 R. Jervis, 'Co-operation under the security dilemma', *World Politics*, 30:2 (1978), p. 199.
109 Yeltsin, for instance, in early 1992 referred to 'minimal defence sufficiency' as the basis of the strength, structure and financing of the Russian armed forces. *Diplomaticheskii vestnik*, 4–5 (29 February–March 15 1992), p. 49.

Recommended reading

R. Allison, *Military Forces of the Soviet Successor States* (London, The International Institute of Strategic Studies, Adelphi Paper, No. 280, 1993).

T.P. Johnson and S.E. Miller (eds), *Russian Security after the Cold War* (Washington, DC, Brassey's, 1994).

RFE/RL Research Report, 2:25 (1993), special edition on 'Post-Soviet Armies'; 2:8 (1993), special edition on 'negotiating nuclear disarmament' and 3:4 (1994), section on 'Ukrainian security issues'.

SIPRI Yearbook. World Armaments and Disarmament (various years, Oxford, Oxford University Press/Sipri).

T. Taylor, *European Security and the Former Soviet Union. Dangers, Opportunities, Gambles* (London, Royal Institute of International Affairs, 1994).

P. van Ham, *Ukraine, Russia and European Security: Implications for Western Policy* (Paris, The Institute for Security Studies, The Western European Union, Chaillot Papers, No. 13, 1994).

5

Diplomacy and conflict resolution: the Soviet legacy and the challenges of the post-Cold War world

Conflict or disagreement was much in evidence over the disposition of military assets within the former Soviet Union (FSU) detailed in the previous chapter. A similar pattern will become apparent when we consider economic issues in Chapter 6. The purpose here is to consider disputes of a particularly intractable nature – those arising from issues of statehood, territory, ethnic/religious solidarity and the composition of governments. These kinds of dispute are the most impervious to co-operative resolution, are usually characterised by active efforts to subvert the status quo and often result in open warfare between states or between rival groups within a state.[1] In this connection, four categories of dispute are relevant to the FSU and the relations of the successor states with the wider world. The first combines aspects of both the FSU's 'inward' and 'outward' orientations, the latter three fall more clearly within the 'outward orientation':

1 disputes involving open warfare, either between or within the successor states;
2 disputed territorial claims involving one or more of the successor states plus an outside party;
3 wars in the Third World, at one time fuelled by the East–West antagonism of the Cold War or Sino–Soviet rivalry; these formerly involved the Soviet Union militarily or diplomatically and since the end of 1991, have entailed a Russian role;
4 the separate case of the former Yugoslavia, where wars of succession have proven the single most important test case, involving Russian participation, of international mediation and peacekeeping in the post-Cold War period.

Efforts aimed at conflict resolution are detailed in the following sections. These correspond to the four categories noted above.

Disputes involving open warfare, either between or within the successor states

The 'internal' frontiers of the USSR were administrative only. With the USSR's collapse they were upgraded, at a stroke, to the status of inter-state borders. Since territorial integrity is a touchstone of independence and statehood, the successor states have been extremely sensitive to any questioning of these frontiers either externally by other states or internally by opposition groups.

In an effort to avoid opening up a Pandora's Box of rival claims, the founding agreement of the Commonwealth of Independent States (CIS) affirmed that members of the Commonwealth would respect territorial integrity and the inviolability of existing borders (see Chapter 3, p. 107). This was, however, only a statement of principle. In the post-Soviet period rival territorial claims have, in fact, bedevilled relations between a number of the successor states. Russo–Ukrainian ties have been severely strained by the wrangle over the Crimea (see Chapter 3, pp. 102–4), while Russia's already poor relations with Estonia and Latvia (two states outside the CIS) have been blighted further by border questions.[2] In Central Asia, parts of Kyrgyzstan's borders with Tajikistan, Uzbekistan and Kazakhstan have also provoked disagreement.

Yet no matter how deep-seated these border disputes, they have remained peaceable and contained. The case studies considered below are different in that they have coupled two important characteristics: violent, often prolonged, armed conflict and third-party intervention. This latter feature is especially significant in that the conflicts themselves are essentially internal in origin, being fuelled by demands for greater autonomy and/or secession amongst minorities. These demands, however, have had external consequences, raising the possibility of a redrawing of inter-state frontiers between successor states, inviting outside military and diplomatic action (both by other successor states and the wider international community), and, in some cases, pitting one successor state against another by virtue of support for political proxies.

The war in Nagorno–Karabakh

Many conflicts first became bloodily apparent during the Gorbachev period, while the circumstances upon which they have fed are the product of inequities committed under earlier phases of Soviet rule. The roots of the Nagorno–Karabakh dispute, for instance, are to be found in the manner of the Bolsheviks' consolidation of power in the former Tsarist territories of the Transcaucasus. Nagorno–Karabakh was initially placed within the boundaries of Soviet Armenia, a decision which seemed entirely rational in view of the territory's overwhelmingly Armenian population. In 1923, however, this decision was reversed and administration was granted to Azerbaijan on the grounds that it was economically better positioned to provide for the Karabakh Armenians. Decades of festering resentment followed, fed by discrimination in education and employment, economic neglect and difficulties in negotiating the patronage and social networks of local bureaucracy.[3] This, in turn, exacerbated an already deep-seated ethnic divide. Some Armenians, for instance, tended to view the ethnically Turkic Azeris as somehow culpable in the Turkish massacre of Armenians during World War I. Perhaps less irrationally, the dilution of the formerly majority Armenian population in Nakhichevan (another territory which had been placed under Azeri rule) was seen as a prelude to the eventual fate of Nagorno–Karabakh itself, where by the early 1980s the Armenian share of the population had fallen by nearly a quarter.[4]

Violence between the two communities erupted periodically throughout the 1960s and 1970s, but it was not until the Gorbachev period afforded the opportunity for relatively open expression that the dispute reached crisis proportions. In 1988 75,000 Karabakh Armenians signed a petition in favour of transferring Nagorno–Karabakh to Armenia. A resolution of the Nagorno–Karabakh parliament demanded the same action. Moscow's response was to affirm the territorial status quo and to impose a temporary form of 'special administration' in the region in order to stem a rising tide of inter-communal violence. By the end of 1989 some 330,000 Armenian and Azeri refugees had fled their place of residence to seek security in their 'home' republics. The Armenian parliament's proclamation in December of a United Republic of Armenia embracing the disputed territory precipitated further hostilities, spearheaded by what were, in effect, private armies equipped by ethnic sympathisers within locally based Soviet armed forces. In the latter months of 1991 the situation continued to deteriorate. In September 1991, the Nagorno–Karabakh parliament announced the creation of an independent Nagorno–Karabakh Republic, to which the Azeri authorities responded by abolishing the autonomous status of the territory which, at least nominally, still fell within its jurisdiction. Side by side with these political moves went a heightening of military engagements, prompting Gorbachev to warn in November that Armenia and Azerbaijan were 'on the brink of real war.'[5]

The independence of Armenia and Azerbaijan at the end of 1991 transformed the Nagorno–Karabakh dispute from one regarded jealously by Moscow as an internal Soviet issue, to an object of international diplomatic activity. A variety of regional powers and international organisations have sought to mediate a settlement. Collectively, these efforts have proven unable to engineer a lasting peace and the war has continued unabated. The reasons for this diplomatic failure will form part of the discussion below on complexities of conflict resolution in the FSU. At this point it is worth considering the motives and limitations of the various actors involved in the conflict in order to ascertain some sense of the increasing complexity of the dispute during its post-Soviet phase.

Turning first to Russia, its entry into the Nagorno–Karabakh peace process began some months prior to the demise of the USSR. In September 1991, Boris Yeltsin, in conjunction with Kazakhstan's President Nursultan Nazarbaev brokered an agreement between Armenia and Azerbaijan, which involved, notably, a pledge by Armenia to revoke its territorial claim to the Karabakh enclave. This statement of principles, however, did not halt the violence. Following a failed ceasefire brokered by Foreign Minister Kozyrev in February 1992, a period of Russian inactivity set in (owing, it was claimed by critics of the Russian Foreign Ministry to Russia's preoccupation with relations with the West).[6] Russia returned to the fray in September, when Defence Minister Pavel Grachev helped mediate a ceasefire. Subsequent efforts during 1993–94 involved Russia in joint initiatives with Turkey, the US, and with Iran. Moscow has also pursued a direct line to the combatants through Yeltsin's personal mediator for Nagorno–Karabakh, Vladimir Kazimirov. The military, however, has arguably been the most effective actor; in May 1994, Grachev mediated yet another ceasefire agreement.

The involvement of Russia in the mediation process has been the result of a number of factors. In the first place, with the disappearance of a Soviet role, Russia simply assumed the status of the dominant force in the Transcaucasus – the only power with sufficient influence over all the warring parties to mediate and possibly enforce a settlement. *Force majeure* alone, however, tells us little of Russian motives. Moscow's activity in the region has not simply been the product of irresistible opportunity, but has been consciously driven by an active appreciation of the possible dangers presented by the conflict and by the gains to be had from influence building in this corner of the near abroad.

For Russia, the war over Nagorno–Karabakh presents a situation in which three unwelcome precedents could be realised. First, recognition of the enclave's independence would signify a process of national self-assertion beyond that sanctioned by the break-up of the USSR into its constituent republics. The dismantling of the successor states on ethnic lines could, it is feared, encourage secessionist claims within Russia itself. Such claims had already assumed alarming proportions with the *de facto* secession of part of the autonomous republic of Checheno–Ingushetia in Russia's northern Caucasus in late 1991.[7] Second, the conflict offers neighbouring Iran and Turkey an opportunity to flex their regional influence. This has been particularly worrying for Russia in the case of Azerbaijan, a country which, under President Abulfaz Elchibey, had eschewed membership of the CIS and had voiced strong affinities with Turkey (see Chapter 3, p. 115). The Turkish secular model of political development, while less alarming than the avowedly Islamic variant offered by Iran, has nonetheless been considered an antidote to Russian influence. The emergence of a Turkish–Azeri axis, moreover, could only encourage a growing role for Ankara further afield amongst the states of Central Asia. A final cause for Russian anxiety has been the growing Western interest in the Transcaucasus. Western attention has in fact been born of similar concerns to those held by Russia (notably a suspicion of Iranian ambition), and Russia has been prepared to co-operate diplomatically with the US over Nagorno–Karabakh. Moscow, however, has strongly opposed any suggestions of a Western peacekeeping role in the area for fear of granting the North Atlantic Treaty Organisation (NATO) and other organisations access to the near abroad.[8]

Turning to Turkish involvement, it has undertaken diplomacy

towards Nagorno–Karabakh through the efforts of the Minsk Group of the Conference on Security and Co-operation in Europe (CSCE), set up in the spring of 1992 to prepare a formal peace conference and, for a period during 1993, via trilateral mediation alongside Russia and the US. It would be easy to simplify such involvement in the Transcaucasus as an expression of pan-Turkic sentiment (aimed at Turkic-speaking Azeris) or as part of some grand struggle for influence amongst Muslim populations waged against Iran. On both counts, however, qualifications are necessary. The notion of a Turkish sphere of influence stretching throughout the Transcaucasus and Central Asia has struck a chord with domestic public opinion but has been embraced only cautiously by the Turkish government. To do otherwise would complicate relations with Turkey's NATO allies, with neighbouring Armenia – a country that had experienced a long and painful relationship with Ankara (see Chapter 3, p. 115) – and, most importantly, with Russia.[9] Turkey has received sufficiently severe warnings from Moscow concerning the Transcaucasus to deter it from an interventionist policy. Then CIS Commander-in-Chief Shaposhnikov stated in 1992 that any military actions mounted by Ankara in favour of the Azeri side would be regarded as an act of war against Armenia and would thus trigger the mutual defence clauses of the CIS Collective Security Treaty. Shaposhnikov's ultimatum was less concerned with solidarity for Armenia than holding Turkey at bay from a traditionally Russian area of interest.[10] This was not just bluster. The removal of Azeri President Elchibey from office in June 1993 was reportedly engineered by the Russian embassy in Baku in order to instigate a shift in Azerbaijan's foreign policy orientation from Turkey to Russia.[11]

Erring on the side of caution, Ankara's policy towards the war over Nagorno–Karabakh has officially been one of neutrality. Lapses into a pro-Azeri position (requests for United Nations Security Council action to punish Armenian belligerence, the mobilisation of troops along the Armenian border and the suspension of humanitarian aid to Armenia) appear to have been largely taken in response to domestic popular opinion.[12] Neutrality has also reflected Turkey's primary, economic interest in the successor states (see Chapter 6, p. 311). An even-handed diplomacy which contributes to peace in Nagorno–Karabakh is a prerequisite for the expansion of Turkey's commercial ties with *both* Azerbaijan and Armenia. Considerations regarding Iran have also been of a practical nature. Turkey's rivalry with Tehran has less to do with a competition between alternative models of governing Islamic societies than with a desire to counter Iranian interference in Turkey itself (in the form of support of Turkish Islamic fundamentalists and the separatist Kurdish Workers' Party).[13]

As for Iran, its interest in Nagorno–Karabakh also reflects a series of practical considerations. The termination of its exhausting war with Iraq in 1988 and the death of spiritual leader Ayatollah Khomenei the following year, spelt an end to the crusading element of Iranian foreign policy. Even if Iran has been inclined towards an expansionist policy in the Transcaucasus, an extension of its influence there on the basis of a religious appeal is problematic. This is obviously so in Christian Armenia. But even in Azerbaijan, whose observant population shares with Iran a Muslim Shia faith, the religious factor is of only marginal significance. Its potential influence as an Iranian bridgehead has been balanced by the importance of Islam for much of the population as a component of national culture rather than religious belief. The ethnic factor too is a dubious basis for extending Iran's influence. The Azeri population has a Turkic, as opposed to Iranian, self-image.

Iran's strategy towards the Nagorno–Karabakh conflict has largely, in fact, been one of containment. Although more inclined towards the Azeri cause, its prime objective is the restoration of stability in the region. It mediated two ceasefires in 1992 and in January 1994 proposed talks on the long-term status of Nagorno–Karabakh. For Tehran, peace in the Transcaucasus would reduce the likelihood of a Turkish military intervention (and thus the slim possibility of a NATO power establishing bases near Iran's northern frontier) and would prevent an overspill into Iran of refugees encamped in southern Azerbaijan who might excite separatist feelings among Iranian Azeris.

Turning to the parties to the conflict itself, in the case of Armenia, the Armenian Pan-National Movement (APNM) had assumed power in 1990 committed to the annexation of Nagorno–Karabakh. It was not without significance that the movement's leader (and subsequent victor of the October 1991 Armenian Presidential elections), Levon Ter-Petrosyan, was a former member of the Karabakh Committee. By late 1991, however, Ter-Petrosyan's position had moderated substantially. Territorial claims were eschewed in favour of a more elastic formulation that stressed the Karabakh Armenians' right of self-determination. The status of Nagorno–Karabakh would be decided by the enclave's population following a cessation of military hostilities (to which end it welcomed international mediation) and negotiations with the Azeri authorities. In line with this stance, the Armenian leadership has recognised neither Azerbaijan's claim to the territory nor the independence of the self-proclaimed Nagorno–Karabakh Republic. Keeping its options open, at the April 1994 CIS heads of state summit, Armenia was the only member state not to append its signature to a declaration on the integrity and inviolability of CIS borders.

The moderation of the Armenian position has been based on a number of considerations. First, a desire to improve relations with Ankara (see Chapter 3, p. 115). Second, a calculation that any solution to the conflict would allow the lifting of the crippling economic blockade imposed against Armenia by Azerbaijan. (Baku had supplied Armenia with around 80 per cent of its gas supplies). Third, the need to reverse the country's diplomatic isolation stemming from military support of the Karabakh cause. Although the Armenian government has denied its armed forces have played any direct role in the war, it has nonetheless been held responsible for the actions of the Karabakh 'defence forces' and the dispatch of 'volunteers' recruited in Armenia.[14] The fact, moreover, that the main channel of arms and other supplies to Karabakh has originated in Armenia indicates a degree of officially sanctioned military involvement, not altogether in keeping with Armenia's disclaimers.

As for Azerbaijan, it too has suffered greatly from the war. Azeri military losses have contributed to the removal of three of Azerbaijan's post-Soviet presidents (the former first secretary of the Azeri Communist Party, Ayaz Mutalibov, in March 1992, his replacement, acting President Yagub Mamedov, in May and the leader of the Azerbaijani Popular Front [AzPF], Abulfaz Elchibey, in June 1993). Despite the huge price of the war, Azerbaijan has remained adamantly opposed to any loss of sovereignty over Nagorno–Karabakh. The stance of the three fallen leaders towards the enclave was essentially similar, embracing a commitment to Azerbaijan's territorial integrity and ruling out any form of self-government for the Karabakh Armenians beyond a degree of cultural autonomy. This position left little room for compromise and rendered Azerbaijan suspicious of diplomatic mediation, which it saw as a process likely to alter the political and legal status quo in Nagorno–Karabakh.

Azerbaijan's strategy, particularly under Elchibey, was based on negotiating from a position of strength. The premises of this approach soon proved fatally misguided. Turkish sympathy, which Elchibey attempted to cultivate, did not extend to credible military support. Any hopes, meanwhile, that the Azeri armed forces would be galvanised into an effective fighting machine under AzPF leadership were dashed in the face of a series of dramatic military victories by the Karabakh 'defence forces'. In May 1992, they defeated Azeri troops in Shusha (the last Azeri stronghold within Nagorno–Karabakh), the following month they established the Lachin corridor linking the enclave with Armenia, and by April of 1993 Karabakh units controlled some 10 per cent of Azeri territory beyond the enclave.

The ouster of Elchibey in June 1993 altered Azeri policy in some respects. His successor, Geidar Aliev, a former first secretary of the Azeri Communist Party, immediately recognised the indispensability of Russia's role in the framing of a settlement. Co-operation with the Russians, however, carried a price. Since it involved the possibility of Russian/CIS peacekeepers, it was construed by the political opposition in Azerbaijan as opening the door to the return of a Russian military presence. In protest Aliev's opponents staged mass demonstrations in May 1994. Hence, a year after assuming power, Aliev's position was no more favourable than that of his predecessors. An internal settlement with the Nagorno–Karabakh forces appeared as distant as ever, Azeri military losses had not been reversed and one of the most credible routes to a settlement appeared cut-off by internal opposition.

The real obstacle to the framing of a settlement, however, has been the secessionist leadership in Nagorno–Karabakh itself, which has displayed a maximalist bent at odds with the more pragmatic inclinations of the Ter-Petrosyan Administration in Armenia. The aggressive military actions of the Karabakh forces and their position that any solution should recognise the independence of the enclave has doomed many peace efforts to failure. The removal of the Nagorno–Karabakh leader, Georgy Petrosian, in mid-1993 following a visit to the enclave by the Armenian President – his first – did pave the way for a somewhat more accommodationist position under the new leadership of Karen Baburyan. His signature of a CSCE peace plan in June 1993 was, however, immediately undermined by a renewed Karabakh offensive to the south-west of the enclave. In subsequent negotiations mediated by Russia and the CSCE, the Karabakh Armenians have shown moderation to the degree that they have been prepared to adhere to the May 1994 Russian-mediated ceasefire agreement and to accept in principle the notion of multilateral negotiations on Nagorno–Karabakh's political status. Observers have noted, however, that this stance is aimed at translating military achievements into political gains.[15] Should the Karabakh Armenians fail to achieve what they might consider due political recognition, this raises the risky scenario that any long-term settlement would have to be imposed upon them. In this light, a possible settlement would be a bilateral Armenian–Azeri matter, and would require either: (1) the forceful disarming of Karabakh forces, involving Armenian and Azeri co-operation, perhaps with Russian or United Nations (UN)-mandated assistance, or (2) the exhaustion of Karabakh resources, through, for instance the pressures of economic collapse or a deliberate strategy by Armenia of turning off the tap of military and economic assistance.

Georgia's three-way civil war

Georgia has been blighted by three devastating armed conflicts. These wars have essentially been internal in nature. Each, however, has had important international dimensions, being subject to outside mediation and/or external military interference.

The first war, that waged against Georgia's erstwhile President Zviad Gamsakhurdia, until his death in January 1994, was primarily political in nature. Gamsakhurdia, who had led the Round Table–Free Georgia coalition to victory in republican elections in October 1990 and had triumphed in presidential elections in May the following year, was ousted from power in January 1992. Gamsakhurdia's period of rule has been described by one observer as 'dictatorial and paranoid'.[16] Arrests of political opponents, censorship of the media, the postponement of local elections and the appointment of prefects to govern the provinces, characterised a ruthless drive to consolidate personal authority. In addition, the Georgian leader abandoned electoral pledges to introduce significant economic reforms such as land privatisation and, out of an inflated sense of Georgian nationalism, adopted a centralising policy towards the three autonomies of Adzharia, Abkhazia and South Ossetia.[17] In conjunction with a temporising attitude towards the August coup (see

Chapter 2, p. 72), these actions whittled away the popular base upon which Gamsakhurdia had been elected and spurred into action the opposition of a diversity of nascent parties, disillusioned government ministers, factions of the Georgian National Guard and unofficial military formations. An attack on the parliamentary building finally forced Gamsakhurdia to flee in January 1992, first to Armenia and, after a brief return to Georgia, to Chechnya in Russia, where he enjoyed the protection of the self-declared republic's leader Dzhokar Dudayev.

The authoritarianism of Gamsakhurdia and the unconstitutional nature of his removal, meant Georgia entered the post-Soviet period as an international outcast. This pariah status was compounded by Gamsakhurdia's refusal to take Georgia into the CIS at the time of the organisation's foundation. Only with the return of Eduard Shevardnadze, Gorbachev's foreign minister and former first secretary of the Georgian Communist Party, to head a 'government of national salvation' in March 1992, did Georgia obtain international diplomatic recognition.[18] Internal legitimacy, however, was more problematic, although parliamentary elections in October and Shevardnadze's simultaneous election as chair of the legislature went some way to returning Georgia's politics to a semblance of constitutional order.

While Shevardnadze was consolidating power, the exiled Gamsakhurdia continued to demand his own restoration to office. This was backed by periodic military actions mounted by armed 'Zviadists' in Mingrelia, a region of western Georgia fiercely loyal to the deposed president. This portion of Georgia's civil war reached a critical juncture in the autumn of 1993. Emboldened by the dramatic victories of Abkhazian rebels against the fast disintegrating Georgian armed forces (see below, p. 234), Gamsakhurdia returned from exile with the aim of 'cleansing' Georgia of the Shevardnadze administration. During October his forces extended their control over western Georgia (Mingrelia and its environs) including the Black Sea port of Poti and the strategic rail junction of Samtredia, thus cutting supply routes to the capital, Tbilisi. These gains were almost immediately reversed, and Georgian forces overran Zviadist positions during the remainder of 1993. In this they were assisted by the logistical assistance of Russian troops (marines from the Black Sea Fleet and paratroopers took control of facilities in Poti and helped guard road and rail links in Mingrelia), following a plea by Shevardnadze for military assistance.[19] Gamsakhurdia's suicide in January 1994, prompted by his perilous position, was the final blow to the Zviadists' military campaign. His followers announced in May their intention to continue their campaign of resistance, but by exclusively political means.

The second of Georgia's armed conflicts raged through 1991–92 and was located in South Ossetia in the north of the country. The Osset, who make up just over 3 per cent of Georgia's total population are ethnically distinct from the Georgian majority and had since 1989 been waging a campaign to unite with the North Ossetian autonomous republic in the neighbouring Russian Soviet Federated Socialist Republic (RSFSR). In September 1990 the South Ossetian parliament proclaimed a South Ossetian Democratic Soviet Republic, to which the Georgian parliament, with its newly elected pro-Gamsakhurdia majority, responded by abolishing the autonomous status the region had enjoyed since 1922. The following May the South Ossetian parliament itself abolished the Democratic Republic, but only as a pretext for placing the region under the administrative jurisdiction of the RSFSR.

This political brinkmanship was accompanied by an escalation of violence. The year 1991 witnessed clashes between Georgian Interior Ministry troops and irregular Georgian militia, on the one hand, and South Ossetian self-defence forces backed by North Ossetian volunteers, on the other. Soviet Interior Ministry troops in the area attempted to separate the warring parties and disarm military formations, but could do little to halt hostilities which, during 1991, resulted in over one hundred fatalities and led to the flight of some 80,000 refugees to North Ossetia. The watershed occasioned by the dissolution of the USSR and the overthrow of Gamsakhurdia initially did little to alter this deteriorating situation. The technically illegal South Ossetian parliament proclaimed the independence of the region from Georgia in December 1991 and ordered the mobilisation of all adults for the war effort. A referendum the following month endorsed, in principle, South Ossetia's union with Russia. This decision, coupled with the withdrawal of the former Soviet Interior Ministry troops (now under Russian command) in April, in turn, prompted Georgian units loyal to the ousted Gamsakhurdia to escalate their attacks on the South Ossetian capital, Tskhinvali.

Gamsakhurdia's departure from power, did, however, eventually smooth the path towards a negotiated ceasefire. Shevardnadze, although committed to Georgian territorial integrity, was, unlike his predecessor, willing to enter into talks with the South Ossetian leadership and with neighbouring Russia. These consultations bore fruit in June and July. Agreements, concluded between Russia and Georgia, provided for a recognition of the rights of the Ossetian minority while upholding the principle of Georgia's territorial integrity. A trilateral peacekeeping force was set up, comprised of Georgian, North Ossetian and Russian units. This combined body, which began to function in July, established a fragile peace in the region and allowed for the safe return of refugees. Little subsequent progress has been made, however, on delineating South Ossetia's political status within Georgia.

The third conflagration, that in Abkhazia, has proven the most intractable of Georgia's multiple conflicts. Abkhazian disaffection with Georgian rule had been characteristic of the entire Soviet period. Having obtained full republic status with the establishment of Soviet power in 1921, Abkhazia was demoted by Stalin (himself ethnically Georgian) to the position of an autonomous republic within Soviet Georgia ten years later. Thereafter, spurred by political and cultural discrimination and an influx of Mingrelian Georgians, the Abkhazians demanded greater autonomy, culminating in an unsuccessful demand in 1978 for incorporation in the RSFSR. A subsequent policy of 'Abkhazianisation' was pursued by the Soviet authorities, which granted the ethnic Abkhazians (by now a minority in their own region) a disproportionate share of local government positions and provided large-scale economic aid. These measures did not satisfy the Abkhazians and, moreover, inflamed resentment amongst local Georgians. In July 1989 clashes triggered off by a dispute concerning university quotas left fourteen dead in Abkhazia's capital, Sukhumi. The following year the Abkhazian parliament issued a Declaration of Sovereignty. With the dissolution of the USSR, the campaign for autonomy continued unabated – in July 1992 the parliament restored the 1925 constitution, which while referring to special ties with Georgia, had also designated Abkhazia as a 'sovereign state exercising state power over its territory independently of any other power'.[20]

Hostilities erupted in Abkhazia within weeks of this constitutional move. Georgian National Guards under the command of Defence Minister Tengiz Kitovani entered Abkhazia in August, ostensibly to retrieve security officials being held by Zviadist forces in the region and to protect road and rail links with Russia. Kitovani's units took it upon themselves (apparently in defiance of Shevardnadze's orders) to storm the Abkhazian parliament building in Sukhumi. A ceasefire was reached in September. This followed Russian mediation, motivated by the need to protect the Russian minority in the region (numbering some 70,000 persons) and, paralleling Russian policy in Nagorno–Karabakh, to minimise the destabilising effects of the war on the Russian Caucasus.[21] This agreement, however, swiftly collapsed owing to the reluctance of Kitovani, a firm adherent of the idea of a unitary Georgian state, to withdraw Georgian troops and to agree to talks on a federal treaty. The following twelve months witnessed a steady escalation of military actions. A further ceasefire brokered by the personal representative of the Russian President was achieved in July 1993. This provided for a planned demilitarisation of the war zone, a Georgian withdrawal from Abkhazia to be overseen by a joint Russian–Georgian–Abkhazian commission, agreement in principle on the deployment of Russian peacekeepers and the inauguration of a joint UN/CSCE observer mission to work out a final settlement. Shortly after, the UN Security Council passed Resolution 858 authorising the establishment of an observer mission. On this occasion, agreement floundered on the inability of Georgian forces to accede to the timetable for troop removals, owing to their ongoing campaign against the Zviadists in nearby Mingrelia. In response, Abkhazian forces (supplemented by local Russians, Greeks and Armenians, plus fellow members of the Confederation of Peoples of the Caucasus drawn largely from Russian republics, and Russian mercenaries and Cossack units) launched a successful attempt to recapture Sukhumi in September. This proved the occasion for a major rupture in relations between Shevardnadze and Moscow, as the Georgian leader charged Russia with abetting the Abkhazian rebellion.[22] Russia in response pointed to economic sanctions it had imposed upon Abkhazia in September following the rebels' violation of the July ceasefire.Whatever the truth of Shevardnadze's accusations, by November the rebel forces had driven from Abkhazia all Georgian forces, along with some 50–60,000 Georgian refugees.

Following this rout, UN-sponsored negotiations were undertaken in Geneva and Moscow involving Russian and American mediation. An agreement reached in April 1994 on a UN peacekeeping force (as distinct from the observer mission), ostensibly to police a ceasefire and permit the return of refugees, came to nothing owing to disagreements between the Georgian and Abkhazian sides on the exact role the contingent should perform. More concrete was an agreement brokered in Moscow in May, providing for a 3,000-strong CIS peacekeeping force, financed by Moscow and made up largely of Russian troops already deployed in the Transcaucasus. Its first units – all Russians – began deployment in Abkhazia in June. The following month the UN Security Council endorsed the CIS/Russian deployment and authorised the dispatch of further UN observers to Abkhazia. The CIS summit in October 1994 provided the CIS/Russian force with a mandate until mid-May 1995. A longer-term political settlement has, however, remained elusive. Negotiations held during 1994 failed to reconcile Abkhazia's preference for a solution based on the principles of the 1925 constitution with Georgia's desire for a more limited autonomy for the region.

Tajikistan

The civil war in Tajikistan has been the most deadly of the conflicts in the FSU. At its height during 1992, the war resulted in approximately 20,000 deaths and half a million refugees. The origins of this conflict certainly defy easy categorisation: ethnicity, regionalism, religion, clan politics and ideology have all played a part in fanning the flames of conflagration.[23]

Tajikistan entered the post-Soviet period in a state of acute political tension. The regime in power consisted of former communist *nomenklatura*, led by Tajikistan's President Rakhman Nabiev. The Islamic-democratic opposition was made up of four main groups: the Democratic Party, *Rastakhiz* or Rebirth (a movement dedicated to a rebirth of Tajik national identity and the restoration of links with Iran based on their common Iranian-speaking roots), *La'l-Badakhshan* (which advocated greater autonomy for the Gorno–Badakhshan autonomous region and upheld the cause of Pamiris, a people distinct in both religion and language from the majority Tajik population), and the Islamic Renaissance Party [IRP] (a party dedicated to the Sunni branch of Islam and thus, not theologically aligned with the Shia variety of Islam dominant in Iran). This disparate opposition drew its support predominantly from areas that had fared poorly under communist rule, setting them apart from the Leninabad region in the north of Tajikistan (an area also home to a large Uzbek population) and the area of Kulab, south-east of the capital Dushanbe.

During early 1992 mass demonstrations were mounted by the opposition in Dushanbe, accompanied by sporadic clashes with government supporters. This upsurge of popular feeling finally persuaded Nabiev to initiate a coalition embracing the opposition in May 1992. The formation of a new government of national salvation, however, simply proved the catalyst for a wave of fighting across the south of the country between the Islamic–democratic opposition (under the nominal leadership of a Front for National Salvation) and the former communists and their allies (grouped under a new organisation, the People's Front of Tajikistan). The war reached a *dénouement* of sorts in December when People's Front forces (assisted by neighbouring Uzbekistan and by forces of the 201st Russian division stationed in Tajikistan) seized control of the capital. This allowed the consolidation in power of political forces drawn from the traditionally dominant Leninabad and Kulab regions, fronted by Imamali Rakhmonov, who was elected chair of Tajikistan's parliament the preceding month.

Upon assuming power, the new government set about ruthlessly repressing the defeated anti-communist forces, forcing their leaders into opposition in Iran, Russia and neighbouring Afghanistan. Insurrection nonetheless continued, mounted primarily by two groups. The first of these, Pamiri separatists in Gorno–Badakhshan, was a diminishing force. The real threat to the Rakhmonov regime was fighters of the IRP, who had fled to north Afghanistan. Here they have enjoyed the protection of a number of Afghanistan's warring *Mujahidin* factions, including those loyal to former Afghan Defence Minister, Abdul Rashid Dustom, and to Gulbuddin Hekmatyar, who was appointed Afghan Prime Minister in June 1993. Benefiting from this sanctuary, IRP forces have mounted a series of cross-border raids on Tajik territory.

International efforts to calm Tajikistan's war have occurred on two levels. The military involvement of Russian and CIS peacekeepers was noted in Chapter 4 (pp. 168–69). These units have borne the brunt of attacks by Tajik rebels and their Afghan allies. Diplomatic activity in seeking a longer-term settlement has also been in evidence. Russia, along with certain Central Asian states (notably Uzbekistan) has sought to bring the regime in Dushanbe and the IRP into dialogue in order to frame an internal settlement. A long-term Russian/CIS presence has also been envisaged in order to police a settlement, possibly alongside UN and CSCE-affiliated peacekeepers. In addition, Russia has seemingly accepted that Iran, Pakistan and Saudi Arabia could play a key facilitating role by virtue of their influence over the Afghan *Mujahidin* and the Tajik opposition.[24]

Diplomatic efforts have, however, achieved very little. Russia's key role as mediator has been compromised by its military involvement, which has created the impression among the rebels that Moscow is a far from disinterested party in Tajikistan. By the same token, an offer to mediate by the Afghan government has been rejected in Dushanbe. The biggest, and apparently insurmountable obstacle, however, has been the attitude of Rakhmonov and his allies towards the opposition. For a combination of reasons, including the enmity created by the war, a desire to preserve a monopoly of political power and a fear of radical Islamic influence, Rakhmonov has doggedly rejected dialogue. Only in March 1994, following pressure from the Russians, did he agree to open talks with moderate representatives of the Islamic opposition. UN-sponsored negotiations held during 1994, mediated by Russia, Iran and Pakistan, finally arrived in September at agreement on a ceasefire to be monitored by the UN. Beyond this, a longer-term political settlement has remained uncertain.

Moldova's Trans–Dniester

The Dniester war, which was waged during 1992, was rooted in the curious blend of ethnic aggrandisement and political conservatism that characterise the Russian population resident on the Dniester left bank, a thin strip of Moldovan territory, bounded on one side by the Ukrainian border and on the other by the Dniester river. Russians here constitute what has been dubbed 'a minority within a minority', comprising 30 per cent of Moldova's overall Russian population and just 25 per cent of the total population of the left bank.[25] Minority status, coupled with a geographic isolation from the RSFSR rendered the left-bank Russians especially sensitive to the growing ethnic separatism which characterised the last years of the USSR. Their fears were compounded by anxieties concerning 'Romanianisation' and the possibility of Moldova's eventual reunification with Romania. (The Moldavian Soviet Socialist Republic had been created in 1940 as an outcome of Soviet conquests under the terms of the 1939 Nazi–Soviet pact. The territory which made up the republic was constituted in large part from what had been Russian Bessarabia under Tsarist rule. Between 1918 and 1939 Bessarabia had been conjoined with Romania. The majority Moldavian population was also essentially ethnically Romanian. The left-bank region, however, had never been part of Romania, and was until 1940 part of the Soviet republic of Ukraine.)[26] The elevation of Romanian to the official language of the republic in 1989, the rise of the pro-unification Moldovan Popular Front (MPF) and Moldova's declaration of independence in August 1991 prompted the left-bank Russians to give strong support to the continued survival of the USSR. Following Moldova's declaration of independence in August 1991, these moves culminated in the announcement by the self-proclaimed 'Dniester Moldovan Soviet Socialist Republic' to seek independence from Chisenau (the Moldovan capital) and to join the USSR as a contracting party in its own right.

While the Dniester Russians have been eager to cast themselves in the role of a beleaguered ethnic minority, the motivation of their political leaders has derived as much from ideological factors. The heavy industrial and military concentrations in the region had, during the Gorbachev period, spawned an anti-reform communist stronghold in Dniester's cities dedicated to the preservation of the 'socialist choice'. Through control of local soviets and the creation of Work Collectives, the communist apparatus held on to power in the region at a time when the Communist Party was losing influence throughout the rest of Moldova. Tellingly, Dniester Russians disliked Gorbachev and the reformist Yeltsin with equal passion and were amongst the most ardent supporters of the abortive coup in August 1991.[27]

The collapse of the August putsch and the USSR's subsequent unravelling encouraged paramilitary units in the Dniester region to seize control of administrative institutions. This was more or less accomplished throughout the left bank by March 1992, whereupon the insurgent forces crossed the Dniester river to claim the city of Bendery (Tighina). Three months of fierce fighting ensued, in which Dniester forces, augmented by Cossack volunteers from Russia and the firepower of the former Soviet Fourteenth Army, inflicted a series of heavy defeats on Moldova's police and nascent armed forces. The violence was finally brought to an end by the signing of a ceasefire agreement between Chisenau and Moscow in July. This followed quadrilateral negotiations held between Russia, Moldova, Romania and Ukraine. The accord provided for the establishment of a security zone along the Dniester and in Bendery to be patrolled by a joint Moldovan–Russian–Dniester force and, in addition, laid down the important political principles of the inviolability of borders (Russia, significantly, recognised the 'Dniester Republic' as part of Moldova) and respect for the rights of minorities.

The agreement brought peace to the region and, in essence, entrenched the political and military gains of the Dniester forces. Reaching a more lasting solution has been rendered difficult by two issues: the long-term political status of the Dniester left bank and the future of the Fourteenth Army. With regard to the former, Dniester positions have all advocated a significant reshaping of the Moldovan state. Dniester President, Igor Smirnov, for instance, has argued in favour of a confederal Moldova made up of a Dniester republic, Gaguazia (a Christian–Turkic region in Moldova's south) and a truncated Moldovan republic.[28] An even more uncompromising stance has been struck by General Alexander Lebed, the Fourteenth Army's commander, who has favoured either Moldova's wholesale incorporation into a renewed Union or the Dniester republic's merger with Russia.[29]

These positions reflect either a lingering communist nostalgia or a pronounced Russian nationalism rather than justifiable fears concerning ethnic discrimination. The Dniester Russians have been offered, according to one observer, 'the most wide-ranging political and cultural rights afforded any ethnic minority in Eastern Europe or the former Soviet Union'.[30] In early 1994, the Moldovan leadership accepted a CSCE plan granting the Dniester region special powers of self-governance. Moreover, the major cause of concern to the Dniester Russians – Moldova's unification with Romania – has receded well beyond the realms of possibility. Admittedly, some groups in Romania remain firmly wedded to the idea. Even in that country, however, the ruling Democratic National Salvation Front has pursued an evasive foreign policy which has kept immediate reunification off its agenda for fear of tension with Romania's own Hungarian minority. In Moldova itself, merger with Romania has become an increasingly unpopular proposition. The MPF, the most insistent advocate of unification, had initially enjoyed widespread support, obtaining through alliances a majority in the Moldovan parliament elected in 1990 and becoming the leading force in the non-communist government formed that year. Its pro-unification stand, however, soon left it marginalised. At the time of the break-up of the USSR, the overwhelming majority of the local population favoured independent statehood rather than merger. Questioned on their identity, they increasingly identified themselves and their language as 'Moldovan' rather than 'Romanian'. A series of practical considerations have also played their part. Romania offers neither a sound economic nor political home (owing to its political instabilities and underdevelopment) and is something of an outcast in the international community. Crucially, Moldovan officials have also been wary of any moves towards reunification or even forms of integration precisely because such steps have elicited a strong 'Romanophobia' amongst Moldova's ethnic minorities.[31]

The growing unpopularity of reunification has been reflected in the changing balance of political forces within Moldova. The MPF effectively collapsed during 1990–91, owing to leadership divisions over the Romanian question, the defection of parliamentary allies and the fall of the government led by the head of the Front, Prime Minister Mircea Druc. The Agrarian Democratic Party subsequently became the governing party and consolidated this position in parliamentary elections in February 1994. Significantly, the Agrarians were elected on a platform that advocated a concept of 'Moldovanism' that stressed ethnic, cultural and historical separateness from Romania.[32] This has been accompanied, moreover, by a specific commitment on the part of the Agrarians to define Moldova as a multi-ethnic state. A non-binding referendum held in early March should have dispelled any lingering doubts concerning Moldova's status. With a turnout of 65 per cent, over 90 per cent voted in favour of Moldova developing as an 'independent, united, indivisible state'.[33]

Turning to the problem of the Fourteenth Army, the presence of this force in Moldova has been analogous in some respects to the stationing of Russian troops in the Baltic states (see Chapter 4, pp. 179–83). Moldova, however, has found it far more difficult to persuade the Russian military to leave. Not until October 1994 was an agreement signed with Moscow on a withdrawal of troops. In some ways, Moscow's stance on this issue appears politically ill-judged. The officers of the Fourteenth Army have not been well disposed towards Yeltsin and have, moreover, voiced strong sympathies towards Alexander Rutskoi, Yeltsin's erstwhile Vice-President and a leader of the parliamentary resistance during the forceful dissolution of the Russian parliament in October 1993. In this light, Yeltsin's uncritical acceptance of the complicity of the Fourteenth Army in the fighting in 1992, his promotion of General Lebed in October 1993 and the bestowing of military honours upon Fourteenth Army combatants can be read as an attempt to ingratiate himself amongst the Fourteenth Army and thereby boost his standing in the Russian Ministry of Defence, itself a keen supporter of the Dniester cause.[34] As well as domestic political considerations, Yeltsin's combative stand has been shaped by a number of foreign policy concerns – notably the protection of ethnic Russians and the desire for basing facilities in the near abroad – which have impeded a Russian withdrawal from the Dniester region. In the negotiations on the troop issue, Moscow has linked a withdrawal to the granting of a special political status for the Dniester left bank and has pressed for a status-of-forces agreement on a 'temporary' presence. Both these conditions were inserted at Russian insistence into the October withdrawal agreement. For good measure, Moscow has also delayed the process of evacuation further by stipulating that the agreement would only take effect after 'the completion of domestic state procedures' (in other words, after the submission for approval or rejection to the Russian government or parliament).[35]

Conflict resolution in the former Soviet Union

In the majority of the FSU's war zones peace of sorts has been achieved following the arrangement of ceasefires and/or the intervention of peacekeeping battalions. While this might be regarded as something of a success one important qualification needs to be borne in mind: in all cases no significant progress has been made towards resolving the underlying causes of antagonism, thus rendering the continuation or re-emergence of open warfare extremely likely. In this light, it is worth considering the reasons why these disputes have been so intractable and the possible methods for advancing viable settlements.

The wars in the FSU have, with the partial exception of Nagorno–Karabakh, not been wars between states, but conflicts waged by ethnically or politically defined groups *within* states. Why have these groups been so adamant in their demands? First, it is worth noting the so-called 'demonstration effect'.[36] By this view, the victorious route to independence of the USSR's republics, abetted in its later stages by a welcoming international community prepared to offer diplomatic recognition, has set off a chain reaction involving demands for self-determination amongst ethnic minorities within the former republics themselves. Minorities in the successor states have also mobilised for protective reasons. As Kamal Shehadi has explained, '(m)any ethnic groups feel insecure at the prospect of belonging to new states with new dominant ethnic groups. They therefore claim or assert their alleged right to self-determination as a defence mechanism against ... a new feared status quo'. These insecurities are that much the worse where the historical background is one of inter-ethnic conflict or perceived ethnic disadvantage. Hence, the claims to 'self-determination as defence' amongst the Abkhaz and Ossetians in Georgia, Karabakh Armenians in Azerbaijan and Dniester Russians in Moldova.[37]

The potency of these claims has, in turn, been compounded in the post-Soviet period by a more general problem observed by Samuel Huntington nearly three decades ago, namely, the difficulties of creating 'political order'. The ability to govern, for Huntington, rests on the development of institutions (of which political parties are considered amongst the most important) that are regarded as authoritative by the populations over whom they presume to administer.[38] In the Soviet Union governance broke down during the Gorbachev period as the Communist Party, the cornerstone of effective government, bifurcated and Gorbachev's executive presidency failed to assume the role of a credible substitute. As the legitimacy of the central authorities waned, popular support was transferred either to nationalist movements (as in Moldova, the Baltics and the Transcaucasus) or to populist politicians, such as Yeltsin, Kravchuk and Nazarbaev, who were able to ride the tide of change. This political sea-change has not yet resulted in durable institutions up to the tasks of creating order in a post-Soviet environment that is characterised by economic hardship, high popular expectations and political cultures intolerant of compromise and bargaining. Post-communist leaderships have found it extremely difficult to erect new edifices of rule, which have sufficient legitimacy to command popular acceptance, or enough coercive power to win national compliance. Only in the Baltic states has a degree of institutional stability been achieved owing to a shared sense of national unity among the titular (but, note, not the settler Russian) population, a permissive political culture and relatively mature civil society. Elsewhere order has prevailed by virtue of the utilisation of pre-existing communist structures by an authoritarian leadership (Turkmenistan, Uzbekistan) or as a consequence of an ostensible commitment to democracy married to authoritarian/populist devices of rule (Russia, Ukraine, Kazakhstan, and to a lesser degree, Kyrgyzstan). In the cases of the successor states that have experienced regional separatism and violence, conflict has arisen because none of these routes to order have proven practicable owing partly to the depths of division and thus, the more dogged and fundamentalist pursuit of minority claims. The parties to most of these conflicts have tended to regard their opposite numbers as totally illegitimate (as an oppressor, on the one hand, or a threat to national unity on the other). This has both quickened the resort to violence and obstructed the framing of peaceable internal settlements through dialogue and negotiation. The relapse into violence in turn creates a vicious circle impeding reconciliation. The enemy-image is deepened and government at the centre is fearful that any concession will be considered a sign of weakness, likely to encourage rather than staunch further demands.

If this were not enough, in the case studies considered above, the problems of ethnic/political division have been affected by two further factors: the militarisation of disputes and external intervention. The former has partly resulted from the disintegration of the former Soviet armed forces, the civil order implications of which have been graphically described by one Russian analyst:

> [disintegration] goes down from military districts to armies to corps to divisions, regiments, and battalions. Left alone by the Moscow General Staff, with lines of communication broken down and supplies terminated, local ("field") commanders have to take care of their enlisted personnel themselves to solve the problems of provision, fuel supply, and so forth on their own. This means they have to strike special deals with local political leaders ... Eventually local units become more and more self-oriented and self-governed, turning into mercenaries ready to sell their support to anybody who is able to pay a good price. They could even try to replace the civilian administration and seize political control in some smaller communities or isolated territories, if the situation permits.[39]

This dangerous trend has been particularly obvious in the case of the Fourteenth Army in Moldova and to lesser degrees in covert support of the Abkhazian separatists by elements within the Russian military.

The weakening of discipline in the former Soviet armed forces has, in turn, encouraged the forceful seizure of arms by both newly formed national armies and irregular units. In the Transcaucasus, to this already dangerous cocktail has been added the violently destabilising effects of the long-standing tradition of private possession of arms and the more recent rise of armed criminal gangs.

Turning to external intervention, this, according to Evan Luard, is more likely to occur in states which are in close proximity to large, powerful neighbours. Intervention is motivated by a desire to aid a particular side in a conflict and to obstruct an opposing side which may be favoured by another external power. As such competition often takes the form of a regional arms race, it serves to prolong rather than to staunch military conflict.[40] In the case of the FSU, these generalisations hold only partially true. The involvement of Russia, Turkey and Iran has not been aimed at aggravating war, but rather at the resolution of conflicts through negotiation and peacekeeping. Moreover, amongst the contiguous countries, Russia has enjoyed a position of *primus inter pares*, which has meant its military interventions have not been met with counterforce and have, in some cases, been successful in dampening hostilities. In fact, the interventions which have most aggravated conflicts have been those of non-state actors as in the case of volunteers in the Transcaucasus and Afghan *Mujahidin* factions in Tajikistan.

While powerful neighbours then have been motivated by a desire to facilitate stability and peace this has been no guarantee of their ability to expedite lasting settlements. This failure relates partly to problems arising from the (im)partiality of external actors (see also below, p. 249). In addition, the fact that the rebellious factions in Georgia and Tajikistan have not been the clients of external governments (or in the case of the Fourteenth Army and Karabakh Armenians, have been largely autonomous of an external patron government) has meant external leverage in conflict resolution has been of limited use. The very nature of ethnic movements has also obstructed lasting settlements. According to Robert Cooper and Mats Berdal, '(l)eaders of [... such] movements are not the same as properly constituted authorities. They are more at the mercy of their followers, and reaching agreement with internal enemies *or with foreigners* may not prove popular'.[41]

In the face of the seemingly intractable nature of the civil conflicts in the successor states what solutions seem feasible? In addressing this question one can divide the possible responses into those which might be pursued at the internal level and those requiring international involvement. At the internal level, a number of scenarios, in ascending order of probability, might be envisaged:

1 The successor states capitulate entirely to minority demands and allow full secession and the formation of new states. This is not only extremely unlikely in view of the adamant resistance to such a course by the states concerned and their regional neighbour Russia, but also a course of action likely to add to, rather than ameliorate problems. The chain-reaction of demands for further partitions likely to ensue could set in motion what has been described as a 'potentially endless process of subdivision'.[42] It also fails to address the problem of the stranded populations in the potential new states (Moldovans in the Dniester region, Georgians in Abkhazia, Azeris in Nagorno–Karabakh) all of whom might themselves resort to violence in self-defence. To deal with this problem the temptation might be to forcefully remove these populations. In Nagorno–Karabakh this has already been largely achieved and was a feasible, if morally unacceptable, proposition given the relatively small number of Azeris there. In Abkhazia and the Dniester, by contrast, where the secessionist populations are themselves minorities in their own localities, such a 'solution' would clearly be resisted with great determination and would lead to the escalation rather than the subsidence of war.[43]

2 Issues of ethnic, religious or cultural preference are stripped of their territorial base. To 'de-territorialise' in this manner, renders matters involving identity much easier to resolve, in that the major motivation of combat – territorial gain, and self-government therein – is removed. In that competing ideologies of nationalism have historically tied identity to territory,[44] this ultimately would require a substantial moderation of the exclusionary nationalism found amongst populations in the FSU. However, the circumstances in which such a dilution of nationalist sentiment would occur, seem very remote. Having only won the opportunity of expression as recently as the Gorbachev period, nationalism seems unlikely to recede in the short term in the FSU through a loss of momentum. Moreover, the antithesis of nationalism, a political culture which encourages tolerance in diversity, bred by a vibrant civil society and

strong democracy, is very far from being realised in any of the successor states affected by conflict.

3 Internal political strategies are pursued which accommodate both the conflicting demands of minority self-determination and the desire of the majority population for the continued territorial integrity of the state. Kamal Shehadi has identified two broad approaches in this regard: 'forging a national identity' and 'designing a political system'. The first is a long-term effort that aims to define the collective identity of the subjects of a state in civic rather than ethnic terms. Citizenship is granted to all permanent residents regardless of ethnicity in return for political loyalty. The optimum shape of the political system, meanwhile, would involve power-sharing arrangements (coalition government), constitutional guarantees for minorities, varying levels of autonomy within a unitary state and ultimately, federalism.[45] These strategies, if effective, amount to a democratic solution. Yet given the incipient nature of democracy in the FSU this is an outcome unlikely in the short term. Only in Moldova has a serious effort been made towards framing an internal political settlement along the lines of devolved powers.

4 Minority rights are repressed through forced assimilation or are insufficiently respected (for example, nominal self-government may be granted to minorities, but with little real substance in practice). Such courses of action have a long pedigree in multi-ethnic states, and was the pattern of rule in the USSR prior to 1985. In the FSU, it also has its attractions. First, it accords with the compelling desire of the leaderships of the successor states to construct new nation-states based on what they regard as the legitimate borders bequeathed by the republican divisions created during the Soviet period. The granting of minority rights is viewed as detracting from this goal. Second, the calculation might be made that if the minority is denied sufficiently long it will lose its sources of support and will dilute its demands. Playing for time also allows the successor states the opportunity to develop the coercive apparatus (national armies, police forces etc.) necessary to carry out repression and to gamble on the fact that economic regeneration might blunt minority grievances. Such a course, however, is replete with potential problems for the governing authority. The root causes of discontent remain unaddressed and thus, the likelihood remains of periodic upsurges of civil

disorder and conflict. As the nationalities issue in the Soviet period demonstrates, even a prolonged period of quiescence can be shattered by a sudden resurgence of tumultuous and often violent ethnic demands. Relying on economic growth as a panacea is also a dubious proposition as the poor record of the post-Soviet economies demonstrates (see Chapter 6).

The destabilising effects of minority issues in the successor states can in the long term only be resolved through the efforts of the contending parties within the countries concerned. Nevertheless, an important facilitating role can be played by outside actors in creating the conditions (the mediation of negotiations and peacekeeping) which facilitate the construction of such long-term solutions.[46] In regard to the FSU, a variety of states and international organisations could potentially carry out this role, although their ability to do so differs widely.

1 The *CIS*, at first glance, appears the most appropriate body to co-ordinate a collective response to the FSU's multiple conflicts. By April 1994 the organisation embraced all the governments experiencing conflagration and could, therefore, act as a forum in which regular multilateral consultations might be undertaken. It had, moreover, built up a tool-chest of provisions related to conflict resolution. Most importantly, two specific agreements on 'Collective Peacekeeping Forces' were adopted in March 1992 and September 1993.

In practice, however, the CIS has performed an extremely limited role, owing to its inability to co-ordinate military co-operation and the preference of CIS member states for bilateral negotiations. Only in the case of Tajikistan has a truly joint CIS force been deployed, and even there it has operated alongside a large Russian presence (see Chapter 4, pp. 168–69). In Abkhazia, the nominally CIS force deployed in June 1994 was both financed and staffed by Russians. In other conflicts, peacekeeping efforts could not be described as CIS operations at all, owing to the fact that the deployments were reached via agreements outside of CIS forums and involved units from states which were not CIS members (Georgian forces in South Ossetia prior to its joining the organisation in December 1993) or from aspirant states unlikely to acquire CIS membership (South Ossetia and the Dniester region). The utility of the CIS, even if fully functional, might also be questioned. Firstly, because it precludes the involvement of a number of interested parties. The use of the CIS as a forum for negotiation on Nagorno–Karabakh, for instance, would exclude both Turkey and Iran, while similar efforts in Tajikistan would rule out Afghani or Pakistani involvement. Secondly, the danger is ever present that an enhanced CIS could act simply as a vehicle for Russian ambition.

2 Could *Russia* act as 'a guarantor of peace and stability'? Where progress has been made towards the cessation of conflict in the FSU, it has usually been through Russian efforts. By March 1994, Russia had at least 9,000 peacekeepers deployed in its near abroad.[47] Furthermore, its assistance in the development of national armies in the successor states could in the long term contribute to local military solutions to internal conflicts or to the formation of local peacekeeping forces. Russia's readiness to become involved in this manner reflects the concern it feels at destabilisation in the near abroad. This combination of Russian efficacy and interest in promoting stability led it during 1993–94 to press the claim that it be granted 'special powers' and financial assistance by organisations such as the UN and the CSCE to carry out its 'special responsibility' to promote 'the cessation of all armed conflicts on the territory of the former USSR'.[48] A Russian campaign to win the CIS formal recognition as a regional and international organisation by bodies such as the UN is also linked to Russian ambitions. A CIS peacekeeping mechanism would, after all, be a framework in which Russia would play the dominant role.[49]

Russian officials have argued that recognition by the international community is, in fact, not a legal requirement of Russian/CIS efforts (simply the agreement of the warring parties is in keeping with international law). In this light, its requests might be seen first, as a means of allaying the huge financial costs of its peacekeeping efforts in the FSU (estimated at 28.5 billion roubles for 1992–93) and second, as an attempt to win tacit approval for what is, in effect, an interventionist policy. By projecting itself as a stabilising factor in the region, Russia can claim to be doing the 'dirty work' the West would prefer to avoid, at the same time carving out a sphere of influence around its borders. The claim to a 'special responsibility', moreover, indicates that Moscow regards itself as having a more important jurisdiction in the FSU than outside powers and international bodies.[50] It has consequently resisted efforts by bodies such as the CSCE to supervise its peacekeeping operations.

While Russia is the most influential state in the FSU it is precisely its vested interest in the region which limits its abilities. While it has been able to promote the temporary cessation of conflicts, its capacity to facilitate more lasting peace agreements is constrained by perceptions of partiality. According to literature on conflict resolution, successful third-party mediation requires that the intermediary possess qualities such as knowledge and skill, access to the appropriate resources and control over face-to-face contacts. These Russia could be said to hold. However, it lacks other, more important attributes such as impartiality, neutrality and a low interest in the outcome of conflicts. In their absence, Russia's influence rests on the awareness by the parties to conflict of its latent ability to impose ceasefire settlements (either through military intervention and/or economic sanctions). Yet such enforced settlements, it is generally recognised, tend to be resented by the protagonists and are usually far from final. They often break down as one side awakens to what it considers an unequal peace and embarks upon attacks on both its erstwhile enemy and local peacekeeping forces.[51]

3 The foremost international organisation with a strong claim to neutrality, and a relatively successful record of mediation and peacekeeping, is the *United Nations*. In the post-war period UN peacekeepers have played a major part in diffusing some of the world's most bitter and protracted conflicts: in the Middle East, in the Indian subcontinent and in Cyprus, the Congo and Cambodia. As of September 1992 the organisation maintained peacekeeping forces in the vicinity of twelve separate conflicts worldwide and observer missions in countless others. As noted below, the organisation has been engaged in a major peacekeeping effort in the former Yugoslavia and has played the role of mediator in Third World conflicts in Angola and Afghanistan.

With the demise of the Cold War, the potential of the UN has been seemingly enhanced as the immobilising effects of superpower veto-wielding in the Security Council have become a thing of the past. Since 1991, the UN has also adopted resolutions and declarations that provide its organs with 'a stronger basis upon which to operate ... in their efforts in conflict prevention'.[52] While this new potential has to some degree been tainted by criticisms that the UN has become a means of providing a framework for American military action (as in the cases of Operation Desert Storm in Iraq/Kuwait, Operation Restore Hope in Somalia and its invasion of Haiti in 1994), it continues to be regarded as the most credible and legitimate body for peacekeeping efforts.[53] This perception extends to governments in the FSU. Both Georgia and Moldova, for instance, have at times voiced a preference for a UN-authorised (rather than a straightforward Russian) presence. UN activities within the FSU have not been without significance. In addition to the UN observer role in Georgia noted above (p. 234), fact-finding missions have carried out work in Armenia, Azerbaijan, Moldova and Tajikistan, and a Special Envoy was dispatched in 1993 to Tajikistan and surrounding states to facilitate negotiations.

The UN is, however, a victim of its own success. Its status as an instrument for impartial third-party management of regional conflict means that greater demands have been placed upon it in recent years to deal with the proliferation of local wars. These needs have severely stretched the financial and human resources of the organisation and have restricted its 'capability to offer plausible means of preventive diplomacy, peacekeeping, protective security or peace-enforcing in many places across the Eurasian land mass'.[54] In the FSU it is also dependent ultimately on Russian goodwill. Russia's Security Council veto remains a potential obstruction to any UN actions which might be seen as supplanting Moscow's self-defined role as peacekeeper in the FSU. Moreover, the UN's cumbersome decision-making and financial machinery has led leaders such as Shevardnadze to balance their admiration for the neutrality of UN peacekeepers with a pragmatic acceptance of the efficacy of more readily available Russian contingents.

4 The *CSCE*[55] is another body that has been reinvigorated by the end of the Cold War. Having facilitated East–West dialogue during the Cold War, during the 1990s, the CSCE set about transforming itself from a series of conferences to a more permanent set of institutions. This process of 'institutionalisation' has given rise to a number of organs pertinent to conflict resolution: CSCE missions, a Conflict Prevention Centre and a High Commissioner for National Minorities. In respect to the FSU, the CSCE has performed a valuable role. A CSCE mission to South Ossetia in December 1992 established commissions for amongst other things the return of refugees

and the strengthening of law and order. In Moldova it has proposed a plan for Dniester self-government and since April 1993 has maintained a Mission of Long Duration aimed at promoting dialogue, encouraging the withdrawal of foreign (that is, Russian) troops and monitoring any future political settlement. In the case of Nagorno–Karabakh, as noted above, the CSCE has pursued the novel step of preparatory talks (the Minsk Group initiative) aimed at the convocation of a peace conference. At the CSCE's Budapest Summit in December 1994 agreement was reached in principle on the dispatch of a 3,000-strong multinational peacekeeping force to the enclave. Like the UN, the CSCE has enjoyed the benefit of neutrality and has attracted some kudos within Russia, where it has been viewed as an alternative to the expansion of NATO structures. Defence Minister, Grachev, for instance, has referred to it as potentially the 'main peacemaking organisation in Europe'.[56]

The CSCE, however, has been severely constrained in other respects. While embracing all the countries of North America, Europe and the FSU, its membership does not extend to Asian states. Iran and Afghanistan – two interested parties in the conflict zones of the FSU – are thus excluded from CSCE initiatives. Moreover, unlike the UN, the CSCE has a limited track record as mediator in war situations. According to one observer, CSCE initiatives tend to be most useful 'at the earliest stages of pre-conflict tension or once the fighting has clearly ended'; it is limited in its abilities to resolve ongoing conflicts.[57] The CSCE also relies almost entirely on moral suasion. Certain of its decisions can be politically binding upon members, but the organisation is poorly equipped to enforce compliance with any decisions reached by its executive or arbitration organs.[58] Furthermore, its mechanisms for undertaking peacekeeping operations are underdeveloped. Some progress in this direction was admittedly registered in the decision of the CSCE's Helsinki summit in July 1992 to sanction the establishment of CSCE peacekeeping forces along the lines of UN operations. This was complemented by a willingness on the part of NATO to make resources available for CSCE missions. These decisions, however, were so qualified as to render them almost useless. Prerequisites for the dispatch of a peacekeeping operation specified in the Helsinki Decisions were far more stringent than comparable UN procedures. Consensus was required on the matter within the CSCE's Council of Ministers for Foreign Affairs (the organisation's highest decision-making body) or its subsidiary, the Committee of Senior Officials. This rendered any deployment subject to a veto by any one of the CSCE's fifty-two members, including, of course, Russia, which might object to any CSCE force seconded from NATO. Even if this veto hurdle was jumped, a force could only be sent *after* the establishment of 'an effective and durable ceasefire',[59] a condition that was applied for instance in the case of the Budapest decision on peacekeeping in Nagorno–Karabakh.

5 A *NATO* role in peacekeeping is envisaged for two of the Alliance's affiliated structures in which the successor states are involved: the North Atlantic Co-operation Council (NACC) and the Partnership for Peace programme (PFP). NACC has provided a forum for discussions on conflicts in the FSU and has forwarded proposals for peacekeeping co-operation amongst its members. At its Athens meeting in June 1993, NACC considered the possibility of joint training and peacekeeping operations under the aegis of the UN or the CSCE. However, NACC, being essentially a consultative body, as yet lacks the operational resources to act upon these discussions. PFP offers more concrete benefits. The 'Partnership for Peace: Framework Document' released in January 1994 suggested subscribing states could co-operate with NATO in operations under the authority of the UN and the CSCE and in 'joint planning, training, and exercises in order to strengthen their ability to undertake missions in the fields of peacekeeping'.[60] Such joint preparations could potentially be of considerable benefit to the nascent armed forces of states such as Moldova, which have undertaken peacekeeping efforts with little prior experience and which have few institutional links to the other major source of advice, the Russian military. PFP however, does not envisage the creation of a permanent peacekeeping arm involving the participation of NATO states in conjunction with PFP signatories. Too overt a role in the FSU, in any case, would not win the acceptance of Moscow, and NATO would court the risk of a major rupture in relations were it to promote operations in Russia's near abroad.

The internal and international aspects of conflict resolution in the FSU prompt important questions relating to the manner in which violent conflict in the post-Cold War period has been perceived in international relations scholarship. This is a debate we shall return to in the conclusion of this chapter, having first considered other conflicts which are germane to the debate.

Disputed territorial claims involving one or more of the successor states plus an outside party

A second category of dispute relevant to the FSU is that relating to questions of borders and territories involving the successor states and outside parties. Disputes of this type have differed in intensity. Amongst the least salient have been potential territorial claims relating to alterations in the western border of the Soviet Union, which occurred immediately before or after World War II. These include possible pretensions to the territories of Lithuania (by Poland), Russia (by Finland), Belarus (by Poland), Ukraine (by Poland, Romania and Slovakia) and Moldova (by Romania). In most cases these have remained largely hypothetical; although taken up by sections of nationalist oppositions, they have not involved a formal claim on the part of government. The only exception has been Romanian aspirations regarding Moldova (see above, pp. 237–38) and Ukraine, which have received some official backing, but only tentatively.[61]

Border disputes in the Transcaucasus involving outside powers have also failed to ignite. Armenian claims against Turkey were defused by inter-governmental agreement, while the Azeri–Iranian dispute was effectively shelved following Elchibey's departure from office and the coming to power of Aliev, a leader more interested in improved relations with Iran (see Chapter 3, p. 115).

Of greater importance, owing to the precedent of the Sino–Soviet border clashes in the late 1960s, are Chinese claims against Russia and the Central Asian states of Kazakhstan, Kyrgyzstan and Tajikistan. These have not, however, given rise to open hostilities. Much of the Russian–Chinese border had been effectively settled by the 1991 Sino–Soviet agreement on the long frontier east of Mongolia (demarcation began in the spring of 1992 and was expected to take five years) and the small 54-km section west of Mongolia has not been an object of contention. As for Central Asia, a tour there in April 1994 by the Chinese Premier, Li Peng, provided the occasion for significant progress on the border question. During his sojourn in Kyrgyzstan, it was announced that a treaty on the common border was imminent. While in Kazakhstan an agreement was signed defining the last disputed stretch of the 1,700 km Kazakh–Chinese frontier.[62] Outstanding issues concern the status of three Russian islands in the Amur and Argun Rivers and Chinese claims to a section of the Pamir mountains in Tajikistan. A resort to force by China in pursuit of its claims appears to be precluded. Russia retains a military presence on the disputed islands and, in the Tajik case, Beijing must weigh up the risks of inciting a Russian intervention (under the terms of the CIS Collective Security Treaty, for instance Moscow might come to Tajikistan's defence to counter Chinese aggression) and being sucked into Tajikistan's civil war.

In many cases then, border issues with outside states have been of diminishing relevance. The same cannot be said, however, of the bitter territorial dispute between Russia and Japan over sovereignty of the southern Kurile Islands (or what the Japanese call the Northern Territories). These four islands make up part of a chain of some thirty islands which stretch from the southernmost point of Russia's Kamchatka Peninsula to within eye-view of Hokkaido, the northernmost of the four main islands that constitute Japan. Under agreements struck between Japan and Tsarist Russia in 1855, sovereignty over the southern Kuriles (Iturup, Kunashir, Shikotan and the Habomai group of islets) was ceded to Japan. A further agreement in 1875 extended Japanese rights to the entire island chain, in return for which Russia acquired the island of Sakhalin. The southern part of this piece of territory was returned to Japan following Russia's defeat in the 1904–5 Russo–Japanese war. All Japan's gains were later overturned in World War II. In return for entering the war against Japan in 1945 on the side of the Allies, the Soviet Union was promised at the Yalta and Potsdam conferences possession of all the Kuriles and the former Japanese parts of Sakhalin. The Potsdam Declarations signed by the US, the UK, along with the Soviet Union, affirmed this by limiting Japan's territorial sovereignty to its four main islands. Japanese resentment over the loss of the Kurile chain, particularly the four southern islands, ruled out the signing of a formal peace treaty between Tokyo and Moscow after World War II.

In the post-war period, the position of the Kuriles was defined by two documents concluded in the 1950s. Under the terms of the 1951 San Francisco Peace Treaty signed with the US, Japan renounced any claim over the Kuriles. Legal title to the islands, however, remained undefined in the agreement (no explicit recognition was given to

Soviet possession) and Tokyo soon after claimed that its renunciation did not include the four southern islands. The 1956 Soviet–Japanese peace declaration initially appeared to break the deadlock. While the declaration simply deferred a settlement of the territorial issue until the conclusion of a full peace treaty, Moscow did concede that once this was signed Russia might hand back the two smallest islands, Shikotan and the Habomai. These concessions marked the high point of Soviet flexibility. In 1960 Foreign Minister Andrei Gromyko suggested that a return of the islands was contingent on the withdrawal of foreign (i.e. American) troops from Japan. By the mid-1970s he was refusing to even discuss the Kuriles issue.

Gorbachev's arrival in power did little to alter the basic Soviet position. The fundamental transformations which occurred in all areas of Soviet foreign policy under the USSR's last leader, found little reflection in regard to the question of the Kuriles. Gorbachev's visit to Japan in April 1991, heralded as a watershed in relations, did result in Moscow's public recognition of the dispute's existence and a pledge on the part of the Soviet leader to initiate a demilitarisation of the islands. This was, however, accompanied by an outright rejection of the 1956 declaration as a starting point for negotiations. Japan, for its part, made clear that large-scale financial assistance for the troubled Soviet economy (beyond that reluctantly extended under pressure from the other G7 countries) would be forthcoming only after a resolution of the territorial dispute.[63]

In the year or so prior to the break-up of the USSR, Yeltsin's attitude towards the controversy departed little from that of the Soviet leadership. During an unofficial visit to Tokyo in January 1990 he revealed a vague five-stage plan which anticipated the concessions offered by Gorbachev. This also contained no reference to the 1956 declaration and rather enigmatically left any settlement of the dispute to the lot of future generations.[64] Greater flexibility was, however, evident in the latter months of 1991 as Russia assumed a growing international profile. Convinced of the necessity of gaining access to Tokyo's finances and creating a favourable climate for private Japanese investment, Russian officials, including Foreign Minister Kozyrev, explicitly recognised the legality of the 1956 declaration and thus, by extension, the eventuality of transferring Shikotan and the Habomai. The optimism engendered by this new approach petered out during 1992. True, Russia's formal entry onto the international stage was occasioned by an active diplomacy towards Japan on the part of the reinvigorated Ministry of Foreign Affairs, aimed at accelerating the demilitarisation of the islands and promoting a long-term solution. By the summer, however, Kozyrev's position had undergone a significant shift; any transfer of territory was now ruled out of the question.[65] The attitude of Yeltsin was similarly ill-disposed. The cancellation of visits to Japan planned for September 1992 and May 1993 only confirmed Yeltsin's unwillingness to be drawn into discussions on the territorial issue. A rescheduled trip finally took place in October 1993, resulting in pledges to find a solution based on 'law and justice', but eliciting no pledges on Russia's behalf to return any of the islands.[66]

The hardening position on the Kuriles reflected the exposure of Yeltsin and Kozyrev to domestic political forces adamantly opposed to any territorial concessions. Opposition has been voiced not just by Yeltsin's foes (one-time Vice-President Rutskoi, and a large proportion of deputies within the old Russian parliament prior to its dissolution in October 1993), but even by ostensible political allies such as Defence Minister Grachev, CIS Commander-in-Chief Yevgenii Shaposhnikov, and Prime Minister Victor Chernomyrdin. Polls of popular opinion have also registered consistent majorities against handing back the islands.[67] A variety of arguments have been forwarded in favour of their retention.

First, the military has continued to regard the islands as having strategic significance. Despite improved relations with the West, the armed forces's Cold War assumption of a hostile US–Japanese axis still influences military perceptions.[68] Hence, a document drawn up by the Russian General Staff in July 1992 suggested that Russia's military presence on the disputed islands served as a deterrent to Japanese ambitions to forcibly seize the territories. During 1993 Russia did withdraw some units from the islands, but the military has continued to regard possession as essential to Russia's strategic posture in East Asia.[69] Any concessions, moreover, have been viewed as an unwelcome precedent that would undermine one of the central tenets of Russian foreign policy: the inviolability of post-war borders. To give up the Kuriles might set off a 'chain reaction' of further Japanese claims (for instance, to Sakhalin) and a revival of territorial issues with China.[70]

The strength of military feeling was shared by a significant portion of deputies within the old Russian parliament (prior to its disbandment in late 1993). Amongst conservative deputies (often referred to as 'national patriots') the Kuriles issue appeared to herald a process of disintegration, which, following the break-up of the USSR, threatened Russia itself. In this regard, opposition to a return of the islands was not simply the reflection of some mystical attachment to Russia's 'sacred land', but more a calculation that territorial concessions would encourage claims against Russia from the successor states and might even lead to demands for secession from some of Russia's own republics. Any economic gains to be had from meeting Tokyo's demands, meanwhile, were considered marginal. Access to Japanese economic assistance was considered scant compensation for the loss of territory containing abundant fishing and mineral resources. More moderate (but also more influential) voices within the parliament shared a number of these opinions, albeit with less ferocity. Figures such as the Chair of the parliament's Committee for International Affairs and Foreign Economic Relations Yevgenii Ambartsumov, played an important role during hearings on the Kuriles in the summer of 1992 in mobilising deputies against Kozyrev and Yeltsin and in creating a climate of opinion which contributed to the cancellation of Yeltsin's scheduled first official visit to Japan.[71]

The issue of the Kuriles has appeared insoluble owing to its location at the centre of the debate on Russia's national interests. The impasse over the issue, however, has not simply been a result of Russian obduracy. Japan too has made the issue a litmus test of foreign policy virility. Since at least 1961 the Japanese position has remained unaltered. It has sought not merely an affirmation of the 1956 declaration, but ultimately the return of all four of the southern Kuriles. This is not a formula which has won friends in Russia and it has ruled out compromise proposals involving joint sovereignty and the submission of the dispute to international arbitration. Moreover, so long as the Japanese line remains a maximalist one, concessions by the Russian leadership court the risk of appearing to be made under duress, thereby undermining both its domestic and international prestige. Tokyo's line, therefore, has encouraged intransigence rather than compromise in Moscow, and has obstructed rather than facilitated a solution based on mutual concessions.

Violent conflicts in the Third World

As examined in Chapter 1, during the Gorbachev period determined efforts were undertaken by the USSR to facilitate the settlement of regional conflicts in the Third World and thereby extricate Moscow from costly foreign policy adventures. In the case of Afghanistan, the USSR's swift exit dealt a fatal blow to Moscow's one-time ally in the country, President Mohammad Najibullah. Russia, which assumed responsibility for the 1991 Soviet–US agreement on a mutual termination of arms (see Chapter 2, p. 77), began implementing the accord in January 1992, thereby depriving the Najibullah regime of its last means of survival. In March the Afghan President announced his intention to leave office, and declared a willingness to co-operate with Russian- and American-backed UN plans concerning the formation of a transitional government. This UN framework proved impossible to implement, however, owing to resistance from a number of *Mujahidin* factions. Sensing Najibullah's exposed position, these groups eschewed a diplomatic solution and in April mounted a successful assault on the capital, Kabul. With the ouster of Najibullah, Afghanistan entered a new phase of war as competing *Mujahidin* factions jostled for ascendancy in an interim administration and sought to promote their own regional, ethnic and clan interests.

Since the *Mujahidin* victory none of the successor states have been willing to enter the snakepit of diplomatic mediation in Afghanistan, calculating that the country's multi-layered conflicts are beyond resolution. Even if a will were present, the successor states, in any case, lack real influence. Russian mediation has been ruled out by mutual suspicions. One legacy of the Soviet intervention is a continuing distrust of Russian intentions amongst Afghanis. Moscow, on the other hand, has been critical of the role of *Mujahidin* factions in the Tajik conflict and the continued detention of former Soviet POWs.[72] With the collapse of the UN plan and the subsequent marginalisation of the United Nations in Afghanistan, even an indirect Russian role via the Security Council has been precluded. Central Asian states have been only marginally better placed than Russia. True, neighbouring Uzbekistan and Turkmenistan have concrete interests in Afghanistan and both Presidents Islam Karimov and Saparmurad Niyazov have forged links with rival *Mujahidin* as part of a competition for regional influence. Neither, however, has carried sufficient weight amongst the Afghan fighters as a whole to act as a viable peacemaker. In light of indifference or impotence amongst the post-Soviet states, diplomatic efforts towards a resolution of the Afghan conflict have been left largely to Pakistan, and to a lesser degree, Iran.

In Cambodia, the involvement of the successor states has been confined to Russia, a result largely of its assumption of the Soviet Union's seat at the UN. As a permanent member of the Security Council, Russia was obliged to participate in the implementation of the UN operation mandated by the Paris Agreements signed in October 1991 (see Chapter 2, p. 77). Lacking any compelling economic, strategic or political interest in the country, it appears to have taken on this task with a degree of resignation.[73] Moreover, Cambodia, having essentially been eliminated as a source of friction between Moscow and Beijing in the Gorbachev period, no longer looms large as an issue in relations with China. UN-supervised elections and the restoration of the Cambodian monarchy in 1993, coupled with the political marginalisation of the Khmer Rouge, China's one-time ally in the country, has completed a process whereby Cambodia has seemingly been removed from the proxy struggles of regional powers.

The relatively peaceful political transition in Cambodia has not been matched in Angola. Here the opposition movement, UNITA, rejected the results of nationwide legislative and presidential elections in September 1992, and relaunched a guerrilla campaign against government forces of the MPLA. Russia's role in conflict resolution in this case has once more been the consequence of its position on the Security Council, and, in addition, an inheritance of Soviet responsibilities towards Angola, stemming from the peace accords reached in 1991 (see Chapter 1, p. 37). During 1992–93 Russia was consequently involved in a secondary role in peace talks between the MPLA and UNITA, mediated by the UN Secretary-General's Special Representative in Angola. It also acted as an official observer to the peace process alongside the US and Portugal,[74] and was instrumental in sanctioning UN Security Council Resolution (UNSCR) 864 of September 1993 imposing an oil and arms embargo against UNITA as punishment for the movement's failure to abide by ceasefire arrangements. Moreover, in a fundamental revision of the 1991 accords, the three observers condoned the Angolan government's rejection of clauses which had prohibited it from seeking arms abroad.[75] Russia soon after entered into negotiations concerning a request for military help. This duly arrived, assisting MPLA forces in making significant gains against UNITA during 1994.

The wars in the former Yugoslavia

The root causes of the 'Wars of the Yugoslav Succession' are complex, but their immediate trigger lay in the drive for secession by four of Yugoslavia's six republics. During 1991–92 these four – Slovenia, Croatia, Bosnia–Hercegovina and Macedonia – declared their independence, moves which the Serb-dominated Yugoslav National Army resisted by force. Once secession had become a reality, a murderous struggle for territory was set in train, pitting Serbs against Croats in Croatia, and Croats, Serbs and Bosnian Muslims against one another in Bosnia. In the midst of this has stood the 'rump' Federal Republic of Yugoslavia (FRY) comprising Montenegro and the more dominant Serbia. The FRY has acted as a vehicle for the expansionist ambitions of Serbia in the former Yugoslavia.

Of the Soviet successor states, Russia and Ukraine have been directly involved in the former Yugoslavia. Of the two, Russian involvement has been the more significant (Ukrainians have taken part in the UN peacekeeping force but Kiev has not played a prominent role in diplomatic mediation). Soviet and latterly Russian historical interests in the Balkans, great power ambitions, and Russia's permanent seat on the UN Security Council have combined to give Moscow a *locus standi* in the former Yugoslavia, which it has exploited to some effect. Russia's role has also been important in the wider context of its relations with the West. These have been severely tested by the Yugoslav imbroglio (specific examples and reasons for this will be noted below). However, while differences in approach have often been very visible, on a number of very basic issues, Russia and the West have been in agreement. It is not without significance that the UN Protection Force in the former Yugoslavia (UNPROFOR) has been the vehicle for the first large-scale participation by Russian units in a UN peacekeeping operation. (The USSR had not undertaken such a role.) Russia has also supported a number of schemes aimed at settling the conflict. The London Conference of August 1992, which inaugurated joint UN/European Community (EC) mediation in Bosnia, for instance, was welcomed by Kozyrev as indicative of constructive international co-operation at a global level.[76] Similarly, the Vance–Owen Peace Plan (VOPP) for Bosnia unveiled at the UN/EC Geneva Conference in January 1993, was fully endorsed by Moscow, which offered to dispatch 12,000 troops to facilitate its implementation.[77] Moscow's commitment to joint solutions continued with the Washington Declaration (signed along with the US, the UK, France and Spain the following May). This provided for the 'progressive implementation' of VOPP via the protection of UN safe areas, the enforcement of an air-exclusion zone over Bosnia and sanctions against the republics of Serbia and Montenegro, who were perceived to be the aggressors owing to the former's backing of Bosnian Serb forces.[78] Even with the major strain in Russian–NATO relations in the spring of 1994 (see below, pp. 262–63), diplomatic co-ordination has remained in evidence. A 'Contact Group' comprising diplomats from Russia, the US, France, Germany and the UK, unveiled in July an international peace plan providing for the division of Bosnia into a Serb territory, a Croat–Muslim federation and areas under temporary UN/EC (now the European Union) administration. In the search of a settlement for Bosnia, a diplomatic division of labour had by this point emerged. Russian diplomacy concentrated on the Bosnian Serbs, while American efforts were directed towards Bosnia's Muslims and Croats. A similar partnership also developed with regard to the conflict in Croatia. A ceasefire between Serb and Croat forces at the end of March being the direct result of joint mediation by Moscow and Washington.

At the same time as seeking to preserve co-operation with the West, a degree of disharmony has also been periodically in evidence. The first area of conflict has concerned Moscow's at times sympathetic treatment of Serbian/FRY interests. The issue of international sanctions illustrates this well. During the first half of 1992, Moscow was reluctant to endorse their imposition against the FRY, arguing that diplomatic measures should be exhausted first and that the Serbs were more likely to compromise if not subject to punitive action. Fearing diplomatic isolation and confronted with Serbian inflexibility, however, Moscow changed tack; in 1992 it twice voted at the Security Council in favour of sanctions.[79] Its adapted line now was to argue that relaxation of sanctions should be used as an incentive for Serbian moderation, arguing, for instance, that the FRY should be rewarded for its severing of financial links with the Bosnian Serbs in late August 1994.[80] At the same time the case was made that the sanctions weapon should be applied equitably. Thus, the Russian envoy to the former Yugoslavia Vitaly Churkin, argued in early 1993 that if sanctions were a means of punishing wrongdoing, the UN should take a firmer line against what was seen as Croatian aggression in Bosnia and in the Serb-held areas in Croatia. The principle of equity was also applied to the UN arms embargo.[81] Russian diplomats argued in response to calls by American President Clinton for a lifting of the boycott against the Bosnian Muslim government, that any influx of weaponry would heighten bloodshed. Privately they conceded it would alter the correlation of forces to the disadvantage of the Bosnian Serbs.[82] Fears of an escalation of conflict were, in fact, shared by France and the UK, and along with Russia, the abstentions of these three helped sink a US-supported vote at the Security Council in June 1993 that would have lifted the embargo against Bosnia.

A second area of dispute has concerned military intervention by NATO, and, in particular, Moscow's opposition to the use of air strikes. This matter came to a head during the spring of 1994 as military measures were utilised for the first time to enforce UN resolutions and halt Serbian aggression in Bosnia. In response to the shelling of the market place in the capital Sarajevo on 5 February, the UN Secretary General asked NATO to ready itself for the use of airstrikes in order to enforce UNSCRs 824 and 836 concerning the establishment and protection of UN safe areas. Two days later, NATO issued an ultimatum to Bosnian Serb forces demanding the withdrawal of their heavy weaponry from the environs of Sarajevo by 21 February or face the threat of air raids. The reaction in Moscow to this turn of events was one of carefully constructed hostility. Having voted for both of the relevant Security Council resolutions it faced the dilemma of having to avert the use of force they apparently sanctioned. Its route out of this conundrum amounted to Russia's most successful diplomatic intervention during the entire Yugoslav crisis. Moscow's initial approach was to argue the case against air strikes. On military grounds these were viewed as an incitement to further hostilities, as threatening to Russian UN peacekeepers in Sarajevo and the probable cause of unavoidable civilian casualties. Procedural issues were also forwarded. In particular, Russia questioned the competence of the Secretary General to request NATO action, arguing that a decision on the use of force ought to be referred back to the UN Security Council. In the event, these arguments failed to impress. Russia consequently undertook a successful *démarche* to defuse the crisis. In addition to offering to transfer 400 Russian UN peacekeepers to Sarajevo, Yeltsin, in a letter addressed to the Serbian President Slobodan Milosevic and the Bosnian Serb leader Radovan Karadzic, requested that Serb forces withdraw their weapons from Sarajevo, a request they subsequently followed. For the Bosnian Serbs this offered a face-saving formula; for Moscow a means of averting NATO action.

Russia was unable to repeat its success. On several occasions in the remainder of 1994, NATO aircraft, operating at the request of the UN, undertook military actions. Without the leeway provided by lengthy ultimatums, Russia lacked in these cases the opportunity to effect diplomatic measures to stave off NATO action or the time to prepare a studied response. In the event, Moscow tended to offer lukewarm acceptance of NATO actions (as a consequence of irrefutable evidence of Bosnian Serb provocation) married with warnings of their dire consequences. In late February for instance, air strikes against Bosnian Serb aircraft to enforce the UN no-fly zone were criticised on the grounds that a political settlement rather than an 'escalation of violence ... the use of aviation' was the best route towards peace in Bosnia.[83] A NATO air strike against a Serb air field in Croatia the following November prompted a similar response. Initially supported by Moscow, Kozyrev went on to complain that such actions should not become a common occurrence and could in future prompt a withdrawal of Russia's UNPROFOR contingent.

To summarise, Russian diplomacy towards the wars in the former Yugoslavia has been characterised by first, co-operation in the search for a diplomatic settlement, second, a sympathetic approach towards Serbian interests, and third, a largely hostile attitude towards Western military intervention. All three features, in turn, have influenced Russia's relations with the major Western states. What factors have conditioned Russia's approach?

An interest in a settlement

The wars in the former Yugoslavia have been characterised by a savagery unseen on the European continent since World War II. The sheer scale of the humanitarian disaster which has befallen the region is reason enough for an active diplomacy to promote a cessation of bloodshed and a resolution of an enormous refugees crisis. *Realpoli-*

tik, however, has also been an important consideration. Sanctions against the FRY, for instance, have been costly to the Russian economy. Sergei Glazev Minister of Foreign Economic Relations, suggested in January 1993 that the international community should compensate Russia for its trade losses. Normality in economic relations, however, could only be fully restored by an end to the war. A possible spread of the conflict beyond the former Yugoslavia also deeply worried the Russian leadership. Greek, Turkish, Bulgarian, Romanian and Albanian intervention presented the possibility of a generalised Balkan conflict. The upsurge of what could be construed as a general war pitting Orthodox, Slavic populations against Muslim states led by Turkey, held implications for harmonious relations between Christians and Muslims in the Transcaucasus and in Russia itself. A Balkan war would also threaten Russia's free passage from the Black Sea to the Mediterranean, an essential warm-water outlet for its merchant and military fleets. In this regard a powerful historical echo is relevant, for it was partly to protect this route that Tsarist Russia entered World War I.

Pan-Slavism

Throughout Moscow's involvement in the former Yugoslavia, the case has consistently been made, particularly amongst Yeltsin's political opponents, that Moscow ought to give support to its Slavic brethren and co-religionists, the Serbs. At its most extreme, this opinion has found expression in the dispatch of illegal Russian volunteers to fight alongside the Bosnian Serbs and suspected covert arms supplies by Russian officers made behind the backs of the civilian leadership in Moscow. Strong pro-Serb sympathies could also be found within the Russian parliament and within the Russian press, who have seen in pan-Slavism a means by which a distinctive 'Russian' identity can be furthered in international affairs. Consequently, no opportunity has been wasted to criticise Yeltsin and particularly Kozyrev for their lack of support for Serbia.[84] Among the wider population, sympathies for the Serbs have not been widespread and the war in the former Yugoslavia has been met with indifference. However, the significance of the pan-Slavist argument has lain in the fact that it has formed part of the general conservative onslaught on Yeltsin's overall foreign and domestic policies. Yeltsin has consequently been sensitive to charges of laxity in the former Yugoslavia.

Indeed, on at least one occasion, the link has been quite explicit; Russia's abstention on UNSCR 820, which tightened sanctions against the FRY, was the direct result of conservative criticism of Yeltsin in the run up to a referendum on his rule in April 1993. Tellingly, once the referendum yielded a victory for Yeltsin, the Foreign Ministry expressed regret that it had abstained in the Security Council vote and declared its backing for sanctions.

Instances of pro-Serbianism have, in fact, been the exception rather than the rule. The influence of the pan-Slavic case on Russian policy as a whole has been marginal. In the first place, the premise upon which its arguments rest – that of Russian–Serbian solidarity – is a questionable one in view of the historical record. Whether one considers Russia's attitude towards Serbian nationalism in the nineteenth century or Soviet–Yugoslav relations, the record reflects self-interest and, in the latter case, acrimony as much as it does healthy intercourse.[85] Moreover, whatever pressure may have been exerted on Yeltsin and his ministers to pursue a shameless pro-Serb policy, they have recognised that such a course is replete with dangers as well as benefits. Kozyrev, for example, has argued that Russia is not simply a Slavic nation, but has a large Muslim population. To pursue a foreign policy based on ethnic and religious calculations would, he claimed, be 'tantamount to shifting the civil war from Yugoslavia to our own motherland'. It could also drive a wedge between Russia and its non-Slav partners within the CIS.[86] Kozyrev has also been aware that the example of a 'Greater Serbia' pursued by force of arms sets an unwelcome precedent in terms of border revisions and the establishment of ethnically uniform areas. The success of 'super-patriotism' of this sort can only stoke the flames of conflict in the analogous cases of the Dniester region and Nagorno–Karabakh.[87] It is also worth pointing out that on several occasions, Russian and Serbian/FRY positions have clearly diverged. When Moscow has run the risk of diplomatic isolation in articulating the Serbian case, it has usually backed down. On the question of sanctions, recognition of Croatia and Slovenia[88] and the expulsion of the FRY from the CSCE, Russia initially resisted the trend of international opinion, only later to fall in line. Russia has also very publicly disassociated itself from Serbian actions when these have confounded its overriding objective of facilitating a settlement. The Bosnian Serbs were criticised for their rejection of the VOPP and the Contact Group's peace plan, while an assault on the Bosnian Muslim enclave of Gorazde in April

1994 evinced condemnation from Yeltsin, Kozyrev and Churkin alike. Indeed, in the latter case, Moscow's ire was directed at the Bosnian Serbs both for threatening an escalation of the conflict, and for the duplicity of Karadzic, who had promised Moscow he would refrain from aggressive actions. Pan-Slavism aside, the Russian leadership has also little in common politically with Serbian leaders. Both Milosevic and Karadzic have been held in equal contempt for their flirtations with Yeltsin's nationalist opponents, Rutskoi, and the ultra-nationalist, Vladimir Zhirinovsky, and for their links with a communist core in the Russian armed forces.[89]

Russia's desire for an independent and influential role

Given the shallowness of pro-Serbian sympathies among the Russian leadership, how then does one explain Moscow's periodic willingness to act as a voice of Serbian concerns? Part of the answer lies in Moscow's desire to pursue a foreign policy course, which, while not necessarily at odds with the West (hence co-operation in the search for a diplomatic solution), nonetheless retains an air of independence befitting what is presumed to be Russia's great power status. In this light, a leaning towards the Serbs has signalled to the West that Moscow has its own distinct interests in the former Yugoslavia and that its co-operation cannot be taken for granted.[90] Moreover, because Moscow has been able at times to exert a positive leverage over the Serbs,[91] Russian foreign policy can be portrayed as having an influence well beyond the country's borders. This strengthens Russia's case for playing an active diplomatic role in other global crises, be they in the Middle East or the Korean peninsula.

A wish to maintain influence and independence also explains other aspects of Russia's policy in the former Yugoslavia. Its objections to NATO intervention, for instance, have often been voiced on the grounds that such actions have gone ahead without Moscow being consulted.[92] Although under the wording of UN resolutions, scope has existed for the Secretary General to request NATO action, Russia has been concerned at the prospect of the Alliance assuming the role of regional peacekeeper in Europe under the guise of a form of sub-contract from the UN.[93] Moscow's preference for the UN proper reflects its ability to exert real influence there via the Security Council, something it cannot do within NATO. A more muscular policy also has domestic implications. Russian initiatives in Bosnia have rebutted criticisms that Moscow has simply followed a Western lead. It is not without significance that the Russian *démarche* over Sarajevo occurred just days before Yeltsin's address to the nation at the Russian Duma – the lower house of the parliament elected in December 1993 with a strong nationalist composition.

Conclusion: conflict resolution in the post-Cold War world

Throughout much of the post-war period, armed conflicts have largely been confined to the Third World. From the 1950s, through to the 1980s, factors such as decolonisation, post-independence power struggles and the intervention of the superpowers, either singly or in combination, contributed to particularly vicious and protracted wars in this region. Those in Korea, Vietnam, Afghanistan and Angola are typical. During the 1990s, wars in the Third World have continued. Indeed, in the Middle East, Africa and Asia their frequency has remained alarmingly high. The overall rate of occurrence of war then has not declined. Two changes have, however, been evident. First the declining incidence of *inter*-state war and the increase in *intra*-state or civil war. According to data collected by Peter Wallensteen and Karin Axell, of the ninety or more armed conflicts that took place worldwide in the period 1988–93, only four were of the 'classical inter-state' variety.[94] The regional pattern of war has also altered. In short, the 1990s have witnessed the return of war to Europe (broadly defined to include the Balkans and the Transcaucasus), a continent which had been largely peaceful during the four decades of the 1950s through the 1980s.[95]

Dealing with this proliferation of discord has posed fundamental challenges for governments in the post-Cold War period. The manner of response has been informed by two overriding problems: the institutional and the normative. The institutional problem refers to the difficulties of reorienting existing international organisations towards tasks for which they have been either ill-suited or ill-prepared, a process akin to 'putting square pegs into round holes'.[96] NATO was designed for defensive purposes and has, therefore, been uneasy with outside conflict prevention or management; the CSCE, initially lacking a permanent organisation, has undergone an as yet incomplete process of institutionalisation; and the UN, a body with experience of peacekeeping, mediation and so on, has not been afforded sufficient resources to adequately deal with the plethora of new demands it has faced. A new institution such as the CIS has proven similarly ill-equipped owing to the weakness of its organisation and controversies amongst its members concerning its purpose.

Normative problems derive from two sources: the recognition of states and intervention in states. The recognition of new states courts the risk of initiating a cumulative demonstration effect as the expectations of yet more aspiring states are heightened. This was a problem noted above in relation to sub-nationalism in the successor states. The second normative problem relates to the centrality of non-intervention as a cardinal principle in international law. Without the consent of the state concerned, external interference is considered an abrogation of sovereignty. As Rein Müllerson points out, this is not an absolute; intervention without consent might be justified on humanitarian grounds. Defining when the political expediency of humanitarian intervention should supersede the legal right of states to profit from non-interference, however, remains an issue of contention. In cases of prolonged internal conflict, should a warring government enjoy the right to do as it pleases in dealing with its internal enemies? Or should it rather submit to the recommendations of outside mediators and the 'right' of the international community to intervene in service of international peace and security?[97] Without clarity on these matters external intervention in the service of conflict resolution might encounter insurmountable obstacles, lacking both rationale and justification.

How institutions and norms might affect conflict has sparked a fervent debate amongst scholars of international politics. Both optimistic and pessimistic judgements have been made. The former tend to group around a pluralist interpretation of international politics, while the latter reflect a realist bent. Both share the view that instability is now a feature of the European periphery (parts of the FSU and in the former Yugoslavia) but differ in their assessment of how and with what likelihood this might be contained.

The optimistic view is based on the premise that, 'norms and institutions matter'.[98] For Kupchan and Kupchan these help to create the expectation among states that co-operation will be both beneficial and forthcoming in their relations. Institutions facilitate co-operation through a number of 'discrete mechanisms'. They increase the level of information available to all states; increase the costs of defection from non-cooperative behaviour (i.e. by punishment regimes); introduce issue-linkages which promote agreement in case of dispute by offering reciprocal concessions; and finally, they promote 'inter-state socialisation' or the dissemination of shared values by virtue of increasing contacts among 'different communities of elites'.[99] Building upon these assumptions several scholars have posited arrangements designed for the management of conflict. To be effective, it is argued that these should embody both normative and institutional aspects. Amongst the former, several principles have been suggested that the international community should seek to further.

1 Clear guidelines for secession should be established. To some degree principles already exist in this regard. The successor states, for instance, only gained international recognition having pledged to abide by the UN Charter and the principles of the CSCE (see Chapter 3, pp. 107–8). Yet now the multi-national USSR has broken up, should these principles be applied to aspiring states within the successor states themselves? Should guarantees from say Abkhazia that it will abide by the UN Charter be sufficient alone to win it international legitimacy? In making a judgement on the virtues of secession a fundamental dilemma is evident. To grant recognition might merely accelerate the demonstration effect, leading to further state breakups with all the attendant dislocation and suffering. To refrain from recognition helps keep in existence a state whose integrity is dubious, thereby perpetuating conflict. Thus, as Jennone Walker argues, while there ought to be a 'strong bias against secession' it should not be 'so categorical that it overrides pragmatism'.[100] Thus, recognition of would-be states might only occur if guarantees are provided that: minority rights will be respected; existing inter-state frontiers will not be challenged; relevant arms control agreements will be abided by; and further problems of state secession be submitted to arbitration. In addition, recognition might only be granted if secession has not involved unnecessary violence and a large proportion of the local population has expressed democratically (i.e. by referendum) a desire for independence.[101]
2 Once established, a new state should seek to promote a civic rather than an ethnic notion of citizenship and the human rights situation should be constantly monitored. Violations should be met by sanctions in the form of the withdrawal of economic

assistance.

3 Potential sources of secession can be discouraged by promoting internal democracy, the rule of law, respect of minority rights and self-restraint. This has been termed a 'code of peaceful conduct', which if followed by the new states might dampen sources of secession within their newly acquired borders. Economic assistance to the successor states can be made conditional upon its observance.[102]
4 The principle of non-intervention should be modified to allow external military intervention without the consent of the state concerned to stabilise a source of regional instability and protect innocent victims of intra-state conflicts. Some movement in this direction has already been made with UN-sanctioned actions in Somalia (Operation Restore Hope) and northern Iraq (to protect the local Kurdish population from Iraqi army actions). In terms of settling an intra-state conflict this would mean a shift from *peacekeeping* (the use of outside forces to police a ceasefire agreed between the warring parties) to *peacemaking* or *peace enforcement* (imposing a solution in situations in which violence is still raging).

The range of institutions that might be utilised to further these aims has been covered in previous sections: the UN, the CSCE, NATO and the CIS. Particular methods of conflict management have also been suggested. Indicative of these suggestions is that of Gareth Evans, the Australian Foreign Minister, who has posited three areas of action: peace-building; preventive diplomacy; and restoring peace. These involve addressing through economic and political measures the root causes of disagreement, upgrading special bodies within the UN to engage in preventive action to prevent a slide into hostilities and dealing with conflicts, if necessary via direct intervention.[103]

Turning to pessimistic views, these have at face value much to commend them. The return of war to the European periphery is in itself cause for pessimism and arguably augurs ill for the long-term stability of the region. The pessimists argument turns on the twin assumptions that the passing of bipolarity in the international system has increased the likelihood of conflict, and that international organisations are a doubtful medium for promoting peace. The first of these claims is considered in the concluding chapter; here we shall focus on the second.

The baldest statement of the marginality of international organisations is provided by John Mearsheimer.[104] He posits several reasons why faith in these bodies is misplaced. Crucially, they can only be effective if they represent the common interests of their members. Only on marginal issues is this likely to be the case (he cites the Incidents at Sea Agreement and points to a preoccupation amongst students of international organisation with economic, not security, issues). He is joined in this opinion by Josef Joffe, who asserts that in crucial issues of security and conflict resolution states will behave as they 'have always done' protecting their particular interests first and foremost. Organisations such as the CSCE and the UN, will only reflect the interests of their constituent parts. When these are in conflict, the organisation is likely to be limited in its effectiveness.[105] Evidence to back this assertion is drawn from what is regarded as the limited success rate these bodies have had in conflict resolution efforts of the last few years (notably in the former Yugoslavia) and the apparent reluctance of the major powers to provide them with sufficient resources and powerful mandates to undertake effective actions. The strength of the UN in ejecting Iraq from Kuwait in 1991 is seen as the exception that proves the rule, a success only because the UN operated essentially as an American surrogate and was free of impediments because of Soviet weakness. Since 1991, Russia has been prepared to allow American leadership in the UN but this, it is argued, will not last beyond Moscow's desire to seek a more assertive foreign policy. Indeed, in the former Yugoslavia this has already become apparent, according to Pierre Hassner, in that Russia's UN Security Council seat has allowed it to exercise 'a *de facto* veto-power over UN and American policies on Bosnia'.[106] Similarly, in its near abroad where Russian interests are more immediate and clear, Moscow has resisted the intervention of international organisations in preference for its own peacekeeping efforts.

What is clear from the debate between the optimists and the pessimists is a fundamental difference of opinion on the virtues of collective action. This returns us to many of the themes outlined in the Introduction on the (neo)realist/pluralist debate concerning anarchy and co-operation. One dimension of this debate has yet to be addressed, that of economic co-operation. It is to this that we now turn.

Notes

1 K.J. Holsti, *International Politics. A Framework for Analysis* (London, Prentice-Hall International, sixth edition, 1992), pp. 353–54.

2 The issue is most acute in the case of Estonia. Its 1992 constitution affirms that the Estonian–Russian border conform to the 1920 Treaty of Tartu. This would mean the transfer of some 2,500 square kilometres of formerly Estonian territory allocated to the RSFSR after World War II. This land is now overwhelmingly Russian populated.

3 T. Dragadze, 'The Armenian–Azerbaijani conflict: structure and sentiment', *Third World Quarterly*, 11:1 (1989), pp. 55–71.

4 H. Smith, *The New Russians* (London, Vintage, 1990), pp. 334–35, 338–39.

5 J. Aves, *Post-Soviet Transcaucasia* (London, The Royal Institute of International Affairs, 1993), p. 33.

6 *Moscow News*, 12–19 April 1992, p. 9.

7 Chechen–Ingushetia declared independence in November 1991, following the coming to power of the National Congress of the Chechen People. The declaration was not supported by the Ingush population in the republic. (Note: The RSFSR, while part of the USSR, had itself been a federal entity. At the time of the break-up of the USSR, the Russian Federation consisted of twenty republics. This increased to twenty-one in June 1992, when the Russian parliament passed constitutional amendments setting up an Ingush republic – a move which implicitly recognised the existence of a separate Chechen Republic [Chechnya], albeit still nominally within Russia.)

8 *Moscow News* 19–26 July 1992, p. 13.

9 M.I. Abramovitz, 'Dateline Ankara: Turkey after Ozal', *Foreign Policy*, 91 (1993), pp. 167–69; G.E. Fuller, 'Turkey's new eastern orientation', in G.E. Fuller *et al.*, *Turkey's New Geopolitics* (Boulder, Colorado, Westview Press, 1993).

10 A. Ehteshami and E.C. Murphy, 'The non-Arab Middle East states and the Caucasian/Central Asian republics: Turkey', *International Relations*, 11:6 (1993), pp. 522–23.

11 U. Halbach and H. Tiller, 'Russia and its southern flank', *Aussenpolitik*, 45:2 (1994), p. 161.

12 E. Fuller, 'Nagorno–Karabakh: can Turkey remain neutral?', *Radio Free Europe/Radio Liberty (RFE/RL) Research Report*, 1:14 (1992), pp. 36–38.

13 Ambramovitz, 'Dateline Ankara', p. 165; G.E. Fuller, 'Turkey's new eastern orientation', pp. 76–85.

14 Thus United Nations Security Council Resolution (UNSCR) 822, while not directly accusing Armenia of aggression, acknowledged

Armenian involvement, demanded an immediate ceasefire and the withdrawal of all Armenian forces from Azeri territory. See *Keesing's Record of World Events*, April 1993, p. 39424.

15 V. Baranovsky, 'Conflict developments on the territory of the former Soviet Union', in *SIPRI Yearbook 1994. World Armaments and Disarmament* (Oxford, Oxford University Press/Sipri, 1994), p. 192.

16 E. Fuller, 'Eduard Shevardnadze's via dolorosa', *RFE/RL Research Report*, 2:43 (1993), p. 17.

17 Under the 1977 Soviet constitution as revised December 1990, Adzharia and Abkhazia were autonomous republics within Georgia and South Ossetia was an autonomous *oblast* or region.

18 See Chapter 3, note, 50.

19 A probable payoff for Russian assistance was Georgia's entry into the CIS in December 1993 and the military provisions of the Russian–Georgian Treaty signed in February 1994.

20 Cited in Baranovsky, 'Conflict developments', p. 193, note 115.

21 C. Dale, 'Turmoil in Abkhazia: Russian responses', *RFE/RL Research Report*, 2:34 (1993), pp. 50–51.

22 There is considerable evidence of Russian military support for the Abkhaz cause. It has, however, been covert and without the official blessing of Moscow. See *ibid.*

23 B.R. Rubin, 'The fragmentation of Tajikistan', *Survival*, 35:4 (1993–94); K. Martin, 'Tajikistan: civil war without end?', *RFE/RL Research Report*, 2:33 (1993).

24 First Deputy Minister of Foreign Affairs, Anatoly Adamishin, cited in *Moscow News*, 13 August 1993, p. 4.

25 V. Socor, 'Moldova's new "government of national consensus"', *RFE/RL Research Report*, 1:47 (1992), pp. 6–7. The remaining population in the left bank is 28 per cent Ukrainian and 40 per cent Moldovan. In Moldova as a whole, according to the 1989 Soviet census, the major population groups are: Moldovans 64 per cent, Ukrainians 14 per cent , Russians 13 per cent, and Gaguaz 4 per cent.

26 B. Nahaylo, 'Ukraine and Moldova: the view from Kiev', *RFE/RL Research Report*, 1:18 (1992), pp. 39–40.

27 V. Socor, 'Creeping putsch in eastern Moldova', *RFE/RL Research Report*, 1:3 (1992), pp. 8–9; *Moscow News*, 19–26 July 1992, p. 5.

28 C. King, 'Moldova and the new Bessarabian questions', *The World Today*, (July 1993), p. 137.

29 V. Socor, 'Russia's army in Moldova: there to stay?', *RFE/RL Research Report*, 2:25 (1993), p. 46.

30 King, 'Moldova and the new Bessarabian questions', p. 138.

31 *Ibid.*, pp. 135–36; V. Socor, 'Why Moldova does not seek reunification with Romania', *RFE/RL Research Report*, 1:5 (1992).

32 'Moldova's political landscape: profiles of the parties', *RFE/RL Research Report*, 3:10 (1994), pp. 8–11.
33 N. Melvin, 'Moldova looks back to the future', *The World Today*, (June 1994), p. 103.
34 'War or peace? Human rights and Russian military involvement in the "near abroad"', *Helsinki Watch*, 5:22 (1993), pp. 8–11.
35 *RFE/RL Daily Report*, 26 October 1994.
36 K.S. Shehadi, *Ethnic Self-Determination and the Break-up of States* (London, The International Institute of Strategic Studies, 1993), p. 54.
37 *Ibid.*, p. 7.
38 S.P. Huntington, *Political Order in Changing Societies* (New Haven, Yale University Press, 1968), pp. 1–91 *passim*.
39 A.V. Kortunov, 'Future strategic relations among the former Soviet republics', in M.I. Midlarsky *et al.* (eds), *From Rivalry to Co-operation. Russian and American Perspectives on the Post-Cold War Era* (New York, Harper Collins, 1994), pp. 156–57.
40 E. Luard, 'Civil conflicts in modern international relations', in E. Luard (ed.), *The International Regulation of Civil Wars* (London, Thames and Hudson, 1972), pp. 18–19.
41 R. Cooper and M. Berdal, 'Outside intervention in ethnic conflicts', *Survival*, 35:1 (1993), p. 137 (emphasis added).
42 M.H. Shuman and H. Harvey, *Security Without War. A Post-Cold War Foreign Policy* (Boulder, Westview Press, 1993), p. 86.
43 In Abkhazia the strategy has been pursued to a degree. The war there in 1993–94 resulted in the flight of much of the local Georgian, Russian and Armenian populations.
44 J.A. Vasquez, 'Building peace in the post-Cold War era', in Midlarsky *et al.* (eds), *From Rivalry to Co-operation*, p. 215.
45 Shehadi, *Ethnic Self-determination*, pp. 68–69.
46 J. Walker, 'International mediation of ethnic conflicts', *Survival*, 35:1 (1993).
47 According to Colonel-General Georgii Kondratev, the military commander responsible for Russian peacekeeping operations, these were distributed as follows: Tajikistan (6,000), Moldova's Dniester region (2,000), Abkhazia and South Ossetia (1,500). See *RFE/RL News Briefs*, 21–25 March 1994, p. 4.
48 These quotes and that at the head of the paragraph are taken from a speech by Yeltsin cited in S. Crow, 'Russia seeks leadership role in regional peacekeeping', *RFE/RL Research Report*, 2:15 (1993), p. 28.
49 S. Crow, 'Russia promotes the CIS as an international organisation', *RFE/RL Research Report*, 3:11 (1994), pp. 33–38.
50 S. Crow, 'Russian peacekeeping: defense, diplomacy, or imperialism?', *RFE/RL Research Report*, 1:37 (1992), pp. 37–40.

51 C.R. Mitchell, *The Structure of International Conflict* (London and Basingstoke, Macmillan, 1981), pp. 292–94.
52 L. Drüke, 'The United Nations in conflict prevention', in W. Bauwens and L. Reycher (eds), *The Art of Conflict Prevention* (London and New York, Brassey's, 1994), p. 23.
53 Cooper and Berdal, 'Outside intervention', p. 136.
54 J.E. Goodby, 'Collective security in Europe after the Cold War', *Journal of International Affairs*, 46:2 (1993), p. 314.
55 Since December 1994 known as the Organisation of Security and Co-operation in Europe.
56 *RFE/RL News Briefs*, 14–18 March 1994, p. 1.
57 K.J. Huber, 'The CSCE's new role in the east: conflict prevention', *RFE/RL Research Report*, 3:31 (1994), p. 28.
58 J. Walker, 'European regional organisations and ethnic conflict', R.Cowen Karp (ed.), *Central and Eastern Europe: the Challenge of Transition* (Oxford, Oxford University Press/SIPRI, 1993), pp. 49, 55–57.
59 'Helsinki Decisions' in *International Legal Materials*, 31:6, (1992), pp. 1400–1401.
60 *RFE/RL Research Report*, 3:12 (1994), pp. 22–23.
61 *RFE/RL News Briefs*, 22–26 February 1993, p. 12, and 6–10 June 1994, p. 20.
62 K. Martin, 'China and Central Asia: between seduction and suspicion', *RFE/RL Research Report* 3:25 (1994), p. 32.
63 The history of the Kuriles issue up to 1991 is traced in S. Foye, 'The struggle over Russia's Kurile Islands policy', *RFE/RL Research Report*, 1:36 (1992), pp. 35–36.
64 H. Kimura, 'Japanese–Russian relations: issues and future perspectives', in T. Taylor (ed.), *The Collapse of the Soviet Empire. Managing the Regional Fall–Out* (London, The Royal Institute of International Affairs/International Institute for Global Peace, 1992), pp. 85, 88–89.
65 *Moscow News*, 26 July–2 August 1992, p. 13.
66 S. Foye, 'Russo–Japanese relations: still travelling a rocky road', *RFE/RL Research Report*, 2:44 (1993), p. 33.
67 *The Economist*, 28 August 1993, p. 50, and L. Buszynski, 'Russia and Japan: the unmaking of a territorial settlement', *The World Today* (March 1993), pp. 52–53.
68 S. Blank, 'We can live without you: rivalry and dialogue in Russo–Japanese relations', *Comparative Strategy*, 12:2 (1993), pp. 185–89.
69 E. Bazhanov and N. Bazhanov, 'Russia and Asia in 1993', *Asian Survey*, 34:1 (1994), pp. 91–92.

70 Foye, 'The struggle over Russia's Kurile Islands policy', p. 38.

71 *Ibid*., p. 39; P.F. Meyer, 'Moscow's relations with Tokyo. Domestic obstacles to a territorial agreement', *Asian Survey*, 33:10 (1993), pp. 958–59; S. Crow, 'Ambartsumov's influence on Russian foreign policy', *RFE/RL Research Report*, 2:19 (1993), p. 40.

72 Russian Deputy Defence Minister, Boris Gromov, revealed in February 1994 that 293 former Soviet soldiers – two-thirds of them Russian – were still held prisoner in Afghanistan. *RFE/RL News Briefs*, 14–18 February 1994, p. 1.

73 E. Bazhanov and N. Bazhanov, 'Russia and Asia in 1992. A balancing act', *Asian Survey*, 33:1 (1993), pp. 100–101; *Moscow News*, 2–9 February 1992, p. 12.

74 This was a hangover from the participation of these countries as observers in a Joint Political–Military Commission set up under the terms of the 1991 peace accords to monitor a ceasefire and the elections. With the dissolution of this body in July 1993, the observer role continued in the form of a 'troika' to assist ongoing efforts towards a MPLA–UNITA settlement.

75 This action and the Security Council measures required a fundamental policy reappraisal on the part of Washington, UNITA's long-time backer. The MPLA's strong showing in the September elections and UNITA's rejection of the democratic process led Democratic President Bill Clinton to reverse over a decade of US policy by extending diplomatic recognition to Angola and openly criticising UNITA's intransigence.

76 *CDSP*, 44:35 (1992), p. 16.

77 *The Guardian*, 5 May 1993, p. 10.

78 *Keesing's Record of World Events*, May 1993, p. 39469.

79 The initial motion was UNSCR 757 of 30 May 1992. This froze Yugoslav assets abroad and banned all trade with Serbia and Montenegro (the Federal Republic of Yugoslavia) with the exception of food and medicine. Russia also voted for UNSCR 787 in November 1992 which outlawed the transhipment through the FRY of major commodities such as oil, coal and iron.

80 The Russian position evidently carried the day; the UNSC voted in early October 1994 for a suspension of sanctions against the FRY in the areas of sport, culture, ferry traffic and air transport.

81 In September 1991, UNSCR 713 established a mandatory arms embargo throughout the territories of Yugoslavia's then six republics.

82 *CDSP*, 45:26 (1993), p. 16; *RFE/RL News Briefs*, 16–19 August 1994, p. 2.

83 Kozyrev cited in Foreign Broadcast Information Service: FBIS-SOV-94–040, 1 March 1994, p. 11.

84 S. Crow, 'Reading Moscow's policies towards the rump Yugoslavia', *RFE/RL Research Report*, 1:44 (1992), pp. 16–18, and A. Lynch and R. Lukic, 'Russian foreign policy and the wars in the former Yugoslavia', *RFE/RL Research Report*, 2:41 (1993), pp. 26–27.

85 The Soviet Union and Yugoslavia are here considered as surrogates for Russian and Serb interests respectively.

86 *Nezavisimaya gazeta*, 20 August 1992; *The Independent*, 27 February 1993, p. 8.

87 *Izvestiya*, 27 May 1992, p. 5.

88 Russia announced its intention to recognise these two former Yugoslav republics in February 1992 having initially demurred as a sign of support for the FRY.

89 M. Glenny, 'The return of the great powers', *New Left Review*, 205 (1994), p. 130.

90 J. Sherr, 'Russia returns to Europe', *European Security Analyst*, 31 (1994), p. 3.

91 The lifting of the siege of Sarajevo is the most obvious case in point. Other examples include Russian pressure on Milosevic to accept VOPP; in winning Karadzic's agreement in March 1994 to lift a blockade of Tuzla airport in Bosnia; and in bringing the Serbian side around to a ceasefire agreement concerning Serb-occupied parts of Croatia the same month.

92 See Yeltsin's reaction to NATO airstrikes on Gorazde, *The Guardian*, 12 April 1994, p. 10.

93 *The Guardian*, 23 February 1993, p. 10.

94 P. Wallensteen and K. Axell, 'Conflict resolution and the end of the Cold War, 1989–93', *Journal of Peace Research*, 31:3 (1994). (The wars in the former Yugoslavia and the undeclared war between Armenia and Azerbaijan do not qualify under Wallensteen and Axell's criteria as inter-state wars).

95 During these years Europe saw no major war, and just two minor conflicts – the Soviet intervention in Hungary in 1956 and the Greco–Turkish war in Cyprus in 1974.

96 S.I. Griffiths, *Nationalism and Ethnic Conflict. Threats to European Security* (Oxford, Oxford University Press/Sipri, SIPRI Research Report, No.5, 1993), p. 91.

97 R. Müllerson, *International Law, Rights and Politics* (London and New York, Routledge, 1994), pp. 51–52; Goodby, 'Collective security', pp. 308–9.

98 J.G. Ruggie, 'Multilateralism: the anatomy of an institution', *International Organisation*, 46:3 (1992), p. 565. (The term 'institution' is used here to embrace both international organisations and regimes – see the Introduction, pp. 9–10).

99 C.A. Kupchan and C.A. Kupchan. 'Concerts, collective security, and the future of Europe', *International Security*, 16:1 (1991), pp. 131–32.
100 Walker, 'European regional organisations', p. 60.
101 *Ibid*., pp. 60–61.
102 G. Evans, 'Co-operative security and intra-state conflict', *Foreign Policy*, 96 (1994), pp. 12–13.
103 *Ibid*., pp. 11–18.
104 S. Hoffmann, R.D. Keohane and J.J. Mearsheimer, 'Back to the future, part II: international relations theory and post-Cold War Europe', *International Security*, 15:2 (1990), pp. 194–99.
105 J. Joffe, 'Collective security and the future of Europe: failed dreams and dead ends', *Survival*, 34:1 (1992), pp. 48–49.
106 P. Hassner, 'Beyond nationalism and internationalism: ethnicity and world order', *Survival*, 35:2 (1993), p. 62.

Recommended reading

R. Allison, *Peacekeeping in the Soviet Successor States* (Paris, The Institute for Security Studies, The Western European Union, Chaillot Papers, No.18, 1994).

V. Baranovsky, 'Conflict developments on the territory of the former Soviet Union', *Sipri Yearbook, 1994, World Armaments and Disarmament* (Oxford, Oxford University Press/Sipri, 1994).

W.R. Duncan and G.P. Holman, *Ethnic Nationalism and Regional Conflict. The Former Soviet Union and Yugoslavia* (Boulder, Westview Press, 1994).

S. Goldenberg, *Pride of Small Nations. The Caucasus and Post-Soviet Disorder* (London, Zed Books, 1994).

V.A. Kremenyuk, *Conflicts in and around Russia. Nation-Building in Difficult Times* (Westport, Connecticut, Greenwood Press, 1994).

6

Post-Soviet external economic relations

As the successor states have embarked upon the journey of independence, amongst the most daunting tasks they have had to deal with is that of economic management. All have faced common problems: catastrophic performance indicators, constraints imposed by interdependence, and the disruption caused by the transition from plan and state ownership to market structures. Some have been more successful than others in meeting these challenges, yet none has truly escaped their Soviet legacy. In this chapter we analyse how the successor states have attempted to address these issues through external economic relations. Attention is given to co-operation among the successor states themselves (that is, part of the FSU's 'inward orientation') and their engagement with the outside world (part of the FSU's 'outward orientation').

The Soviet economy: crawling from the wreckage

Standing at the threshold of independence, the leaders of the successor states confronted a daunting economic inheritance as a consequence of what was, in effect, a collapse of the Soviet economy during 1991. Plummeting output provides one indicator of the severity of the crisis, one from which none of the Soviet republics was immune (see Table 6.1).

This steep decline in production was in fact only one dimension of Soviet economic breakdown. Shortages of basic goods and plummeting capital investment plagued all the republics during 1991 and annual retail price inflation was nowhere less than 80 per cent. Budgetary devolution meanwhile had resulted in the accumulation of weighty deficits, amounting in the case of the RSFSR to some 9 per cent of its GDP.[1] An equally gloomy situation prevailed in external economic relations. A drop in overall Soviet foreign trade during 1991 was replicated at the republican level. The eleven founding members of the CIS experienced falls in trade with the outside world ranging from 30 per cent in Armenia, through 37 per cent in the RSFSR and up to 46 per cent in the case of Moldova.[2] The USSR's large foreign debt was a further, burdensome inheritance, in this case made all the more unwelcome by the complicated matter of apportioning liability among the former republics.

Table 6.1 *Economic performance of the Soviet republics: 1991 over 1990 (% change, selected indicators)*

	Real GDP	*Industrial output*	*Agricultural output*
USSR	–9.0	–7.8[a]	–7.0
RSFSR[b]	–9.0	–2.2	–5.0
Ukraine	–11.2	–4.5	–12.0
Belarus	–0.9	–1.5	–3.0
Moldova	–18.0	–7.0	–11.0
Azerbaijan	–0.7	3.8	0.0
Georgia	–20.6	–19.0	—
Armenia	–11.8	–9.6	11.0
Uzbekistan	–0.9	1.8	–5.0
Kazakhstan	–13.0	0.7	–8.0
Turkmenistan	–0.6	4.1	–2.0
Tajikistan	–8.7	–2.0	–10.0
Kyrgyzstan	–5.0	0.1	–8.0
Latvia	–8.3	0.0	–4.0
Lithuania	–13.4	–1.3	–4.0
Estonia	–11.8	–9.0	–16.0

Notes: [a] aggregate of CIS states only (excludes Georgia and Baltic states). [b] Russian Soviet Federated Socialist Republic

Sources: J. Noren and L. Kurtzweg, 'The Soviet economy unravels: 1985–91', in R.F. Kaufman and J.P. Hardt (eds), for the Joint Economic Committee, Congress of the United States, *The Former Soviet Union in Transition* (New York and London, M.E. Sharpe, 1993), p.25; International Monetary Fund, *World Economic Outlook, May 1993* (Washington DC, 1993), p. 138.

The common response of the successor states to the challenge of economic recovery has been macroeconomic stabilisation (involving limits on expenditure to reduce budget deficits, restrictions on monetary issue and spending to reduce inflation etc.) and the construction of market-based economies (involving privatisation, reducing the directing role of the state, and so on). The degree of commitment to this course has varied. The pioneers of market reform (notably, Estonia, Latvia, and the reformist ministers in Russia grouped around acting Prime Minister Gaidar during 1992) regarded the economic and moral bankruptcy of the Soviet economy as so complete by 1991 as to require a revolutionary transformation, which would wipe out the institutions of socialism and replace them with those of capitalism. Gorbachev's ill-fated attempts to introduce market mechanisms into what remained an essentially state-owned economy appeared to bear out the wisdom of this observation. Such enthusiasm for the market was not uniformly shared throughout the FSU. Not only was the abandonment of state direction seen as entailing painful economic and social costs (unemployment, inflation, plant closures), but it suggested a loss of the all-embracing political control formerly enjoyed by the numerous echelons of government and bureaucracy engaged in the running of the enormous state sector. However, even the cautious were not opposed to some movement away from the planned, state-owned economy. In countries such as Ukraine, Turkmenistan, Uzbekistan, the emphasis might have been on gradualism, but a transition from centrally planned and state-owned economies towards market capitalism was nevertheless accepted in principle as the only long-term corrective to their grave economic predicament.[3]

Alongside fundamental domestic reforms it was also accepted that regeneration would be strongly influenced by external economic relations, whether these be with other successor states or with the wider world. The extreme centralisation of the former Soviet economy meant that all the successor states were bound together by a myriad of connections, which, coupled with the regional weight of Russia, provided a strong case for co-operation. Integration with the international economy, meanwhile, provided a route towards modernisation and prosperity through economic assistance, trade and foreign investment.

Economic viability

Acquiring the attributes of statehood is often seen as being first and foremost a political task. At a domestic level this involves, most importantly, the emplacement of an indigenous leadership in positions of government and the pursuit of legitimacy and authority through a process of nation-building, involving the revival of language, local histories and the potent symbols of flag and anthem. These goals, as noted in Chapter 2 were partially realised by a number of Soviet republics during the Gorbachev period. The external aspects of statehood followed with the USSR's demise. The granting of diplomatic recognition by the international community and the pursuit of independent defence and foreign policies have been covered in Chapters 3, 4 and 5.

Equally important, a state will also seek to pursue economic objectives. Its ability to do so, however, is often severely limited. The experience of a number of Third World countries, notably in Africa, demonstrates that the euphoria of 'flag independence' soon dissipates once the difficulties of pursuing national development priorities are confronted. An international economic system in which trading patterns, raw material prices and financial conditions are beyond influence has been the downfall of many a Third World economy. National development in such a hostile environment is, however, not an impossibility, as demonstrated by the countries of the Pacific rim and, to a lesser extent, those in parts of Latin America. Economic well-being in part depends on judicious economic policies, a favourable political climate and, equally important, in maximising the potential benefits to be had from endowments such as natural resources, geographic location and human reserves. The presence or absence of these factors contribute to *economic viability*, defined by Gertrude Schroeder as 'the capability to exist and develop as a separate state in a world of highly economically interdependent states'.[4]

In relation to the successor states, economic viability has been affected by a number of factors. It has been most damagingly influenced by warfare. War destroys infrastructure, disrupts transport links, lays waste to arable land, brings trade to a standstill and diverts the workforce into economically unproductive military duties. It also acts as a powerful disincentive to foreign investment and international financial assistance. Not surprisingly, the successor states with the most woeful levels of economic performance have been those at war: Tajikistan, Armenia, Azerbaijan and Georgia.

More peaceful political competition can also exert a detrimental influence. Effective political leadership and policy-making institutions are essential for the success of economic policy, the more so when such policies are aimed at a fundamental restructuring of the economic order. Yet in much of the FSU, the political realm has been far from stable. In Russia, for instance, successful reform has been hampered by a chaotic series of political reshuffles. As *The Economist* commented in January 1994, in two years of economic reform, Russia had had 'three prime ministers, four finance ministers, two central-bank governors, two parliaments, five governments and umpteen changes of policy', a 'mess' which seemingly put the country 'beyond help'.[5] In Ukraine, the situation has been equally grave. During 1993 a three-way political battle between President Leonid Kravchuk, the Ukrainian parliament and the Prime Minister Leonid Kuchma, hampered consensus on marketisation and accelerated the country's slide into a 'hyper-depression' of shrinking output and runaway inflation.[6] Kuchma, who resigned in September, had his revenge the following July. Against a backdrop of widespread popular dissatisfaction prompted by shortages, inflation and the threat of unemployment, Presidential elections were held which saw Kravchuk defeated by his erstwhile Prime Minister. Such crises, however, have not always been the norm. The Baltic states have managed to minimise the immobilising effects of political in-fighting largely because an overall consensus has existed on the benefits of a swift transition towards the market. In Turkmenistan and Uzbekistan, meanwhile, political stability has been bought at the price of a creeping authoritarianism and a cautious market reform strategy. This, it has been claimed, allows for economic change involving minimum social dislocation while at the same time fostering an environment favourable to foreign investment.[7]

Demographic factors are further indicators of economic viability. The Central Asian states, for instance, possess fast-growing, predominantly rural and under-educated populations. This presents a challenge familiar in parts of the developing world: the need for economic growth in order to foster job creation and to avert the social discontent occasioned by rising unemployment. The Slavic and Baltic states face an entirely different situation. Their inhabitants are mainly urban and a majority of the workforce is employed in industry. The historical overstaffing and industrial obsolescence of the Soviet economy means restructuring in these countries will inevitably result in a shedding of labour. The consequent rise in unemployment, however, will at least not be aggravated by an influx of new entrants to the workforce. In all these countries the natural rate of population increase is very low, and in the case of certain Russian regions actually negative.[8]

Alongside the urban–rural balance, ethnic composition can effect economic performance. Where a minority occupies a strategic position within the workforce, its sudden departure can be harmful. In the Transcaucasus and Central Asia the large Russian technical intelligentsia has since the late 1980s been leaving in large numbers, fearful for their security in the midst of warfare or upset by a loss of political and social privileges. The departing Russians have left behind understaffed industries and a dearth of local technical skills. In the comparable cases of Estonia and Latvia the large Russian workforce has remained where it is. Despite the difficulties experienced by new citizenship and language laws, the relative prosperity and civil stability of the Baltic states has prevented a Russian exodus. This, however, can create additional problems for the host state. Grievances among the large resident minority has led in the Baltics to politically motivated strike actions in key industries, worker opposition to government economic policies and resistance to alterations of labour and employment legislation.

Geography can also play a part in influencing economic fortune (see also Chapter 3, pp. 111–20). The proximity of the Baltic states to the Nordic countries, for instance, presents favourable conditions for the development of both trade and investment. Russia's Far East enjoys a similar positioning in relation to the dynamic economies of the Asian–Pacific region. Kazakhstan's long frontier with China offers potential for thriving trans-border commerce. Location can also give weight to claims regarding international affiliation and co-operation. Arrangements which allow access to the markets and financial assistance of the European Community/European Union (EC/EU), for example, are far more likely for states such as the Baltics, Ukraine and Russia, than the geographically and culturally distant Central Asian countries.

Any assessment of economic viability of course must take into account the sectoral structure of the post-Soviet economies. Industrialisation, the *leitmotiv* of early Soviet economic development affected the USSR's republics quite differently. Parts of Russia, Ukraine, Belarus and the Baltics are sites of heavy industrial and mining belts whose origins go back before the 1917 revolution and which developed further under Soviet rule. Central Asia experienced, for a time, a rapid rate of industrialisation under Soviet direction. During the 1920s and 1930s, industrial development, which had hardly begun prior to 1917, occurred at an impressive rate, and in the case of Kazakhstan continued long after, boosted by a massive influx of Russian migrants. For all these efforts, however, levels of industry remained far below those in the Slavic and Baltic republics. During Soviet rule, a clear division was also apparent in agriculture. In Central Asia figures for 1990/91 indicate that agricultural production accounted in each republic for the largest portion of net material product.[9] Yet in gross terms the industrialised republics too were important agricultural producers. In the Russian case, this was a function of sheer territorial size and in Ukraine a consequence of the possession of particularly fertile land. In the Baltics meanwhile, an emphasis on more intensive forms of agriculture meant the export of dairy products, meat and processed food to other Soviet republics. Sectoral differentiation, coupled with the varying rates of natural population increase, in turn, gave rise to further divisions. The Slavic and Baltic republics, for instance, enjoyed above average rates of per capita investment and higher standards of living whether measured by income or consumption levels.

Finally, endowments of mineral and energy resources also affect viability, offering a lucrative avenue of wealth generation. During the Soviet period the RSFSR was, in fact, the major producer of all forms of energy in the USSR. Ukraine contributed sizeably to Soviet coal and electricity output. The Central Asian states and Azerbaijan also made a not insignificant contribution. Output per capita was above the Soviet average in Kazakhstan (electricity, oil, coal), Uzbekistan (natural gas),Turkmenistan (natural gas) and Azerbaijan (oil). Uzbekistan was also the source of one-third of the USSR's gold production (making it the world's eighth largest producer), and Kazakhstan was a site of significant uranium deposits and one-third of the Soviet Union's silver. By contrast, the remaining successor states are less well blessed. The Baltic states, along with Belarus, Moldova, Armenia, Georgia and Kyrgyzstan are, for instance, all greatly deficient in energy resources.

Interdependence

Among the factors which bear on economic viability perhaps none is as significant to the successor states as their degree of mutual dependence. All had formerly been part of the highly integrated and centralised Soviet economy, in which planning was largely carried out by sector and republican interests were subordinated to the interests of the USSR as a whole. Alongside the emphasis placed on attaining economies of scale through the operation of large enterprises, this resulted in the concentration of production in a limited number of enterprises and high levels of republican specialisation. This might have made sense within the Soviet economy, but once the USSR disintegrated it left many of the republics with severely imbalanced economies, ill-equipped for local needs. The potential problems can be seen in Central Asia. Here, a large agricultural sector did not render these republics anywhere near self-sufficient in foodstuffs. A satisfactory diet was confounded by a cotton monoculture and agrarian specialisation involving a limited number of edible crops. A dependency index calculated by Ihor Stebelsky shows that Turkmenistan, Uzbekistan and Tajikistan were, in fact, amongst the most reliant of the Soviet republics for food *imports* from other republics.[10]

Interdependence can also be illustrated by reference to trade. The Soviet republics were, with the exception of the RSFSR, poorly oriented towards transactions with the outside world. Mutual exchanges accounted for nearly 72 per cent of all trade carried out by the republics.[11] Trade interdependence was paralleled by an intimate distribution and transport network. This, once more, paid little heed to republican priorities. Take the case of Kazakhstan. In aggregate terms, it enjoyed a near-sufficiency in natural gas, yet could only utilise this for its industries in the north after it had been processed in the RSFSR. The bulk of consumption in the centre and east of the country was satisfied not by domestic production at all but by supplies from neighbouring Uzbekistan and Turkmenistan. Kazakhstan's electricity meanwhile was supplied by grids controlled in Moscow and in Tashkent in neighbouring Uzbekistan.[12] Even the RSFSR, which was the hub of the Soviet transport system, was affected, in that over half its sea freight was transported from ports in other republics. Of course, one would have expected inward-looking trade relations and transport links, given the republics' common development within a single economy, the vast geographical size of the USSR and the patterns of republican specialisation noted above. Yet, in the post-Soviet period, such a state of affairs has exposed certain of the successor states to a disadvantageous dependency on their erstwhile Soviet partners.

Patterns of income redistribution within the USSR provide a further measurement of interdependence. Many republics benefited substantially from the redistributive effects of trade pricing. The practice of underpricing energy and raw materials while overpricing food and manufactured goods, resulted in an outflow from the RSFSR amounting to some 66.8 billion roubles in 1989 alone.[13] Income transfers through the state budget were a further means of redistribution. All five Central Asian republics benefited from this, while the net budgetary donors included the RSFSR, Azerbaijan, Byelorussia and Ukraine.[14]

Interdependence, integration and the formation of the CIS

The interdependence of the republics within the framework of the Soviet economy, coupled with their common commitment to market reforms, might at first sight have provided a strong case for continued co-operation as the USSR fell apart. Leaders such as Nursultan Nazarbaev, Stanislau Shushkevich and Mircea Snegur, respectively the Presidents of Kazakhstan, Belarus and Moldova, were, in fact, quite explicit in supporting such a line of reasoning. That said, a trend towards inter-republican economic dislocation was already painfully apparent well before the USSR's political demise. The collapse of Soviet output during 1990-91 was both cause and effect of a trend towards regional autarky. In many cases, the authorities in the republics impelled by growing shortages, the increasing ineffectiveness of central procurement, and rising political expectations sought to restrict exports to other areas of the USSR in service of local needs. In total, inter-republican trade fell by some 15 per cent during 1991. This resulted in acute shortages of fuel, consumer goods and material inputs, and inevitably, in a marked decline in industrial output. Some of the harmful effects of trade disruption were offset by the conclusion of bilateral trade agreements. But the basic point remains; the assertion of short-term republican interests augured ill for co-ordination beyond the Soviet era.

There were other factors likely to impede co-operation. For some, co-operation meant regulation. In areas of inter-republican trade, monetary issue and the regulation of migratory labour this might have a straightforward economic rationale, but politically it was unacceptable. The exercise of powers by a co-ordinating economic body ran counter to the process of consolidating sovereignty and was viewed as an attempt to preserve the old 'centre' in some form. For these reasons the Baltic states and Georgia, despite considerable energy dependence, resolved to deal with the other successor states on a largely bilateral basis rather than through membership of the CIS. Considerations of this nature were compounded by an awareness of Russia's economic muscle. This fuelled suspicions, notably in Ukraine, that any economic mechanism would simply entrench Russian influence throughout the territory of the FSU. Kravchuk in the run up to his election as President in December 1991 suggested that future prosperity could only be guaranteed in a truly independent state, arguing falsely that Ukraine under the Soviet system was a net exporter of resources to Russia.[15]

Turning to Russia, it appeared to have sound economic reasons for loosening some of the bonds which connected it to the other former republics, not least staunching the net outflow of resources described above. In this light it might seem surprising that Moscow emerged as a strong advocate of economic co-ordination. Its position on this matter was not, however, born of altruism. Russia was prepared to shoulder some of the costs formerly borne by the Soviet budget (subsidies to Central Asia, trade credits to other republics) as a necessary price of strengthening the attractions of the CIS and bolstering Russia's dominant position within the organisation.[16] More obvious economic calculations were also important. A rapid switch away from the artificial low prices of the Soviet period might offer Russia the prospect of increased revenues, but if the successor states were unable to meet the new trading terms, this would further dislocate intra-FSU trade. A sudden upward revision of the price of Russian oil and gas might force the closure of plants outside Russia, producing goods upon which it depended, or result in retaliatory price hikes which would increase the cost of materials such as cotton and foodstuffs essential for Russian consumers.

Given then, the divergent attitudes of the republics at the end of 1991, how was co-operation to be achieved? The division between the 'economic pragmatists' (who favoured continued integration in some form, if only because of the reality of interdependence) and the 'national romantics' (who sought to maximise local powers and extend national economic interests) appeared one that was impossible to resolve within a common framework.[17] In this light, the formation of the CIS was a largely fortuitous occurrence; the result of a temporary meeting of minds amongst a majority of republics on the necessity of repairing inter-republican links as a means of halting the spiral of economic collapse. An initial attempt with the same end, the Economic Community Treaty signed by ten republics in October and November, had become bogged down in intractable discussions, and was, despite its granting of wide republican autonomy, still a solution conceived within a Union framework. The CIS founding agreements sought to improve upon this by outlining a form of economic co-ordination free of a 'centre' and compatible with full political independence. Added urgency was given to this task by the almost literal financial bankruptcy of the USSR, and fears of unilateral Russian actions, aroused by its declared intention to introduce a comprehensive price liberalisation.[18]

These good intentions saw their realisation in the CIS founding agreements. The most comprehensive economic provisions were contained in declarations by the Commonwealth's initiators – Russia, Ukraine and Belarus. Having made clear their aspiration to develop a 'common economic space', these three adopted a declaration on the co-ordination of economic policies that baldly affirmed the need to develop close links 'in order to stabilise the economy and set the basis for economic recovery'.[19] To this end, a parade of measures was suggested, which, at first sight, reflected a triumph of pragmatism over economic self-interest. The impression of compromise was strengthened by Russia's willingness to put off price liberalisation from December 16 until January 2 to permit Ukraine and Belarus time to prepare. Tentative steps were also taken towards the creation of institutional mechanisms of co-ordination, in the form of the councils of heads of state and government and ministerial committees. Despite this auspicious beginning, dark clouds loomed on the horizon. The CIS could make no claim to comprehensiveness; the Baltic states, three of the more economically advanced of the former republics were adamantly opposed to membership. Moreover, the CIS agreements contained an apparent consensus on broad issues, but the details were still to be negotiated. Subsequent efforts to define workable mechanisms of co-operation have proven largely unsuccessful.

Economic issues and the CIS

The rouble zone

Nowhere have the complexities and contradictions of the Soviet legacy been more apparent than in the failed attempts to maintain a common currency. At the end of 1991, the continued use of the rouble (the currency throughout the whole USSR prior to its collapse) appeared a practical means of promoting intra-FSU trade and keeping a check on inflation. To these ends, the Minsk summit of the CIS in December decided to set up a 'common rouble zone' in which the former Soviet rouble would continue to be used by all CIS member states. The absence of national currencies anywhere in the FSU at this point meant the non-CIS members of the Baltics and Georgia were also effectively included within this zone.

During 1992-93 the common currency area suffered a series of fatal blows. A major problem concerned control of the money supply. The location of monetary issue in Russia (it had liquidated the former Soviet state bank and transferred its issuing powers to the Central Bank of Russia) was circumvented in the other successor states by the issue of credit money by individual central banks and the running of government deficits. This uncontrolled creation of money had inflationary consequences throughout the FSU. In addition, it resulted in a huge haemorrhage of commodity resources from Russia as enterprises in other successor states simply purchased goods in Russia on the basis of rouble credits issued by their own national banks. This soon proved intolerable to Russia. In July, it unilaterally tightened up the rules governing inter-bank rouble settlements.

Russia's attempted imposition of monetary discipline illustrated to the members of the rouble zone that so long as the rouble remained the common currency Moscow reserved the right to determine financial policy. This prompted them to take action to boost their economic freedom. From mid-1992 a variety of different national monetary forms was introduced. This step also had a strong political content; a currency was, after all, an important symbol of independent statehood. It should be of no surprise, therefore, that the Baltic states and Ukraine were among the first of the successor states to break with the rouble. The Estonian kroon made its entrance in June 1992, to be joined within the next twelve months by the Latvian lat, the Lithuanian lit, the Ukrainian karbovanet and the Kyrgyz som. In addition, five countries (Belarus, Moldova, Azerbaijan, Armenia and Georgia) while retaining use of the rouble introduced parallel currencies. As of July 1993, only in the Central Asian states of Kazakhstan, Uzbekistan, Tajikistan and Turkmenistan, and in Russia itself, was the rouble the sole currency.

Moves towards monetary independence prompted further Russian action. In July 1993, the Central Bank announced that pre-1993 roubles would be immediately taken out of circulation on Russian territory. Only Russian citizens, enterprises and foreign visitors would be allowed to exchange old roubles for new ones. This step, which could be interpreted as a rather drastic move to curtail inflation within Russia, held inflationary implications for those still in the rouble zone, threatening as it did an outflow of pre-1993 notes from Russia to the other states. In this sense, Russia's 'demonitisation' appeared to be an ultimatum: either submit to full monetary subordination to the Russian Central Bank or seek a swift exit from the rouble zone. The effects were immediate. Four states (Georgia, Azerbaijan, Turkmenistan and Moldova) declared their intention to introduce fully independent national currencies by year end. Russia, Armenia, Belarus, Kazakhstan, Tajikistan and Uzbekistan, by contrast, signed a framework agreement in September, which envisaged the unification of monetary, fiscal, banking and customs policies within a revamped rouble zone. This new arrangement offered benefits such as preferentially priced Russian exports and seemed the only option on offer to those states ill-prepared for the introduction of national currencies. However, the terms demanded by Russia for supplying new roubles were soon revealed as totally inimical to economic independence. Kazakhstan, for one, blenched at the demand that Moscow control its import–export operations and that it deposit gold and hard currency reserves in Russia. It, along with Uzbekistan and Armenia, effectively left the new rouble zone in November following the introduction of national currencies. By the end of 1993 only Tajikistan, Belarus and Russia remained committed to the idea of a common currency. Thereafter, negotiations amounted to sorting out terms whereby economic dependency on Russia was to be given a formal monetary dimension. The draft agreement on Russian–Belarusian Monetary Union reached in April 1994 gave the Russian Central Bank the sole right to issue currency and determine Belarusian monetary policy.[20]

Trade relations

Controversies over currency have been more than matched by issues of trade. Disputes in this area contributed to a 50 per cent drop in intra-CIS trade during the period 1991 and 1993. The greatest bone of contention here has been the pricing of goods, particularly energy commodities. The prices of oil, gas and coal have not been subject to regulation by CIS or other inter-governmental institutions, but have rather been determined by national governments, which have retained a controlling stake in energy production. By far the most important producer is Russia.

As noted above, at the birth of the CIS, Russia was, for a combination of political and economic reasons, prepared to countenance a drain on its resources as the price of CIS economic co-ordination. In the trading sphere this took the form of grossly underpriced energy and raw material exports to the other successor states. The immense cost of this underpricing, however, was unsustainable. When coupled with the proportionately higher prices that made up the bulk of Russian imports from the FSU, it was estimated that during 1992 alone, Russia gave away a staggering 2 trillion roubles in such subsidisation – a sum equivalent to 14 per cent of its GDP.[21] This alone was reason enough to tighten the trading regime. Additional incentives also existed: a sharp decline in oil and gas production during 1992 and the ever-present temptation to sell a greater proportion of Russia's dwindling production on the more lucrative international market.

Influenced by these factors, Russia began to inflict an 'energy shock', involving simultaneous reductions in the supply of, and increases in the price for, energy supplied to customers in the FSU. The Baltic states have been particularly hard hit. Their non-membership of the CIS and eagerness to withdraw from the rouble zone, meant Russia, from an early stage, had little incentive to offer preferential trading terms. Political calculations have also been at work. Moscow has used the 'energy card' to punish alleged discrimination against local Russian-speaking populations and to exact concessions in negotiations on military withdrawals. Since 1992, energy exports have dropped dramatically and prices have soared. The impact upon the Baltic economies has been uniformly detrimental, requiring from them draconian conservation measures, increases in charges for both domestic and industrial users and the mothballing of industrial capacity.[22]

At least in the Baltic states the effects of energy shock have been partly offset by overall positive trade balances with Russia. Such has not been the case with Ukraine and Belarus, two other states highly dependent on Russian energy. Ukraine was the victim of a tenfold increase in the price of natural gas in February 1993 and a doubling in the charge for oil a few months later. Price rises of such magnitude have contributed to a growing debt to Russia, estimated in October 1994 at $2.7 billion (of which $1.75 billion was for supplies of natural gas). To make matters worse, indebtedness has been accompanied by cutbacks in deliveries. The approximate 50 million metric tons of oil delivered during 1991 was reduced to 33.5 in 1992. Planned supplies for 1993 were a mere 20 million, less than half Ukraine's estimated annual requirement.[23]

In the face of Russian pressure, Ukraine has recognised the necessity of diversifying its sources of energy imports. Its dependency on Russia has been partly alleviated by deliveries from new suppliers. During 1992 it bartered metals for Iranian oil. In 1993 a number of oil and gas deals were signed with Central Asian producers. In May 1994 Kiev signed an agreement to construct a pipeline for shipping oil from Turkey to the Ukrainian port of Odessa. However, while Ukraine's entry into the international market allows of diversification, it will not in the long-run provide a cheap alternative to Russian energy. Other suppliers are as commercially minded, a point well illustrated by Turkmenistan's severance of gas deliveries in February 1994 after Ukraine had failed to clear debts for shipments made during the latter part of the previous year. In this light, Kiev's energy strategy might best be directed towards cutting consumption (much energy in Ukraine is wasted owing to antiquated heavy industry and an under-utilisation of conservation measures).

Belarus, which is almost completely bereft of domestic energy resources, has been even more reliant on Russia for its fuel supplies. Owing to this acute dependency it has sought to avoid frictions in its relations with Moscow and has been one of the strongest advocates of closer economic co-operation within the CIS. Belarus has not, however, escaped the pernicious effects of Russia's energy shock. Its answer to this predicament has been to explore a number of alternative policies: seeking new Middle Eastern suppliers, importing oil through a new port in the Polish city of Gdansk, linking up with a prospective Baltic natural-gas market that would supply Norwegian gas and switching to nuclear power.[24] Belarus has also attempted to negotiate new terms with Russia, although with little success. In August 1994 its debt for gas supplies alone stood at the equivalent of $425 million, a sum Russia was demanding be repaid in full by April 1995 on pain of suspensions in supply.

Even other energy suppliers have fallen victim to Russia's use of the energy weapon. Moscow's control of pipelines leading to the Baltic and Black Seas and thence on to the Mediterranean and Europe has been exploited to exact concessions from other producers. In Azerbaijan, negotiations between the Azeri authorities and Western companies have been complicated by a Russian campaign to limit overseas involvement in developing oil fields in the Caspian Sea. A contract finally reached with a consortium of seven Western firms and the Turkish Petroleum Corporation in September 1994 granted the Russian state-owned Lukoil Company a 10 per cent equity share. In Kazakhstan, Russia has pursued similar tactics, setting limits on oil passing through Russian pipelines as a means of forcing access to oil and gas projects being carried out by Western companies. It has also been adept at gaining entry to pipeline schemes linking the Central Asian states and Azerbaijan with the contiguous states of Iran and Turkey. Moscow's involvement, ultimately, could thwart the ambitions of non-Russian producers to acquire transportation independence.[25]

Energy disputes have not been the only source of trade disruption. A failure to agree upon a workable payments and customs regime in the FSU has also been a negative influence. The collapse of the rouble zone and shortages of convertible currency have hindered trade. A CIS Inter-State Bank was set up in January 1994 to overcome the barriers to trade posed by the proliferation of unconvertible currencies. As of mid-1994, its multilateral clearing mechanism remained unrealised. Moreover, free trade on the basis of commercial transactions across borders unencumbered by tariffs, duties and other restrictions has been slow to develop in the FSU. Even allowing for the growing commercial sector, governments have retained an important directive role in trade either through the imposition of direct barriers (import duties and export limits to keep scarce goods for domestic consumers) or, in Russia's case, through the manipulation of commodity prices. In fact, a great deal of transactions in the FSU have been conducted in much the same manner as inter-republican trade during the USSR's latter years. That is, via bilateral intergovernmental agreements, usually involving barter or credit.[26]

Where free trade has emerged it has been through bilateral channels or regional arrangements. With regard to the former, during 1992–94 Russia established free trade arrangements with all the CIS member states bar Ukraine through a series of bilateral treaties and protocols. Concerning the latter, success is, generally speaking, contingent on a number of factors: political amicability, geographic proximity, economic complementarity and a shared perception that co-operation is necessary to overcome a common predicament.[27] By these criteria, the Baltic Free Trade Agreement reached in September 1993 seems amongst the most promising. Inaugurated in April 1994, it provides for the abolition of all customs duties and quotas on imported goods. In Central Asia, meanwhile, efforts directed at co-operation date back to the first summit of regional leaders in June 1990. In early 1994 a 'Common Economic Space' was formed enveloping Kazakhstan, Kyrgyzstan and Uzbekistan. This provided for the dismantling of trade barriers and co-ordinated economic policies. Its creation reflected straightforward economic judgements. Uzbekistan seemed impressed by Kazakhstan's achievements in introducing market reforms; Kyrgyzstan wanted to open up trade with Uzbekistan to avoid a threatened collapse of its economy; Kazakhstan's leader, Nazarbaev, meanwhile, viewed the arrangement as a step towards greater integration within the CIS as a whole.[28] Despite this arrangement, economic co-operation in the region has been dogged by a series of problems. The war in Tajikistan has been an obviously disruptive influence. The leaderships in the region also hold differing views on how to approach economic management. Kazakhstan and Kyrgyzstan have been much more enthusiastic towards market reforms than their neighbours in Turkmenistan and Uzbekistan. Furthermore, despite sharing a common interest in loosening dependence on Russian energy imports, the Central Asian states have been reluctant to pool their own substantial energy resources in furtherance of regional self-sufficiency. Currency issues have also impeded co-operation. Kyrgyzstan's unannounced introduction of the som in 1993 was met by temporary trade boycotts mounted by both Uzbekistan and Kazakhstan, who claimed that a Kyrgyz national currency would hinder the settlement of debts.

The CIS Economic Union

Regional arrangements are, ultimately, no substitute for a CIS-wide trading regime that involves Russia. In this connection, the most ambitious economic arrangement has been the CIS Economic Union set out in a treaty initialled by the then nine CIS member states in September 1993.[29] This document provided for the gradual creation of a 'common economic space on the basis of market relations', by such means as the eventual abolition of customs tariffs and other trade barriers.[30] For countries such as Kazakhstan and Belarus, persistent advocates of close economic co-operation, the Economic Union offered a means of repairing damaged trade links, notably with Russia, thereby boosting overall economic performance. For all such hopes, the chances of success were slight. Earlier CIS agreements with a similar purpose, such as the March 1992 accord on a customs union, had done nothing to halt the decline in trade. The September agreement, moreover, amounted only to a framework for future developments. The signing and implementation of thirty-five further documents was envisaged to make the Economic Union a reality. Subsequent CIS summits have attempted to put flesh on this framework. In April 1994 an agreement was reached on the creation of a free trade zone. At the subsequent summit in October several documents were accepted including a memorandum on 'integration development in the CIS', and agreements on the establishment of a payments and customs union and the inauguration of an Interstate Economic Committee to promote economic union. However, while Yeltsin described these measures as liberating co-operation from 'artificially created obstacles' he was the first to concede that they amounted to only the first steps towards integration.[31]

One of the greatest sticking points has been the semi-detached position of Ukraine. Ostensibly, Kiev shares an interest in preserving the links of the former Soviet economy, in order to guarantee supplies of the Russian raw materials and energy essential to its industries and to ensure a market for its own products that are uncompetitive on the wider international market. The case for close co-operation with Russia has some influential friends within Ukraine. During 1993, Prime Minister Kuchma emerged as a firm advocate. Even Kravchuk has been touched by the inescapable logic of ties to Russia. In July 1993 Ukraine, along with Russia and Belarus, signed a 'declaration on economic integration'. The Ukrainian parliament, however, has been deeply sceptical of any arrangement which might compromise Ukrainian sovereignty. By this view, the Economic Union smacks of a supranational body dominated by Russia. Russian policy has, in various ways, added to such suspicions. Moscow's hard line on energy prices and the rouble zone was compounded for the Ukrainian parliament by Yeltsin's attempt at Massandra to use economic leverage to resolve the issues of the Black Sea Fleet and Ukrainian nuclear weapons (see Chapter 4, pp. 154, 186–88).

Following Massandra, Kuchma's advocacy of greater links with Russia grew increasingly unpopular. The Prime Minister's isolation on this issue, coupled with mounting parliamentary and presidential resistance to his economic reforms precipitated his resignation in September. President Kravchuk, meanwhile, aware of the flow of opinion in parliament and fearful of ruining his nationalist credentials in future presidential elections felt able to sanction Ukrainian accession to the Economic Union only as an 'associate' member, pending the approval of his legislature.[32] Kuchma's replacement of Kravchuk in July 1994 seemed to offer the possibility of a more determined presidential effort to restore economic ties with Russia and to reinvigorate Ukraine's involvement in the CIS. Yet at his first CIS summit in October 1994 Kuchma too treated the concept of economic integration with some suspicion (see Chapter 3, p. 101), mindful perhaps of nationalist feeling in the Ukrainian parliament.

The Economic Union is the great unrealised hope of the CIS. Its prospects are limited not just by the potential for disagreement among its members, but by the increasingly obvious pursuit by Russia of a form of economic diplomacy. This has been directed less at the strengthening of the multilateral mechanisms of the CIS and more at deriving unilateral economic benefits. In this regard, it forms part of Russia's overall assertive approach to the near abroad, which began to emerge in the latter part of 1992 (see Chapter 3, pp. 98–100). Two important strands of this strategy have already been detectable above: Russia's use of the energy weapon and the stringent conditions attached to the new rouble zone. Russia's actions, the suspicions and animosity these have aroused in states such as Ukraine, and tendencies towards regional arrangements among the successor states indicate that a CIS economic agenda has become less and less significant. The CIS has been marginalised further by the efforts of the successor states to orientate themselves towards new partners entirely beyond the FSU. This is the subject of the following section.

The former Soviet Union and the international economy[33]

The efforts of the Gorbachev leadership to rectify the damaging effects of the USSR's economic isolation were noted in Chapters 1 and 2 (pp. 34, 50–1). The case for extensive involvement with the international economy is arguably even more compelling for the successor states. International economic interactions take many forms. Those of particular relevance to the successor states include foreign economic assistance ('aid'), foreign trade and direct (i.e. commercial) foreign investment.

Economic assistance ('aid')

In the parlance of international relations the term 'foreign aid' has a rather flexible meaning, encompassing a variety of different activities. Geoff Berridge offers the following definition:

> 'Foreign aid' ... normally means the transfer of goods, services or investment capital from one state to another without charge or (more frequently) at a rate somewhat below the market price. This may be done directly ('bilateral' aid) or via the medium of some international organisation ... ('multilateral' aid).[34]

Much of what is commonly regarded as 'aid', however, falls outside the more precise definition suggested by the Organisation of Economic Co-operation and Development's (OECD) Development Assistance Committee, which limits the term to resource flows containing a grant element of at least 25 per cent.[35] This excludes both loans which have only slight concessionary terms and, equally important, export credits, whereby a government offers a loan which is tied to purchases of goods in the donor state. The status of debt relief is also problematic. In the short term this amounts to a grant. The deferral of debt repayment relieves a state of a financial obligation and, therefore, effectively delivers it a resource it would not otherwise have had. This relief is usually, however, only temporary. Debt is rarely forgiven entirely and must eventually be repaid. In the FSU, as we shall see, the term 'aid' is largely inaccurate. Export credits, debt relief and loans with poor concessionary terms have abounded. For this reason, it is perhaps more useful to use the term 'economic assistance'.[36]

The provision of economic assistance has been commonplace throughout the post-war period. Little precedent, however, exists for the assistance efforts directed towards the successor states.[37] The Marshall Plan, by which the US provided massive financial assistance to Western Europe's post-war reconstruction, offers some analogies. However, even advocates of a latter-day plan point out that while the political will and generosity embodied in the original deserve emulation, the FSU presents unique problems. The *creation* of a market-based economy in the successor states, in the midst of catastrophic economic decline and social disintegration, is a far more daunting challenge than the *restoration* of the pre-existing market structures that the Marshall Plan effected in post-war Western Europe.[38] Furthermore, in some successor states, overseas involvement is a potent political issue. Suspicion often arises concerning the motives of foreign donors. The close association of assistance with painful structural reform has led to a popular belief in Russia that Western nations and international financial institutions are bent upon the imposition of policies designed to weaken, if not destroy, the Russian state.[39] The Russian political leadership, meanwhile, has been jealous of any interference in its domestic economic management. Prime Minister Victor Chernomyrdin has been unenthusiastic about help that is conditional on domestic reform. Yeltsin, seeking a scapegoat for economic crisis, has criticised assistance provided by the International Monetary Fund (IMF).[40] Resentment has also been generated by the often explicit connection the US has made between the allocation of funds and Russian policy towards its near abroad. In September 1993 the American Senate passed legislation appropriating $2.5 billion in assistance to the states of the FSU. An amendment to the relevant bill required the US President to certify at six monthly intervals that Russia was proceeding with its military withdrawal from Estonia and Latvia. Stung by this apparent encroachment on its freedom of action, the Russian Foreign Ministry condemned such linkage as a relapse into the Cold War.

As for the donors, they too have had doubts concerning the efficacy of assistance. One general motive for assistance is to facilitate recovery in the recipient state, thereby boosting trade and investment opportunities for the donor country. Yet in the case of the crisis-ridden economies of the FSU recovery appears far off at best (see also the conclusion below, pp. 327–30). Caution has also followed from the economic difficulties experienced by the wealthier industrialised nations themselves. With the USSR's collapse, the US has been in no position to repeat the effort of the Marshall Plan. The economic ascendancy the US enjoyed in the immediate post-war period had, by the 1990s, long evaporated. The yawning federal deficit (which stood at $360 billion in December 1991), Congressional resistance to costly foreign policy commitments and the turn, following President Clinton's inauguration in January 1993, towards urgent domestic priorities, has placed severe financial and political limits on American economic engagement with the successor states.[41] The German economy has been no better placed, owing to the gigantic cost of integrating the former East Germany (estimated to have amounted to $100 billion by the end of 1992). Japanese funds, although more plentiful, are alone inadequate and prisoner to the dispute with Russia over the Kurile Islands. Finally, the modest size of the so-called 'peace dividend' enjoyed by the NATO powers has meant these economic restraints cannot evidently be overcome by a massive diversion of funds away from military expenditure.[42]

Yet whatever the reservations, with the initiation of a transition towards capitalism, external assistance in some form has come to be regarded both within and beyond the FSU as an essential support. For the successor states it offers a means of compensating for the lack of alternative sources of funding, be these domestic savings[43] or the massive, but uncollectable debts, that had been owed to the USSR by Third World states. Assistance can be put to use to cushion the painful side effects of structural reform (price liberalisation, falling real living standards, unemployment etc.) and to promote, through technical advice, the development of the institutional foundations of market economies. In addition, where a country lacks foreign reserves or is experiencing a balance-of-payments deficit, foreign assistance offers a means to finance imports, whether these be items such as foodstuffs, or the plant, equipment and technology necessary for industrial modernisation. In the case of the poorer successor states, assistance provides a form of compensation for the loss of the generous subsidies provided by the old Soviet budget.

For both those seeking assistance and those extending it, economic motives are not the only consideration. Knorr suggests that the political imperative of governments to remain in office might be well served by gaining access to foreign resources.[44] The context of this observation is that of international security, and indeed, large-scale economic assistance has often proven material in ensuring the survival of certain regimes. Soviet support of Cuba and Vietnam bear obvious testimony to this. In these examples, assistance was rendered in order to prop up regimes which laboured under almost complete American economic boycotts. The position of the successor states, however, is different. They require help not to compensate for a hostile international environment, but to counter a domestic threat. To the extent that such resources promote development and lessen the dangers of political opposition fuelled by economic decline, the survival of a government is that much more guaranteed. Yeltsin has, in fact, been explicit in this regard, arguing that the success of economic reform and thus the survival of democracy in Russia are contingent upon large-scale Western assistance.[45] Such claims should be taken with a pinch of salt in that the Russian President has tended to regard the endurance of democracy as synonymous with a strengthening of his own personal powers. Nonetheless, a link between economic misery and the rise of political extremism has clearly been discernible in Russia, most publicly in the strong showing of the neo-fascist Liberal Democratic Party in the parliamentary elections held in December 1993.

The spectre of political instability stemming from economic collapse has also vexed Western governments. In this regard, the strategy of Western donors rests on the assumption that the creation of market economies offers the best long-term guarantee of prosperity, concomitant democratic consolidation and thus, international peace and security. At a rather atmospheric level, such reasoning has been evident in President Clinton's attachment to the Kantian notion that republics (i.e. democracies) do not face each other in war.[46] More practically, assistance is viewed as a means of alleviating the social costs of the transition to capitalism, thereby guarding against the danger of a resurgent authoritarian/nationalist right feeding off the popular dissatisfaction of economic dislocation. In the case of Russia, such a strategy has accorded well with the West's strong interest in the political survival of Yeltsin, a leader who is seen as the personification of Russia's commitment to stable relations with the NATO powers.

Economic assistance to the FSU has occurred largely through the joint efforts of bilateral donors, acting in concert with three international financial institutions (the IMF, the World Bank and the European Bank of Reconstruction and Development [EBRD]) and the European Community/Union (EC/EU) (see Box 6.1). An informal oversight role has been played by the Group of Seven (G7). During 1992 co-ordination was carried out through the medium of three international conferences held in Washington (January), Lisbon (May) and Tokyo (October).

Box 6.1 *International organisations and economic assistance to the former Soviet Union*

The Group of Seven (G7)
The world's seven largest economies (Canada, France, Germany, Italy, Japan, the United States and the United Kingdom) have met at world economic summits since 1986. President Yeltsin attended the G7 summits in 1992, 1993 and 1994 as a guest. The 1994 Naples summit enhanced this status, allowing Russia full consultation on matters other than those concerning economic co-ordination among the G7. In this partial sense, the G7 was elevated to the G8.

International Monetary Fund (IMF)
Founded in 1945, it acts as an overseer of the international financial system and extends loans to countries experiencing balance-of-payments difficulties. These require macroeconomic reforms, often including the alteration of fiscal, monetary and exchange rate policies. The G7 countries account for approximately 45 per cent of the IMF's quota resources and voting weight . During 1992/93 all the successor states became members of the Fund. As of November 1992, Russia's voting weight ranked ninth overall (2.89 per cent) behind the US (17.66 per cent), the other G7 countries and Saudi Arabia. Its quota was set at 3 per cent of Fund resources, allowing a potential annual borrowing of slightly more than $4 billion.

The World Bank
Founded in 1945, the 'World Bank' refers to two distinct entities: the International Bank for Reconstruction and Development (IBRD) and the International Development Association (IDA). The Bank's decision-making structures and voting procedures mirror those of its sister organisation, the IMF. It finances development projects, as well as economic policy-reform programmes by extending both market-rate loans and concessional loans to governments. All fifteen successor states have joined the IBRD. As of June 1993 Russia and five others (Kazakhstan, Kyrgyzstan, Latvia, Uzbekistan and Tajikistan) had joined the IDA.

The European Bank for Reconstruction and Development (EBRD)
Founded in 1991, with the purpose of extending financial and technical assistance to

Eastern Europe and the (former) Soviet Union. Its conditions for loans are stricter than both the IMF and World Bank, and its resources are much smaller (its founding capital amounted to $730 million). It expressly requires progress towards multiparty democratic politics as a condition for providing loans.

The European Community
(This body became the European Union with the formal entry into force of the Maastricht Treaty in November 1993.) The Baltics states signed free trade accords with the EC in 1992 and 1994; Russia and Ukraine signed 'Partnership' agreements with the European Union in June 1994. All the successor states have received economic assistance under the PHARE or TACIS programmes.

The inaugural international conference, held in Washington, was an American initiative, organised by Secretary of State James Baker, ostensibly to bring some co-ordination to the provision of emergency assistance. A sense of urgency was brought to this task by the recent collapse of the USSR and the immediate requirements of easing grave shortages of food and medicine in Russia. While the gathering was primarily concerned with humanitarian aid, the acceptance of the principle of co-ordination extended to economic assistance in general. The growth of bilateral and multilateral efforts since 1990 had resulted in financial commitments of various kinds to the USSR/successor states worth some ECU 63 billion ($79 billion) in the period September 1990 to January 1992 (although actual disbursements amounted to just one-quarter to one-third of this figure). Little of this had been committed by the US. More than half was furnished by Germany, and pledges by the EC and its member states as a whole accounted for some three-quarters of the overall total.[47] The political break-up of the USSR and the likelihood of an acceleration towards market economies in the FSU placed this assistance in an entirely new context. Donor nations were aware of the need first, for harmonisation in order to avoid the duplication of effort, and second, for a strategic direction aimed at promoting macroeconomic stabilisation and market transition in the new successor states.[48] Attendance at the conference was impressive. Forty-seven countries were present, together with seven international organisations. In terms of new commitments, however, the results of the meeting were rather modest, an American offer of $600 million in humanitarian aid being the most notable development. The gathering's most concrete achievement lay in the establishment of sectoral working groups concerned with food aid, energy, medical aid, technical assistance and housing construction (for military personnel returning from abroad) and with laying down plans to assess future requirements and co-ordinate assistance efforts.[49]

The follow-up conference in Lisbon, held under the auspices of the EC, sought to shift the emphasis away from emergency measures towards longer-term assistance. In this sense, it followed closely upon, and indeed was largely overshadowed by, developments in the intervening months concerning first, the entry of Russia and the successor states into the IMF and the World Bank, and second, the launch of a large-scale assistance programme on behalf of the G7. Amongst the advantages of the former was access to previously untapped lending facilities. For the successor states as a whole, these were estimated at $6.5–9 billion per annum from the IMF and up to $40 billion from both bodies during the initial four years of membership.[50] Access to these funds was not, however, automatic, but depended on approved reform programmes. In the Russian case, this resulted in the submission of a Memorandum on Economic Policy to the IMF in March 1992 (one month after its formal request for membership). The Memorandum provided for the lifting of almost all price controls by the end of the following month, the freeing of domestic oil prices, and a reduction in the budget deficit to 1 per cent of GNP by year end. The latter would be achieved through cutting defence expenditure and subsidies to industry and through a tightening of the Central Bank's monetary and credit policies. According to one observer, the Russian proposals followed IMF recommendations 'to the letter'.[51]

Russia's enthusiasm for IMF norms had, in fact, been anticipated the previous January with the launch of a policy of economic 'shock therapy', overseen by acting Prime Minister Yegor Gaidar, that embraced both price liberalisation and a tight monetary policy. This display of resolve appeared to pay dividends almost immediately. On 1 April the IMF accepted Russian membership (formal entry occurred on 1 July) and this was followed soon after by the announcement of a three-year $24 billion assistance package that was to be adopted by the G7 summit in July. That said, little of this package was ground-breaking; much of it was made up of largely recycled commitments ($11 billion worth of trade credits and the $2.5 billion in deferred interest on debt repayments) or simply reflected Russia's drawing rights as a new member of international financial institutions ($4.5 billion in loans to be provided by the IMF, World Bank and the EBRD). The only novel element was an IMF-financed, rouble-stabilisation fund worth $6 billion as a step towards stimulating trade and foreign investment. The entire amount was contingent upon the full implementation of a programme of reforms agreed between Russia and the IMF along the lines of the Memorandum.[52]

Despite Russia's accommodation of IMF guidelines in early 1992, the next twelve months witnessed an increasingly strained relationship between the Russian government and the Fund. Domestic political pressures, notably opposition to Gaidar's economic policies within the Russian parliament, meant a constant trimming during 1992 of the radical policies laid down prior to April. Gaidar's replacement in December by the far more conservative Victor Chernomyrdin only personified a moderation of shock therapy which had already begun just days after Russia's entry into the IMF. Such 'backsliding', however, was ill-received by donor institutions. After IMF approval for the release of a 'stand-by' loan of $1.04 billion in August, negotiations on further financial support reached an impasse following Fund dissatisfaction at Russia's inability to sufficiently curtail inflation and the budget deficit owing to the relaxation of its monetary policy. The $6 billion rouble-stabilisation fund also came to nothing. Its initiation was dependent on establishing some prior degree of steadiness in the value of the rouble within a floating exchange-rate regime. A combination of factors, including most crucially the expansion of credit (and consequently inflation) within the rouble zone during 1992, meant currency stability was not attained; the value of the currency plummeted from 140 roubles to the dollar on 1 July to 740 by April the following year.

Russia's divergence from IMF norms during 1992 illustrated well the problems of the entire assistance effort. The member states of the G7 demanded adherence to IMF guidelines in order to establish a propitious economic framework for their efforts. Yet to deny Russia help on the grounds that these criteria were not being met ignored the pain the country had already experienced in introducing structural reform and threatened to worsen its already dire economic situation. Hence, despite Russia's domestic policy failures, the G7 continued to lobby for increased assistance, but made sure that this was made up of largely risk-free items. The IMF and World Bank, meanwhile became subject to increasing pressure from Western governments to relax (but not to abandon) its tough conditions in order to ease Russia's access to the funds of these financial institutions.

The summit between Yeltsin and America's newly installed President Bill Clinton, in Vancouver in April 1993, was indicative of this approach. Yeltsin dubbed the occasion 'the first economic meeting of the leaders of the two states in history' and appropriately it departed from the traditional summitry preoccupation with security matters, concentrating almost entirely on economic issues. The $1.6 billion American assistance package for 1993 unveiled by Clinton, with its carefully targeted provisions and harnessing of funds unspent by the Bush Administration or already appropriated by Congress, reflected, however, a sober American assessment somewhat at odds with Yeltsin's sense of occasion. The American package complemented parallel measures being undertaken by the G7 as a whole at that point. The day before the summit, the Paris Club of creditor nations rescheduled Russia's official debt, lightening the country of $15 billion of debt service obligations during the remainder of the year. These sums, in turn, formed part of a programme of measures worth some $43 billion announced by a special meeting of G7 Foreign and Finance Ministers in Tokyo later that month. Amongst the new commitments of this meeting were a $1.82 billion pledge from Japan (consisting mainly of credits, but also humanitarian aid worth $300 million) and $600 million from the UK. The remainder of the $43 billion consisted of largely recycled items: $10 billion in bilateral export credits from the G7 countries, most of which reiterated previous offers; the unreleased $6 billion rouble stabilisation fund; $4 billion in unused IMF loans; and finally, nearly $5 billion in World Bank loans which had been under negotiation for several months.[53] A further $3 billion fund to support Russian privatisation unveiled at the G7 summit in July was similarly made up, in the main, of old pledges.

Meanwhile, the disbursement of IMF/World Bank facilities remained contingent on criteria concerning Russian economic performance. The World Bank, while able to issue a credit of $610 million to assist the oil industry, gave up on negotiations in September on the disbursement of a $600 million 'rehabilitation' loan originally agreed upon in August 1992. The IMF did, under pressure from the G7 countries, exhibit a degree of belated flexibility. In April 1993 it created a new, temporary arrangement – the systemic transformation facility – which allowed Russia (and the other successor states) easier access to funds designed to cover balance-of-payments deficits. Even the new softer terms, however, were far from easy. A loan of $1.5 billion was approved in June only after Moscow had agreed to implement further measures aimed at curbing inflation, cutting the budget deficit through reductions in government expenditure and speeding up the privatisation of land. A second $1.5 billion instalment was only unlocked in March 1994 after prolonged negotiations with the IMF. Other parts of the Tokyo package also proved difficult to access. By the time of the G7's Naples summit in July 1994, approximately $30 billion of the $43 billion had been released.[54] Table 6.2., which concerns data up to February 1994, indicates progress on the disbursement of total Western assistance to Russia agreed at the G7 summits in 1992 and 1993.

Table 6.2 *Official financial assistance to Russia (billion US dollars)*

	1992		*1993*		*1992 and 1993*[a]	
	A[b]	*D*[c]	*A*	*D*	*A*	*D*
Bilateral creditors and EC/EU[d]	11	14	10	6	21	20[e]
IMF (including stabilisation fund)	9	1	13	1.5	14	2.5
World Bank, EBRD	1.5	0	5	0.5	5	0.5
Official debt relief	2.5[f]	—	15	15[g]	15	15
Total	24	15	43	23	55	38

Notes: [a] Excludes most double counting, i.e. amounts announced but not disbursed in 1992 and announced again in 1993. The largest of these elements is the $6 billion rouble stabilisation fund from the IMF. [b] Announced. [c] Delivered. [d] Does not include approximately $4 billion of grants from Germany to rehouse Russian troops. [e] Excludes some items in the announced packages for which reliable data are not available (e.g. technical assistance, nuclear facilities rehabilitation). [f] This amount of interest deferral was not formally granted during 1992. [g] Includes $6.5 billion that was deferred or went into arrears in 1992.

Source: IMF Survey, 7 February 1994, p. 45.

The assistance gathered on Russia's behalf has had no equivalent in the other successor states. While lacking the co-ordination and scale of Russian assistance, help for these states has nonetheless been based on very similar criteria. Consequently, those economies that have lagged in structural transformation or exhibited a lack of macroeconomic stability have fared poorly in gaining access to Western funds. Ukraine is a case in point. Although it is the FSU's second largest economy and one in dire need of funds to ease the shocks of Russian energy price increases, and to finance the shutting down of Chernobyl (which, according to Ukrainian calculations, would cost $14 billion) it was not until 1994 that it received serious financial attention in the West. During 1992-93 it received a mere $27 million from the World Bank and it was only in October 1994 that it first obtained IMF assistance (approval for a loan worth $371 million). According to IMF officials, the reasons for Ukraine's delayed access to funds lay in profligate economic management that involved the continuation of large government subsidies to industry, delayed privatisation and an inability to stem galloping inflation.[55] Kiev's case for assistance, moreover, has not been helped by its unwillingness to strike a deal with Russia over the repayment of former Soviet debts to external creditors. Here Ukraine has adopted a position distinct from the other successor states, all of whom have acceded to a 'zero option' in negotiations with Russia that involves a renunciation of all claims on former Soviet foreign assets (embassies and debts owed to the USSR) in return for Russia assuming full responsibility for Soviet debt.[56] Kiev's stance reflects resentment at the implicit recognition the deal gives to Russia's claim to be the continuing state of the USSR, rather than any economic logic. Ukraine's share of Soviet debt was calculated at the end of 1991 as 16.4 per cent of the total. By December 1994 this percentage amounted to a debt of $3 billion. Given Ukraine's budget deficit (projected at 15 per cent of its GDP in 1993) and a lack of foreign currency reserves, it would be unable to service, let alone repay, this sum. A further obstacle to assistance has been Kiev's policy on nuclear weapons. Only after its belated initiation of denuclearisation in the spring of 1994 (see pp. 156–57) was major G7 assistance forthcoming – the Naples summit of the industrialised countries in July earmarked a package worth $4.2 billion.

Those successor states that have been able to demonstrate a clear commitment to IMF/World Bank approved policies have fared somewhat better than Ukraine in attracting funds. All three Baltic states have received IMF stand-by funds and World Bank rehabilitation loans. Kyrgyzstan, in July 1993, obtained funds under the IMF's systemic transformation facility and became the first of the Central Asian states to receive a pledge from the World Bank – a credit of

$60 million in May 1993. Moldova obtained an identical commitment the following October. Finally, Belarus and Kazakhstan reached agreement with the IMF in July 1993 on reform programmes necessary for the receipt of systemic transformation funds. A total of $255 million in loans was approved for Kazakhstan the following January. In November the World Bank followed suit and agreed to a three-year credit allocation of $1 billion to be used for projects such as the restoration of the Kazakh oil and gas industries.

The EC has been a further source of help, in this case to virtually all the successor states. The TACIS programme of technical assistance agreed with the USSR in August 1991 was extended to a number of the successor states in 1992. Its budget for that year was ECU 450 million (of which about a third was earmarked for Russia), rising to ECU 510 million in 1993. This amounted to some 70 per cent of all Western technical help to the region. TACIS funding for 1992 covered 400 separate projects, involving some 750 consultants offering training and advice to both governments and individual firms, banks and farms. The Baltic states meanwhile have been included in the EC's PHARE programme, established in 1989 to provide assistance to Hungary and Poland, and subsequently extended to other East European countries. During 1992, this was worth ECU 135 million to them. The EC has also provided loans. A ECU 1.25 billion medium-term credit for the purchase of food and medicines by the USSR, originally agreed at the EC's Maastricht summit in December 1991, was divided in early 1992 between twelve of the successor states, of which Russia was to receive less than half.[57] The three Baltic states, meanwhile, have again been treated separately and during 1992-93 were the beneficiaries of ECU 220 million ($259 million) in loans.

The EBRD ranks far behind the EC as a source of funds. Given its precise remit (see Box 6.1) the Bank appears a tailor-made vehicle for encouraging the development of fledgeling market-based economies in the FSU. In January 1992, the EBRD decided that 40 per cent of its total lending (up to $500 million per annum), should be targeted at the successor states. Its subsequent record, however, has been disappointing. By April 1993, only $152 million had been disbursed in total to all post-communist countries, little of which ended up in the FSU (over half the loans went to Hungary). Taking commitments into account, its record is somewhat better. The Baltic states, for instance, have been the beneficiaries of $109 million for their energy industries and Uzbekistan won $60 million in November 1993 to support privatisation. Pledges to Moscow have been more substantial – an agreement involving $43.8 million to assist Russian privatisation was reached in March and in August a loan of $254 was announced for the development of the country's oil industry.

While the funds detailed above appear impressive, overall, external assistance to the FSU has made at best a marginal contribution to economic development. These efforts compare very poorly with the scale of assistance directed towards post-war reconstruction in Europe. In the period between April 1948 and December 1951 assistance provided under the Marshall Plan amounted to $12.4 billion in grants and concessionary loans ($65 billion in 1991 prices) or 5–6 per cent of the GNP of recipient countries. Assistance equivalent to 5 per cent of Russia's GNP in 1991 would require funds of some $45 billion per annum – a figure well in excess of the amounts actually provided in 1992-94 (much of which, in addition, had far less concessionary terms than Marshall Plan provisions). For the FSU as a whole, it would require a massive $75 billion per annum.[58] Without a fundamental political reappraisal of expenditure priorities (involving, for instance, a diversion of funds from defence spending) these will remain amounts well beyond the capacities of Western economies.

Economic assistance is not, however, the only means of encouraging development. For the successor states there exist two further potential external sources of growth – trade outside the FSU region and direct foreign investment.[59]

Foreign trade

In the case of trade, the major potential benefits, it is argued, are to be had from increasing exports, in order to generate hard currency, and in gaining access to much-needed imports (consumer goods, food, plant and technology for industry). A healthy exporting sector might also stimulate foreign investment, lessen the dependency of domestic enterprises upon government subsidies and boost the credibility of market reform programmes. Readily available imports meanwhile open up domestic producers to foreign competition and can spur innovation and restructuring.[60] The consolidation of trade ties has, in addition, a political dimension, in that trade is often seen as a method of promoting amicable relations between states. In the case of the successor states this applies to relations not simply with Western nations, but also with large, influential neighbours such as China, Turkey, Iran, India and so on.

As noted earlier, prior to the dissolution of the USSR, the trade pattern of the Soviet republics was inward-looking, in the form of inter-republican transactions, rather than towards foreign markets. For the reasons outlined in the previous paragraph, the successor states have sought to place a greater emphasis on trade outside the FSU region. In doing so they have been compelled further by the disintegration of trade within the FSU in the post-Soviet period. Success in shifting the direction of trade has depended on a variety of factors touched upon in our discussion of economic viability. For instance, Estonia, and to lesser degrees, Latvia and Lithuania, have been able to reorientate trade partly as a consequence of their higher level of economic development and closer proximity to Europe. During 1992, the Baltic States signed trade accords with the EC and with Sweden, Norway and Finland. Agreements were signed in July 1994 between the Baltics and the EU permitting free trade in certain industrial and agricultural goods from January 1995. By increasing its trade with the West, Estonia's overall foreign trade turnover (including that with the FSU) in 1993 was more than double the level for 1992. Regional factors have pertained to a lesser degree in Central Asia. Kazakhstan and Kyrgyzstan have profited from the blossoming of trans-border trade with China. Turkey has been a source of large trade credits. In 1992, the Central Asian states and Azerbaijan joined the Economic Co-operation Organisation (ECO), a body embracing Iran, Turkey, Pakistan and Afghanistan. ECO's Istanbul Declaration, issued in mid-1993, envisaged the creation of a free trade zone and the construction of a transportation system to allow land-locked states easier access to ports.[61] For the Central Asian states, favourable resource endowments have also been of benefit in promoting profitable exports. Kazakhstan, which in the Soviet period exported virtually no metal, emerged during 1992-93 as a significant supplier to the West of chrome, copper, lead and zinc. Along with oil and grain sales, this contributed to an overall positive trade balance with countries outside the FSU during the first half of 1993. Uzbekistan, meanwhile has successfully diverted cotton fibre exports away from Russia towards Chinese and European customers. The wealth to be had from oil and gas exports, however, has yet to reach its full potential, owing to problems of transportation to world markets and the cost of exploiting as yet untapped reserves. Turkmenistan, Uzbekistan and Kazakhstan do supply some oil and gas to international markets, but their major customers are within the FSU.

Adjusting to the new trading environment has been particularly difficult in the Transcaucasus. The economies of the region have been severely disrupted by war. Only Azerbaijan has a potentially lucrative export earner, in the form of oil. Membership of regional economic organisations, notably the Black Sea Economic Co-operation (BSEC) project formed in 1992, has also had limited rewards. BSEC mechanisms for promoting trade have been slow to take shape, owing to the organisation's diverse and quarrelsome membership (it embraces both Armenia and Azerbaijan, and Turkey and Greece). Ukraine and Belarus have also encountered serious problems. During the Soviet period these two were respectively the second and third largest exporting republics to international markets. Both were particularly hard hit by the collapse of intra-CMEA trade in 1991. In the case of Ukraine, exports have also been stymied by the problems of gaining access to protected Western agricultural markets, the slow progress of trade liberalisation, and the generally parlous condition of the domestic economy. Attempts by these two states to revive trade with East European neighbours and increase transactions with Western partners have met with mixed success. Belarus's largest European trading partners have been Germany and Poland. During 1993, in overall trade outside the CIS, Belarus ran a deficit, a state of affairs which offered no help in accumulating funds to ease the burdens of its huge debt to Russia for energy supplies. The Ukrainian predicament is similar. Trade agreements with East European countries and China have had only a marginal impact on trade turnover, and little progress has been made in boosting trade with East European partners. According to one estimate, by late 1993, Ukrainian exports were worth $15 million a week; the cost of financing its gas and oil imports from Russia, meanwhile amounted to some $20 million a day.[62]

During the Soviet period only Russia engaged in foreign trade that was of equal magnitude to its inter-republican transactions. By virtue of possession of the bulk of Soviet energy and raw material wealth, the RSFSR accounted for over 80 per cent of Soviet hard currency exports. In 1991 it was the only Soviet republic with a trade surplus with the outside world (valued at $7.1 billion).[63] This positive balance, however, could not conceal an overall slump in trade turnover, mirroring the collapse of overall Soviet external trade at this point. This trend continued during 1992 and was to be explained by: the collapse of the CMEA trading regime, a contraction in output of major hard currency earners such as oil and gas, shortages of hard currency, and the dislocation in the domestic economy occasioned by the Russian reform programme introduced under Gaidar. Only in 1993 was the decline in trade in any sense arrested. That year witnessed a recovery in turnover with major international partners, such as the US, Japan and China. Trade also increased with regional partners such as Iran and Turkey. Less lucrative trade relations with long-time customers in Cuba, Vietnam and India fell away considerably. Exchanges with Eastern Europe, meanwhile, continued the precipitous decline begun in 1990, owing to the preference of both parties to reorientate trade westward and slow progress in establishing new payment arrangements. In total, Russian exports grew by 4 per cent during 1993, largely as a result of the diversion of raw material deliveries, notably oil, away from other successor state economies. This modest increase, coupled with a policy of restricting imports contributed to a positive trade balance in 1993 estimated at $17.5 billion.[64]

Overall, in the post-Soviet period, Russia could hardly be described as a major trading nation. During 1992, the country failed to appear in the list of the world's top twenty-five traders and assumed the trading status of a middle-ranking economy, exporting less than Norway and importing less than Portugal.[65] Russia's relatively lowly position has not, however, prevented it from becoming embroiled in a series of disputes with the West over trade issues. In this connection, Russia has voiced two major concerns. First, that its commercial activities have been hindered by a lingering political distrust handed down from the Cold War. And second, that it has been confronted with unfair trade restrictions designed to protect Western markets and give advantage to Western producers.

The survival of trade barriers first imposed upon the USSR has occasioned both these grievances. Some of these barriers had, it is true, undergone change in the latter Soviet period. The 1974 Jackson–Vanik Amendment, which linked American Most-Favoured Nation (MFN) trade status to Soviet emigration policies, was waived by the Bush Administration on two occasions, in 1990 and 1991. Following the dissolution of the USSR, Presidential waivers were extended to Russia. These permitted the coming into force in June 1992 of the 1990 Soviet–American Trade Agreement granting MFN status to Russia. While flexibility has been evident, and has created a propitious framework for increased trade, Moscow has been irked by the fact that the restrictions themselves have not been removed, simply suspended. The terms of Jackson–Vanik could be reimposed at any time. Their survival, even in repose, was criticised by Yeltsin at the 1993 Russian–American summit in Vancouver. Such restrictions did not just hinder 'honest competition', but were an offence to Russia's political accomplishments, which ignored the suffering the country had undergone 'to achieve democracy'.[66] Yet as was made clear at the Yeltsin–Clinton summit of September 1994 (where another waiver was granted) the permament lifting of the restrictions depended on Congressional action, something an increasingly beleaguered President Clinton was unable to guarantee.[67]

Technology controls have been viewed in a similarly hostile manner by Moscow. Exports in this field had, through the Cold War period, been regulated by the Co-ordinating Committee on Multilateral Export Controls (COCOM), an organisation established in 1949 at America's behest to control sales of military-sensitive items to the communist countries. The controls enforced by COCOM were relaxed as the Soviet threat collapsed and US companies sought to exploit new markets in the former communist bloc. Nonetheless, Western governments remained reluctant to allow the transfer of advanced products ('stealth' technology and high-speed computers) for fear these might enhance Russia's still powerful military capabilities. The decision taken in November 1992 to admit the twenty-five former communist countries to a new COCOM affiliate, the Co-operation Forum, a body entrusted with the task of expediting technology transfers, reflected a judicious mix of political and commercial considerations. Loosening up the market could only benefit large Western and Japanese exporters, while exemptions from normal COCOM restrictions were to apply only if individual countries pledged not to re-export sensitive materials to third countries and to utilise new technology solely for civilian ends.[68] COCOM's formal abolition in March 1994 liberalised the technology control regime still further, but left certain restrictions in place. A new arrangement embracing Russia and the other previously proscribed states was intended, but in the interim controls were to be implemented at a national level. In tandem, the Clinton Administration announced the lifting of export curbs on most commercial computer and telecommunications equipment to Russia. Restrictions were to remain on dual-use technologies.

Arms sales have given rise to further controversies. With the collapse of the USSR, the share-out of the Soviet defence complex created a number of new arms supplier nations. The potential exports from Ukraine, Belarus and possibly Kazakhstan, however, paled into insignificance next to those from Russia where the bulk of the Soviet defence industry had been concentrated. Here arms exports offered a means of keeping production lines open and compensating for the drop in domestic arms procurement. Such considerations were buttressed by the Russian government's search for hard currency. Funds from arms sales, however, have proven difficult to obtain. Russia's entry into the international arms market occurred at a particularly inauspicious juncture. Many of the most important and long-standing clients of the Soviet arms industry were not commercially viable customers. Countries such as Cuba and Vietnam, to whom most arms had been provided on credit, found it impossible to adjust to a new, harsher payment regime introduced first by the Soviet Union in 1991 and later continued by Russia. Trade with other important clients, moreover, was ruled out by diplomatic considerations. Adherence to UN sanctions against Libya, Iraq and the rump Yugoslavia, according to the Russian newspaper, *Pravda*, had by February 1993 resulted in lost arms sales worth $16-18 billion. Purchases by East European countries of new arms, (as opposed to spare parts to service old Soviet-supplied equipment) were also reduced following the dissolution of the WTO. Countries such as Poland, Bulgaria, the Czech Republic and Slovakia, facing the prospect of the dislocation of their own defence industries, were more concerned with the *export* of weaponry and emerged as potential competitors of Russia rather than customers. During 1992 Russia earned an estimated $4 billion from arms exports. This figure did appear to match the annual 'real' earnings (i.e. minus subsidies to major purchasers) of the USSR in the decade or so up to 1991, but in absolute terms represented a negligible influence on the Russian economy.[69]

In the face of a shrinking market for arms, Russia has followed a twin-track strategy. On the one hand it has consolidated potentially profitable ties with important customers inherited from the Soviet Union, in particular China, Iran and India. On the other, it has attempted to break into markets dominated by Western suppliers and largely neglected in the Soviet period (in the Gulf and the Asian–Pacific Region). Both tracks have occasioned controversy. With regard to the former, the US has been opposed to two notable deals, the first involving diesel-powered submarines to Iran and the second, liquid-fuelled rocket engines to India. These have been seen as antithetical to American security interests, giving rise to demands by Washington that the deals be terminated. The dispute concerning India resulted in the imposition of American sanctions against the Russian space agency in May 1992 and the issue was only resolved in March 1994 when a restructured deal was agreed, involving less sensitive technology and Indian pledges not to modify or re-export the supplies. As for the deal with Iran, Moscow was also forced to back down, agreeing at the Yeltsin–Clinton summit in September 1994 to withhold further arms deliveries to Iran only when threatened by the US with exclusion from participation in a post-COCOM technology control regime.

As well as falling foul of the US, disputes relating to trade issues have also arisen between Russia and the EC/EU. Trade relations here are in fact of no small benefit to Russia. In 1993, the EC accounted for over 35 per cent of Russian trade outside the FSU. That year Russia enjoyed a surplus with EC countries of $3.9 billion. Russia has, however, been subject to EC-wide restrictions on its steel, cast-iron, uranium and textile exports. Greatest controversy has centred around aluminium. A massive upsurge of cheap Russian exports during 1992-93 led to the introduction of EC quotas on CIS member-country exports in the latter half of 1993. This decision generated considerable ill-feeling in Russia. Interviewed shortly after the EC action, Russia's Deputy Minister of Foreign Economic Relations, Georgi Gabunia, claimed Russia's price advantage in the commodity was not the consequence of unfair practices, as the EC claimed, but reflected a comparative advantage stemming from cheap hydroelectric power. In this light, Gabunia continued, the EC's 'antidumping' measures were a form of covert protectionism aimed at safeguarding the markets of European, and specifically French, producers.[70]

The aluminium controversy complicated negotiations on a partnership and co-operation agreement during 1993-94. Russia demanded it be given the same treatment the EC accorded to member countries of the General Agreement on Tariffs and Trade (GATT), a body to which Moscow submitted a formal application of membership in June 1993, having assumed the observer status granted the USSR in 1990. The EC responded by claiming that until Russia complied with GATT guidelines on freeing energy prices and allowing the unrestricted movement of capital, membership was impossible. To this, the EC demanded the partnership accord include qualifying clauses, which would permit first, the reimposition of certain barriers to avoid 'serious injury' to domestic producers and second, the complete suspension of any agreement in the event of human rights violations.[71] A partnership agreement was finally signed by Yeltsin at the European Union's Corfu summit in June 1994. Once ratified, this would grant mutual MFN status and would regulate trade up until the end of 1997, at which point the EU and Russia will decide whether to embark on the more ambitious objective of a free trade area. Other, more detailed, provisions marked qualified gains for Russia. The European Union pledged to support full Russian accession to GATT and to remove previous quotas on over 600 Russian exports (those on certain textile products and steel remained).

Investment

The third external source of growth for the successor state economies is direct foreign investment. This has taken a number of forms: acquisitions, the establishment of subsidiaries and branches of American, European or Far Eastern parent companies and, most commonly, joint ventures with local private enterprises or, in the case of energy, with state concerns. Such methods of foreign economic involvement offer to the successor states possible benefits such as job creation, transfers of technology and the introduction of new managerial skills. In certain sectors, it may expose domestic enterprises to competition, thereby impelling them towards greater efficiency and product innovation. For the consumer the establishment of foreign concerns presents increased choice and an improvement in standards, albeit at inflated prices.[72] All the successor states have sought to attract overseas investment funds, with varying degrees of success.

One indicator of foreign participation is the presence of joint ventures. At the end of 1991, registered joint ventures were to be found in greatest number in the RSFSR and Ukraine, followed by Estonia and Latvia, which had proven particularly successful in attracting Scandinavian partners. In the year following the USSR's collapse, a rapid expansion of operations occurred in the Baltics, with moderate increases apparent in Russia and Ukraine. At the other end of the scale were the Central Asian states of Tajikistan, Kyrgyzstan and Turkmenistan. In many cases, joint ventures have been significant success stories, particularly where they have filled an obvious market gap and have been able to exploit a relatively highly-skilled local workforce.[73] In the case of Russia, major activities have been fairly evenly divided between services (retail distribution, banking, business consultancy, security services) and manufacturing (computers, machine tools, medical equipment). Their early concentration on Moscow and St Petersburg has since given way to a greater exploration of other centres of economic activity.

Even accounting for joint ventures, with the exception of the Baltic states, the overall contribution of foreign investment to the post-Soviet economies has been far from significant. Figures released by the Russian government at the end of 1993 showed that less foreign money had been invested in Russia during the year than in tiny Estonia. Russia had attracted only 0.1 per cent of the world's total investment.[74] During a visit to Russia by US Secretary of Commerce, Ronald Brown, in April 1994, it was reported that of a total of $490 billion invested abroad by American investors only $1 billion had located in Russia. Ventures in Russia with foreign capital accounted at the end of 1993 for just 1 per cent of total production of goods and services and employed 0.2 per cent of the workforce.[75]

Beyond the obvious deterrents of political instability, civil strife and economic decline, the paucity of external engagement in the FSU can be explained by a wide variety of factors: unclear tax and investment laws, uncertain ownership rights to property, antiquated labour legislation and, in Russia, widespread crime and corruption.[76] The Baltics and a number of Russia's regions have striven through the establishment of free economic zones to overcome many of these barriers. Russia's Far East has successfully attracted Japanese, Korean and Chinese funds in this manner. The FSU as a whole, however, has been regarded by Western investors as an unenticing prospect and one which ranks well below the other economies in transition in Eastern Europe.

The difficulties of foreign investment are nowhere more apparent than in the energy sectors of the post-Soviet economies. In the energy-rich states of Central Asia, Russia and Azerbaijan, decrepit infrastructure and a lack of domestic resources to prospect for, and exploit, untapped resources, have severely hampered the development of a potential engine of growth. The cost of reviving these industries is staggering. Taking just the oil sector in Russia, the opening up of new fields has been estimated to require $130 billion in new investments. The cost of simply maintaining and modernising existing operations is placed at $25–45 billion per annum.[77] While some official assistance has been directed towards the energy sector of the FSU, the only realistic source of such enormous sums of money is the major multinational oil and gas concerns. Yet despite being home to an estimated 40 per cent of the world's unexploited oil and gas reserves, the FSU has not seen a flood of foreign partners. In Russia, small-scale joint ventures with local producers have been the norm. By their very nature, these have not generated large amounts of investment. Foreign oil companies seeking larger-scale joint ventures or access to wholly foreign-run tenders have encountered numerous difficulties; not least capricious tendering procedures, oil export levies and uncertainties over the location of administrative and political authority in oil-rich, but independently minded republics and regions of Russia such as Tatarstan and Tyumen.[78]

Outside Russia, the picture has been mixed. One problematic case is Azerbaijan, where foreign companies have had to deal with the vicissitudes of chronic political instability. In 1993 British Petroleum reached an initial agreement on the exploitation of oil fields in the Caspian Sea. Due for signature by President Abulfaz Elchibey in June, the agreement had to be renegotiated following the assumption to power of Geidar Aliev, resulting in a profit-sharing ratio more favourable to the host government. Kazakhstan, by contrast, has provided a much more conducive environment, aided by political stability, and the clear priority President Nazarbaev has attached to market reform and attracting foreign investment. This Central Asian state has seen the largest oil and gas deals in the FSU, involving foreign participation in exploiting the massive Tengiz and Karachaganak fields and prospecting for new reserves in the Caspian Sea.

Conclusion

Post-Soviet economic interdependence: two views.

The reality of economic interdependence among the successor states stems from their common origin within the USSR command economy. In the post-Soviet period interdependence has been relaxed, but still exists to a significant degree. As was noted in the introductory chapter, it forms an important defining characteristic of the FSU's inward orientation. The specific consequences of economic interdependence amongst the successor states are apparent in the sections above; here it is worth pausing to consider two different perspectives on the phenomenon of economic interdependence in general.

For those working within a neorealist perspective economic interdependence is not considered necessarily beneficial. For scholars such as Kenneth Waltz, interdependence involves a degree of vulnerability and thus exposure to the possible exercise of leverage by others. Fear of such influence-wielding and thus subordination impedes economic co-operation even when the economic benefits of participation in an international division of labour appear straightforward. Fear in this context is a product of the anarchic nature of the international system. As Waltz argues, '(s)tates do not willingly place themselves in situations of increased dependence. In a self-help system, considerations of security subordinate economic gain to political interest'. In such an environment states are driven to either 'control what they depend on' ('imperial thrusts') or 'lessen the extent of their dependency' ('autarchic strivings towards greater self-sufficiency').[79] The insecurities of anarchy also hinder co-operation in a further sense. While co-operation raises the prospect of absolute gains among all states, in a self-help system where a state is unsure of the intentions of a potential partner, a problem of 'relative gains' arises. As explained by Joseph Grieco, 'a state will decline to join, will leave, or will sharply limit its commitment to a co-operative arrangement if it believes that partners are achieving, or are likely to achieve, relatively greater gains'. Gains of this type raise the prospect that 'the partners will surge ahead ... in relative capabilities; and ... that their increasingly powerful partners could become all the more formidable foes at some point in the future'.[80] In the neorealist perspective co-operation is not ruled out, but it will entrench rather than level out power capabilities. Strong states will exploit their relative advantage, while those whose capabilities are limited (economically weak, in other words) will have little choice but to engage in economic relations which increase their dependency.[81]

The pluralist perspective holds a far more sanguine view of interdependence. Scholars such as Robert Keohane and Joseph Nye do recognise the existence of inequalities or what they term 'asymmetries in dependence' and thus the potential for influence. They also admit to the disadvantages of the 'vulnerability dimension of interdependence'. Nonetheless, they argue that a situation of 'complex interdependence' has clear benefits. In particular, a greater diversity of foreign policy issues means matters of military security, with all their attendant risks, tend not to dominate interstate relations. Moreover, the existence of a range of issue areas allows of a process of linkage between them. This operates to the benefit of weak states as well as strong ones owing to the former's utilisation of international organisations as a forum to legitimise their demands and to form coalitions.[82] In short, in complex interdependence, states operate in a manner divorced from realist assumptions: 'actors other than states participate directly in world politics ... a clear hierarchy of issues does not exist, and ... force is an ineffective instrument of policy'.[83]

This is a world in which distinctive incentives exist towards co-operation. States bound together by many mutual links find themselves in a situation where they swim or sink together. Economic interdependence gives one state a stake in the economic fortunes of others. One cannot export goods and services to others if their economies are so weak they cannot afford to buy them. A depression in one state has detrimental knock-on effects in others. Conversely, economic buoyancy in one state can contribute to prosperity in others.[84] Moreover, as Keohane has recently remarked, '(a)t higher levels of interdependence, the opportunity costs of not co-ordinating policy are greater'.[85] In other words, if economic transactions between states are to be conducted with the minimum of disruption, then a reliable framework of regulation needs to be in place in order to fulfil functions such as regulating trade, promoting monetary stability and keeping open lines of transport and communication. To foster such a propitious environment for economic activity, pluralists consequently place a premium upon international organisations and regimes.[86]

How relevant are these competing views of economic interdependence to the FSU? At the outset the general, and perhaps obvious point, needs making that neither of these views was explicitly formulated with the successor states in mind. It could be plausibly argued that only the Waltzian view has any applicability to the region; it claims to have a universal application, whereas the pluralist model was formulated with reference primarily to the advanced economies of the industrialised West. Indeed, many neorealist insights have a certain ring of truth about them when applied to the successor states. Russia's heavy-handed exploitation of its superior economic resources has led to a form of economic interdependence whose outcomes are far from mutually beneficial. The resource weaknesses of many of the successor states allows them little scope to resist Russian leverage by recourse to self-reliance and, thus far the institutions of the CIS have offered little in the way of a mechanism for moderating Russian economic self-aggrandisement nor a reliable medium of long-term institutionalised co-operation. Furthermore, the interdependence among the successor states is something quite distinctive from the pluralist model. Interdependence, which is normally an effect of growing contacts between states is, in the FSU, a legacy of a previously integrated but now defunct economic system. Interdependence exists in an awkward space between the one-time centralised Soviet command economy and the disintegrative effects of Soviet dissolution. For the majority of states – with the exception of Russia – it is, moreover, something whose costs arguably outweigh its benefits.

Is then the pluralist conception of interdependence irrelevant when referring to relations between the successor states? It might be argued that in the short term the assertion of national priorities will impede co-operation, but eventually the effects of such a free for all will prove injurious to a number of states, compelling them towards greater joint efforts. Three factors consistent with pluralist thinking will influence the degree to which such co-operation develops. First, a readiness on the part of Russia to act as the guarantor of any economic mechanism (e.g. the CIS Economic Union).[87] We have seen above how Russia helped prop up the CIS during its early stages at some cost to itself, but soon switched to a strategy which was more exploitative in its attitude towards monetary and trade relations with other CIS states. For mutually beneficial co-operation to be furthered, a situation has to be reached whereby Russia recognises that its own economic self-interests are inextricably bound up with those of the other successor states. Unilateral measures may allow Russia to reap immediate rewards, but these will not permit it lasting benefits if such measures help to sever pre-existing economic links within the FSU. The consequences of Russia's energy shock policy illustrates this well. Russia's hiking of prices serves its own short-term revenue requirements but is not in its long-term economic interest in that it encourages its customers within the FSU to seek other suppliers in world markets and/or to exploit their own indigenous energy supplies to a greater degree. Both courses of action diminish the demand for Russian energy in the long term. A more mutually acceptable outcome would be a moderate price rise that would protect Russia's export markets while continuing to guarantee the other successor states a reliable and relatively cheap source of energy.

A second factor concerns the development of institutional mechanisms or regimes, through which co-operation can be conducted. Their development depends on Russian acquiescence and thus this second factor is linked to the first. A free trade regime as foreseen under the CIS Economic Union, offers potential benefits to Russia and the other successor states, yet has been stymied by the animosities engendered by Russia's policies on energy and the rouble zone. Greater leeway by Russia on these issues could facilitate the development of trading or monetary regimes, which might reverse the precipitous decline of intra-FSU trade and which would be of benefit both to itself and to the majority of successor states. The success of regimes in these areas, in turn, would provide an impulse to the development of further economic regimes in related fields.[88]

A final factor concerns the level of international diversification attempted by the successor states. As noted above, this has already been considerable in some cases. In this connection, it might be argued that the greater the drive of a particular state towards involvement with the international economy, the less the likelihood of increased co-operation within the FSU. This has clearly been the case with the Baltic states, among the more successful of the diversifiers. Here one form of interdependence is being substituted for another, ostensibly more beneficial one. Should relations with external powers prove rewarding then the desire for strengthening relations with the international economy will increase and the enthusiasm for intra-FSU arrangements will flag. Should the reverse occur and the benefits of external assistance, investment and trade prove unable to live up to their initial promise then a stronger interest in co-operation within the FSU seems likely.

Post-Soviet economic transformation: two views

It was suggested earlier in this chapter that a preference for economic reform based on a transition to capitalism has been the desired course of action of the successor states (see p. 281). The fundamental premise that this is the only feasible strategy is shared by Western governments, international financial institutions and mainstream academic opinion. All recognise that the transition is not easy and that a 'valley of tears' will have to navigated before the economic payoff is achieved. Yet all also consider that with the correct domestic policies complemented by the appropriate outside advice and assistance the transition will, in the long run, succeed. While a debate exists on the sequencing and speed of the transition,[89] opinion is united on two fundamentals: the desirability of the objective (a free market economy – capitalism) and the means to achieve it (macroeconomic stabilisation; liberalisation of prices and exchange rates; privatisation; the development of a legal framework and market-supporting institutions such as commodity markets and commercial banks; and external economic assistance and integration in the international economy via trade and investment).[90]

The introduction of capitalism and the concomitant integration of the successor states into the international economy is considered both desirable and necessary *per se*. Why? Several reasons have already been touched upon during the course of this chapter. A full list would include the following:

- the Soviet economy at the end of 1991 was near to collapse; something drastic and innovatory had to be done;[91]
- the alternatives to capitalism – state ownership/planning and market socialism (*à la* Gorbachev) – are viewed as economically wanting and morally bankrupt;
- free markets are more efficient and productive than state planning and, therefore, more likely to deliver enduring prosperity;[92]
- a state-controlled economy goes hand in hand with communist authoritarianism, whereas a free market economy is compatible with democracy;[93]
- the spread of democracy in the FSU is compatible with the Kantian notion of a 'pacific union' of states;
- recovery in the FSU will remove a 'drag on global growth' and have a beneficial effect on 'the world economy as a whole'.[94]

This orthodoxy is not, however, the final word on the subject. An alternative school of thought, derived from the globalist frame of reference outlined in the introductory chapter and other radical views, offers a far more critical perspective. The arrival of capitalism in the

FSU by this view represents an ongoing process of 'globalisation'.[95]

As outlined by Andrew Glyn and Bob Sutcliffe, globalisation can be understood to refer to two different things: the 'spread of capitalist relations of production' and 'an increase in the interdependence of the world economic system'. In the globalised system national economies are increasingly interlinked, patterns of production and consumption are interdependent such that each nation depends on others for supplies of goods and for markets for its own products, finance capital is internationalised to a greater degree, and corporations are rooted not in national economies but are global in terms of the location of their assets, their markets and their personnel.[96] This interdependence, is, however, seen as greatest amongst the core economies of the advanced industrial world. In the Third World periphery, many countries are economically so underdeveloped and insignificant that they 'are failing to participate in the growing globalisation of the rest of the world ... they are increasingly marginalised within the system of which they form a part'.[97] They are dependent economies in the sense discussed in the introductory chapter. Globalisation forces these 'weak, indebted and dismembered nations to accept policies that radically expose them to fierce competitive pressures ... (u)nder these conditions they are often unable to maintain the delicate political balances on which social cohesion, political stability and cultural coexistence so often depend'.[98]

How does the notion of globalisation relate to the FSU? Most fundamentally, the 'liquidation of the Communist economic model' and the embrace of market economies amongst the successor states amounts to 'their incorporation as subordinate elements within the economic, cultural and military/strategic networks of the international capitalist system'.[99] Capitalism, which even during the existence of the socialist bloc had assumed a global sway (see Introduction, pp. 11–12) has, with the passing of its rival form of social organisation, now fully embraced new sectors and previously unintegrated areas in the FSU. In doing so, the status of the successor states will be that of peripheral or semi-peripheral economies. Their dependence on the core has already become evident in the form of IMF-led structural adjustment policies designed to enforce adherence to 'the neo-liberal rules of capitalist global competition'.[100] Amongst the less developed successor states the prospect exists that they will become entirely dependent on external sources of finance (whether in the form of investment or assistance) and linked to core state export promotion. In return they will become the providers of raw materials (for instance, energy supplies) for the core. Development on the lines of the 'Asian tigers', exporting cheap, technically advanced manufactures is not seen as feasible. The successor state economies are woefully uncompetitive and would be entering an already saturated world market.[101] While the more advanced economies of say Russia and Ukraine are not so vulnerable (and indeed, Russia is itself a regional economic power within the FSU) their subordination to the exigencies of the core has already become apparent in the embrace of external investment and Western policy prescriptions. Moreover, as Michael Burawoy and Pavel Krotov have written of Russia: '(o)nce the barriers are down, international capital becomes predatory on new entrants into the capitalist world, plundering those countries for their resources without making commensurate investment ... The later a society launches into capitalism the more its surplus is drained away to the more advanced surrounding economies'.[102] Finally, the political future for the successor states is not regarded as democratic. The introduction of market capitalism will be attended by massive economic and social dislocation in the form of mass unemployment and plummeting living standards. This creates a legitimation problem for the new post-communist regimes at a critical time of raised expectations amongst their populations, resulting in the venting of 'economic and political frustrations in radical, often violent, ethnic nationalism, populism and, at the margins, fascism'.[103] To the degree that civil society (the tradition of rights, well entrenched civil institutions and so on) in all the successor states is at a formative stage, little popular resistance can exist to the destructive effects of economic transition other than in the form of these radical, maximalist solutions. The social and political costs of transition, in turn, provide ruling regimes with the temptation to resort to authoritarianism in order to impose economic change regardless of popular opposition.[104]

Two quite different perspectives, therefore, can be applied to post-Soviet economic transformation. The first of these still remains the orthodoxy. Nonetheless, the second, by drawing attention to the harmful effects of transition and, indeed by questioning its very desirability, does raise some stimulating issues, although the alternative it implicitly posits, that of a radical, global restructuring of wealth, appears at best a distant prospect. Yet while the two views have quite different outlooks on the benefits of economic transition, both are as one in recognising that marketisation in the FSU is an apparently irresistible phenomenon. While elements of state control and ownership still persist in the post-Soviet economies these have tended to become more and more marginal. The old structures of the centrally planned economy have been pretty well eradicated in the successor states. Any oversight that remains is in the form of strategic direction (e.g. of trade, energy exploitation) or the result of political and economic aggrandisement (e.g. factories and farms that remain under the direction of local political elites). It is not part of a conscious and comprehensive planning regime or of ideological hostility to market capitalism. For this reason, the future economies of the FSU will undoubtedly be ones in which market forces play an increasing role.[105]

We began this chapter with an examination of the grave economic situation of the successor states at the time of the USSR's dissolution. How has their position altered in the post-Soviet period?

With rare exception, since 1991 all the successor states have experienced an overall contraction in output and an explosion of inflation (see Table 6.3). In its 1993 annual report, the IMF suggested that even in the more promising cases such as the Baltic states, the drop in economic output was unlikely to be reversed until at least the mid-1990s.[106] Economic decline in the post-Soviet period has been largely the consequence of the structural transition from the predominantly state-owned and planned Soviet economy to new economies oriented around market mechanisms. Curtailments in subsidies, the depletion of capital investment and the disruption of inter-enterprise links stemming from the demise of the planning mechanism have all contributed to sharp falls in output.[107] This process is bound to continue. In Russia, Ukraine and Belarus, the end of state subsidies to unviable industries, mines and farms, which began tentatively in 1994 will result in bankruptcies, further economic contraction and large increases in unemployment. To make matters worse, the economic transition in the FSU has been particularly difficult owing to the peculiar legacies of the Soviet period, notably inter-republican trade dependency and the common currency. The framework of the CIS has struggled to create a coherent mechanism of economic integration to address these problems. These factors have rendered change in the FSU that much more painful than, for example, the comparable cases in Eastern Europe.[108]

The common experience of economic misfortune amongst the

states of the FSU should not blind one to the fact that a considerable divergence in performance has become apparent across the region. In some cases this has reflected the consequences of policy choices of government. On the one hand, those countries such as Uzbekistan and Turkmenistan, that have pursued conservative policies towards market transformation, have been able to stabilise output. This arguably amounts only to a delay rather than an avoidance of economic restructuring with its attendant drops in output. The more radical transformers, on the other hand, have been buffeted by severe short-term shocks. Kyrgyzstan's poor performance in 1993 reflected in part the destabilising effects of the sudden introduction of a national currency. The pronounced decline in output during 1992 in Russia was partly a consequence of the expenditure-reducing measures associated with the early, austere phase of shock therapy. The poor performance of the Baltic states, meanwhile, has much to do with the disruptions occasioned by their determined attempts to escape from trade and energy dependence on Russia.

To return to some of the themes touched upon in earlier sections, differences in economic performance have also been the consequence of factors connected with economic viability, including the varied manner in which the Soviet legacy has impinged upon the successor states. Those heavily dependent on energy imports (Belarus, the Baltics, Kyrgyzstan and to some degree Ukraine) have been vulnerable to the energy diplomacy practised above all by Russia and, to a lesser degree, by Turkmenistan. Conversely, Turkmenistan's pursuit of economic independence and its apparently enviable economic performance would have been impossible without its rich natural gas endowment. The experience of warfare and the accompanying breakdown of civil and political authority in Georgia, Armenia, Azerbaijan and Tajikistan largely explains their position amongst the most woeful economic performers in the FSU (see Table 6.3).

In the longer term, the increasing differentiation of economic performance amongst the successor states will be buttressed by their ability to obtain official assistance and to cultivate private investment and trade with countries beyond the FSU. Certain trends in this regard have already been apparent. The Baltic states, for instance, seem the most likely to enjoy a reasonable level of integration with the advanced economies of Europe. Russia, by virtue of its size, strategic importance and imperfectly utilised, but vast natural

Table 6.3 *Economic performance of the successor states (annual rates of change, %)*

	Real GDP		*Industrial output*		*Agricultural output*		*Consumer prices*[a]	
	1992	*1993*	*1992*	*1993*[b]	*1992*	*1993*	*1992*	*1993*
Total FSU	–18.2	–11.9	–18.8	–16.5	—	—	1,292	1,226
Armenia	–52.0	–28.0	–52.5	–39.9	–13.0	–5.0	790	2,500
Azerbaijan	–26.8	–14.4	—	—	–25.0	–17.0	611	797
Belarus	–11.0	–11.7	–9.6	–14.6	–9.0	2.0	969	1,188
Estonia	–19.3	–3.5	—	–26.6	—	—	1,069	89
Georgia	–45.6	–30.0	—	—	—	—	887	1,480
Kazakhstan	–14.0	–10.0	–14.8	–12.1	1.0	–3.0	2,568	2,146
Kyrgyzstan	–19.1	–16.4	–26.8	–27.0	–5.0	–8.0	855	1,207
Latvia	–33.8	–10.1	—	–36.0	—	–16.0	951	109
Lithuania	–37.7	–16.2	—	–46.0	—	–8.0	1,023	410
Moldova	–21.3	–15.0	–21.7	7.0	–16.0	3.0	1,276	1,340
Russia	–18.5	–11.5	–18.8	–16.5	–9.0	–4.0	1,353	896
Tajikistan	–30.0	–30.0	–24.3	–25.5	–9.0	–4.0	1,157	1,870
Turkmenistan	–5.3	8.5	–16.7	18.8	–9.0	9.0	493	1,860
Ukraine	–17.0	–17.0	–9.0	–8.0	–8.0	–1.0	1,445	4,928
Uzbekistan	–9.5	–4.2[c]	–6.2	2.5	–6.0	0	528	761

Notes: [a] rounded to nearest whole number. [b] With the exception of the Baltic states, January to September 1993 as compared to January to September 1992. [c] National Income Produced (i.e. GNP) from January to July as compared to January to July 1992.

Sources: International Monetary Fund, *World Economic Outlook, 1994* (Washington DC, 1994), pp.118, 126; E. Whitlock, 'The CIS economies: divergent and troubled paths', *RFE/RL Research Report*, 3:1 (1994), p.14; S. Girnius, 'The economies of the Baltic states in 1993', *RFE/RL Research Report*, 3:20 (1994) pp.6–7; 'Ekonomicheskoe razvitie stran SNG v 90-e gody', *Mirovaya ekonomika i mezhdunarodnye otnosheniye*, No.6, 1994, p.138.

resources, will always weigh heavily on the calculations of Western governments, international financial institutions and investors. Certain Central Asian states, notably Turkmenistan and Kazakhstan, promise to progress rapidly on the basis of foreign involvement in energy development and, by some accounts, are poised to become Central Asia's equivalent of the prosperous, oil-rich Gulf states. By contrast, the war-affected Transcaucasus, and the exposed states of Belarus, Ukraine and Moldova seem destined to endure continuing economic hardship and dependence on their neighbours within the FSU, notably Russia.

Notes

1 United Nations, Economic Commission for Europe, *Economic Survey of Europe in 1991–1992* (New York, 1992), p. 142. (Hereafter, UNECE, *Economic Survey of Europe*.)

2 International Monetary Fund, *Economic Review. Common Issues and Interrepublic Relations in the Former USSR* (Washington, DC, 1992), p. 53. (Hereafter, IMF, *Economic Review*) (The figures refer to percentage changes in 1991 compared to 1990.)

3 G.E. Schroeder, 'Post-Soviet economic reforms in perspective', in R.F. Kaufmann and J.P. Hardt (eds) for the Joint Economic Committee, Congress of the United States, *The Former Soviet Union in Transition* (New York and London, M.E. Sharpe, 1993), pp. 70–76, and International Monetary Fund, *Annual Report, 1992* (Washington, DC, 1992), pp. 30–34, provide overviews of policies in the FSU.

4 G.E. Schroeder, 'On the economic viability of new nation states', *Journal of International Affairs*, 45:2 (1992), p. 549.

5 *The Economist*, 29 January 1994, p. 17.

6 *The Financial Times*, 1 September 1993, p. 3.

7 B. Brown, 'Central Asia: the economic crisis deepens', *Radio Free Europe/Radio Liberty (RFE/RL) Research Report*, 3:1 (1994), pp. 66–68.

8 M.. Bradshaw, *The Economic Effects of Soviet Dissolution* (London, The Royal Institute of International Affairs, 1992), p. 9; J.P. Cole, 'Republics of the former USSR in the context of a united Europe and a new world order', *Soviet Geography*, 32:9 (1991), p. 589.

9 S. Marnie and E. Whitlock, 'Central Asia and economic integration', *RFE/RL Research Report*, 2:14 (1993), p. 36.

10 'Panel on patterns of disintegration in the former Soviet Union', *Post-Soviet Geography*, 33:6 (1992), pp. 389–90.

11 IMF, *Economic Review*, p. 37.

12 J.W. Schneider, 'Republic energy sectors and inter-state dependencies of the Commonwealth of Independent States and Georgia', in Kaufman and Hardt (eds), *The Former Soviet Union in Transition*, pp. 487–88.

13 *The Guardian*, 21 February 1992.

14 M.V. Belkindas and M.J. Sagers, 'A preliminary analysis of economic

relations among Union republics of the USSR: 1970–1988', *Soviet Geography*, 31:9 (1990), pp. 638–41.

15 The reverse was the case. Ukraine was a major recipient of cheap oil and gas from Russia. Kravchuk would have been more accurate had he been referring to Ukraine's contribution to the *Soviet* economy, for as was noted on p. 287, Ukraine was a net donor to the Soviet budget.

16 This argument is made by J. Steele in *The Guardian*, 21 February 1992.

17 *Current Digest of the Post-Soviet Press (CDSP)*, 44:37 (1992), p. 23.

18 The common use of the rouble meant that price liberalisation in Russia would exert considerable pressure on other republics to do likewise. Any republics that retained old (i.e. cheaper) prices would soon be exposed to a haemorrhage of its goods into Russia where they might be sold at a premium, and an influx of Russian consumers in search of bargains. The options to deal with this were all problematic – dissuading Russia from liberalisation, lifting price controls and risking social unrest, and abandoning the rouble in favour of local currencies. See J.H. Noren and R. Watson, 'Interrepublican economic relations after the disintegration of the USSR', *Soviet Economy*, 8:2 (1992), p. 91.

19 *Agreements on the Creation of the Commonwealth of Independent States Signed in December 1991/January 1992* (London, Russian Information Agency/Novosti, January 1992), pp. 8–9.

20 Progress on this agreement subsequently floundered. The head of the Belarus Presidential Administration described monetary union in October 1994 as an illusion owing to the slower pace of economic reform in Belarus. Russian Prime Minister Chernomyrdin has also expressed doubts, owing to the burden union would impose upon the Russian budget.

21 E. Whitlock, 'Obstacles to CIS economic integration', *RFE/RL Research Report*, 2:27 (1993), p. 35.

22 J.M. Kramer, '"Energy shock" from Russia jolts Baltic states', *RFE/RL Research Report*, 2:17 (1993), pp. 41–49.

23 E. Whitlock, 'Ukrainian–Russian trade: the economics of dependency', *RFE/RL Research Report*, 2:43 (1993), pp. 39–40.

24 K. Dawisha and B. Parrott, *Russia and the New States of Eurasia* (Cambridge, Cambridge University Press, 1994), p. 183.

25 J.P. Carver and G. Englefield, 'Oil and gas pipelines from Central Asia: a new approach', *The World Today*, (June 1994), pp. 119–21.

26 Bradshaw, *The Economic Effects of Soviet Dissolution*, pp. 42–45; International Monetary Fund, *Annual Report, 1994* (Washington, DC, 1994), p. 73.

27 R. Gilpin, *The Political Economy of International Relations* (Prince-

ton, Princeton University Press, 1987), p. 294; E. Luard, *Economic Relations Among States* (London and Basingstoke, Macmillan, 1984), p. 196. Among the most successful contemporary examples of such an arrangement is the single market of the European Community/Union.

28 B. Brown, 'Three Central Asian states form economic union', *RFE/RL Research Report*, 3:13 (1994), pp. 33–35.

29 Non CIS members at this point were the three Baltic states, Moldova, Azerbaijan and Georgia.

30 *The Financial Times*, 25–26 September 1993, p. 2; *Moscow News*, 1 October 1993, p. 3.

31 British Broadcating Corporation, Summary of World Broadcasts, SU/2134 A/2-5, 24 October 1994.

32 On the day the Economic Union agreement was initialled, the Ukrainian parliament voted to hold legislative elections the following March and a Presidential poll in June.

33 The term 'international economy' is used here in the context of relations between the states of the FSU and the wider world (the 'outward orientation'), as distinct from economic relations between the successor states themselves (the 'inward orientation').

34 G.R. Berridge, *International Politics. States, Power and Conflict since 1945* (New York, Harvester Wheatsheaf, second edition, 1992), p. 121.

35 A grant is an outright gift for which no repayment is expected. The grant element is usually calculated on the basis of how concessionary an official loan is by comparison with funds provided by commercial lenders. Unlike their commercial counterparts, many official donors typically furnish low interest loans, often with extended periods of grace before repayment falls.

36 M. Light, 'Economic and technical assistance to the former Soviet Union', in T. Taylor (ed.), *The Collapse of the Soviet Empire. Managing the Regional Fall-Out*, (London, The Royal Institute of International Affairs, 1992), p. 61.

37 Assistance to the post-communist countries of Eastern Europe offers some precedent, particularly the IMF-supported stabilisation policies pursued in Poland since 1990. However, chronologically, developments in Eastern Europe and the FSU have been, for all intents and purposes, simultaneous.

38 G. Allison, *The Guardian*, 24 April 1992, p. 18.

39 J.E. Mroz, 'Russia and Eastern Europe: will the West let them fail?', *Foreign Affairs*, 72:3 (1992), p. 47.

40 *RFE/RL Research Report*, 1:29 (1992), p. 41.

41 L.A. Patterson, 'A "Marshall Plan" for the former Soviet Union: ideological, economic and political considerations', *Arms Control*, 14:2 (1993), pp. 181–95.

42 S. Deger, 'World military expenditure', in *SIPRI Yearbook 1993, World Armaments and Disarmament* (Oxford, Oxford University Press/Sipri, 1993), pp. 367–86.

43 The so-called 'rouble overhang' of private savings had been wiped out by inflation and, in any case, could only have been poorly utilised owing to the underdevelopment of a commercial financial sector to channel these monies into investment.

44 K. Knorr, *The Political Economy of International Relations* (New York, Basic Books, 1975), pp. 171–72.

45 *The Financial Times*, 17 March 1993, p. 18.

46 W.C. Bodie, 'The threat to America from the former USSR', *Orbis*, 37:4 (1993), pp. 509–10. The Kantian notion of a 'pacific union' was discussed in Chapter 3, p. 129.

47 UNECE, *Economic Survey of Europe*, pp. 184–86.

48 *Ibid.*, p. 177.

49 In addition, South Korea offered $800 million in loans and Thailand $450 million for food purchases. See Light, 'Economic and technical assistance', pp. 62, 74.

50 *RFE/RL Research Report*, 1:19 (1992), p. 43.

51 L. Boulton in *The Financial Times*, 3 March 1992, p. 2.

52 P. Desai, 'From the Soviet Union to the Commonwealth of Independent States: the aid debate', *The Harriman Institute Forum*, 5:8 (1992), p. 13, note 30; Light, 'Economic and technical assistance', pp. 63–64; *Izvestiya*, 1 April 1992, p. 1; *IMF Survey*, 11 May 1992, pp. 150–51.

53 *Keesing's Record of World Events*, April 1993, pp. 39423–24.

54 H.-H. Hoehmann and C. Meier, 'The world economic summit in Naples – a new political role for Russia?', *Aussenpolitik*, 45:4 (1994), pp. 336–38.

55 *IMF Survey*, 8 November 1993, pp. 349–51. The large increase in inflation was due, in part, to Russian energy price increases. The IMF, however, viewed the major cause – and one for which Kiev was directly culpable – as a lax monetary and credit policy.

56 *The Economist*, 3 April 1993, pp. 104–5. The Baltic States did not participate in this arrangement since, as noted in Chapter 3, pp. 107–8, they did not consider themselves responsible for Soviet debts.

57 *The European Focus*, January 1992, p. 5, and September 1992, p. 15.

58 Calculated on basis of figures in A. Smith, *Russia and the World Economy. Problems of Integration* (London and New York, Routledge 1992), pp. 231–32 and R.Sakwa, *Russian Politics and Society* (London, Routledge, 1993), p. 206.

59 A further possibility is commercial bank lending. This had, however, come to a virtual standstill in 1990, owing to the high risk of return and the difficulties of the USSR and then Russia, in meeting interest

payments and reaching agreement with private creditors (grouped in the so-called 'London Club') on debt rescheduling.

60 *IMF Survey*, 21 February 1994, p. 58; *Trade Policy Reform in the States of the Former Soviet Union* (Washington, DC, IMF Economic Review Series, No.2, 1994).

61 *Moscow News*, 23 July 1993, p. 3. ECO remains largely an aspiration rather than a reality, its inclusion of both regional and commercial rivals Iran and Turkey is a major impediment to cooperation. Following its Istanbul meeting, ECO has lapsed into inactivity. See Brown, 'Central Asia: the economic crisis deepens', p. 59.

62 *The Economist*, 27 November 1993, p. 17.

63 'Panel on patterns of disintegration', pp. 363–64; K. Bush, 'An overview of the Russian economy', *RFE/RL Research Report*, 1:25 (1992), p. 49.

64 *Russian Economic Trends*, 2:3 (1993), pp. 50–52; *RFE/RL News Briefs*, 14–18 March 1994, p. 2.

65 *The Financial Times*, 29 March 1993, p. 6.

66 Foreign Broadcast Information Service: FBIS–SOV–93–064, 6 April 1993, p. 5.

67 *US Department of State Dispatch*, 5:41 (1994), p. 666, 672. The election of Republican majorities to both houses of Congress in November made the repeal of Jackson–Vanik a distant prospect.

68 S. Alam, 'Russia and Western technology control', *International Relations*, 11:5 (1993), pp. 486–89.

69 For detail of Russian arms sales, see S. Foye, 'Russian arms exports after the Cold War', *RFE/RL Research Report*, 2:13 (1993).

70 *Moscow News*, 20 August 1993, p. 7.

71 *The European Focus*, May 1993, p. 16 and July 1993, p. 14; *The Economist*, 3 July 1993, p. 42.

72 D. Lipton and J. Sachs, 'Prospects for Russia's economic reforms', *Brooking's Papers on Economic Activity*, 2 (1992), p. 264.

73 See the case studies of computer hardware and software joint ventures in P. Lawrence and C. Vlachoutsicos, 'Joint ventures in Russia: put the locals in charge', *Harvard Business Review*, (January–February 1993), p. 54 and D.A. Dyker and G. Stein, 'Russian software: adjusting to the world market', *RFE/RL Research Report*, 2:44 (1993), pp. 50–53.

74 *RFE/RL News Briefs*, 27 June–1 July 1994, p. 3.

75 *Moscow News*, 15–21 April 1994, p. 9; *CDSP*, 45:40, (1993), p. 33.

76 R. Starr, 'Structuring investments in the CIS', *Colombia Journal of World Business*, 38:3 (1993), pp. 13–19.

77 *The Independent on Sunday* (Business Section), 30 August 1992, p. 10.

78 United Nations, *World Economic Survey, 1993* (New York, United

Nations, 1993), pp. 134–35; *The Financial Times*, 6 March 1992, p. 19; *The Economist*, 13 March 1993, pp. 93–94.

79 K. Waltz, *Theory of International Politics* (Reading, MA, Addison-Wesley, 1979), pp. 106–07.

80 J.M. Grieco, 'Anarchy and the limits of co-operation: a realist critique of the newest liberal institutionalism', *International Organisation*, 43:2 (1988), p. 499.

81 Waltz, *Theory of International Politics*, p. 143.

82 R. Keohane and J. Nye, Jr, *Power and Interdependence. World Politics in Transition* (Boston and Toronto, Little Brown, 1977), pp. 24–37.

83 *Ibid.*, p. 24.

84 S.Gill and D. Law, *The Global Political Economy. Perspectives, Problems, and Policies* (New York, Harvester Wheatsheaf, 1988), p. 8; B. Russett and H. Starr, *World Politics. The Menu for Choice* (New York, W.H. Freeman, fourth edition, 1992), p. 387.

85 R.O. Keohane, 'The analysis of international regimes. Towards a European–American research programme', in V. Rittberger (ed.), *Regime Theory and International Relations* (Oxford, Clarendon Press, 1993), p. 35.

86 H. Milner, 'International theories of co-operation among nations. Strengths and weaknesses', *World Politics*, 44:3 (1992), pp. 475–78.

87 This assumption stems from the hegemonic stability thesis. This holds that a leading economic power (a hegemon) is essential to provide 'public goods' (for instance, monetary stability and a trading regime) from which all benefit, and to enforce the rules governing economic co-operation. Both neorealist and pluralist versions exist of this thesis. The former stresses the 'self-regarding' or coercive nature of the hegemon in establishing order, while the latter refers to an 'other-regarding' or benevolent hegemon. See, R. Keohane, *After Hegemony. Co-operation and Discord in the World Political Economy* (Princeton, Princeton University Press, 1984), Chapters 1–3; R. Higgott, 'International political economy', in A.J.R. Groom and M. Light (eds), *Contemporary International Relations. A Guide to Theory* (London, Pinter, 1994), pp. 159–60.

88 According to Keohane, the prior success of existing regimes 'will tend to lead both to an expansion of institutional tasks and to an increase in the number of functioning international regimes'. See 'The analysis of international regimes', p. 36.

89 B. Slay, 'Rapid versus gradual economic transition', *RFE/RL Research Report*, 3:31 (1994).

90 M. Mandelbaum, 'Introduction' and S. Islam, 'Conclusion: problems of planning a market economy', both in M. Mandelbaum and S. Islam

(eds), *Making Markets. Economic Transformation in Eastern Europe and the Post-Soviet States* (New York, Council on Foreign Relations Press, 1993).

91 Lipton and Sachs, 'Prospects for Russia's economic reforms', pp. 216–29.

92 Mandelbaum, 'Introduction', pp. 8–9, 13.

93 *Ibid.*, p. 10; A. Åslund, 'Russia's road from communism', *Daedalus*, 121:2 (1992), pp. 82–83.

94 IMF Managing Director, Michael Camdessus cited in *IMF Survey*, 27 April 1992, p. 134.

95 The interpretation of globalisation as used in this current section reflects a particular, radical viewpoint within the discipline of International Political Economy. It is characterised by a critical view of globalisation and capitalism in general. Other, less critical, interpretations of globalisation also exist. For a discussion, see R. Higgott, 'International political economy'.

96 A. Glyn and B. Sutcliffe, 'Global but leaderless? The new capitalist order' and H. Magdoff, 'Globalisation – to what end?' both in *Socialist Register 1992* (London, Merlin Press, 1992), pp. 56, 76–78.

97 Glyn and Sutcliffe, 'Global but leaderless', p. 91.

98 M. Bienfeld, 'Capitalism and the nation state in the dog days of the twentieth century', *Socialist Register 1994* (London, Merlin Press, 1994), p. 95.

99 L. Panitch and R. Miliband, 'The new world order and the socialist agenda', *Socialist Register 1992*, p. 2.

100 *Ibid.*, p. 12.

101 Magdoff, 'Globalisation – to what end?', pp. 68–69.

102 M. Burawoy and P. Krotov, 'The economic basis of Russia's political crisis', *New Left Review*, 198 (1993), pp. 66–67.

103 M. Williams and G. Reuten, 'After the rectifying revolution: the contradictions of a mixed economy? The political and economic transformations in Central and Eastern Europe', *Capital and Class*, 48 (1993), pp. 81–82, 91.

104 R. Cox, 'Global perestroika', *Socialist Register 1992*, p. 33.

105 For a similar conclusion see P. Rutland, 'The economy: the rocky road from plan to market', in S. White *et al.* (eds), *Developments in Russian and Post-Soviet Politics* (Houndsmills and London, Macmillan, 1994), p. 161.

106 International Monetary Fund, *World Economic Outlook, 1993*, (Washington, DC, 1993), p. 60.

107 United Nations, *World Economic Survey, 1993*, p. 35.

108 According to IMF figures the worst annual output performance of the economies of Eastern Europe (including the former Yugoslavia) was

1991 when the figure was –12.7 per cent. The region registered negative growth in the period 1990–93 inclusive. It was projected to experience positive growth of 1.8 per cent in 1994 and 3.5 per cent in 1995. The lowest point so far for the FSU has been 1992 with a growth rate of –18.2 per cent. Taking into account USSR performance, the FSU has experienced negative growth in the years 1990–1993 inclusive. A figure of –9.8 per cent is projected for 1994 and a positive growth of just 0.4 per cent in 1995. International Monetary Fund, *World Economic Outlook May 1994* (Washington, DC., 1994), p. 109.

Recommended reading

A. Åslund (ed.), *Economic Transformation in Russia* (London, Pinter Publishers, 1994).

M. Bradshaw, *The Economic Effects of Soviet Dissolution* (London, The Royal Institute of International Affairs, 1993).

S. Islam and M. Mandelbaum (eds), *Making Markets. Economic Transformation in Eastern Europe and the Post-Soviet States* (New York, Council on Foreign Relations Press, 1993).

R.F. Kaufmann and J.P. Hardt (eds), for the Joint Economic Committee, Congress of the United States, *The Former Soviet Union in Transition* (New York and London, M.E. Sharpe, 1993).

C. Michalopoulos and D. Tarr (eds), *Trade in the New Independent States* (Washington, DC., International Monetary Fund, 1995).

G.E. Schroeder, 'Observations on economic reform in the successor states', *Post-Soviet Geography* 35:1 (1994), pp. 1–12.

Conclusion

Perspectives on the post-Cold War world and the former Soviet Union

The drama of international politics in the 1990s leaves one breathless. The ordered stability that accompanied the Cold War, post-1945 order has been replaced by a world of flux and thoroughgoing transition. Despite this uncertainty, many would quibble with the view that the years of the Cold War should be regarded with nostalgia. The period up until the late 1980s was, in effect, one of imposed order, a result of the stalemated military and ideological competition between a communist bloc led by the USSR and a liberal–democratic bloc headed by the US. This achieved a harmony of sorts, but arguably at a huge price, placing the whole of humanity under the shadow of nuclear holocaust. True, the two superpowers were prepared to exercise restraint owing to a shared perception of the threat of mutual annihilation. Yet even this did not prevent periods of considerable tension, notably during the Cuban missile crisis in 1961 and for a time during the early 1980s, when nuclear war came to be regarded by both sides as a conceivable eventuality. Moreover, during this period the order occasioned by the East–West divide, while bringing a stability to Europe and the Eurasian landmass generally, prompted destabilisation elsewhere. In much of the Third World, the Cold War found a channel of ventilation in the form of proxy wars and competitive support for varieties of left-wing and right-wing authoritarianism.

However, for all the disadvantages of the Cold War period, it did bring with it a degree of certainty, particularly in Europe where the post-war settlement of a continent divided in two halves militarily and ideologically came to be regarded as almost immutable. As well as affecting the calculations of governments either side of the divide, in the academic community also, assumptions were made and frameworks laid down which took as given the perceived verities of international politics. Few people prior to the arrival of Gorbachev in the Kremlin in 1985 were willing to consider either that the antagonism of the Cold War would be short lived or that the days of the Soviet Union as a unified state were numbered. Consequently, the twin demise of Cold War and the USSR, two coincident and closely related developments, caught many on the hop and occasioned a considerable degree of intellectual soul searching (see, Introduction, p. 13). This has not yet given rise to a new theoretical framework for the study of international politics.[1] As outlined below, frameworks laid down during the Cold War have also been used to explain the new order of things. Indeed, advocates of these approaches would argue that, for all the change that has occurred, certain elements of the international system remain essentially unaltered. The neorealist would point to the abiding condition of anarchy and the rivalry of states, the pluralist to the continuation of 'complex interdependence' and the imperative toward co-operation, while the globalist would highlight the onward march of the capitalist world economy. How these frameworks stand up to the test of time in the new environment has yet to be decided and debates between their scholarly advocates rage on unabated.[2]

Where the successor states fit into these debates is a question as yet without a satisfactory answer. No single framework seems adequate to comprehend the new international politics within the former Soviet Union (FSU) or the region's interaction with the wider world. The three approaches considered below offer a partial, but far from complete, means of understanding. It may, in fact, be more fruitful to combine the insights of a number of approaches. As Hugh Miall has suggested 'like the elephant illuminated by the torchlight of several close observers, the same phenomenon may make more sense if different partial views are put together'.[3]

Here then, we return to the theoretical discussion of the introductory chapter, utilising the three-fold distinction advanced there between realism (or more specifically, neorealism, its contemporary standard bearer), pluralism and globalism. Our concern is to outline how these approaches perceive contemporary international politics and to consider their relevance as frameworks for studying the place of Russia and the successor states in the post-Cold War order. We are now in a position to fully consider these themes having anticipated much of the discussion in previous chapters.

(Neo)realism

As discussed in the introduction, neorealist analysis emphasises the condition of anarchy in the international system. Neorealism holds that under anarchy a bipolar distribution of power offers more propitious conditions for maintaining peace than a multipolar arrangement. Bipolarity is, therefore, forwarded as a major factor in explaining the 'long peace' of the post-war era.[4] The late 1980s and early 1990s witnessed the decline of bipolarity. This was a consequence of the waning of Soviet power under Gorbachev and the subsequent collapse of the USSR. Coincident with this phenomenon, the Cold War was effectively ended. The passing of bipolarity has given rise to three major preoccupations among analysts working within the neorealist framework. First, the likely trends in the distribution of power within the international system. Second, the prospects for peace in this newly configured system. And third, prescriptions for dealing with the new uncertainties.

Turning to the first of these concerns, Christopher Layne has suggested that '(t)he Soviet Union's collapse transformed the international system from bipolarity to unipolarity'. Although other states may be formidable militarily (Russia) or economically (Germany, Japan), only the US is of sufficient strength to enjoy 'a pre-eminent role in international politics'.[5] Kenneth Waltz, by contrast, has argued that 'bipolarity endures'. Measured in terms of capabilities (population, territory, economic potential and military strength) the US and Russia are at present the world's only two great powers. Even though Russia's military capabilities are being undermined by economic weakness, and its internal political order is subject to instability, it will continue to enjoy this rank almost indefinitely. While for Waltz, Russia is limited in its ability to project force beyond its own borders on land or sea,[6] its nuclear capability, coupled with a sizeable conventional force ensure that no state can successfully attack it. Russia, therefore, remains a great power, albeit one oriented toward a defensive or deterrent role. Only its complete disintegration as a unified state will alter this ability.[7]

Both Layne and Waltz, while differing in their opinion of the *current* distribution of power, are as one in their opinion that a multipolar international system will *eventually* emerge as new great powers arise. One consequence of the demise of the Cold War has been the loosening of the Western alliance (in the form of the North

Atlantic Treaty Organisation [NATO] and the US–Japanese military relationship) owing to the absence of a clear adversary either in the form of the USSR or in the guise of a Russian state with a military presence in continental Europe. In this environment, states such as Germany and Japan, previously held in check by alliance discipline, will be increasingly assertive in international politics and will, given their possession of the appropriate capabilities, strive for great power status. Having once been prepared to succumb to American leadership in order to obtain protection against the USSR, these states will be suspicious of the international preponderance of American capabilities and will seek to balance the US now the Soviet threat has disappeared. In the short term this will be done through the exploitation of economic strength and the articulation of a more assertive international diplomacy. In the long term they will aspire to nuclear status. Meanwhile, the inexorable rise of China will continue, creating by the first decade of the next millennium a multipolar world of 'five or so' great powers – the US, Russia, China, Germany (or possibly a united Europe) and Japan.[8]

With regard to the second concern, that of the prospects for peace, neorealism argues forcefully that a post-Cold War world characterised by multipolarity will be a world that is more complicated, more uncertain, and ultimately more dangerous. Writing in 1990, Jack Snyder suggested that a 'Hobbesian pessimism' characterises neorealist thought. By this view, a multipolar system of several great powers will result in fluid balance of power politics that could, as in 1914 and 1939, lead to general war. This danger could be exacerbated by the creation of zones of instability (in particular an Eastern Europe free of Soviet oversight) in which the conflicts of local minor powers 'may help catalyse war among the great powers'.[9] For Barry Buzan, the fading of the Cold War and its associated bipolar structure could increase the incentives for great powers to intervene in the affairs of weak states. Consequently, as the number of weak states increases, the level of insecurity in the international system as a whole is heightened.[10] The swift collapse of first Yugoslavia and then the USSR, the outbreak of nationalist wars within and among new states in the former communist federations, and finally, the faltering process of democratisation in these states has only deepened the sense of pessimism.[11]

In order to moderate the destabilising effects of multipolarity, neorealist analysis has recommended a number of policy prescriptions.

Initially, considerable emphasis was placed on maintaining the bipolar order that was considered to be weakening. Hence, during 1990, it was argued that the Cold War should be perpetuated in some form, primarily through supporting the continued existence of a powerful Soviet Union. This would ensure stability in Eastern Europe, the continued cohesion of NATO and an ongoing American commitment to West European security.[12] The passing of this as a realistic option led to other, equally bold suggestions. In particular, Waltz has claimed that a limited proliferation of nuclear weapons (that is, to Germany and Japan) by raising the costs of military conflict among the (emerging) great powers to unacceptable levels would restore to a considerable extent 'the stark symmetry and pleasing simplicity of bipolarity'.[13] Mearsheimer, as noted in Chapter 4, has applied a similar logic in advocating a Ukrainian nuclear deterrent as a counter to Russian ambition (see p. 160).

Pluralism

The pessimism of the neorealist is not shared by the pluralist view of the post-Cold War world. Dangers are certainly recognised, but the pluralist argues that: (1) neorealist pessimism is overstated and based on false assumptions; and (2) that threats to peace can be contained and indeed ameliorated through a process of international institutionalisation, that is, through the operation of international organisations and regimes.

The pluralist assault on neorealism usually begins with an assertion of the latter's failure to convincingly account for the end of the Cold War and the coincident demise of Soviet power (see Chapter 1, pp. 41–42). The Soviet Union's wilful withdrawal from Eastern Europe and the collapse of the Soviet federation shortly after is taken to contradict two fundamental tenets of neorealism and its classical realist progenitor: that states are lustful for power and that they will protect their own survival at all costs (if necessary through the execution of war). For scholars such as Charles Kegley this falsification of neorealism augurs well in that it suggests that relations between states need not be conflictual, and that co-operation in the anarchic international system is as likely as competition.[14]

A further aspect of neorealist thought that has been subject to criticism is its emphasis on the destabilising effects of multipolarity. According to Stephen Van Evera, sufficient argument can be mounted in support of both bipolarity and multipolarity as supportive of peace. Preference for one or other configuration forms 'a frail basis upon which to argue that the risk of war will rise sharply in the new Europe'.[15] In the view of Stanley Hoffmann the whole debate has been accorded an unnecessary importance. It is not the number of 'poles' that explains the incidence of war or peace, it depends as much 'on the domestic characteristics of the main actors, on their preferences and goals, [and] ... on the relations and links among them'.[16]

The upshot of this attack on the theoretical premises of neorealism is that the pluralists have a far more sanguine view of the prospects for peace in Europe after the Cold War. It is not inevitable that Russia (or for that matter the US) will embark on an aggressive pursuit of power that will return us to the Cold War. Neither is it fated that multipolarity will involve a slide to war redolent of the years leading up to the First and Second World Wars. The outbreak of conflagrations in the Balkans and the FSU is recognised as significant, but these have been interpreted less as inter-state wars than 'civil conflicts or post-colonial conflicts'. From this it follows, that 'the threats to European security are not a consequence of the characteristics of the new system of states, which requires the formation of new Alliances and a new balance of power. Instead, we are confronted with problems which arise out of the specific conditions of the collapse of a political and economic system'.[17] This characterisation does not diminish the gravity of conflict in these areas, nor the urgency of finding solutions to them, but it does suggest that threats to stability are local and unlikely to give rise to escalation capable of menacing the entire European continent.

A cornerstone of the pluralist approach is its emphasis on the sobering effects of organisations and regimes and the ability of these international institutions to promote co-operation between states. In the post-Cold War world, pluralists have accorded institutions a central role. For Robert Keohane and Joseph Nye, the stability of Western Europe since 1945 has resulted from the development of a 'densely institutionalised' network of relations between states. The durability of this network will ensure that here the gloomy premonitions of neorealism will remain unrealised. But what of elsewhere? The task in this connection is to extend the model to Eastern Europe and the FSU in order to set in train 'a continuous pattern of institutionalised co-operation'.[18] For advocates of this approach, it has been seen primarily as a process of co-opting the successor states into existing arrangements. This serves to stabilise the potentially disruptive international consequences of the collapse of the USSR and the attendant end of the Cold War. The involvement in the FSU of organisations such as NATO (and its offshoots – the North Atlantic Co-operation Council and Partnership for Peace) the European Union (EU) and the International Monetary Fund (IMF), the World Bank and the Group of Seven (G7), the preservation and extension of arms control and disarmament regimes, and the role of the United Nations (UN) and the Conference on Security and Co-operation in Europe (CSCE) in conflict resolution are all seen as germane in this regard.[19] In contrast to the neorealists, who view established international organisations as being weakened by the end of the Cold War, the pluralists argue that although the rationale of these bodies has altered, their fundamental organisational strengths remain. Indeed, in the case of the UN and the CSCE they have been freed from the paralysis which gripped them during the period of East–West stand-off. The CSCE, for instance, has been viewed as the potential embodiment of a truly pan-European framework of collective security, embracing the NATO countries, Eastern Europe and the successor states.[20]

The pluralist view has a good deal to commend it. International organisations, regimes and norms proved to be powerful influences on Soviet foreign policy under Gorbachev and have played a key role in the areas of military and security affairs, conflict management and economic relations explored in Chapters 4, 5 and 6. A degree of caution, however, remains on the basis of three important qualifications to the pluralist view. First, the emphasis on the salutary effects of international institutions. While appropriate in terms of the involvement of organisations and regimes originating outside of the FSU, this appraisal is less relevant when considering institutions originating within the FSU, notably the Commonwealth of Independent States (CIS) and its associated arrangements. The latter have proven fragile and far from efficacious in dealing with the disagreements which have beset the successor states. In other words, institutions operating at the level of the FSU's 'outward orientation' have had a relatively greater impact than those at the level of the 'inward orientation'. Moreover, even the former have been presented with serious obstacles. True, the international nuclear and conventional arms control regime has been successfully applied in the FSU, and Russia and the other successor states have moved some way toward the acceptance of regulated involvement in the liberal economic order. But in other regards, notably conflict resolution and the elaboration of a framework of European security capable of satisfying Russia, much remains to be done. The survival of an East–West nexus, in the form of Russian–American bilateralism over issues such as nuclear arms control, disagreements over the former Yugoslavia and Moscow's objections to an extension of NATO also suggest institutions might be impeded by great power calculations.

This leads us to our second qualification – the behaviour of Russia and the US in the post-Cold War period. Even critics of the neorealist persuasion recognise that the two states 'continue to pursue power and rely on military might'.[21] In the Russian case this has been evident in its effective capturing of the CIS after 1992, the carving out of a sphere of influence in its near abroad and the exploitation of economic and military advantage in relations with the other successor states. In terms of relations further afield, the passing of the short honeymoon period of especially close Russian–American relations in 1992 and the emergence of what Yeltsin has dubbed a 'cold peace' might suggest that the realist framework, with its emphasis on the competitive dynamics of great power interaction, has not been exhausted.

A third qualification concerns the existence of economic and political preconditions for the unfolding of the optimistic pluralist scenarios. As pluralists are willing to recognise, the ability of institutions to facilitate co-operation is dependent on complementary interests between states; 'they are not sanguine about co-operation where such interests do not exist'.[22] Pluralists are, therefore, keen to identify those conditions under which such common interests will arise. Two important arguments are relevant in this regard, both of which have been touched upon in earlier chapters. First, interests are seen as increasingly convergent in a liberal economic order. Here common prosperity and interdependence are promoted, both of which enhance the possibility of co-operation and moderate the motives for war. Second, similar effects are generated by the spread of democratic values. This is the 'pacific union' argument noted in Chapter 3. The fall of communism in the Soviet Union created an optimism on both these counts. Not in the sense that the victory of democratic capitalism was assured in the successor states, but rather that communism, its main ideological competitor, had been vanquished.[23] Yet four years on the prospects for both economic prosperity and democratic development seem far from assured within the FSU. The demise of communism has been followed by economic collapse and the rise of equally potent obstacles to democratic governance in the form of particularist nationalism and varieties of post-communist authoritarianism. These lack communism's ideological flavour and its inherent hostility to democratic capitalism, hence, the old ideological East–West divide has not been resurrected. However, so long as functioning liberal democracies propped up by developing economies remain absent from the FSU, the danger is ever present of the emergence of ultra-nationalist regimes, heralding a return to expansionism and hostility toward the West.[24] Political and economic conditions are also important in influencing relations among the successor states themselves. The logic of co-operation forced upon them by the legacy of Soviet interdependence has lingered on, but has been accompanied by a growing tendency toward discord and the exercise of Russian leverage. The thin spread of both prosperity and democratic rule has only exacerbated this state of affairs.

The political and economic conditions that have given rise to peace in the developed world centred on the industrialised West and Japan remain unestablished in the FSU. In this light, Keohane and Nye have characterised the post-Cold War international system as one in which a 'zone of peace' in the West coexists with a 'zone of conflict' in the East.[25] Positing a similar demarcation, James Goldgier and Michael McFaul have suggested that in the West and Japan co-operation and peace is virtually assured – that is, relations between states operate along the lines emphasised by pluralism – but elsewhere the interaction of states seems to be better described by the postulates of realism. Here states are preoccupied with threats to their security, both internal and external, and lack the common interests provided by shared political norms. Consequently they shy away from co-operation with their neighbours and are kept at arm's length by the West. By this view only Russia, by virtue of its great power status, seems capable of elevating itself to the role of a bridge between the two regions.[26]

Globalism

Elements of this approach when applied to the FSU were outlined in the conclusion of the last chapter, in terms of the impact of 'globalisation' upon the post-Soviet economies. Here it is worth reiterating some of these points in terms of the wider world system framework posited by scholars such as Immanuel Wallerstein described in the introductory chapter.

For Wallerstein,[27] the post-Cold War era will be marked by trends that stem from two separate but coincident developments: the end of the Cold War itself – a contest that had 'shaped all interstate relations' in the post-1945 era; and the end of the 'US hegemonic era' of American dominance of the capitalist world economy. Wallerstein's tentative prognosis of future trends suggests 'a time of great world disorder'. This will be a world of two 'likely poles of strength ... a Japan–US axis, to which China will be attached, and a pan-European axis, to which Russia will be attached'. In this scheme of things Russia will sink to the status of a semi-peripheral region (see Introduction, p. 11 for Wallerstein's location of the USSR as part of the 'core') in which only privileged sectors of Russian society will benefit from the economic expansion in the core. While Wallerstein is not explicit on the status of the other successor states, we can surmise that the European oriented among them (Moldova, the Baltics, Ukraine) will be similarly linked to the pan-European axis. The remainder can be envisaged either as peripheral countries, in which some (Azerbaijan, Kazakhstan, Turkmenistan) will acquire enclave status by virtue of core exploitation of their energy riches, or as making up a 'semi-semi periphery', linked to the core indirectly via a lingering dependence on Russia.

The tendency toward global disorder is located, for Wallerstein, in an increasingly 'intense North–South conflict' owing to the economic marginalisation of the periphery and the more acute polarisation of global wealth. The countries of the South will be a source of major destabilisation in international politics on three fronts. First, some will reject the rules of the inter-states system, a situation most likely in Islamic states ('the Khomeini option'). Second, some will attempt to challenge militarily the dominance of the North ('the Saddam Hussein option'). Third, 'an unstoppable mass movement of people from South to North' will eventually occur. Given the South's rejection of the legitimacy of the capitalist world system, the North's only credible reaction to these challenges is coercion. However, a weakening of American military power and the limited possibilities for combined military actions by core countries, owing to their intense economic rivalries, means that force will prove difficult to mobilise. The long-term survival of the capitalist world system, therefore, cannot be assured, and it may well pass from the historical stage within half a century. Again, Wallerstein offers little in the way of analysis of the FSU in this scenario. However, developing his argument, one might surmise that those successor states such as Russia closely linked to the core will perceive their best interests as lying in an orientation toward the North, both for economic reasons and because they too are fearful of destabilisation from the South. In areas such as Central Asia, by contrast, a failure of economic development will increasingly set them against the North and incline them towards a more forthright southern orientation.

Prospects

Just as the larger theoretical debates remain unresolved, future trends regarding the FSU remain equally uncertain. In this section, we will conclude by positing some possible scenarios concerning developments in the region and its interaction with the wider world.

1 *A revival of Russian power*

To a large degree this is already observable. Moscow has manipulated the CIS to its own ends and set about the creation of a zone of influence in its near abroad. However, when the Russian leadership talk about Russia's destiny as a great power, they have more in mind than simply a hegemonic role in the country's backyard. It seeks a condominium with the US in dealing with matters of international significance. Consider the following statement by Yeltsin: 'we do not acknowledge ... that the US should, as it were, be the leader and the world's number one. No. Let us tackle things on an equal footing and jointly ... We are two great powers'.[28] A statement of Yeltsin's press secretary Vyacheslav Kostikov made in the context of Russia's role in the former Yugoslavia is also illuminating in this regard: 'no small or great power can fail to take account of Russia's position and national interests ... no international organisation ... can make effective decisions unless it takes account of Moscow's voice. The illusory nature of the notion that any major problem can be resolved behind Russia's back has become apparent'.[29] This is almost a direct paraphrase of a statement made by Soviet Foreign Minister Andrei Gromyko in 1971, itself a near carbon copy of comments made by Foreign Minister Molotov in 1946.[30] All of this goes to show that Russia has inherited a preoccupation with status, a desire to play a role in international politics commensurate with its geographic size, historical influence and military strength. The encroachment of the West and China onto areas of traditional Russian/Soviet interest such as Eastern Europe, the successor states of Ukraine, the Baltics and Moldova, and Central Asia might stimulate this desire further. It could prompt a more vigorous drive by Moscow to strengthen its standing in the near abroad and to bolster mechanisms of economic and military integration such as the CIS through which this might be achieved. Hand in hand, Russia will resist international engagement in the region under the guise of conflict resolution and will adopt an increasingly hostile attitude to attempts such as the Partnership for Peace initiative aimed at engaging the successor states in Western military initiatives. It will also continue to question areas of East–West co-operation which it considers disadvantageous (for instance, the CFE Treaty or IMF/G7-led economic assistance programmes) and will prove a less willing partner in areas of diplomatic co-ordination (the war in the former Yugoslavia). If Yeltsin should be replaced by a more nationalistically inclined leader in the Presidential elections set for June 1996 these trends will be accentuated.

2 *A saturated Russia*

An alternative scenario suggests that Russia may well lack both the means and the motivation to play out the role of a great power. Just as Gorbachev discovered during the last years of the USSR, the ability to pursue such a role is dependent ultimately upon underlying economic strength. When this is in decline foreign policy must adjust to more modest ends. Given the turmoil in the Russian economy, Moscow lacks the means to pursue an ambitious, expansionist foreign policy. The economic and consequently the military means are simply not at hand to convert any but a few of the weaker successor states to satellite status, to embark upon an active policy further afield, say, in Eastern Europe or relatively near areas of the Third World (the Gulf region, southern and south-east Asia) or to maintain military parity with the NATO alliance. Moreover, it is also dubious that a political logic exists for such a policy. A messianist element, formerly provided by communism or Tsarist imperialism, is absent from contemporary Russian foreign policy. Russia's oversight of the near abroad reflects a lingering imperial impulse, but little rationale can be found for the resurrection of a Russian presence elsewhere. Domestic political developments might also rule out an assertive foreign policy. The likely successor to Yeltsin, Prime Minister Viktor Chernomyrdin, is regarded as an arch pragmatist and is likely to pursue a policy toward the West that judiciously mixes a preference for continued co-operation where this serves Russian interests with the right amount of international posturing to appease domestic criticism. Meanwhile, the current (1995) Russian leadership has ample domestic preoccupations in the face of economic crisis, threats to its territorial integrity (e.g. in Chechnya), and institutional in-fighting (in the form of rivalries between the military and the Ministry of Foreign Affairs on the one hand, and between the separate arms of government – President, Prime Minister, cabinet and parliament, on the other), to divert it from new, potentially costly, external commitments, either in the near abroad or further afield. For the same reasons, and because of continued reliance on Western economic assistance and investment, the close relationship with the West initially established by Yeltsin and Kozyrev in 1991–92, while moderated to a degree by Russian assertiveness, will not in essence be reversed (see also the sixth scenario below).

3 Integration within the FSU

Levels of military and economic interdependence within the FSU have remained remarkably high as a consequence of the shared origins of the successor states within the USSR. These links form an imperative for co-operation. Moreover, the disruptive consequences that have attended the efforts of some successor states to forge independent development will lead to a sobering of minds and a growing desire to repair links severed in the initial post-Soviet period. For Russia, reintegration will be driven by a host of additional factors, some of which have been noted above: fear of Western and Chinese encroachment on a traditional sphere of influence; the urgent need to staunch destabilisation around its borders; and the practical benefits to be had from a strengthening of military and economic ties. The initial disorientation that the majority of Russians felt at the dissolution of the USSR has been overcome and a 'powerful delayed reaction' is now apparent, impelling Moscow toward 'imperial reconsolidation' in its near abroad.[31] This will be pursued through a selective strengthening of the CIS (the Economic Union, the mooted Defence Union etc.) and the construction of a network of tight bilateral ties with certain successor states.

Efforts toward greater integration emanate not only from Russia. In the opinion of Andrei Zagorsky, many of the new states on the territory of the FSU 'seek a certain degree of reintegration ... in order to cope with the problems resulting from former economic dependencies'.[32] This thinking is married with a loss of faith on the part of many non-Russian elites on the possibility of going it alone either economically or in the development of military capabilities, and a perception that the outside world is not rushing in to furnish the massive aid and resources that might provide an alternative to Russian assistance.[33]

4 Disintegration within the FSU

The consolidative tendencies within the FSU have definite limits. The three years since the dissolution of the USSR have demonstrated the potency of nationalism in the successor states and the desire to establish the credentials of independence (for example, national currencies and armed forces). A number of successor states have jealously guarded their independence in the face of Russian pressure and have displayed a marked reluctance to participate within the CIS in anything but a semi-detached manner. Ukraine, in particular, has doggedly resisted Russian diktat on sensitive military issues (the fate of nuclear weapons and the Black Sea Fleet) and on the territorial question of the Crimea. Kuchma's replacement of Kravchuk has not fundamentally altered Ukraine's suspicious attitude toward Russian intent. Elsewhere, a similar attitude has been apparent. Georgia and Moldova have entered into the CIS only in the face of considerable Russian pressure.

In the long term, Russia may be unwilling to act as a regional hegemon, forcing reintegration upon the successor states. In some cases, most obviously the Baltic states, Moscow regards the new states as beyond persuasion. While it seeks to preserve certain interests here (protection of the Russian minority, access to Kaliningrad) the reality of Baltic independence is fully accepted. Moldova, provides a parallel case and once the thorny issue of the Fourteenth Army in the Dniester is settled, it will be less of a preoccupation to Russia. In the Transcaucasus and Central Asia, there are also limits to Russian involvement. As Sergei Karaganov has suggested, 'no sane politician in Moscow would choose to take over the weak economies and turbulent societies' of these neighbouring states.[34] Russia is currently propping up governments in Tajikistan and Georgia, simply for reasons of expediency (to prevent the spread of destabilisation within its own borders and to exact military benefits while these states are vulnerable). The longer conflicts continue in these states, the more costly will Russian involvement become and the greater the pressure will be for Moscow to withdraw. Not for nothing has Tajikistan been labelled 'Russia's Afghanistan'.

Trends toward divergence between the states of the FSU will to some degree be moderated by 'localisation' (for instance, in Central Asia) and 'bilateralisation' (centring on Russia). With regard to the latter, very close relations can be envisaged between Russia, and partners such as Belarus, Kazakhstan, Turkmenistan, Uzbekistan and Armenia. These tendencies, however, will lead to the evolution of patterns of integration and co-operation quite distinct from the multilateralism embodied in the CIS.

5 *The international isolation of the successor states*

Should trends toward integration become more pronounced than those toward greater divergence, certain of the successor states are likely to forswear giving priority toward links outside the FSU. In Central Asia and the Transcaucasus, for instance, ties with neighbouring states have, in any case, developed slowly. Bilateral ties with Turkey, Iran and China and links with organisations such as Economic Co-operation Organisation (ECO) have proven a poor substitute for an inward orientation – intimate relations with Moscow, the development of the CIS and the promotion of initiatives such as the Central Asian Regional Union. As regards relations with the West, these will also be less than dynamic. The geographic remove of the successor states in the Transcaucasus and Central Asia from the European heartland will render them of only marginal concern to organisations such as the EU, the Western European Union and NATO. These states do have an untapped economic potential but Western investors will remain cautious about involvement, owing to political uncertainties and a wariness of Russian interference. Even the Baltics and Ukraine will slip from the Western agenda now that sensitive military issues (the Russian troop presence and the fate of nuclear weapons) have been all but settled. A realistic acceptance that these states fall within a Russian sphere of influence will deter Western capitals from pushing initiatives in the military or political arenas. Arrangements such as Partnership for Peace and partnership agreements with the EU are purely symbolic; they do not presage concerted integration with Western organisations and are certainly not a step toward full membership of either NATO or the EU. As for Russia itself, should it eschew the role of a great power (see the second scenario above), its foreign policy will, by default, become preoccupied with its near abroad.

6 *An international profile for the successor states*

Since the dissolution of the USSR, the outward orientation of the FSU has developed apace. In the period since the end of 1991, international organisations such as NACC and PFP have been developed to deal specifically with issues thrown up by the post-Soviet transition. The successor states have also developed important relationships with extant organisations such as the CSCE and the UN on issues of conflict resolution and with the IMF, the EU, and the G7 on matters of economic reform. In addition, the scope of important international treaties such as START 1 and CFE has been successfully extended to the territory of the FSU. These links have proven fruitful to both the successor states themselves and to the states of the West, who remain fearful at the consequences of destabilisation in the FSU. In that these institutions serve mutual interests and have proven their worth, they are likely to endure and develop further.

The successor states have also developed regional profiles. The Central Asian and Transcaucasian states have, to varying degrees, forged close ties with China, Turkey and Iran. Ukraine has displayed a keen interest in Eastern Europe. The Baltic states have been particularly active, seeking tighter relations with their Nordic neighbours and with the member-states of the EU. Russia, finally, has pursued a largely co-operative relationship with the West and with China. The legacy of decades of hostility during the period of Communist rule has been overcome remarkably swiftly. On issues such as arms control and disarmament, external economic relations, border issues and regional conflicts, Russia has displayed a willingness to co-operate that extends the *rapprochement* begun during the late Soviet period under Gorbachev. After nearly a decade of accommodation, Moscow has now fully emerged as a 'normal great power', to use Kozyrev's phrase. 'Its national interests will be a priority. But these will be interests understandable to democratic countries, and Russia will be defending them through interaction with partners, not through confrontation'.[35]

These six scenarios offer conflicting pictures of the FSU and its place in the world. Yet elements of all of them can be discerned from the brief history of the post-Soviet period. Uncertainty, contradiction and even confusion remain the stuff of the international politics of Russia and the successor states. This makes the subject infernally difficult to study, but ultimately an exciting and rewarding one. If the reader now feels able to make even slightly better sense of the complexity of changes, this book will have achieved its purpose.

Notes

1 See F. Halliday, *Rethinking International Relations*, (Houndsmills, Basingstoke, Macmillan, 1994).
2 See A.J.R Groom and M. Light (eds), *Contemporary International Relations: A Guide to Theory* (London and New York, Pinter, 1994).
3 H. Miall, *Shaping the New Europe* (London, Royal Institute of International Affairs/Pinter, 1993), p. 18.
4 J.J. Mearsheimer, 'Back to the future. instability in Europe after the Cold War', *International Security*, 15:1 (1990), p. 11. (See also Chapter 1, pp. 7–8.)
5 C. Layne, 'The unipolar illusion: why new great powers will rise', *International Security*, 17:4 (1993), p. 5.
6 Presumably with the exception of the 'near abroad', which Waltz fails to mention.
7 K. Waltz, 'The emerging structure of international politics', *International Security*, 18:2 (1993), pp. 50–52; K. Waltz, 'The new world order', *Millennium: Journal of International Studies*, 22:2 (1993), p. 191.
8 Waltz, 'The emerging structure', pp. 55–69; Waltz, 'The new world order', pp. 192–94; Layne, 'The unipolar illusion', pp. 8–16. France and the UK will rank somewhat behind despite their nuclear capabilities, owing to relative economic decline.

9 J. Snyder, 'Averting anarchy in the new Europe', *International Security*, 14:4 (1990), p. 9. See also Mearsheimer, 'Back to the future', pp. 14–15.

10 B. Buzan, *People, States and Fear. An Agenda for International Security Studies in the Post-Cold War Era* (New York, Harvester Wheatsheaf, second edition, 1992), p. 156.

11 Snyder, 'Averting anarchy', pp. 18–38; J. Joffe, 'Collective security and the future of Europe: failed dreams and dead ends', *Survival*, 34:1 (1992), p. 46; P. Hassner, 'Beyond nationalism and internationalism: ethnicity and world order', *Survival* 35:2 (1993), pp. 49–53.

12 Snyder, 'Averting anarchy', p. 13; Mearsheimer, 'Back to the future', p. 52.

13 Waltz, 'The emerging structure', p. 74. (Mearsheimer in his article published in 1990 had already advocated the extension of nuclear weapons to then West Germany. Mearsheimer, 'Back to the future', p. 38).

14 C.W. Kegley, Jr., 'The neoidealist moment in international studies? Realist myths and the new international realities', *International Studies Quarterly*, 37 (1993), pp. 137–38; see also F. Kratochwil, 'The embarrassment of changes: neo-realism and the science of Realpolitik without politics', *Review of International Studies*, 19:1 (1993), pp. 63–64.

15 S. Van Evera, 'Primed for peace. Europe after the Cold War', *International Security*, 15:3 (1990/91), p. 40.

16 S. Hoffmann, R.O. Keohane and J.J. Mearsheimer, 'Back to the future, part II: international relations theory and post-Cold War Europe', *International Security*, 15:2 (1990), p. 192.

17 C. Bluth, *The Future of European Security* (University of Essex, Occasional Papers in European Studies, 1, 1993), pp. 6, 9.

18 R.O. Keohane and J.S. Nye, 'Introduction: the end of the Cold War in Europe', in R.O. Keohane *et al* (eds), *After the Cold War. International Institutions and State Strategies in Europe, 1989–1991* (Cambridge, Massachusetts and London, Harvard University Press, 1993), pp. 5–6; Hoffmann *et al.*, 'Back to the future, part II', p. 194.

19 C. Archer, *Organising Europe. The Institutions of Integration* (London, Edward Arnold, second edition, 1994), pp. 281–82; R.W. Cox, 'Multilateralism and world order', *Review of International Studies*, 18:2 (1992), pp. 164–65; J.G. Ruggie, 'Multilateralism: the anatomy of an institution', *International Organisation*, 46:3 (1992), p. 561; Kegley, 'The neoidealist moment', p. 136.

20 M. Chalmers, 'Developing a security regime for Eastern Europe', *Journal of Peace Research*, 30:4 (1993), pp. 427–44, passim; J.E. Goodby, 'Collective security in Europe after the Cold War', *Journal of International Affairs*, 46:2 (1993), pp. 299–321, passim. B.M. Russett, Thomas Risse-Kappen and J.J. Mearsheimer, 'Back to the future, part III: realism and the realities of European security', *International Security*, 15:2

(1990/91), p. 219.

21 Kegley, 'The neoidealist moment', p. 139.

22 Keohane and Nye, 'Introduction: the end of the Cold War in Europe', p. 6.

23 B. Denitch, *After the Flood. World Politics and Democracy in the Wake of Communism* (London, Adamantine Press, 1993), p. 84. This echoes Francis Fukuyama's thesis on the triumph of liberal democrcy as the 'end point of mankind's ideological evolution'. See his, *The End of History and the Last Man* (London, Penguin Books, 1992), p. xi.

24 Bluth, *The Future of European Security*, p. 38.

25 Keohane and Nye, 'Introduction: the end of the Cold War in Europe', p. 6.

26 J.M. Goldgier and M. McFaul, 'Core and periphery in the post-Cold War era', *International Organisation*, 46:2 (1992), pp. 467–92, passim.

27 The summary presented here is derived from Wallerstein's 'The collapse of liberalism', in R. Miliband and I. Panitch (eds), *Socialist Register 1992* (London, The Merlin Press, 1992) and his 'The world-system after the Cold War', *Journal of Peace Research*, 30:1 (1993), pp. 1–6. A similar approach is also apparent in N. Chomsky, *World Orders, Old and New* (London, Pluto Press, 1994).

28 *Radio Free Europe/Radio Liberty (RFE/RL) Daily Report*, 5 October 1994.

29 Cited in M. Mihalka, 'European–Russian security and NATO's Partnership for Peace', *RFE /RL Research Report*, 3:33 (1994), p. 39.

30 Gromyko: 'there is not a single important question which could be settled without the [co-operation of] Soviet Union'. (*Pravda*, 4 April. 1971, p. 8). Vyecheslau Molotov: 'One cannot decide now any serious problems of international relations without listening to the voice of our Fatherland.' (Cited in A. Ulam, *Expansion and Co-existence. The History of Soviet Foreign Policy, 1917–67* [London, Secker and Warburg, 1968], p. 405).

31 S. Shenfield, 'The post-Soviet strategic space: trends and problems', in *Brassey's Defence Yearbook, 1994* (London and New York, Brassey's, 1994), pp. 83–84

32 A. Zagorsky, 'Reintegration in the former USSR?', *Aussenpolitik* 45:3 (1994), p. 263.

33 S. Karaganov, *Where Is Russia Going? Foreign and Defence Policies in a New Era* (Frankfurt, Peace Research Institute, Report No. 34, 1994), p. 31.

34 *Ibid*., p. 33.

35 A. Kozyrev, 'Russia: a chance for survival' *Foreign Affairs* 71:2 (1992), p. 10. In an article published two years later, he made a similar point: 'the only policy with any chance of success is one that recognises the

mutual benefit of partnership for both Russia and the West, as well as the status and significance of Russia as a world power ... a firm and sometimes aggressive policy of defending one's national interests is not incompatible with partnership'. 'The lagging partnership', *Foreign Affairs*, 73:3 (1994), pp. 61–62.

Recommended reading

M. Klare and D.C. Thomas (eds), *World Security. Challenges for a New Century* (New York, St Martin's Press, second edition, 1994).

S.M. Lynn-Jones (ed.), *The Cold War and After. Prospects for Peace* (London, MIT Press, 1991).

H. Miall (ed.), *Redefining Europe. New Patterns of Conflict and Co-operation* (London, Pinter, 1994).

T. Taylor and S. Sato (eds), *Security Challenges for Japan and Europe in a Post-Cold War World. Vol. IV. Future Sources of Global Conflict* (Washington, DC, The Brookings Institute, 1995).

Index